The Silk Industries of Medieval Paris

THE MIDDLE AGES SERIES

Ruth Mazo Karras, Series Editor

Edward Peters, Founding Editor

The Silk Industries of Medieval Paris

Artisanal Migration, Technological Innovation, and Gendered Experience

Sharon Farmer

PENN

UNIVERSITY OF PENNSYLVANIA PRESS

PHILADELPHIA

Published by
University of Pennsylvania Press
Philadelphia, Pennsylvania 19104-4112
www.upenn.edu/pennpress

Printed in the United States of America on acid-free paper
10 9 8 7 6 5 4 3 2 1

A Cataloging-in-Publication record is available from the
Library of Congress
ISBN 978-0-8122-4848-7

Contents

A Note on Nomenclature and Money

It is always difficult, in a project such as this, to come up with a single set of rules for nomenclature. For names of elites who have been discussed in modern scholarship, I have chosen what I perceive to be the most common English usage: King Philip the Fair, King John II of France. In some cases, as far as I can tell, the most commonly used form of the given name, even in English-language scholarship, is the modern French form, thus: Queen Jeanne of Navarre; Jean, the son of King Louis IX.

For names of individuals who have not been discussed in modern historical literature, I have attempted, instead, to stay close to the form of the name (or, at least, to one of the forms of the name) that one encounters in the sources. This is true as well for street names. In some cases, however, when the orthography is both slippery and very close to the modern version, I have simply opted for the modern spelling.

Money in Paris was calculated in both livres tournois and livres parisis: 4 livres parisis equaled 5 livres tournois. In both systems, 1 livre equaled 20 sous or 240 deniers. The French franc was first coined in 1360; it was the equivalent of 1 livre tournois.

Abbreviations

ADS   Chambéry, Archives départementale de Savoie
AN   Paris, Archives Nationales de France
PdC A Arras, Archives du Pas-de-Calais, Centre Mahaut d'Artois, Série A

Introduction

At some point before the last decade of the thirteenth century a luxury silk cloth industry emerged in Paris. In chronological terms, this development is not particularly surprising. By the end of the thirteenth century at least four towns in northern Italy had developed commercial silk cloth industries, and in Paris itself the commercial production of silk yarn and smaller silk mercery goods had been around for at least fifty years.[1] It is, rather, geography that might give us pause. In the period before the fifteenth century European production of luxury silk cloth was generally confined to the Mediterranean region; and, indeed, until that century, Paris remained the only western European town north of the Mediterranean basin to produce luxury silk cloth.[2] At least one major historian of the silk industry of Renaissance Italy has drawn the conclusion, moreover, that the Parisian silk industry of the thirteenth century could not have amounted to anything other than the production of haberdashery.[3] One goal of this book, then, is to establish that Paris really did have a silk cloth industry and to demonstrate that, together with the other silk textile industries there, it played a major role in the local economy, especially because it was one of the most important sources of employment for women.

Another goal of the book is to explain how the technology of luxury silk cloth production reached Paris and, in so doing, to address the question of long-distance immigration from the Mediterranean basin to medieval northern France. In the premodern period, luxury silk technologies tended to spread in conjunction with the movement of skilled artisans and entrepreneurs who understood the peculiar characteristics of silk fiber and of the complex looms that could create patterned and piled textiles with that fiber.[4] Understanding the origins of the luxury silk cloth industry in Paris thus entails an analysis of patterns of migration in medieval France, most especially patterns of migration from the Mediterranean basin—where the closest luxury silk cloth workers resided—to northern France. In examining those patterns of migration, I hope that this book will recast our understanding of the French medieval past.

Since the publication of Gérard Noiriel's *Le creuset français* in 1988, a number of historians of modern France have attempted to assert the importance of immigrants and immigration in the history of France and thus to redefine powerful national myths about what it means to be French. Only by reorienting our understanding of the French past, Noiriel believed, could the enormous numbers of French citizens who are themselves immigrants, or the children and grandchildren of immigrants, come to feel, and to be perceived, as fully French.[5]

While Noiriel focused on waves of immigration in the nineteenth and twentieth centuries, other scholars, such as Jean-François Dubost and Peter Sahlins, have pushed the inquiry back into the seventeenth and eighteenth centuries.[6] Medievalists, however, have been slower to come to grips with the magnitude and socioeconomic breadth of immigrant communities in France, especially communities of immigrants who came to northern France from various parts of the Mediterranean. It seems especially important that historians of medieval France do so, however, given the huge role that French medievalists of the Annales school played—in the decades following World War II, when the French peasantry was rapidly disappearing—in perpetuating the myth that the French landscape and the peasants who once worked it gave birth to the people who eventually constituted the modern French nation.[7] Indeed, despite Noiriel's work, the myth continued to inform French historical scholarship into the early 1990s and beyond. In an essay titled "La terre" in Pierre Nora's collective work on French realms of memory, for instance, Armand Frémont claimed that "with only a few rare exceptions, every French family sinks the roots of its genealogical tree into peasant soil."[8] Perpetuating such a view requires putting on blinders when it comes to modern, early modern, or medieval immigrants who became permanent residents of France.

The one category of Mediterranean immigrants to medieval northern France that has received considerable attention—to which I will return in Chapter 5—is that of northern Italian merchant-bankers and pawnbrokers. But the problem with these merchant-bankers and pawnbrokers is that, for the most part, they did not integrate into French society—their immigration was usually temporary, they clustered in their own neighborhoods, and they were subject to distinct and often discriminatory treatment by the king. Focusing on the temporary status of the majority of these Italians, as well as on their volatile relations with the crown, a number of social historians of medieval Paris have come to the conclusion that Italian immigrants to Paris never integrated with the rest of the community and that Paris thus "remained a northern city," with a foreign migrant population consisting almost exclusively of people originating in England, Germany, and the Low Countries.[9]

Through a focused analysis of immigrants who contributed to the origins and early development of the Parisian silk industry in the late thirteenth and early fourteenth centuries, this book challenges that conventional wisdom. The Mediterranean immigrant entrepreneurs and artisans who contributed to the early development of the Parisian silk industry took up permanent residence in Paris, paying taxes not as foreign "Lombards" but as "bourgeois of Paris." The evidence concerning these immigrants suggests that from at least the thirteenth century, if not before, the melting pot of France consisted of much more than the three iconic groups—Gauls, Romans, and Franks—whose role in the making of France was first highlighted and idealized by Jules Michelet.[10] The influx of these immigrants into Parisian society and the contributions that they made to that society suggest, moreover, that during and just after the age of the crusades, and of Latin Christian Europe's expansion into Iberia and the Byzantine empire, human movement across the Mediterranean transformed not only the frontiers of Latin, Greek, and Muslim cultures but also the northern regions from which many of the crusaders and settlers emerged.

The second major focus of the book is that of gender and work status. A majority of the Mediterranean immigrants who participated in the early development of the silk cloth industry in Paris came from towns in northern Italy where inheritance customs, legal systems, and guild regulations worked to restrict women's access to property and to high-status labor. Large numbers of women in these Italian towns worked in the silk industry, but they were almost always in positions at the very bottom of the labor hierarchy. In Paris, by contrast, the industry that these immigrants helped start ended up providing unusual opportunities for women. By examining, and attempting to explain, the prominence that women came to play in the Parisian silk industry—not only as workers with relatively modest incomes but also as prominent mistresses of ateliers and as prosperous entrepreneurs—I hope to add new perspectives on gender and work in the Middle Ages. The discussion of women's high-status labor in the Parisian silk industry will draw useful comparisons with women's roles in Italian centers of silk production, as well as with their roles in the wool industries of northern France and the Low Countries. Those comparisons emphasize that Parisian silk women were able to rise to levels of prominence that we do not find in other textile industries. The presence in Paris of the French royal court, I argue, may help explain the unusual gendered patterns in Paris's silk industry.

The final chapter of the book brings together issues of migration, cultural difference, and gender by looking at Jewish and foreign Lombard interactions with Parisian silk women—both through relationships of production and through relationships of credit.

*   *   *

Chapter 1 sets the stage for the rest of the book by providing a broad overview of late thirteenth-century Paris as a city with a significant range of luxury industries and with a significant population of Mediterranean immigrants. Part of the context for Mediterranean immigration into Paris is already well-known, although it bears repeating here: in the thirteenth century, the French royal dynasty and the aristocrats who associated with that dynasty were tied to Mediterranean regions through dynastic marriages and through familial histories involving a variety of military conquests. Additionally, the University of Paris, which first took shape in the twelfth century, drew large numbers of international students and scholars, including a very large number from Italy and a significant number from Iberia. Beginning in the mid-thirteenth century, moreover, Italian merchant-bankers became semipermanent residents of Paris in order to finance royal projects, lend money to elite and modest borrowers, and supply wealthy consumers—royal, aristocratic, and ecclesiastical—with exotic luxury goods, many of which originated in the Far East.

As I further elaborate in Chapter 1, Paris reigned supreme among northwest European centers of luxury consumption, so much so that in the late thirteenth and early fourteenth centuries even the English king sent his agents there to buy luxury goods. Some of those goods, like silk cloth from Lucca and the Levant, were imported. Others, however, such as gold and silver plate, jewelry, illuminated manuscripts, and fine linens, were produced locally; and it was within this context of skilled luxury production that Paris became both a magnet for talented immigrant labor and a place in which luxury silk textiles were produced.

Chapter 2 turns to the production processes within the interconnected silk textile industries that took root in Paris over the course of the thirteenth century. The production process began outside of Paris, in centers of silkworm cultivation in Central Asia, China, and around the Mediterranean. By first describing the original transformation of silk cocoons into raw silk and then following the journey taken by silk fiber, from the centers of silkworm cultivation to Paris, the chapter calls to our attention the trade networks that linked Paris and its silk industry not only to the Mediterranean world but also to Asia and Central Asia. It then goes on to elucidate the ways in which silk work differed from or resembled work with other textile fibers, thereby enhancing our understanding of why the spread of silk technologies usually involved the migration of skilled workers. Those migrants are the focus of Chapter 3. The technical discussions in Chapter 2 also provide useful background information for understanding gendered hierarchies of production, which are a major focus of Chapter 4.

Chapter 3, an investigation of the role of immigrants who contributed to the Parisian silk industry, begins with a discussion of the Parisian mercers—entrepreneurs who both sold silk and, in some cases, managed the production of silk yarn, textiles, and mercery goods. It then turns to a variety of source materials in an effort to locate, among mercers who resided in the most important mercery neighborhoods of Paris, those who had immigrated to Paris from the Mediterranean region. I then search, in the evidence provided by Parisian tax assessments, for immigrant silk artisans whose tax addresses place them in relative proximity to mercers from the same towns or regions. Immigrant mercers, we learn from Parisian tax assessments and other sources, had come to Paris from nearly every important zone of silk production in the Mediterranean: the Levant, Cyprus, the former Byzantine empire, Iberia, Venice, and Lucca. Silk artisans—including some artisan women—migrated to Paris from Venice, Lucca, and Cyprus.

Chapter 4 looks at gendered hierarchies and the importance of women in the Parisian silk industries. The tax assessments from late thirteenth- and early fourteenth-century Paris indicate that in Paris, as elsewhere, women predominated among silk workers; silk work, moreover, predominated among women's forms of employment. Nevertheless, men predominated among high-status silk workers and among silk entrepreneurs. The first section of Chapter 4 discusses the evidence supporting this point, emphasizing five different markers of labor status. The second and third sections of the chapter, however, shift our perspective, comparing and contrasting the status of Parisian silk women with the status of other working women: specifically, silk women in Italian towns, and women in Paris and other northern French and Flemish towns who participated in the wool industry. Looked at from this perspective, Parisian silk women appear to have had extremely high status. After attempting to explain why Parisian silk work was able to offer unusual opportunities for women—and why the gendered hierarchies of silk work changed when silk production traveled from Italy to Paris—the chapter returns to silk women of low income and status, thereby highlighting the enormous gap in wealth and opportunity between silk women who owned their own workshops and those who remained mere employees throughout their lives.

Chapter 5 looks at relations that arose between silk women, on the one hand, and two groups that were considered outsiders to Parisian bourgeois society but whose members, nevertheless, had a relatively strong presence in Paris at the end of the thirteenth century: Jews and foreign Lombard moneylenders. In the first section I argue that although thirteenth-century Parisian silk women probably turned to both Jewish and Lombard money-lenders when they were in need of credit, they would have been more inclined—if they had a reasonable choice—to do business with Jewish mon-eylenders rather than Lombard moneylenders. A perception that foreign Lombards were sexually dangerous, I suggest, contributed to that preference. In the second part of the chapter, I turn to other relations that developed, in the second half of the thirteenth century, between Parisian silk women and Jews, some of whom became involved in the production of various silk prod-ucts. The fact that Parisian Jews were involved in textile production points, I suggest, to contacts between northern French Jews and Jews of Mediterra-nean regions. In the third and final section of the chapter I explain and describe transformations that took place during the fourteenth century, when the French king began to pass and enforce increasingly repressive policies toward Jews and foreign Lombards.

In the conclusion to the book I review the political and economic chal-lenges that Paris faced in the fifteenth century, with a view toward providing a context for the eventual disappearance of Paris's silk cloth industry, which took place at some point before 1467.

*   *   *

In developing the analysis in the chapters that follow I have drawn, for the most part, on three distinct types of sources: Parisian guild statutes that were generated between c. 1266 and 1365, seven Parisian tax assessments that were generated between 1292 and 1313, and household accounts and inventories from the courts of France, England, Artois, Savoy, Flanders, Hainaut, Sweden, Navarre, and Rome. Where appropriate, I have also drawn on narrative evidence from the fragmentary civil and criminal court records of late fourteenth-century Paris and from miracle stories of the late thirteenth century. These sources offer windows into the daily lives of immigrants, Parisian Jews, apprentices, and working women who fell into hard times.

The few historians who have mentioned the silk industry of medieval Paris in their work have drawn almost exclusively on published editions of the collection of Parisian guild statutes known as the *Livre des métiers*. Most of those statutes (those for 73 of the 101 guilds whose statutes are now included in published editions of the *Livre des métiers*) were codified between 1266 and 1275 by the royal provost of Paris, Étienne Boileau, or by his immediate successor. As I will discuss more fully in Chapters 2 and 3, however, the statutes for the two most important silk-weaving guilds were not codified until after 1280, thus suggesting that those two guilds, and most likely the activity of weaving silk cloth, did not take shape in Paris until after 1275.[11]

Étienne Boileau held the office of royal provost of Paris from 1261–1270. He was appointed to that office by King Louis IX (r. 1226–1270), who instigated a number of reforms both for the governance of his realm and for the governance of Paris itself. Those reforms helped create the political context for the flourishing of artisanal production and commercial activity in Paris. Louis helped limit abuses of royal administrative power in Paris by transforming the office of royal provost into a salaried position rather than one that was remunerated through a "farming" system, in which administrators owed a fixed amount of their administrative revenue to the king but could keep for themselves the rest of the revenue that they generated; Étienne Boileau was the first royal provost to be remunerated with such a salary. Louis IX also created the administrative structure through which the bourgeois elite of Paris came to exercise independent governance over civil and commercial aspects of life in the municipality. Beginning with Louis's reign, that governance was exercised by the newly created provost of the merchants and four bourgeois *échevins* who assisted him.[12] This group of bourgeois magistrates is important to us because it came to include a number of mercers—entrepreneurs who sold silk textile products and managed part of the production process. We will encounter a number of mercers from *échevin* families in the chapters that follow.

Like the *Livre des métiers*, the Parisian tax assessments of 1292–1313 are emblematic of the particular concerns of a particular king—those of King Philip the Fair (r. 1285–1314)—whose military skirmishes with Flanders and England created a need for more organized forms of taxation. But the assessments are also indicative of the successful formation of the city's bourgeois leadership: the bourgeois citizens of the town chose to fulfill their financial obligations to the king through an assessment of the value of their property, rather than having to pay a tax on all commercial transactions, which they apparently felt would have been harmful to commerce. Although no document ever spells out how the assessors (who were bourgeois residents of the neighborhoods that they assessed) arrived at their conclusions concerning the tax obligations of particular households, it seems that they based their assessments on the value of a household's movable and immovable property, including business inventory.[13]

The tax assessments of 1292–1313 constitute the most extensive demographic source for the population of Paris from the entire Middle Ages, and they are among the best fiscal records that we have for any medieval town. The first assessment, that of 1292, which seems to have been a preliminary list of people who would later be taxed, was the largest of all of the assessments because it included citizens who were assessed for only 1 sou (or 12 deniers); it includes approximately 15,000 heads of household. The assessments of 1296–1300, which included taxpayers owing 2 sous or more, represent the last 5 years of a collective tax obligation of 10,000 livres parisis per year that began in 1293.[14] Each of the assessments of 1293–1300 originally included approximately 10,000 taxpaying heads of household; however, the lists for 1293–1295 have been lost, as has that part of the 1296 assessment that included the names of the most modest taxpayers—those who paid between 2 and 5 sous. The assessment of 1296 thus includes only around 6,000 names rather than 10,000. Similarly, the more restricted assessment for the year 1313, which was drawn up for the knighting of the future Louis X, also includes approximately 6,000 names.[15]

All of the taxpayer information from the seven tax assessments of 1292–1313 has been entered into a computerized database by Caroline Bourlet of the Institut de recherche et d'histoire des textes in Paris. Over the past dozen years, she has generously created at my request numerous electronic files containing the names and taxpayer information of various categories of workers and various categories of immigrants. Those lists provided the starting point for the appendices at the back of this book, as well as for other statistical arguments that I have developed in the text and in the notes.

As I explain in Chapters 1, 3, and 4, the tax assessments do not provide consistent information for generating statistics. Nevertheless, they have enabled me to draw conclusions concerning patterns of migration, the relative size of various professional groups, and relative incomes across professions and between genders. Moreover, unlike many other tax lists of this period, the Parisian tax assessments locate taxpayers in their parishes and on their streets. Since some 75 percent of the population was never taxed, the information about taxpayers' precise locations on their streets is only approximate; nevertheless, it is clear that the tax assessors moved up and down the streets of Paris in an orderly fashion, so we do get important information about approximate locations and about individuals who either lived or worked in proximity to each other. Because the tax assessments provide geographical information, and because it is possible to collect cumulative information about individuals and neighborhoods across the seven assessments, I have been able to chart individual taxpayers' locations on maps of medieval Paris, to determine who their neighbors were, and to follow them (and sometimes their business partners and families) from one tax assessment to another.

Unlike the *Livre des métiers* and the Parisian tax assessments, household account books did not result from a single set of administrative innovations coming out of a single court. Instead they emerged broadly across Europe, as a manifestation of the growth of pragmatic literacy and improved record keeping in the twelfth and thirteenth centuries. The earliest surviving aristocratic or royal household account books are those of the count-kings of Catalonia, from the 1150s.[16] By the late thirteenth century, most kings and many aristocratic households were keeping such records—in order to keep track of the amount of money that household administrators were spending on food, provisions for horses, clothing, jewelry, and plate. The accounts, or sections of accounts, that most interest us were known as the "wardrobe accounts," in the case of the English royal household, the "Comptes de l'argenterie," in the case of the French royal household, and "mises extraordinaires," "grosses parties," or "parties foraines," in the case of various aristocratic households. In these accounts, or sections of accounts, the administrators of elite households recorded purchases of textiles for the clothing for the head of household, for members of his or her family, and for liveries to all of the retainers within the households.[17] Textile purchases for interior decorations of residences and for military banners and outfits (for both mounted warriors and their horses) sometimes appeared in these accounts, but they were also recorded in separate accounts for building and stable expenses, which I have drawn on, in places, as well. For the decades surrounding the end of the thirteenth century, I have consulted two of the most extensive sets of unpublished accounts from this period for the region north of the Alps: those of the English royal household and the comital house of Artois. I have also consulted the published and unpublished records of the French royal household, the comital houses of Flanders and Hainaut, and the published inventories of Pope Boniface VIII. For that period, and the later fourteenth century, I have also made an effort to examine all of the published sources mentioned in Frédérique Lachaud's survey article on textiles in medieval household accounts, and I have bene-fited, as well, from references provided by colleagues working with the royal and comital accounts of Sweden and Savoy.[18]

Combining prosopographical evidence from the account books and the Parisian tax assessments has proven to be invaluable for constructing minia-ture biographies of a number of Parisian silk entrepreneurs. The aristocratic accounts also provide precious evidence concerning the consumption of Pari-sian silk textiles, and they occasionally offer hints concerning production processes. Contrary to the assumption that Paris produced only haberdash-ery, the account books indicate that luxury silk cloth that was produced in Paris showed up in such diverse places as France, England, Sweden, and the county of Savoy.[19] To be sure, those same accounts also indicate that Paris's silk industry never reached productive capacities that competed with those of the four main Italian centers of thirteenth-century production, but it is clear, nevertheless, that there was indeed a luxury silk cloth industry in medieval Paris and that it lasted for at least a hundred years.

Chapter 1

Paris, City of Immigrants

With a population that exceeded 200,000 by the end of the thirteenth century, Paris was the largest city in western Europe.[1] As we see in a small slice of the Parisian tax assessment of 1300, which shows the taxpayers on one side of the "Grand Rue" (also known as "Street of the Saddle Makers"), that population was fed in large part by an influx of immigrants from both near and far (fig. 1).[2] Of greatest interest to us is the presence on that street of a chest maker from Iberia named Richart of Aragon.

We will return to Richart of Aragon, and to other artisans who immigrated to Paris from the Mediterranean region, in the second half of this chapter. In order to understand why Richart and others like him would have been drawn to Paris, however, we need to begin at the top of the social hierarchy, with the royal family and with some of the most powerful members of the French nobility, who, while based in other parts of France, nevertheless maintained expensive residences in Paris. As a result of marriage alliances and military conquest, these individuals had wide-ranging connections in the Mediterranean region. Those connections drew royal and aristocratic immigrants to Paris, and royal and aristocratic immigrants often brought servants and retainers along with them.[3]

Members of the royal family and the circle of wealthy aristocrats who surrounded it were joined in Paris by the most powerful bishops and abbots of France, and all three of those wealthy groups had expensive tastes for imported goods, which were conveyed to them by merchants from Italy, who constituted yet another significant group of foreign residents in Paris. Members of the royal family, nobility, and ecclesiastical elite also commissioned and purchased luxury goods that were produced right at home, in Paris itself, thereby providing the impetus for the growth of local luxury industries. Indeed, in the second half of

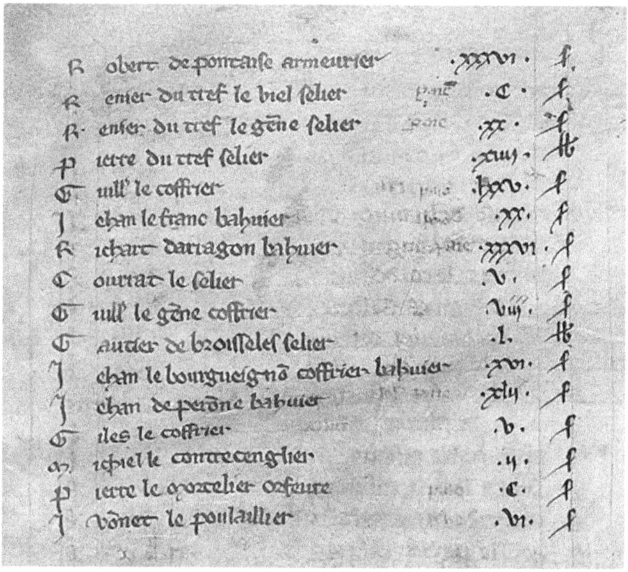
R obert de pontoise armeurier .xxxvi. s.
R enier du tref le viel selier .c. s.
R enier du tref le gēne selier .xx. s.
P ierre du tref selier .xiiij. lb
G uill' le coffrier .lxxv. s.
J ehan le franc bahuier .xx. s.
R ichart darragon bahuier .xxxvi. s.
C onrrat le selier .v. s.
G uill' le gēne coffrier .viij. s.
G autier de brousseles selier .l. lb
J ehan le bourguegnō coffrier bahuier .xvi. s.
J ehan de perōne bahuier .xlij. s.
G iles le coffrier .v. s.
M ichiel le contrecenglier .ij. s.
P ierre le mortelier orfeure .c. s.
I vonet le poulaillier .vi. s.

Figure 1. Parisian taxpayers on the west side of the "Grand Rue," the section also known as the "Street of the Saddle Makers" (now the lower portion of the rue Saint Denis): Robert of Pontoise, armorer, 36 sous; Renier of Utrecht the elder, saddle maker, 100 sous; Renier of Utrecht the younger, saddle maker, 20 sous; Pierre of Utrecht, saddle maker, 14 livres; Guillaume the chest maker, 75 sous; Jehan the Frank, chest maker, 20 sous; Richart of Aragon, chest maker, 36 sous; Conrrat the saddle maker, 5 sous; Guillaume the Younger, chest maker, 8 sous; Gautier of Brussels, saddle maker, 50 livres; Jehan the Burgundian, chest maker, 16 sous; Jehan of Peronne, chest maker, 42 sous; Giles the chest maker, 5 sous; Michiel the maker of counter-cinches, 2 sous; Pierre le Mortelier, goldsmith, 100 sous; Ivonnet the poulterer, 6 sous. AN KK 283, fol. 239. Photo courtesy of Archives Nationales, site de Paris, reproduced with permission.

the thirteenth century Paris became one of the most important centers in all of northern Europe for luxury production. For that reason, Paris was able to attract a large population of skilled immigrant artisans, including significant numbers from various regions of the Mediterranean.

Royal and Aristocratic Immigrants in Paris

During the thirteenth century, the French royal family formed a whole series of marriage alliances with three kingdoms in Iberia: Castile, Aragon, and

Navarre. Moreover, through the military conquests of Charles of Anjou, the younger brother of King Louis IX, the royal family also formed strong ties with southern Italy, and those ties also came to be reinforced through marriage alliances (fig. 2). Royal women and men who came to Paris from Iberia and southern Italy played important roles in transforming the culture of the French capital; it is also likely that servants who came with those royal immigrants helped transform the broader population.

French royal ties with Castile first took shape in 1200, when the future king Louis VIII (r. 1223–1226) married Blanche of Castile (1188–1252), the daughter of King Alfonso VIII of Castile and of his queen, Eleanor of England. After Louis VIII died, Blanche of Castile continued to exercise a great deal of influence over her son, King Louis IX. Working both independently and alongside her son, Blanche introduced a number of Castilian cultural preferences into France. Scholars have argued, for instance, that Blanche was responsible for introducing the Capetian dynasty to Castilian proclivities for patronizing Cistercian monasteries and for choosing to be buried among the Cistercians.[4] In Castile, it was the royal Cistercian monastery of Las Huelgas, founded by Blanche's parents, that came to play the role of the royal necropolis. For the kings of France, the Benedictine monastery of Saint Denis already enjoyed that position, but royal women and cadet members of the royal family were free to be buried elsewhere. After her son Louis IX founded the Cistercian abbey of Royaumont (perhaps due to her influence), Blanche seems to have played a major role in assuring that two of Louis's children, Blanche and Jean of France (who both died young), were buried there. According to art historian Kathleen Nolan, Blanche also played a role in commissioning the funerary sculptures for those two children, and she may have influenced the design of those sculptures as well.[5] The sculptures portray the two royal children in checkered textiles with alternating heraldic symbols—the Capetian fleur-de-lis and Castilian castles. The textiles represented on these sculptures—originally housed at Royaumont but now included among the royal tomb sculptures of the Abbey Church of Saint Denis—very much resemble textiles that were worn in Iberia by members of the Castilian royal house (fig. 3).[6] Blanche herself went on to found two additional Cistercian monasteries—Lys and Maubuisson—and she chose Maubuisson as the location of her own burial.[7]

King Louis IX had two daughters whom he named Blanche of France. In 1267 the second of those two married the Crown Prince of Castile, Fernand de la Cerda, thereby reinforcing French royal ties to her grandmother's natal home. When Fernand predeceased his father, King Alfonso X,

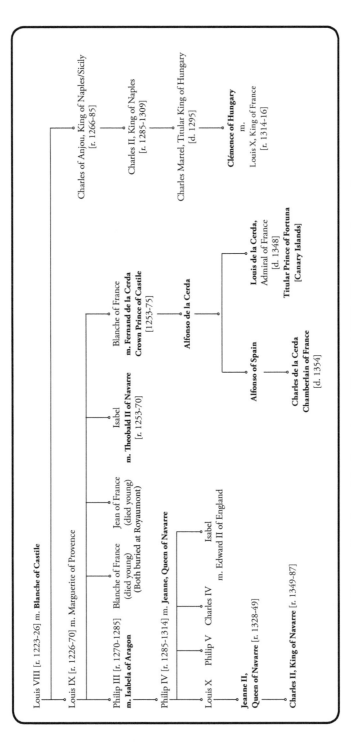

Figure 2. Genealogy of the descendants of King Louis VIII of France, showing marriage relations with Iberia and Italy. Eddie Peralta, Artworks, University of California, Santa Barbara.

Figure 3. Line drawing of the tomb effigy of Jean of France, third son of King Louis IX (d. 1247). Jean is depicted wearing a textile with a checkered pattern of diamonds containing, in alternating rows, the heraldic fleur-de-lis of the Capetian royal family and the heraldic castle of his grandmother's natal family, the royal house of Castile. Similar textiles can be found in contemporary representations of members of the royal house of Castile, as well as in Castilian royal tombs. Oxford, Bodleian Library, Ms. Gough Drawings, Gaignières 2, fol. 25. Reproduced with permission of the Bodleian Library.

in 1275, Fernand's brother, Sancho, claimed the right to the throne. Blanche and her two young sons fled first to Aragon, where the boys remained under the protection of their paternal grandmother, Violante of Aragon.[8] Eventually, however, Blanche returned to France, and her older son, Alfonso de la Cerda, followed her there, marrying the daughter of the Viscount of Narbonne.

Manuscript evidence suggests that upon her return to France princess Blanche may have been responsible for stimulating the transmission and translation from Castilian into French of the story of *Cléomadès*, which was adapted from one of the Arabic stories that is associated with the *Thousand and One Nights*.[9] Well into the generation of her grandchildren, moreover, Blanche's marriage to Fernand de la Cerda continued to weave a web of connections between France and Iberia, largely through the careers of the children of her son Alfonso. Four of Alfonso's children married members of Iberian royal or noble families and returned permanently to Iberia. Three of his sons, by contrast, remained in France, where they had prominent careers. Alphonse of Spain was a favorite of King Charles IV; his son, moreover, Charles de la Cerda, would hold the office of Chamberlain of France under King Charles V. Henry of Spain, another son of Alfonso, would become archdeacon of Paris. Finally, Louis of Spain—or Louis de la Cerda—fostered ties on both sides of the Pyrenees. After marrying the daughter of a major figure of the Castilian Reconquista, Alonso Pérez de Guzmán el Bueno, and participating in the defense of Gibraltar not long after it had been taken from the Muslims, Louis de la Cerda returned to France, where he fought in a number of battles of the Hundred Years' War and was named both Count of Talmont and Admiral of France. Nevertheless, he had not given up aspirations to the south: in 1344 he sought and received papal recognition as titular sovereign of "Fortuna," one of the recently discovered Canary Islands, located in the Atlantic Ocean off the coast of Morocco. Although Louis began to put together a maritime expedition to establish his reign in the Canaries, opposition from several Iberian kings, and the resumption of the Hundred Years' War, prevented him from bringing the project to fruition. Not long after Louis died, however, two other Frenchmen—Jean of Béthencourt and Gadifer de la Sale—would finally conquer the Canaries, in 1402.[10]

Much like the ties between the French royal house and the kingdom of Castile, those between the French royal house and the kingdom of Navarre endured for several generations. Ties between the French and Navarrois royal families were first forged in 1255 when Isabel, the daughter of King Louis IX, married Theobald II, Count of Champagne and king of Navarre. When Theobald died without issue in 1271 the kingdom devolved to his younger brother, Henry I, who incited the anger of the people of Navarre by ignoring local traditions that placed restraints on royal power. Indeed, when Henry died in 1274 and the kingdom devolved to his very young daughter, Jeanne, she and her mother were forced to flee the realm, taking refuge in the French court.[11] Ten years later Jeanne married the soon-to-be king of France, Philip the Fair. Neither Jeanne of Navarre nor her husband ever returned to Navarre. Nevertheless, Jeanne must have known something about Iberian cultural trends, since she commissioned a Latin translation of King Alfonso X of Castile's Castilian translation (from Arabic) of the ancient collection of South Asian moral tales known as *Kalila and Dimna*.[12] We also find a few Navarrois—a knight and a crossbowman—working for King Philip the Fair's household. Moreover, because Jeanne conveyed to her husband and their descendants jurisdiction over the kingdom of Navarre, French officers were regularly sent to administer that Iberian kingdom, and Navarrois ambassadors were regularly sent to Paris to negotiate with their king or to urge him to come to Pamplona to be crowned as king of Navarre.[13] Eventually the kingdom devolved to Jeanne, the daughter of King Louis X of France, and Jeanne's son, King Charles II of Navarre, would take up residence in Navarre in 1361.[14]

French engagement with the kingdom of Sicily/Naples began in 1266 when Charles of Anjou, the younger brother of King Louis IX, conquered the kingdom of Sicily and southern Italy. In 1282, when the people of Sicily rebelled against Charles's rule, a significant number of Frenchmen answered his call for help, taking up arms and traveling to the southern Italian kingdom, where they helped him preserve his rule over the peninsular part of the kingdom of Sicily/Naples.[15] Despite the precarious situation in southern Italy, Charles I maintained a residence in Paris, which lent its name to the rue du roi de Sicile. After Charles died in 1285 his widow, Marguerite of Burgundy, established Tonnerre, in Burgundy, as her principal residence, but she nevertheless retained the Parisian residence until her death in 1308. Charles I of Anjou's son, Charles II of Anjou and Naples, also spent a good deal of time in Paris.[16] In 1304, moreover, Charles II sent Francesco Caracciolo, a member of an important Neapolitan family, to Paris as his ambassador. Caracciolo made such a good impression that he was named chancellor of the University of Paris in 1309.[17]

Links between the French and the kingdom of Naples were reinforced in 1315 when the great-granddaughter of King Charles I of Sicily, Clémence of Hungary, who had been raised in Naples, traveled north to become the second wife of King Louis X of France. In Paris, Clémence patronized artwork that drew on religious and cultural sentiments that she had known before coming to France. In her will, for instance, she bequeathed a reliquary of Saint Louis of Toulouse to the French king, Philip of Valois, thereby promoting in France the cult of the most important saint of the Angevin royal line of Naples.[18] Clémence also commissioned, for the Dominican church of Paris, a funerary sculpture of her great-grandfather King Charles I of Sicily.[19]

Like the French royal family, members of the most elite northern French noble families also forged ties in the Mediterranean region, both through marriage and through military engagement. One of the most spectacular examples of aristocratic marriage ties is that of the counts of Champagne, who ended up inheriting the throne of Navarre when King Sancho the Strong died childless in 1234 and the kingdom thus devolved to Sancho's sister Blanche, the wife of Count Theobald III of Champagne. Blanche's son, Count Theobald IV of Champagne, thus became King Theobald I of Navarre.

The career of Count Robert II of Artois (1250–1302), a nephew of King Louis IX, is illustrative of French noble ties with the Mediterranean through military engagement. Count Robert spent almost half of his adult years advancing the interests of the French royal family in North Africa, southern Italy, and northern Iberia. When he returned to northern France in 1292, after spending nearly a decade as a major military leader and administrator for the Angevin kingdom of southern Italy, his entourage included close to two dozen servants, administrators, and household familiars from southern Italy, Spain, and northern Italy. Many of the men in that group contributed to the physical and administrative transformation of the county of Artois.[20] Some, however, like Robert's physician Palmerius of Riso, who was from Sicily, would have spent time in Paris as well.[21]

Foreign Lombard Bankers, Merchants, and Administrators

Because proximity to the French king could bring favor and increase one's wealth, every major French aristocrat, as well as several Francophone nobles who were not subject to the French monarch, had a residence in Paris, as did a good number of archbishops, bishops, and abbots. A recent list compiled by historian Boris Bove indicates that by 1320 some 90 wealthy aristocrats and ecclesiastical leaders had major residences in Paris.[22] Like the royal family, those aristocrats, bishops, and abbots brought wealth and extravagant consuming habits to the French capital.

Largely because of that wealth and those consuming habits, Paris emerged, in the second half of the thirteenth century, as a major magnet for branch offices of large northern Italian merchant-banking companies, which held dominance, in western Europe, not only in the fields of banking and credit but also in the long-distance importation of luxury goods from the East. The Italians who managed branch offices in Paris only rarely moved their families there, thus their residence was considered only temporary and they were categorized, for the purposes of policy and taxation, as foreign "Lombards." Nevertheless, they often remained in the French capital for long stretches of time, sometimes for several decades.[23]

The settlement of Italian bankers in Paris seems to have begun around 1225, when King Louis VIII invited Lombard pawnbrokers to establish themselves in Paris.[24] Two decades later, while he was preparing for the seventh crusade, which began in 1248, King Louis IX turned to a number of northern Italian banking firms to finance the venture, and some of those firms established branch offices in Paris.[25] By 1292, when the first Parisian tax assessment was created, the two lists of foreign Lombard taxpaying units (one for foreign Lombard taxpayers in Paris itself and another for those residing on the lands of the abbey of Saint-Germain-des-Prés) included 180 entries. Many of those entries included the names of multiple individuals, all of them working for the Parisian branch of a large Italian merchant-banking firm.[26] By the beginning of the fourteenth century, there were more Italian merchant-bankers in Paris than at the Champagne Fairs.[27]

Some of these firms—like those of spice dealers—specialized in the importation of exotic goods from the East. The tax assessments of 1296–1300 include the names of seven Italian spice companies. By 1313, the leader of one of those companies, Girart of Soleret, emerged as one of the ten wealthiest taxpayers in all of Paris.[28] As a spice dealer, Girart would have sold not only spices from the Far East but also raw silk, cotton, imported dyes, wax, dates, sugar, rice, and nuts.[29] Other Italian merchants sold luxury textiles, most especially silk. Still others, like Andrea Simonetti of Lucca, were eclectic in their mercantile activities. An inventory of Simonetti's Parisian possessions, which he himself drew up in 1362, indicates that he sold figured silk and cloth of gold (both of which were probably made in Lucca), velvet (which may have come from Venice), wool cloth from Brussels and Ghent, linen from Reims, embroidered garments, carved wooden devotional statues, gold rings with precious gemstones, luxury books from Italy, metal armor, the expensive red dye known as "grano" (which came from an insect that grew on Mediterranean live oak trees), raw silk from the Caspian Sea region, and unwound silk cocoons.[30]

The sections of the Parisian tax assessments of 1292–1300 that listed foreign Lombard taxpayers included not only the names of international bankers and merchants but also those of some of the chief financial officers of the royal administration, such as Biche and Mouche Guidi of Florence.[31] Beginning in 1290, Biche and Mouche served as receivers of France and then as royal treasurers. The king also sent them out as ambassadors to Rome and Germany, and they played a major role in organizing the king's 1303 campaign against Pope Boniface VIII. The nephews of Biche and Mouche, Tot and Vanne, also worked for the royal financial administration, and at least two other foreign Lombards who appeared in the tax assessments—Quinquenelle (or Quinquiellus Corraldi) and Guy Fauconnier (or Falconieri)—worked for them as well.[32] Another important Italian administrator, Betin Caucinel of Lucca, served as master of the royal mint, and indeed we find a number of men of Italian origin listed in the tax assessments as mint workers or money changers.[33] Betin married a Frenchwoman, thereby establishing a noble French dynasty whose members continued to hold royal offices into the sixteenth century.[34] Additionally, the tax assessments identify one of the foreign Lombards of Paris as a collector of the *maltôte*—the tax that Philip the Fair instituted in 1292.[35]

Foreign Scholars

The presence in Paris of the oldest university in Europe, which included both a prestigious school of theology and a prestigious medical school, also attracted a number of foreign residents to Paris, most of whom remained in France only temporarily. The most famous of the Italians who flourished at the University of Paris in the thirteenth century were the Dominican and Franciscan theologians Thomas Aquinas and Bonaventure, both of whom died in 1274. Toward the end of the century, one of the most well-known Parisian scholars from the Mediterranean basin was the Augustinian friar

Giles of Rome, a student of Aquinas who wrote what has been described as "the most successful 'mirror of princes' of medieval political thought," the *De regimine principum*, which he dedicated to King Philip the Fair. Giles went on, in 1287, to become the Augustinian order's first regent master of theology at the University of Paris.[36] Of similar renown was Lanfranc of Milan, who became the first surgeon to join the medical faculty at the University of Paris, thereby bringing to France Italian traditions of text-based surgery. Although King Philip the Fair ended up deciding that Parisian surgeons would continue to apprentice under guild masters rather than training at the university, Lanfranc's treatise on surgery, which he wrote in Paris in 1296, gained a large audience and was printed many times in the fifteenth and sixteenth centuries.[37]

A list of secular scholars (those not in religious orders) at the University of Paris that was compiled for a special tax on the university community in 1329–1330 provides evidence concerning the relative size of the foreign university population at that time. Among the names on the list, which constituted around one-quarter of the total population of secular masters and students, 29 were from Scotland, 25 from Italy, 17 from Germany, 11 from Denmark and Sweden, 14 from England, and 9 from Spain and Portugal. If these numbers are proportionally representative of the total numbers of masters and students from each foreign region, we can extrapolate that there must have been around 100 Italians and 36 Iberians among the 3,000 or so secular masters and students at the university. The Italians on this list were concentrated in the medical school, and indeed, a number of them were on the faculty. Among the Iberians, by contrast, all were students—but they tended to be students with extremely powerful connections. One of the Iberian students was the illegitimate son of a member of the Portuguese royal family; he would go on to earn doctorates in both medicine and theology and end up with a post as bishop of Évora. Another Iberian student in Paris, the dean of the cathedral chapter of Avila, was a familiar of the king of Castile; yet another was treasurer of the cathedral of Seville; and another was a protégé of the archbishop of Taragona whose studies in Paris were sponsored by the king of Aragon. These Iberians tended to pay taxes that were substantially higher than the average tax on the 1329–1330 list, so we can expect that their presence in Paris entailed the presence, as well, of a number of household servants, including some from Iberia.[38]

In addition to the secular students at the university, there were also students and masters who belonged to various mendicant religious orders.

Those students resided in the Parisian convents of their respective orders during their scholarly sojourns in Paris. Each of the mendicant orders required each of its administrative provinces to send one or more students to study as "lectors" at the order's Parisian convent. Additionally, some students moved on to study and in some cases to eventually teach at the university itself. In 1303 that system resulted, at the Franciscan convent in Paris, in the presence of 41 friars from Italy, 2 from Greece, and 2 from Iberia. We do not have any complete lists for the Dominicans and Augustinians, but we know that they, too, sent students from their various provinces to Paris.[39]

Immigrant Artisans

The presence in Paris of a large population of aristocrats, clerics, and students—not to mention the royal court itself—helped stimulate its emergence as one of the most important centers (if not the most important center) of luxury consumption in all of Europe. Most aristocrats in northern France and the adjacent Francophone counties, as well as most members of the French royal family, maintained itinerant lifestyles, moving several times a month from one residence to another. Nevertheless, they tended to linger the longest in Paris, and it was there, in the French capital, that the agents of their households made most of their luxury purchases for nearly everything except woolen cloth; by the second decade of the fourteenth century, with the establishment of the Parisian Cloth Hall of Brussels, Paris became a major retail center for luxury woolens as well.[40] Indeed, in the last quarter of the thirteenth century and the first quarter of the fourteenth, even the English king and queen sent their agents to Paris to purchase linens, silk textiles, cushions, saddles, jewelry, and gold and silver plate.[41] Similarly, the Angevin kings of southern Italy sent agents to Paris to purchase clothing, jewels, headdresses, and crowns.[42] Moreover, as Agnes Geijer has suggested concerning a spectacular embroidered silk cope now in the cathedral museum of Uppsala, Sweden, members of the church hierarchy, especially those who had been educated in Paris, must have joined the French nobility in commissioning luxury goods from Parisian artisans. The embroidered vestment, which was clearly made in France and dates from the last third of the thirteenth century, was probably produced in the 1270s for the consecration of Fulk Johansson Ängel, archbishop of Uppsala. Fulk, Geijer suggests, had probably been a student in Paris before assuming his position as archbishop of Uppsala.[43]

Paris, then, was not only a center of administration, scholarship, and aristocratic consumption. It was also a center of artisanal production. Indeed, its role as the capital of luxury consumption in northwest Europe provided a major stimulus for the development of many of its industries and crafts. Its luxury manuscripts and gold work were unmatched in quality, its linens—which were sold in large quantities to the English king—rivaled those of Rouen and Reims, its silk and gold embroideries rivaled those of England and Cyprus, and its tapestries were matched only by those of Arras (see fig. 9 in Chapter 2).[44] Paris also excelled in the production of luxury saddles, chests, and armor.[45] And it produced two types of woolen cloth. One of them, "tiretaine of Saint Marcel"—a mixture of linen and wool—was purchased by kings, queens, counts, and countesses, who used it for their summer clothing. The second woolen, known as "biffe of Paris," dominated the international market for modestly priced woolens in the second half of the thirteenth century.[46]

These industries created a magnet for both the skilled and unskilled labor markets of the late thirteenth century. As other scholars have already pointed out, large numbers of laborers came to Paris from England, Brittany, Germany, Flanders, and Burgundy.[47] Among the saddle and chest makers whose names show up in figure 1, we find three from Utrecht, one from Brussels, and one from Burgundy. We learn from the tax assessment of 1297, moreover, that Conrat the saddle maker, also on that street, was from Germany and that a certain embroiderer on that street was from Lausanne, in Switzerland.[48]

Significant numbers of artisanal immigrants also came to Paris from Italy and Iberia. Thus among the saddle and chest makers residing on the Street of the Saddle Makers we find a certain "Richart of Aragon, chest maker" (fig. 1).[49] As I indicate later in the chapter, Richart was not the only man from Aragon living on that street. Other neighborhoods, moreover, included craftspeople from more distant places of origin around the Mediterranean, such as Tunis and Cyprus. Given the distances that some artisans had traveled and the particular economic niches that they ended up filling, we have to suspect that for certain industries some form of organized labor recruitment must have been involved: how else can we explain the presence of a whole cluster of Cypriot silk workers and embroiderers in late thirteenth-century Paris? I return to that question in the concluding section of Chapter 3.

Sources from the last decade of the thirteenth century and the first three of the fourteenth enable us to identify around 200 nonelite and nonclerical Parisians of Mediterranean origin who had settled permanently in the French capital, shedding their legal identity as foreigners. Most of those 200 immigrants appear as heads of household, listed under the category "bourgeois of Paris" in the seven Parisian tax assessments that were generated between 1292 and 1313.[50]

On first consideration, 200 immigrant heads of household does not seem like very many in a town of 200,000 or more people. However, given the gaps in the sources, we can be sure that those 200 represent a much larger group. First of all, the tax assessments did not even come close to listing all of the residents of Paris: the largest of the tax assessments included the names of around 15,000 heads of household; the smallest had less than 6,000. Since only heads of household were listed, most women and all children were left out. Moreover, most Parisian heads of household were not assessed at all: around 15 percent were not assessed because as nobles or members of the church hierarchy they were exempt from taxation, and some 60 percent do not show up in the assessments because they were too poor to pay taxes.[51] Then there is the problem of how people were identified: fewer than half of the male taxpayers were given surnames indicating a place of origin; and among female taxpayers, fewer than 25 percent were so identified.[52] In the absence of surnames specifically indicating place of origin we might expect to be able to spot Italians or Iberians because of other distinguishing characteristics in their names. However, because French documentary sources usually translated foreign names into their French equivalents, that is not the case. Thus, for instance, Lando Belloni, a silk merchant from Lucca who shows up in a number of Parisian sources from this time, was usually identified as "Lande Belon" or "Laude Belon."[53] When it comes to studying immigrants, then, especially immigrants of modest means, we have to recognize the multiple ways in which documentary sources often erased the evidence of their presence or of their geographical origins.

Of course, not every toponymic surname was indicative of an individual's personal place of origin. In some cases, such names referred to the place of origin of progenitors or spouses rather than of individuals; fortunately, however, the Parisian use of surnames was still in its emerging stages in the last decade of the thirteenth century—so in most cases, if a place-name surname did not refer to the individual's personal place of origin the person associated with that place-name was an extremely close relation.[54] According to medieval jurists, moreover, toponymic surnames using variations of the pronoun "of" were more reliable, as indicators of place of origin, than were other forms of toponymic surnames.[55] There is reason to believe, however, that regional surnames such as "the Lombard" were, in fact, reliable indicators of place of origin, since they often made reference to recognizable cultural differences, such as primary language or accent.

*   *   *

Who, then, are the identifiable Mediterranean immigrants who became permanent members of Paris's bourgeois community, and what contributions did they make to the Parisian economy? Within the group of 200 Mediterranean immigrants of Parisian bourgeois status who show up in the sources, around 130 were identified either as Lombards (i.e., northern Italians) or as coming from particular northern Italian towns, such as Lucca, Venice, or Pavia.[56] Significantly—given earlier scholars' tendency to assume that most Italian immigrants in France were prominent bankers or international traders—over half of the northern Italians who were taxed as "bourgeois of Paris" rather than as foreign "Lombards" paid below-average taxes (less than 1 livre, or 20 sous), and over a third of them were in the lowest stratum of taxpayers (those paying 5 sous or less). Most of these artisans of modest means who were taxed among the "bourgeois of Paris" were given the surnames "le Lombart" or "la Lombarde" even though they were decidedly *not* being identified with the foreign merchants and pawnbrokers who were taxed as foreigners. These northern Italian immigrants who had gained permanent rights as citizens of Paris included a porter and a woman who earned her living as an itinerant peddler,[57] but they also included a good number of people who made substantial contributions to several Parisian textile industries as well as to the armor-making industry.

Two former Florentines apparently played a major role in enhancing the reputation of the dyeing and weaving industries that were growing up along the banks of the stream known as the Bièvre, in the Left Bank suburb of Saint Marcel. The weaving industry there produced the prestigious summer textile known as "tiretaine." In 1317 those two men—"Berthelinus Quercitani" and "Jacobus Fava" (or Berthelin Cresseten and Jacques Faves in French)—were included in a group of four Florentines who were granted a royal letter recognizing them as "townsmen of our kingdom of France" (*burgensium nostrorum regni nostri francie*); it appears, moreover, that Berthelin may have already been residing in Saint Marcel in 1292.[58]

In 1292 there were also two *tiretaine* weavers in Saint Marcel. Beginning around 1315, moreover, we find Jacques and Berthelin selling *tiretaine*, or "tiretaine of Saint Marcel," to Countess Mahaut of Artois and Count Raoul of Eu.[59] In 1315 one of Countess Mahaut's purchases, from Berthelin, was for *tiretaine* that her son was to wear to the king's coronation.[60] In 1319, when she bought *tiretaine* from Jacques Faves of Saint Marcel, it was then sent to "madame Blanche à Gaillart." The Blanche in question was Mahaut's daughter, the wife of King Charles IV, who had been imprisoned at Chateau Gaillard in 1314 after being found guilty of adultery.[61]

In addition to selling *tiretaine*, and probably managing its production, Jacques Faves was also involved in finishing and dyeing the very best wool textiles from the Low Countries. Thus in 1317, after purchasing 11 pieces of white *camelin* and one piece of "fine white wool" in Brussels, Countess Mahaut of Artois then conveyed the wool to Jacques Faves in order to have the cloth dyed in scarlet. Both the cloth and the dyeing were extremely expensive: the 12 pieces of cloth cost 120 livres; dyeing them cost 216 livres.[62]

The weaving and dyeing industries that Jacques Faves and Berthelin Cresseten apparently managed in the suburb of Saint Marcel resembled similar industries in their former hometown: one of the most well-known guilds of thirteenth-century Florence was the *arte di calimala*, which specialized in dyeing and finishing wool cloth that had been woven in Flanders and northern France.[63] Aristocratic account books from northern France also suggest that up until the time when the *tiretaines* of Saint Marcel began to dominate the luxury market for lightweight summer cloth, Florence had also been famous for its high-status *tiretaines*.[64]

Workers and entrepreneurs from northern Italy also constituted a strong presence among the Parisian stocking makers—textile workers who made hosiery out of silk, linen, or possibly wool, cutting the fabric on the diagonal in order to enhance the elastic qualities of the garment.[65] Three "Lombards" whose town of origin is never indicated, a fourth man from Pistoia, and a fifth who was a prominent mercer from Lucca all show up on a list of members of the Parisian stocking makers' guild.[66] Another two stocking makers who were not included on the guild list were taxed, in 1292, as foreign Lombards.[67] So seven Italians were definitely involved in stocking making in Paris. Additionally, over twenty other stocking makers (many of whom lacked a topographic surname) resided on or very near the rue de la Buffeterie, which would soon be renamed the "rue des Lombards" because so many Italians resided there. I suspect, therefore, that twenty or more Parisian stocking makers originated in northern Italy.[68]

Other Parisian textile workers who originated in northern Italy included a woman who was a member of the embroiderers' guild, three women who were members of the guild of makers of silk alms purses that were said to be made in the "Saracen" (Muslim) style, a cloth dyer, and a maker of luxury cushions and other quilted items.[69]

In addition to making a substantial contribution to the textile industries of Paris, Italian immigrants made a significant contribution to the armor industry there. Eight northern Italians—most of whom were probably from Milan—were identified in the Parisian tax assessments as either makers or suppliers of armor. Only one of the eight paid an above-average tax, thus suggesting that he was an entrepreneur who supplied armor rather than an artisan who made it; the other seven must have been artisans.[70]

These workers made mail armor and the quilted clothing that had to be worn under it, and they may have made some of the earlier forms of plate armor as well.[71] Moreover, because military equipment included embroidered banners and embroidered silk coverings for horses, armorers also worked as embroiderers. Quilting and sewing were mentioned in the original statutes of the Parisian armorers, which were written between 1268 and 1270; the statutes of 1364 mentioned embroidery and appliqué, specifying that the thread employed for such decorations had to be made of silk.[72] The embroidered accoutrements that a nobleman and his horse wore into battle could be extremely expensive. In July 1302, for instance, in preparation for the battle of Courtrai, Count Robert II of Artois, who would command the French troops there, spent over 60 livres on the embroidered silk "couverture," or caparison, for his horse; that covering was made of red and blue silk *cendal* cloth and gold thread.[73]

Milan produced the most prestigious cotton textiles in Europe—and the quilted clothing that military men wore under their armor was often stuffed with cotton, a textile fiber that had come to Europe from the Islamic world in the twelfth century. Additionally, the most prestigious metal armor in Europe was produced in Milan; and indeed, in 1295 a prominent Milanese, Frederic the Lombard, delivered to Bruges a huge order of armor, including both mail coats and plated armor, for King Philip IV of France.[74] Some of the Lombard armorers who show up in the Parisian tax assessments may have come to Paris as a consequence of Frederic the Lombard's contract with the king. Nevertheless, two armorers were already listed on the 1292 Paris tax assessment, even before Frederic delivered his order to Philip IV. The fact that the work of armorers included embroidery and quilting may help explain the presence in Paris of a quilter ("courtepointier") named Nicolas the Lombard and of an embroiderer named Ermengart the Lombard.[75]

The second largest group of Parisian immigrants from Mediterranean regions consisted of over thirty men and women from various parts of Iberia, most of whom were identified as being from Aragon. Six men in this group engaged in some kind of leather work: two worked with cordovan leather (a leather made from goat's skin), one made saddles, and three, including Richart of Aragon, whose name appears in figure 1, were chest makers. Three of those six, including Richart of Aragon, resided on opposite sides of the Street of the Saddle Makers (now the lower end of the rue Saint Denis) in a neighborhood that had a high concentration of cordovan leather makers, prestigious saddle makers, and chest makers. A felt and blanket maker from Aragon also resided on that street, presumably because felt was useful for the work of saddle and chest makers.[76]

Saddle making and chest making were closely related to each other because the objects consisted of a wooden framework that was covered with leather; those objects, moreover, often incorporated cordovan leather. Indeed, because some saddles incorporated cordovan leather, Parisian saddle makers were allowed to become members of the guild of cordovan leather workers.[77] We know, in fact, that some of the best saddles were decorated with this soft, supple leather: in 1292 the Count of Flanders purchased two saddles covered with vermillion cordovan leather from Conrrat the saddle maker, who resided on the Street of the Saddle Makers; in 1304, moreover, Countess Mahaut of Artois ordered, from Gautier of Brussels, who was a close neighbor of Conrrat and of Richart of Aragon, eleven embroidered saddles that were to be covered with vermillion cordovan leather.[78] Gautier of Brussels was one of the most sought-after saddle makers in Paris, as were his neighbors Pierre and Renier of Utrecht.[79] By the second decade of the fourteenth century, moreover, their neighbor, the chest maker Richart of Aragon, had joined them in receiving multiple commissions from elite consumers, including the king, the Countess of Artois, and the Count of Eu.[80]

The presence of men from Aragon in a prominent neighborhood of saddle, chest, and cordovan leather workers, and the prominence of Richart of Aragon as a prestigious chest maker, is hardly surprising, since the name for cordovan leather associated it with the town of Cordoba, in Iberia, and early fourteenth-century Parisian statutes gave specifications for softening this kind of leather according to the methods of Valencia, Barcelona, Toulouse, and Navarre.[81] Both Valencia and Barcelona were in the kingdom of Aragon. We learn from a case that came before the royal court of the Châtelet in 1399, moreover, that Parisian cordovan leather merchants sometimes (or perhaps often) purchased their untreated goat skins from Iberian merchants who, presumably, had brought the skins from Iberia.[82]

Two additional men from Aragon were included on a list of members of the sword makers' guild.[83] Significantly, in addition to those two from Aragon, the list of 105 members of the guild included eight Germans and eight Englishmen. Together, these men from Aragon, England, and Germany constituted 17 percent of the total membership.[84] At that time, the towns of Toledo, in Castile, which was adjacent to Aragon, and Sölingen, just outside of Cologne, produced the most prestigious swords in all of Europe. Moreover, the area around Siegen, in the Hesse region of Germany, was the leading area in Europe for the production of high-quality steel because of the manganese content in the iron ore there.[85] In England, the Forest of Dean, near Gloucester, and Yorkshire also produced weapon-quality steel.[86] While it is possible that some Iberian, German, and English sword makers migrated to Paris spontaneously, the concentration of so many sword makers from the best centers of sword and steel production suggests that someone with the authority to help them gain entry into the sword makers' guild and with the resources to make the move worthwhile for them—such as a member of the royal court—may have engaged in a process of active recruitment.

Three other Parisian bourgeois taxpayers who had originated in Aragon were identified as cooks, and one of those two, Guillaume of Aragon, was included on an undated list of five members of the cooks' guild.[87] All three of these cooks must have been among the more prominent cooks in the city since they practiced their craft at the center of town, on, or very near, the Petit-Pont. On the guild list, only two of the five guild members practiced their craft there. The other three members of the guild did business at three different entrances to the city.[88]

The Parisian tax assessments included the names of three Mediterranean immigrants who worked with horses: a "sergent a cheval" named "Jehan the Spaniard'" and two horse brokers (*courtiers*) from northern Italy.[89] This is no mere coincidence. Beginning in the early Middle Ages and continuing into the fourteenth century, northern Iberia was associated with the breeding of excellent horses; in the late thirteenth century, moreover, the most prestigious war horses, known as "great horses," came out of Lombardy.[90] In 1294–1295, more than 1,700 horses destined for market crossed the Alps from Italy; in the two years that followed, 2,500 horses were brought north over the Alps for sale.[91] Aristocratic account books affirm that these horses were held in high esteem. In 1313, Countess Mahaut of Artois purchased a "great horse" from a merchant from Milan, and in 1319 she bought a horse from a certain Lappe of Pistoia. Similarly, in the 1330s, Raoul, the Count of Eu, who was the king's constable, regularly purchased horses from Meche Canevas of Milan. We also run into frequent references to valuable horses from Iberia. In 1302, in preparation for the battle of Courtrai, for instance, Count Robert II of Artois—who led the French forces at that battle—spent 300 livres on a bay-colored "great horse" from "Spain." In 1311 Robert's daughter, Countess Mahaut, sent a squire to Aragon to procure some horses, and in 1320 she bought horses from Pasqualoppe the Spaniard and Jehan of Pamplona.[92] In the 1330s, the Count of Eu purchased horses from Simon des Roses of Pamplona. Count Robert II of Artois also employed experts from both Iberia and northern Italy to help manage his horses and his stud farm in Normandy: in the decade between 1292 and 1302 he employed five Iberians and two "Lombards" in his office of the stables. Similarly, at the end of the fourteenth century, we find a man from Valladolid, in Castile, Spain, working in the office of the stable of Louis II, Duke of Bourbon—the uncle of King Charles VI.[93]

There were ten people residing in Paris who were identified as being either from Cyprus or from the town of Limassol, which was on Cyprus.[94] Since most of these immigrants from Cyprus were involved with silk textiles, I will return to them in Chapter 3. One of the Cypriots, however, Madame Bienvenue of Cyprus, was the concièrge of the Parisian residence of Count Robert II of Artois. In addition to working as a concièrge, Bienvenue, like several other Cypriots in Paris, may have worked as a merchant of luxury goods. Indeed, experience as a merchant and furnisher of luxury goods seems to have been a frequent career path for individuals who became concièrges of aristocratic households: the prominent goldsmith and mercer Mahy of Arras, whom we will encounter again in Chapter 2, also served as a concièrge for the Count of Artois, as did a spice dealer named Jehanne l'Espicière.[95] It appears, as well, that the prominent saddle maker Pierre of Utrecht must have served as concièrge for the count, since he penned a small account roll recording carpentry and masonry expenses related to repairs at the Parisian residence of the count.[96]

One concièrge account that was penned by Madame Bienvenue herself in 1303, but for expenses ending in 1302, indicates that she not only took care of major repairs and interior decorations for the Parisian residence of the Count of Artois but also purchased luxury goods for her employer, including some silk to cover a book that had once belonged to the queen and a set of embroidered silk textiles for the chapel. It seems, then, that the count put his trust in Madame Bienvenue's abilities to assess and choose luxury silk textiles.[97]

The Parisian population also included a smattering of people from Islamic lands including at least one converted Muslim and a few individuals with the last name "Mahommet." There were six taxpayers whose names suggest that they came from Tunis. One of them was a glassmaker who was taxed just a few doors down the street from the king's glassmaker. This seems significant, since Tunis was known for its glass.[98] One additional Parisian, who was taxed just next to someone from "outremer," was identified with the surname "of Babylon," which was a premodern name for Old Cairo (and, indeed, the name lives on in the Fortress of Babylon there).[99] Another Parisian resident was identified in royal account books as "Martina de ultramare baptizata, morans Parisius" ("Martina of Outremer, the baptized convert, residing in Paris").[100] According to Guillaume de Saint-Pathus, King Louis IX converted around forty Muslim men, women, and children during his time in Egypt and Acre between 1248 and 1250. Those "baptizati" were brought back to France and remained dependents of the king—thus they, and their descendants, show up intermittently in later royal accounts. However, it is usually difficult to determine the origins of baptizati in royal accounts: some were converted Muslims, but some were probably individuals of Jewish origin who had been baptized as children. In the case of Martina of Outremer, however, her origins in the Levant are relatively clear.[101]

The Parisian tax assessments reveal the presence in the city of at least three individuals with the last name Mahommet.[102] Moreover, a list of individuals residing at the Parisian hospital for the blind in 1302 included a woman named Hersente la Mahommette.[103] Two of the men with the last name Mahommet were wool weavers. One of them signed an agreement between the Parisian weavers' guild and the guild of wool dyers in 1291; the second was included in a prestigious group of about ten Parisian weavers whom Queen Jeanne of Burgundy enticed, in 1318, into moving to the town of Gray, in Burgundy, in order to start a wool industry there.[104] The third man with the last name Mahommet was a harness maker; he lived across the street from Richart of Aragon—and it seems quite possible that he, too, was from Iberia.[105]

One final group of Parisian immigrants from the Mediterranean consisted of nineteen people from either Acre or "Outremer."[106] Most of these would have been descendants of former crusaders who had been born in the Levant but then returned to France after the fall, in 1291, of the final crusader holdout at Acre. Among the nobility, however, some individuals held this name even if they never actually resided in the Levant. Jean II of Acre, cousin of the king and Grand Butler of France under Louis IX, was the grandson of Jean of Brienne, who had become king of Jerusalem in 1210 and king of the Latin kingdom of Jerusalem in 1229; Jean II's son, who was also Grand Butler of France, resided in the Parisian Hôtel of Acre at the end of the thirteenth century.[107]

The nineteen taxpayers who were identified as either "of Acre" or "of Outremer" were of more modest means than were the descendants of Jean of Brienne. Their numbers included three tavernkeepers, a money changer, a draper, a cordovan leather worker, a metal worker, and a baker. Three of the Parisians from Acre, moreover, were Jewish: a physician named Lyon of Acre, his wife, and his son.[108] Like a number of other Jews from Paris, Lyon and his family had probably decided to settle in the Holy Land at some point in the thirteenth century. They may have numbered among the survivors of the destruction of Acre in 1291, when the Jewish community was destroyed along with that of the crusaders, but it is also possible that they decided to leave Acre even before 1291.[109] As the discussion in Chapter 5 suggests, the Parisian Jewish community may have included other Jews of Mediterranean origin as well.

Parisian documentary sources, most especially the tax assessments, thus offer us a window into the presence in Paris of immigrant workers from a variety of locations in the Mediterranean region. Given the fact that most Parisians never show up in the tax assessments at all and most of those who were taxed were never identified by place of origin, we can surmise that the group that we can identify constitutes only a small fraction of workers who immigrated to Paris from Mediterranean regions.

Degrees of Assimilation

What do the fragmentary sources tell us about the ways in which these immigrants coped with the experience of dislocation or the degree to which they ended up assimilating into the broader community? Did they tend to cluster in the same neighborhoods, marry among themselves, or remain loyal to forms of religious devotion from their places of origin?

Sources concerning Italians in Paris indicate that many of them clustered together in two different Italian neighborhoods: the zone around the rue de la Buffeterie, which would soon be renamed the "rue des Lombards," and an area that included the southern part of the Île-de-la-Cité as well as the Petit-Pont, which crossed over to the Left Bank.[110] Those sources also suggest that some children of Italian immigrants married within the immigrant community and that merchants from Lucca tended to cohere around the most important religious symbol of their hometown: the cult of the "Volto Santo," or "Holy Face" of Lucca.[111]

In towns all over Europe prominent businessmen from Lucca tended to found chapels and confraternities dedicated to the "Volto Santo."[112] In Paris, the brothers Lando and Ugolino Belloni founded such a chapel in the 1340s; it would remain a center of religious identity for Lucchese merchants in Paris throughout the rest of the Middle Ages. For the Belloni family, moreover, the chapel provided a place to honor and bury their dead: along with their spouses, Lando and Ugolino established daily masses for their family at the chapel of the "Volto Santo," and when they did so, they secured written assurance that they had the right to be buried there.[113] Epitaph evidence indicates that even Ugolino's daughter and her husband, who was also from Lucca, were buried in that chapel.[114] Religious devotion, and the financial means to create sacred space to go with it, thus helped the merchants of Lucca maintain their cohesion and identity.

But the tax assessments indicate that many of the Italians living in Paris resided in neighborhoods other than the Lombard zones. Moreover, evidence concerning merchants from Lucca indicates that they or their descendants eventually assimilated into Parisian society. The Parisian mint master Betin Caucinel married a Frenchwoman and founded a dynasty of French nobles. Members of the Spifami family of Lucca also married Frenchwomen and settled permanently in Paris.[115] Similarly, the granddaughters of Ugolino Belloni married Frenchmen rather than men from Lucca.[116]

Some first-generation Italian merchants also became integrated into religious institutions that served, and were served by, the broader community of Parisians. Jacques Bondos, for instance, another merchant from Lucca, became a lay warden at the Parisian parish church of Saint-Jacques-de-la-Boucherie; and it appears that another Italian, named Aubert Bertaut, did so as well. Their fellow lay wardens included the *échevins* Estienne Haudri,

Jehan of Rueil, and Geoffroi Dammartin.[117] Along similar lines, Barthelemy Castaing, a spice dealer and moneylender from either Florence or Genoa, became a member of the board of governors of the Church of the Holy Sepulcher on the Grand Rue (now the rue Saint Denis); he and his wife also founded a chapel there, where they were (or perhaps only he was) buried.[118] To be sure, the Church of the Holy Sepulcher housed the Lucchese chapel of the Volto Santo—but the larger governing body of that church included a number of prominent members of the Parisian merchant community, including one man, Guillaume Toussac, who served as a Parisian *échevin*.[119]

Unlike these prominent entrepreneurs, workers and artisans rarely left behind the kinds of records that enable us to trace their marriage patterns or religious loyalties. Moreover, since they did not control the kinds of resources that were available to Lando and Ugolino Belloni, they could not endow the kinds of devotional and burial spaces that enhanced the sense of cohesion among wealthy Lombard merchants and bankers. Nevertheless, as a story from the *Miracles de Saint Louis* makes clear, even immigrants whose primary daily contacts were with native French people, and who had no consecrated space to call their own, could cling tenaciously to cultural symbols of their places of origin. The story, which was based on the sworn testimony of multiple witnesses, concerns an English artisan rather than one from the Mediterranean, but it is illuminating nevertheless.

In 1275, a leather worker named Hugh (or Hue) of Northampton who had been residing for some thirty years in Saint Denis, just north of Paris, became impatient with the new religious devotion that was building up around the tomb of King Louis IX, who was buried in the Abbey Church of Saint Denis. Hugh began to mock the people who came to pray or to seek miraculous cures at the king's tomb, declaring that King Henry of England had been a better man than King Louis IX of France. In his frustration with the local devotion, Hugh even went so far as to seize some of the candles that were burning at Louis's tomb and throw them on the ground. When he subsequently lost the ability to walk, his wife and fellow workers told him that this disability was a divine punishment for the insult that he had hurled at the saintly king. After a sleepless night of physical suffering and reflection, Hugh came to see things in the same way. Repenting his behavior, he made a vow to King Louis IX asking him to forgive the insult and heal his impaired legs. Hugh then asked a fellow leather worker, who was from the village of Gonnesse near Saint Denis, to carry him to Louis's tomb. Consequently, we are told, he soon regained his ability to walk.[120] Only through a traumatic experience of illness, which he came to perceive as the result of divine punishment, did Hugh of Northampton abandon the sense of competitive pride that he had felt for the English king and the distance that he had attempted to create between his own loyalties and those of the native French people around him. The transformation of Hugh's attitude was so great that he later led his feverish children to Louis's tomb in quest of a cure.[121]

While we know very little about marriage patterns among Parisian artisan immigrants from the Mediterranean, the tax assessments do enable us to say something about the degree to which they clustered in the same neighborhoods. As I have already indicated, a number of northern Italians who were taxed among the bourgeois of Paris continued to reside in the two Parisian neighborhoods that had high concentrations of foreign Lombards. We also find some neighborhood cohesion among the Cypriot immigrants, five of whom clustered on the rue de la Courroierie on the right bank.[122]

In general, however, artisan immigrants to Paris tended to settle into sections of town that were defined by craft activity rather than by the regional origins of the workers themselves. Thus, as I have already indicated, a number of the saddle and chest makers from Aragon lived on the Street of the Saddle Makers, which had a high concentration of leather workers, saddle makers, and chest makers, who had immigrated to Paris from a broad spectrum of places, most of which were in France, the Low Countries, and Germany.

Similarly, immigrant silk mercers, whom we will encounter in Chapter 3, resided in neighborhoods that were defined by merchant activity rather than by the regional identities of the merchants. Indeed, one of our major pieces of evidence that silk mercers from Venice, Lucca, the Levant, and possibly the former Greek empire were extremely successful is the fact that they ended up working, residing, and paying taxes on the rue Troussevache and the rue Quincampoix—the two Parisian streets that were occupied by the wealthiest mercers in Paris, many of whom were members of échevin families.

For both mercers and craftspeople, craft guilds probably provided a major avenue for assimilation. Only a few lists of guild members survive from this period, but, as I have already suggested, those lists point to a number of members who had migrated to Paris from Mediterranean regions. Five northern Italians became members of the stocking makers' guild. The embroiderers' guild included one man from Cyprus, a woman from northern Italy, and another who was identified as "the Spaniard." The guild of makers of silk alms purses included three women from northern Italy, the sword makers' guild included two men from Aragon, and another man from Aragon was a member of the chefs' guild.[123] In order to gain access to membership in these guilds, craftspeople needed to build relationships of trust with masters who already practiced the craft. Thus we find that when Jehan Vanne, who was from Lucca, wanted to join the stocking makers' guild he needed to find three masters who would vouch for his competency. Those masters, Girvese the Stockingmaker, Jehan de Chevreuse, and Pierre de Vitry, were apparently of French background.[124]

*   *   *

There were, then, significant numbers of people from the Mediterranean living in Paris at the end of the thirteenth and the beginning of the fourteenth centuries. Most were of Italian origin, but there were people from a range of other areas in the Mediterranean as well. It seems logical that this was the case. As Robert Bartlett argued in *The Making of Europe*, French speakers played a major role in the movement of northwest European expansion of the eleventh through the thirteenth centuries. Individuals from northern France fought in crusades, they settled in the Levant and the former Byzantine empire, and they took over the rule of the island of Cyprus. Charles I of Anjou, moreover, the younger brother of King Louis IX of France, conquered the kingdom of Sicily and southern Italy in 1266, and when the Sicilians rebelled against his rule in 1282 large numbers of knights from northern France answered his call for help.[125] Additionally, the Capetian dynasty was linked through marriage to the Iberian dynasties of Castile, Aragon, and Navarre.

French settlers who remained abroad maintained ties in northern France, and those who returned to France brought servants and associates home with them.[126] French clerics who held church offices abroad also made an effort to stay in contact with the French capital. Thus, in 1303, when King Philip the Fair asked the secular and religious leaders of the realm to sign on in support of his campaign against Boniface VIII, one of the bishops who was able to add his signature was the bishop of Nicosia, in Cyprus.[127]

As a result of this tissue of connections, and through the contacts of prominent Italian merchants who settled in Paris, artisans from the Mediterranean world moved to Paris (and to other parts of northern France as well), bringing technical knowledge and skill with them. As I have suggested concerning the members of the sword makers' guild, moreover, and as I will suggest again in the conclusion of Chapter 3, the royal court may have offered incentives to some of these workers to entice them to bring their specialized skills with them to Paris. Once they settled in Paris, these immigrant artisans, unlike many prominent merchant-bankers from northern Italy, assimilated relatively quickly with the broader population, thus becoming a part of the medieval French melting pot.

Chapter 2

From Persian Cocoon to *Soie de Paris*: Trade Networks and Silk Techniques

In 1294 a Parisian named Mahy of Arras, who was both a goldsmith and a silk entrepreneur (or "mercer"), traveled to the Champagne fair of Lagny-sur-Marne where, working as an agent for Isabel of Luxembourg, Countess of Flanders, he purchased some raw silk fiber from an Italian merchant named Cote Salmon (fig. 4). The fiber was from Lahijan, in the province of Gilan, on the south coast of the Caspian Sea; Cote Salmon was from Lucca, which was the most important center of luxury silk cloth production in Europe (fig. 5).[1] Cote had probably bought the fiber from one of the Genoese merchants who supplied raw silk fiber for the textile industry of Lucca. In turn, the Genoese merchant would have purchased the silk fiber either in Gilan province itself or in the entrepôt town of Tabriz, which, like Gilan province, constituted part of the Mongol Ilkhanate, which overlapped with Persia. Genoese and Venetian merchants flocked to Tabriz in order to buy spices, silk, and jewels from the Far East, as well as silk fiber that was more locally produced.

From Tabriz the Genoese merchant who first purchased the silk fiber from Lahijan would have traveled to Trebizond, on the Black Sea. Before 1285, he would have chosen a shorter route, through the Armenian port of Ayas, on the Mediterranean coast of Asia Minor. In the wake of the Mamluk sultan's extension of control over Cilisian Armenia in 1285, however, the Genoese refused to pay the tribute taxes demanded by the Mamluks, so, in cooperation with the Mongol Ilkhanate ruler, they transformed Trebizond into the most important western "end point" for the southern branch of the trans-Asian Silk Road.[2]

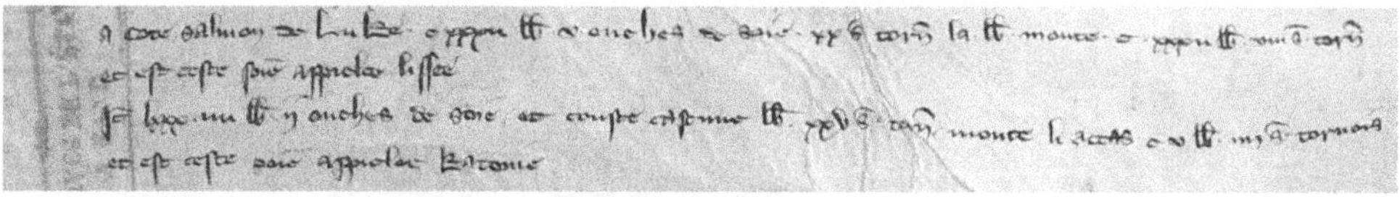

Figure 4. Account of Isabel of Luxembourg, Countess of Flanders, 1294, showing the purchase of some silk fiber from the Caspian Sea region: "A Cote Salmon de Luke cxxxii livres v onches de soie . . . et est ceste soie appielee lissee; Item lxxxiiii livres ii onches de soie et couste chacune livre . . . Et est ceste soie appielee Katonie" (To Cote Salmon of Lucca [for] 132 pounds, 5 ounces of silk . . . and this silk is called "Lissee" ["Liggee" is the more likely name]; And again, for 84 pounds 2 ounces of silk, and each pound [costs . . .], and this silk is called "Katonie"). Ghent, Rijksarchief, fonds Gaillard 52, membrane 8. Photo by author.

After purchasing the Gilan silk from a Genoese merchant, Cote Salmon needed to travel for around a month to get from Lucca to Lagny. If he took the route that was prescribed by the French king, he would have gone from Lucca to Nimes, then into the Cévennes mountains, through Alès, and on to Clermont and beyond.[3]

Back in Paris, as we learn from another entry in the Countess of Flanders's household accounts, Mahy of Arras bought another batch of raw silk from his wife, then oversaw its transformation as it was thrown into usable yarn, cooked to remove the natural gums, and dyed. Fiber that had begun as cocoons of silkworms that were raised somewhere on the shores of the Caspian Sea, or perhaps in China, Greece, or southern Italy, was now ready to be woven into luxurious belts or used in embroidery projects in the countess's household.[4]

*   *   *

Focusing on the late thirteenth and early fourteenth centuries, this chapter recounts the journey of silk fiber that was destined for the Parisian silk industry, from the moment when the silkworms were killed, in various centers of silkworm cultivation in China, Central Asia, and around the Mediterranean, to the moment when Parisian mercers assumed possession of the finished silk textiles and put them up for sale. Through an examination of the actual routes that the silk traveled, we gain a better understanding of the trade networks that linked Paris and its silk industry not only to the Mediterranean world but also to Asia and Central Asia. Discussion of the

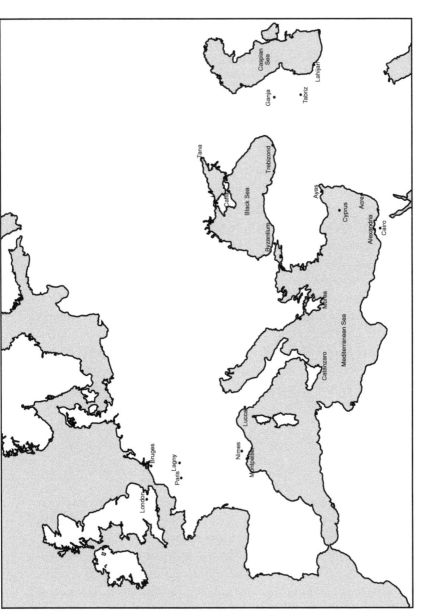

Figure 5. Major centers of silk production and exchange in Europe, North Africa, the Middle East, and the Caspian Sea region, late thirteenth century. Map created by Eddie Peralta, Artworks, University of California, Santa Barbara.

techniques that were employed in transforming the fiber into luxury textile products elucidates the ways in which silk work differed from or resembled work with other textile fibers while highlighting the evidence that we are able to tease out concerning specialized production techniques in Paris. Both discussions enhance our understanding of why we should expect to find skilled immigrants among the silk workers of late thirteenth-century Paris. The discussion of techniques of production thus provides essential background for our discussion, in Chapter 3, of immigrants who may have played a central role in the development of the Parisian silk industry. It also helps lay the groundwork for our examination, in Chapter 4, of gendered roles within the production process.

Historians of the silk industries of fifteenth- and sixteenth-century Italy have at their disposal the internal business records of the entrepreneurs who organized the silk industry, extensive guild regulations, and a fifteenth-century treatise on the way in which silk was produced in Florence.[5] Our sources for late thirteenth- and early fourteenth-century Paris are limited, by contrast, to the names of silk workers and silk entrepreneurs that show up in the Parisian tax assessments that were generated between 1292 and 1313, a few passages in aristocratic household account books recording payments to silk entrepreneurs such as Mahy of Arras, and the somewhat opaque Parisian guild statutes, starting with those that were first recorded in the *Livres des métiers* between 1266 and 1275. None of these sources ever spells out the techniques or organizational structure of the Parisian silk crafts. The guild statutes tend to focus on quality control, requirements for becoming a master and completing an apprenticeship, and the size of the workshop; the aristocratic account books record purchases of products for which only vague descriptions are ever provided. We are thus forced to read between the lines and to extrapolate from non-Parisian sources in order to gain some idea of what went on in Parisian silk workshops. Nevertheless, as will become apparent in Chapters 3 and 4, there appear to have been important differences between the organization of silk production in Paris and the organization of silk production in the major silk textile centers of Italy.

From Cocoon to Raw Fiber

By the late thirteenth century, silk fiber that reached western European centers of silk textile production, including Paris, came from a variety of centers of silkworm cultivation in China, the region around the Caspian Sea, the Levant, various parts of the Greek Mediterranean, and southern Italy.[6] Evidence from Italian notarial sources indicates that among the silk fibers that were available around the year 1300, fiber from the Caspian Sea region—from places such as Lahijan in the province of Gilan in modern Iran (the name "Lahijan" means "place to obtain silk fiber") and from Ganja in modern Azerbaijan—usually garnered the highest prices; raw silk from Catanzaro in Calabria, southern Italy, drew the lowest prices; and silk fiber from China, while relatively abundant, garnered low to moderate prices, apparently because its quality was not as good as that of silk fiber from the Caspian region (fig. 5).[7]

In the premodern era (and indeed, in the modern era as well) nearly all silk fiber was reeled off of the cocoons in the rural areas where the worms themselves were raised.[8] Chinese, Central Asian, Levantine, Greek, and southern Italian peasants who raised the silkworms placed a number of cocoons in warm water in order to soften the gummy sericin that hardened the cocoons and held them together. Once the softening process had loosened each cocoon's filament end, the peasant reelers then loosely reeled together four or more filaments to create a single strand (fig. 6).

Good reelers took care to assure that only the good, middle part of each filament was wound into the strand and that the reeled threads included a consistent number of filaments. Whenever a filament broke off, they stopped the reeling process in order to add a new filament, thus maintaining the consistency of the reel.[9] Once the filaments had been reeled off the cocoons the skeins of raw silk were removed from the silk-reeling devices and prepared for shipping, probably by hanging the loose skeins on a horizontal bar, twisting them, and then bundling up a number of twisted skeins into a long bale called a fardel (fig. 7).[10]

The low price of Chinese raw silk in the early fourteenth century, along with evidence concerning raw Chinese silk in the modern era, suggests that some Chinese peasants may not have been as careful as were Caspian peasants in reeling the silk off of the cocoons. According to the Florentine merchant Francesco Pegolotti, who wrote a merchants' manual in the 1330s, silk fiber that came to Europe from China suffered in quality because of the friction that it endured while traveling the great distances to reach western Europe.[11] To be sure, friction does diminish the quality of silk, especially when it is wet,[12] but nineteenth- and early twentieth-century evidence suggests that low standards of production may also have been at play in China, at least in the

qui la maestra mette dentro a una gran' caldara
piena d'aqua calda le galle et quella altra fem
mena l'aspa et ua tirando su la seda in filzolo

Figure 6. Giuseppe Arcimboldo (Italian, 1527–1593), reeling off of raw silk from the cocoons. From *Treatise on Silk Culture and Manufacture* (about 1586). Pen and blue ink with brush and blue wash on paper. Sheet 30.8 x 19 cm. (12 1/8 x 7 1/2 in.). Museum of Fine Arts, Boston, William A. Sargent Fund, 50.6.15. Photograph © 2016 Museum of Fine Arts, Boston.

production of fiber that was destined for export: according to Hollins Rayner, a British silk manufacturer who was active toward the end of the nineteenth century, the oldest and commonest form of Chinese raw silk that was imported into Britain, known as Tsatlee reel, was reputed to be of low quality because the reelers in China, who worked domestically, did not always take care to produce threads of even consistency, sometimes allowing threads that had started out with filaments from ten or eleven cocoons to run down until they contained filaments from only two cocoons. Other types of hand-reeled raw silk from nineteenth-century China were also considered "coarse and uneven."[13]

The principal long-distance suppliers of the silk fiber that reached Paris around the end of the thirteenth century and the beginning of the fourteenth were the major shipping merchants and international merchant companies of northern Italy. Anchoring in the ports of Laiazzo/Ayas in Cilician Armenia in Asia Minor (up until 1285), Acre (up until 1291), Trebizond (after 1285), Cyprus (largely after 1291), Tana and Caffa on the north shore of the Black Sea, Byzantium, the western Peloponnese, Morea, Alexandria, and southern Italy, merchants on Genoese and Venetian ships purchased skeins of raw silk fiber, silk fiber that had been spun into usable yarn and then "cooked" in order to remove the sericin, silk yarn that was spun, cooked, and dyed, and, occasionally, silk cocoons. They also had merchant representatives who acquired silk fiber at the inland trading center of Tabriz (fig. 5).[14] Between 1257 and 1344—when the Mongol Empire became more fragmented and trade with the Far East became more difficult—the Genoese imported to Europe significant quantities of Chinese silk, and by the third decade of the fourteenth century merchants from both Venice and Genoa had traveled to China.[15] After the Mongol Empire fragmented in 1344 the price of raw silk from China and the Caspian region rose significantly, and raw fiber from China pretty much disappeared from western markets. Raw silk from the Caspian region, however, continued to reach western destinations in significant quantities. In the meantime, moreover, raw silk from Greek lands rose to fill some of the gaps in the market, as did high-quality raw silk from central Italy and Iberia.[16]

In the thirteenth and early fourteenth centuries, most of the raw silk fiber that was purchased by Genoese merchants was destined for Lucca, which had western Europe's most thriving silk cloth industry; and much of the silk fiber that was purchased by Venetian traders would have been sold to those who created silk textiles in Venice.[17] Nevertheless, as the example of Mahy of

Arras's purchase from Cote Salmon of Lucca demonstrates, despite the high demand for silk fiber in Lucca itself, some Lucchese merchants—whose companies had branches all over northwest Europe—carried some of the raw fiber that had come to their city to the Champagne Fairs. Venetian, Genoese, and Florentine merchants also carried raw fiber to destinations north of the Alps—either transporting it by land and river to the Champagne Fairs or, by the last quarter of the thirteenth century, sailing through the Straits of Gibraltar and then on to Bruges, London, and Antwerp.[18] In the latter part of the twelfth century the Genoese had perfected a ship—the *tarida*—that employed both sails and oars and was thus capable of making the difficult east-west passage through the Straits of Gibraltar, a journey that required sailing against the wind. By the later thirteenth century the direct ocean voyage from the Mediterranean to the North Atlantic became an increasingly attractive means of transporting goods between the Mediterranean and ports in the English Channel and North Sea.[19]

Our earliest reference to Chinese silk north of the Alps comes from a London customs record of 1304 indicating that members of the Florentine Frescobaldi company paid customs dues for "serico vocato Catewy" ("silk called Cathay").[20] Other early references to silk from China suggest that merchants from Piacenza and Pistoia may have served as intermediaries between Genoese suppliers and consumers north of the Alps and that merchants from Montpellier also played a role in the diffusion of Chinese silk.[21] We also know that silk from the Caspian region was finding its way to northern Europe. A late fourteenth-century Italian merchants' manual specifically mentioned that Venetian and Genoese galleys were transporting to Bruges raw silk known as "ghella," which would have come from the province of Gilan south of the Caspian.[22] From Bruges, that raw silk would have been shipped primarily to Paris and Cologne.

A list of customs tariffs that were charged on goods sold in Paris at some point in the first half of the fourteenth century indicates that at least two kinds of raw silk from Persia were known by name there: the document indicated that there was a tariff of three pennies on each pound of raw silk ("soie escreue") that was sold in Paris. It qualified the "soie escreue" as "ligée et catonière"—presumably referring, in the first case, to silk from Lahijan ("seta leggia" or "seta leggi" in Italian sources) in Gilan province and, possibly in the second case, to "seta catanji," a contemporary Italian name for silk from Ganja, in Azerbaijan.[23] That same tariff list went on to mention "soie mermite de gerant et pampée": silk of Malmistra, in Asia Minor, silk from

Georgia, and a third silk whose name I have not been able to identify.[24] Mahy of Arras purchased from Cote Salmon two of the varieties of raw silk mentioned on the Parisian tariff list, paying a slightly higher price for "soie Katonie" than for "soie liggee."[25]

In addition to transporting silk from China, Central Asia, and the Mediterranean to the Champagne Fairs and Bruges, Italian merchants also played a role in bringing silk fiber directly to Paris. Thus in 1294, Mahy of Arras, who was in Paris at the time, purchased 18 pounds, 5 ounces of raw silk from a Lombard merchant named Bonnis.[26] And in 1362 the Parisian inventory of a Lucchese merchant, Andrea Simonetti, included raw silk called "ligi" ("serici crudi ligi nuncupati")—that is to say, silk from Lahijan in Gilan province.[27] There were certainly a lot of foreign Lombard merchants in Paris—and a statute that was passed in 1275 at the request of the mercers' guild suggests that a significant number of those Lombards must have traded in silk fiber.[28] As mentioned in Chapter 1, the Parisian tax assessment of 1292 included 180 foreign Lombard taxpaying units, many of which were business enterprises, with several members of each company residing in Paris at one time.[29] The tax assessments point to the presence of at least seven companies of Lombard spice dealers—whose inventories would have included raw silk. But other Italian merchants carried a variety of goods, and we are most interested, within that group, in those who were from towns whose merchants engaged in long-distance trade involving goods from the Far East. The tax assessment of 1296 specifically identified, among the foreign Lombard taxpaying units in Paris, a number of foreign Lombards from such towns, including thirteen individuals or companies from Lucca, fourteen from Genoa, six from Venice, and two each from Pistoia and Florence.[30] The wealthiest of all the taxpayers, moreover, was a foreign Lombard named Gandoulfe d'Arcelles (or Gandolfo di Arcelli), who was from Piacenza, which was yet another town whose merchants carried raw silk fiber to markets north of the Alps.[31]

Many of these Lombards were concentrated in the Lombard zone that stretched across and below the rue de la Buffeterie, which would be renamed the rue des Lombards in 1322.[32] Others were concentrated on the Île-de-la-Cité and on the Petit-Pont, which connected the Cité to the Left Bank.[33] The Lombards who lived on, or near, the rue de la Buffeterie were in close proximity to the wealthy Parisian mercers concentrated around the rue Troussevache and the rue Quincampoix who, as I will indicate in Chapter 3, would have been eager to purchase raw silk fiber (see fig. 19 in Chapter 3). Lombard merchants on the Cité and the Petit-Pont were not particularly close to any important mercers or to any known silk weavers, but they were surrounded by over a dozen hosiery makers who probably needed silk for their work.[34]

Although Lombards played an important role in the last stage of the movement of silk fiber from East Asia, Central Asia, and the Mediterranean to its final destination in Paris, Parisian mercers—who, as I will argue in Chapter 3, were instrumental in organizing silk production—also participated in that movement. As I have already pointed out, the Parisian mercer-goldsmith Mahy of Arras, who resided on the rue Quincampoix, purchased silk for the Countess of Flanders at the Champagne fair of Lagny in 1294. In Paris, moreover, Mahy purchased additional silk fiber from two other Parisian mercers—Jehan le Pellier, who resided on the rue Quincampoix, and Phelippe Anketin, who resided nearby, in the Troussevache mercery. Mahy also purchased silk fiber from his own wife, who must have been a mercer as well. On one occasion Mahy indicated that raw silk sold to him by Phelippe Anketin had been purchased at the fair of Lagny.[35] Although we have no direct evidence for Parisian mercers buying silk fiber in Bruges, we do know that the Parisian mercer Jehan Tabarie the younger did business in Courtrai—which was not far from Bruges.[36]

From Raw Silk to Final Product

Silk fiber differs considerably from other natural fibers in several important ways that affect both the manner in which it is processed and its final performance and value as a luxury fiber. One of the most important differences is the fact that it is the only natural fiber consisting of continuous filaments. In order to create its cocoon, the silkworm produces a single pair of extremely fine, and extremely long, filaments known as brins, which are up to 1,600 meters in length, with up to 900 meters of fiber that can be used, unbroken, to produce pure silk. Up until the time when the fiber is finally "cooked," the two brins are joined together into a single filament known as a bave, which is held together by a gum called sericin. As long as the filaments are covered with the sericin, the fiber is somewhat stiff, like the hairs of a horse's tail. Once the sericin has been removed, the smoothness and luster of the fibers—features that also distinguish silk from wool, cotton, and linen—become apparent, but the cooking cannot take place until first four or more baves have been reeled together as raw silk and then several of those raw silk threads have either been twisted into yarns or, if the yarns are left untwisted as "no-throw" yarn, until after the cloth has been woven.[37]

The most common method for preparing silk fiber for textile production involved the sequential processes of throwing—or twisting—several strands of raw fiber into durable yarns, "cooking" the twisted yarns in order to remove the gums, and then dyeing or bleaching the yarns.[38] While we know that some silk had already been spun, "cooked," and dyed before it ever reached Paris, a high proportion of silk fiber arrived in Paris as raw silk. That is the impression to be gained, in any case, from the accounts of the Countess of Flanders, which refer to the expenses of purchasing silk fiber and then having it spun and dyed in Paris.[39] It is also the impression that we gain from the large numbers of silk throwsters in the Parisian tax assessments: the 93 throwsters who show up in the seven Parisian tax assessments of 1292–1313 (all of them women) nearly equaled the sum total of 6 silk dyers, 26 weavers of silk cloth, 24 weavers of silk narrow ware known as "tissu/z de soie," and 54 makers of ribbon and laces.[40] Moreover, because women were far more likely than were men to be underrepresented in the tax assessments, and because over half of the 113 women who were identified as "ouvrières de soie" were probably throwsters as well, the throwsters probably outnumbered the total number of silk dyers and weavers.[41] Indeed, we can safely estimate that there were probably around 900 silk throwsters in Paris toward the end of the thirteenth century.[42]

Once the skeins of raw silk reached Paris, the mercers who organized silk production would have inspected the silk for its qualities, perhaps deciding which combinations of fibers should be twisted together to make various kinds of yarn. Since silk fibers from worms that were raised in different geographical locations can have vastly different characteristics that affect their performance during the various stages of production, this inspection stage was extremely important. The mercers needed to evaluate the color, luster, elasticity, tenacity, neatness, evenness, and thickness of each batch of skeins (fig. 8).[43]

In classifying, or grading, the silk skeins, Parisian mercers may have drawn, in part, on their knowledge about the place of origin of the fiber, as would later be the case in fifteenth-century Florence.[44] Indeed, Florentine silk entrepreneurs—the *setaioli*—placed so much stock in distinctions among fibers from different regions that they tended to supply each of their silk winders with raw fibers from only one such region.[45] We have no evidence concerning the ways in which Parisian mercers evaluated silk fiber. Nevertheless, we can be certain that in order to minimize the possibility of theft of

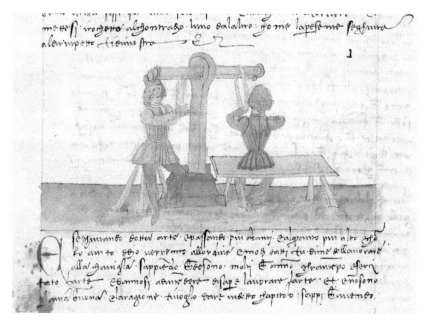

Figure 8. Fifteenth-century Italian silk entrepreneurs inspecting skeins of raw silk. From anonymous fifteenth-century treatise on silk production, Florence, Biblioteca Medicea Laurenziana, Plut. 89 sup. Cod. 117, fol. IV. Reproduced by permission of MiBACT (Ministero dei beni e delle activitá culturale e del turismo).

valuable fiber during the throwing process the mercers would have inspected and weighed their raw silk before sending it out to the throwsters. After the silk was returned to them, moreover, they would have inspected and weighed both the thrown yarn and the discarded waste silk that was an inevitable by-product of the throwing process.[46] The waste-silk fragments would then be used as stuffing in quilted materials or degummed, combed, and then spun into waste-silk yarn. We know there was at least one silk comber in late thirteenth-century Paris, which suggests that there must have been spinners of waste silk as well.[47] The guild of makers of "draps de soye," velvet, and silk purses allowed for the use of waste-silk yarn in minor works and in the warp of silks woven with two warp beams. Similarly, the statutes for the armorers' guild mentioned the use of either waste silk ("borre de soie") or cotton as the stuffing material for padded jackets and leggings.[48] Apparently, as we learn from Jean de Meung, waste silk was also used for making wigs and hairpieces.[49]

After their initial evaluation of the raw silk fiber, the mercers sent the good fiber out to the silk throwsters, who turned the fiber into usable yarns, not by spinning it but by twisting together several long strands of reeled raw silk. This was done before the silk was degummed.[50] John of Garland's *Dictionarius* suggests that already in the 1220s professional throwsters were working in Paris.[51] By the time the earliest set of guild statutes was compiled, at some point between 1266 and 1275, there were two guilds of silk throwsters in Paris: one for throwsters using large "spindles" and one for those using small ones ("filleresses de soye a grans fuiseaus" and "filleresses de soie a petiz fuizeaux").[52]

The technical history of silk-throwing techniques that preceded the arrival or invention of mechanized silk-throwing machines has yet to be written, and it probably varied considerably from place to place, depending on local traditions for spinning other fibers.[53] For that reason, we have no clear indication concerning the reasons for the distinction between the two guilds of silk throwsters in thirteenth-century Paris: did one group of throwsters work with drop spindles and the other with a spinning wheel? Did the term refer to two different-sized drop spindles or to two different-sized spinning wheels? The statutes for the throwsters working with large spindles named the usual variety of tasks that throwsters perform—reeling, throwing, doubling, and retwisting the yarns.[54] The statutes for the throwsters working with small spindles, by contrast, do not bother to spell out the particular tasks, so we have no way of comparing the work that the women in the two guilds did.[55] Nor do the tax assessments help in any way: while the assessments mention several spinners, presumably wool spinners, who worked with spinning wheels, they never mention the equipment of silk throwsters.[56] We should not conclude from this silence, however, that none of the silk throwsters used the spinning wheel. In fact, just the opposite could be the case: if spinning wheels were common among silk throwsters, then the tax assessors would have no reason to mention them.

Before the fiber could be thrown, the skeins needed to be opened, untangled, and broken down into workable sections (known as "slips" in modern parlance) in order to minimize the possibility of breakage during the throwing process. The throwsters, or women who worked as reelers for the throwsters, then separated slips of coarse strands from slips of fine strands and set aside sections of the filaments that were unsuitable for throwing, either because they came from the outside of the cocoons, where the filaments were too rough, or because they came from the inside of the cocoons, where the filaments were too weak.[57] The winders then wound the threads onto bobbins, constantly watching for knots or breaks, working back along the strands to find the places where broken filaments began to weaken in the first place and then working in new, stronger filaments to replace them.[58] The adhesive qualities of the gummy sericin, which had not yet been removed from the filaments, helped the winders integrate the new ends into the continuous strands.

After the strands of filaments had been wound onto bobbins, the throwsters created the yarns. In some cases tram, or weft, yarn was given very little twist so that it would remain soft and lustrous. Such yarns could be created without a spindle by simply pulling off several strands of reeled raw silk over the end of a reeling wheel, thereby introducing a single twist with each turn of the wheel.[59] Other types of weft yarn and all warp yarns were twisted with some kind of spindle—either with a spinning wheel or without, we do not know which. In order to create heavier, doubled yarns, the throwsters then needed to take two previously thrown yarns and twist them together with a spin that went in the opposite direction from that of the original yarns.[60]

While we do not know much about the tools of production that were employed by silk throwsters of Paris, we do know that the ultimate product of their work must have been of excellent quality. The quality and variety of the yarns that they produced played a major role in determining the value and variety of silk textiles and mercery goods that were produced in Paris in the late thirteenth and fourteenth centuries. Working with high-quality yarns of a variety of thicknesses and degrees of twist, Parisian weavers were able to create nearly diaphanous, featherweight veils, lustrous, lightweight, *cendals* and heavier silks requiring doubled, or even tripled, yarns, such as taffeta, cloth of gold, and velvet.[61] In the absence of high-quality yarns, their final products would have been nubby, irregular, and varying in thickness, and they would not have been able to compete with the fine silk textile products of Lucca, Venice, Cyprus, the Mongol empire, and the Levant.[62]

While no source of the late thirteenth century directly attests to the reputation of the silk yarns that were produced in Paris, the elevated reputations and extended markets of silk belts, embroideries, and alms purses that were made in late thirteenth- and early fourteenth-century Paris suggest that, in fact, the handiwork of Parisian throwsters was of excellent quality. One silk belt of "work of Paris" shows up in an account from early fourteenth-century Naples; two packs of goods that were confiscated in Aix-en-Provence in 1343 included 216 silk and gold purses from Paris; and a clerical cope that was probably embroidered in Paris ended up in Uppsala, Sweden, in the late thirteenth century (fig. 9).[63] In 1317, moreover, Queen Jeanne of Burgundy

Figure 9. French purse, c. 1340, depicting "the return of the hunter." Cut velvet embroidered with silk, gold, and silver thread. Musée des tissus/Musée des arts décoratifs, Lyon, MT 30020, 2. © Lyon, MTMAD–Pierre Verrier.

wore a cape made with three pieces of "draps d'or de Paris, ouvré" (cloth of gold of Paris, worked [probably meaning embroidered]) to her coronation in Reims; between 1324 and 1333, the English royal household made nearly annual references to a piece of luxury silk cloth that had been woven in Paris; and the postmortem inventory of Blanche of Namur, queen of Sweden, who died in 1363/4, indicates that she had a piece of silk of Paris among her possessions. Additionally, in 1397 the Count of Savoy purchased a piece of "red, green, and purple" silk of Paris.[64] We also know that the tradition of producing fine silk yarn continued in Paris until at least the sixteenth century. In the late fourteenth century, the household of the Count and Countess of Savoy made several purchases of silk yarn that was produced in Paris, and in the fifteenth century, silk yarn that was produced in Paris garnered substantially higher prices in London than did silk yarn that was produced in London itself.[65] "Fine silk [yarn] of Paris," dyed in at least four different colors, also shows up in a mid-sixteenth-century contract for a tapestry that was commissioned by the Parisian abbey of Ste.-Geneviève.[66]

After being thrown, most silk yarn was then "cooked" to remove the sericin so that the yarn could then be properly dyed or bleached.[67] In some cases, however, silk veils and monochrome silk cloth, such as *cendal*, were woven before the cooking and dying occurred. An early fourteenth-century account of Countess Mahaut of Artois refers to *cendal* that had not yet been "washed," and the 1294 account of the Countess of Flanders refers to the purchase of "une pieche de soie esorne" (a piece of raw silk cloth). In both cases, the silk cloth in question had apparently been woven with raw silk yarn that had not yet been boiled or dyed.[68] This was appropriate for lightweight monochrome silks, such as *cendal*. Leaving the sericin on until after the weaving was completed protected the yarn during the weaving process. It also enhanced the desired lightweight quality of the textile, since the final washing away of the sericin reduced the weight of the fiber by around 25 percent and left air pockets in the weave.

In fourteenth-century Lucca a separate group of *coccitore* cooked—or degummed—the yarn or cloth before it was sent to the dyers; in fifteenth-century Florence, by contrast, both the cooking and the dyeing were performed by the dyers.[69] In Paris the arrangement seems to have anticipated that of Florence. Thus when Mahy of Arras bought raw silk fiber and turned it into yarn for the Countess of Flanders, he listed separate expenses for the throwing and the dyeing but none for the degumming, presumably because the cost of degumming was folded into the cost of dyeing.[70]

There was no separate guild of silk dyers in Paris, and, as I will elaborate in Chapter 3, the mercers passed a number of regulations regarding silk dyeing processes.[71] This has led some scholars to conclude that the mercers themselves did the silk dyeing.[72] While this may have been true in a few cases, the tax assessments indicate that between 1296 and 1300 Paris had at least five artisans who specialized in silk dyeing; a sixth dyer, moreover, turns up in the tax assessment of 1313.[73] Given what we know about the number of silk dyers relative to the number of silk weavers in fifteenth-century Florence, we can conclude that the six dyers of Paris constituted an appropriate number for the size of the silk textile industries there.[74] As was the case in Florence, the silk dyers of Paris tended to reside in a single part of the city: the five silk dyers who show up in the tax assessments of 1296–1300 resided in an area just east of the Troussevache and Quincampoix merceries, in a part of the parish of Saint Merri that was bounded by the rue Neuve Saint Merri, the rue de Biau-Bourc (now known as the rue Beaubourg), the rue Geoffroi l'Angevin, and the rue du Temple (see fig. 19 in Chapter 3).[75] The Parisian silk dyers also resembled the later Florentine dyers in that they were more prosperous than the silk weavers: the average tax assessment for the four silk dyers who were taxed in 1297–1300 was 8.4 sous.[76] By contrast, the average tax assessment for the eleven male weavers of silk cloth who were taxed in 1297–1300 was 5.6 sous, and the average tax assessment for the seven female weavers of silk cloth who were taxed in those years was 2.8 sous.[77]

Like the silk dyers of Florence, those of Paris had to develop skills that were distinct from those of wool dyers. In order to remove the sericin from the fiber without ruining its luster and without leaving streaks or blotches of the gum on the yarn or cloth, which would cause the fiber to absorb the dyes unevenly, they needed to use a special kind of soap. They needed to understand, moreover, that different kinds of silk fiber needed to be "cooked" in the soapy water for differing lengths of time (fig. 10).[78]

Silk dyers also needed access to water with a low mineral content because "hard" water could prevent the total removal of the natural sericin, thereby causing the dyes to be absorbed unevenly.[79] This need for especially pure water may explain why the silk dyers were concentrated not near the Seine, on the east side of Paris (as was the case with the wool dyers), or on the Left Bank stream of the Bièvre (as was the case with the dyers of Saint Marcel) but in the northeast quadrant of the city, in a cluster of locations that were in close proximity to the Fontaine Maubuée, which was constructed at some point in the thirteenth century when the aqueduct linking the abbey of Saint-Martin-des-Champs to the aquafer under the hill of Belleville was extended farther into the city (see fig. 19 in Chapter 3).[80]

In order to dye the fiber without ruining it, the silk dyers also needed to learn recipes that were distinct for each color: dyeing with kermes (or "grano"), the famous dye for making "scarlets," often involved the use of "sour water" (water in which boiled bran had gone sour); dyeing with woad, to make deep blues, required cooking the powdered dye for twenty to thirty-seven hours.[81] It is likely, moreover, that in Paris, as in Florence, each silk dyer worked with a full palette of colors rather than specializing in a single hue, as was the case with wool dyers in Florence and probably in other centers of wool cloth production as well.[82] Precision and skill were absolutely

Figure 10. Cooking raw silk. From anonymous fifteenth-century treatise on silk production, Florence, Biblioteca Medicea Laurenziana, Plut. 89 sup. Cod. 117, fol. 3v. Reproduced by permission of MiBACT (Ministero dei beni e delle attività culturale e del turismo).

essential, since each color required a different recipe and soaking time, and mistakes could result in the loss of both valuable silk fiber and expensive dye (fig. 11). In the fifteenth century an anonymous entrepreneur recorded recipes for various silk dyes, but, as is the case with many artisanal activities, actual skill could only be learned on the job: only through sensual experience— including smell and taste—could the dyers know when a dye bath was ready for the fiber or when the fiber needed to be removed from the bath.[83]

We have no records concerning the range of colors used by the silk dyers of Paris, but we do know that they worked with the expensive red dye known as "grano," which was also used to dye the expensive wool cloth known as scarlet.[84] The mercers' guild passed a statute in 1324 indicating that all red *cendals* and samites that were sold in Paris had to be dyed "in grano"; and in 1326–1327 the English royal household possessed a piece of luxury silk cloth that had been woven in Paris that was both striped and dyed "in grano."[85]

Figure 11. Dyeing silk with red dye. From anonymous fifteenth-century treatise on silk production, Florence, Biblioteca Medicea Laurenziana, Plut. 89 sup. Cod. 117, fol. 27r. Although the text did not associate this image with the use of the red dye kermes, the artist may have been inspired by the process of dyeing with kermes, which usually involved the use of sour water; note that one of the dyers seems to be holding his nose. Image reproduced by permission of MiBACT (Ministero dei beni e delle attività culturale e del turismo).

Fragmentary evidence suggests that from the 1290s to the 1350s the specialized talents of Parisian silk dyers stood out among the talents of cloth dyers north of the Alps. In 1294 the Countess of Flanders purchased a batch of raw silk fiber, which she then had thrown in Paris. Apparently believing that the wool dyers of Flanders would be willing and able to dye her silk yarn, the countess shipped it there, but the undyed yarn was soon shipped back to Paris, where the dyeing finally took place.[86] In 1359, moreover, a Parisian silk dyer relocated to Cologne, thereby providing us with our earliest evidence for the presence of silk dyers in that town.[87]

Metallic thread was also important for the Paris silk industry: we know that some of the male weavers made "cloth of gold," for which they would have woven together silk yarns and yarns that contained gold. We can also surmise that some of the veil makers used gold thread, since literary texts describe veils woven with gold; and we know from both aristocratic account books and surviving samples of narrow ware that it was often woven with both silk yarn and gold or silver thread.[88]

Two types of metallic thread were employed in this period: the first type was made with a substratum of animal membrane onto which gold or silver foil had been beaten. After being cut into strips, the gilded membrane was then wrapped around a silk or linen core. The second type involved cutting thin metallic strips from sheets of gold, silver, or gilded silver and then wrapping the metallic strips around a silk or linen core. As far as we can tell from the surviving fragments of woven cloth of gold that was produced in Lucca and Venice during the late thirteenth or early fourteenth century, the weavers who made cloth of gold almost always used the first type of gold thread, that which employed a gilded animal substratum.[89] By contrast, many surviving examples of narrow ware and embroidery employed gold or gilded silver thread that was made with metallic strips that were wrapped around a fiber core.[90]

By the end of the thirteenth century the island of Cyprus became an important center of production for gold thread. The documentary evidence, as well as the thread used on one surviving embroidery that is thought to have been made in Cyprus, suggests that this thread, known as "gold of Cyprus," was of high quality and made with metal strips rather than with gilded animal membrane.[91] Two Parisian mercers' statutes of 1324 suggest, moreover, that a type of gold thread made in Paris, known by the name "gold of Paris," must have been similar to "gold of Cyprus": the statutes forbade embroiderers and makers of *tissu* (silk narrow ware) to use any kind of gold thread except "gold of Cyprus" or "gold of Paris," and it specifically forbade the use of "gold of Lucca," by which the authors probably meant gold thread made with a gilded animal membrane.[92] The gold thread that was woven into larger cloth of gold in Paris may have been made with gilded animal membrane, but it appears that the mercers wanted to assure that embroidered works and woven narrow ware were made with the more valuable metallic thread.

The production of gold thread was managed by gold beaters ("orbateurs"), who made the gold foil that was beaten onto the animal membranes and the strips of metal that were used to make the more expensive type of gold and silver thread. The earliest collection of Parisian guild statutes, which was compiled before 1275, divided the gold foil makers and the gold strip makers into two different groups, but documents of practice indicate that some gold beaters, like Odeline of Courson, engaged in both types of production.[93] Once they had created the metallic strips or the gilded animal membrane that was to be used in gold thread, the gold beaters sent it out to the "fileresses d'or," who spun the strips around fiber cores. In Paris, as elsewhere, the process of spinning gold thread was carried out almost exclusively by women.[94] The 1294 account of the Countess of Flanders suggests that the gold spinners used a steel spindle to make gold thread: the account tells us that the countess purchased a number of spools of gold and silver wire, as well as metal cutters and steel spindles "to spin gold."[95] Most surviving medieval spindles, by contrast, were made of wood.

Once the silk yarn and metallic thread were ready for use, some of it was sold to aristocratic households, where the ladies of the household either directed, or themselves engaged in, a variety of textile activities, including tablet weaving and weaving. We have evidence for a variety of textile implements from French royal and aristocratic households of the late thirteenth and early fourteenth centuries, and we know that several English royal women engaged in tablet weaving.[96] Additionally, a good amount of silk yarn and gold and silver thread must have been sold to craftspeople other than weavers. These included over 90 Parisian embroiderers, over 125 makers of luxury silk and gold alms purses ("aumonières sarrazinoises"), and approximately 75 stocking makers, not to mention makers of luxurious embroidered saddles, cushion makers, the makers of women's fashionable silk hairnets (known as "crépines"), makers of silk and gold hats, and arms makers, who made not only silk and cotton padded clothing for warriors to wear under their armor but also decorative embroidered garments and banners that warriors and their horses wore and carried into battle.[97]

Nevertheless, much of the silk yarn and metallic thread that was produced in Paris was destined for the workshops of Parisian silk weavers—those who produced narrow ware and ribbons, those who produced veils, and those who wove several types of silk cloth. Since the skeins of dyed silk yarn had to be transferred to bobbins before they were sent to the weavers, the yarn would have been sent back to the throwsters' workshops before arriving at the workshops of the various weavers (fig. 12).

The most numerous group of professional silk weavers in Paris consisted of those engaged in the production of narrow ware—an art that was not at all new to Paris at the end of the thirteenth century. In the 1220s John of Garland had indicated that Parisian women were weaving a range of silk and gold narrow ware products: belts and hair bands for rich women, as well as clerical stoles for priests.[98] At some point in the late 1270s many of the women who produced narrow ware were organized into the guild of makers of "tissuz

Figure 12. Silk winders winding silk onto bobbins. From anonymous fifteenth-century treatise on silk production, Florence, Biblioteca Medicea Laurenziana, Plut. 89 sup. Cod. 117, fol. 29r. Image reproduced by permission of MiBACT (Ministero dei beni e delle activitá culturale e del turismo).

de soie"—for which the guild statutes assumed a female membership.[99] The tax assessments affirm that nearly all of the producers of *tissu/z de soie* were indeed women.[100] However, there was a second guild of makers of narrow ware, that of the "Laceurs de fil et de soie," whose members were frequently called "dorelotiers." The statutes for that guild assumed a predominantly male membership, and the tax assessments affirm that men did indeed constitute a majority of taxpayers who were identified as "dorelotier," "laceur," "laciere," "laceresse," or "qui fait laz de soie."[101] The statutes do not allow us to determine why *dorelotiers* and the makers of *tissu/z de soie* constituted two different guilds: they merely tell us, on the one hand, that the "Laceurs de fil et de soie" made silk and linen laces as well as ribbons and "trouses" for saddles, while the makers of "tissuz de soie" both wove and embroidered "tissu." Nor do account books and literary sources provide much clarity: while they tell us that "tissu" was often decorated with silver or gold thread, they also apply the name "tissu" to the full range of narrow ware products, including the ribbons and laces that were presumably made by the "Laceurs de fil et de soie."[102]

According to Elisabeth Crowfoot, Frances Pritchard, and Kay Staniland, archaeological evidence suggests that at least four different methods were employed to create narrow ware at this time: tablet weaving, finger looping, plaiting, and tabby weaving. They also suggest that tablet weaving was especially associated with women.[103] This close association of tablet weaving with women's work may supply a clue as to the technique employed by makers of "tissuz de soie," since, indeed, their guild was almost entirely female while that of the "laceurs" had a majority of male members.

Tablet weaving is a very ancient form of narrow ware weaving in which the warp threads are threaded through a set of ivory, bone, wood, or (in the modern era) cardboard tablets or cards, all of which have been identically cut and perforated with the same number of holes. The shape of the tablets and the number of perforations vary, but the most common technique involves the use of square cards containing holes in each corner. A belt or trim that has been woven on a tablet loom warped with ten tablets, all containing four holes, would have a warp of forty yarns. Each twist of the cards (which might consist of a quarter turn in which all of the cards are rotated forward, a half turn in which all of the cards are rotated forward, or a more complex turn with some cards rotating forward and others rotating backward) changes the lift of the warp threads, thus preparing the warp for a new pass of the weft yarn. The rotation of the cards also causes the warp threads to wrap around each other, thereby introducing a braided pattern to the weave (fig. 13). Because of the braiding effect, tablet-woven narrow ware is denser and stronger than tabby-woven ribbons and laces and thus more suitable for making belts and orphreys.[104] Several medieval texts associate belts with *tissu/z de soie*, thereby supporting the idea that the women who made "tissuz de soie" may have engaged in tablet weaving.[105] We find some evidence, moreover, that Beguines sometimes wove orphreys.[106]

Because various numbers of cards and perforations, and various combinations of turns, are possible with tablet weaving, the method lends itself to the creation of an endless variety of patterns. In this period, many tablet-woven bands were woven with silk and metallic thread. The belt of "work of Paris" that showed up in Naples in the early fourteenth century may well have been a product of Parisian tablet weaving. Certainly by the latter part of the century the term "work of Paris" was being applied to tablet-woven narrow ware items. Thus an inventory of the Church of the Holy Sepulcher

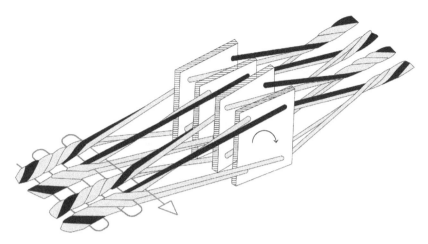

Figure 13. Tablet-woven warp in which alternate cards are being twisted in opposite directions, one-quarter of a turn each time, in order to create both z-twists and s-twists. Adapted from Desrosiers, *Soieries et autres textiles*, 476, by Eddie Peralta, Artworks, University of California, Santa Barbara.

in Paris, compiled in 1379, referred again and again to orphreys "made *au tavel* of work of Paris." In most cases, the inventory does not describe the actual designs that were woven into these works, but we do know that one tablet-woven orphrey was "sprinkled with fleurs-de-lis from the coat of arms of France."[107]

In 1294, the Countess of Flanders made numerous purchases of narrow ware items in Paris. In at least one case, the account recording these purchases makes it clear that the weaver who produced the *tissu* was also the vendor from whom it had been purchased.[108] Well into the fifteenth century, narrow ware from Paris continued to hold a prestigious position in the luxury markets of northern France and the Low Countries: between 1430 and 1455, for instance, Philip the Good, the Duke of Burgundy, purchased all of his silk cloth in towns other than Paris, but it was in Paris that he purchased most of his *tissu de soie*.[109]

The second major group of weavers in Paris were the women who wove head coverings. These included women's veils; barbettes, which women wrapped under their chins; and wimples, which they draped over their faces and chests (fig. 14). I include in this group of textile workers women who are identified in the tax assessments as "qui carie soie," as well as a Beguine who shows up in a mid-fourteenth-century account book as a maker of *cendal*.[110]

Figure 14. Noble lady at prayer. "Psalter-Hours of Yolande de Soissons," France, Amiens, between 1280 and 1299. Pierpont Morgan Library, MS M.729, fol. 232v, purchased in 1927. The praying lady's head is covered with a gold caul over which she has draped a diaphanous silk wimple, which also covers her neck. The Pierpont Morgan Library, New York.

In all likelihood these women wove lightweight, tabby-woven monochrome silk. Tabby weave is the simplest kind of loom weaving, in which "the wefts go alternately over and under one warp end, so that the weave unit is 2 x 2."[111]

Like the makers of "tissuz de soie" and the *dorelotiers,* the makers of silk head coverings had a guild, for which the statutes appear in all of the surviving manuscripts and printed editions of the *Livre des métiers.*[112] However, it seems that this guild, as well as that of the men who wove various kinds of silk cloth, did not exist when the earliest Parisian guild statutes were compiled. Published editions of the *Livre des métiers,* which include statutes for 100 guilds dating from the thirteenth century and one from the fourteenth, are indicative of the size that the collection eventually reached. However, as Caroline Bourlet has persuasively argued, in its earliest form (which probably dates to the years 1266–1275) the collection contained statutes for only 73 guilds: the guilds whose statutes conform to a single format and use a similar terminology throughout. Bourlet suggests as well that the statutes for another 15 guilds, which resemble the original 73, must have been compiled before 1280. However, Bourlet argues, the statutes for 12 of the guilds, for which the terminology and format differ significantly, must have been written at some point between 1280 and 1300. Included among those 12 guilds were the 2 governing the work of women who wove silk head coverings ("tesserandes de queuvrechiers de soie") and men who wove silk cloth.[113]

The statutes for the makers of silk head coverings do not mention the weaving techniques that the women used, but archaeological evidence suggests that medieval silk weavers were able to achieve a light gauzy effect with tabby weave, and illustrations in French manuscripts suggest that veils from this time could be nearly diaphanous (fig. 14).[114] Moreover, literary texts indicate that some wimples were dyed with saffron and some were elaborately decorated with gold thread. For instance, the medieval French translation (and embellishment) of Guillaume de Nangis's Latin description of the 1275 coronation of Queen Marie, wife of King Philip III, mentioned noble ladies whose heads were adorned "de riches guymples toutes tixurez a fin or" (with rich wimples all woven with fine gold); and the "Dit des merciers," a text describing the mercers of Paris that was written in the late thirteenth or early fourteenth century, mentioned "guimples ensaffrenees" (wimples dyed with saffron).[115] It is quite possible that some of the Parisian women who wove women's head coverings did the saffron dyeing themselves, as was the case in sixteenth-century Venice.[116]

Five women show up in the tax assessments as weavers of silk head coverings, and another four are identified as "qui carie la soie," an expression that probably refers to weaving simple monochrome silks.[117] As I will argue in Chapter 4, however, women in general, and especially those at the lower end of the income pool, were vastly underrepresented in the tax assessments. In the case of the embroiderers, for whom we can compare a list of guild members with embroiderers who show up in the tax assessments, it appears that over 80 percent of the women who practiced the craft either never appeared in the tax assessments or were never identified by trade.[118] If that was also the case for women silk weavers, then the nine women who were identified in the tax assessments as silk weavers represent a group that consisted of at least forty-five such weavers.

The final group of Parisian silk weavers included those whose guild statutes identified them as "ouvriers de draps de soye, de Paris, et de veluyaus et de bourserie en lice" (weavers of silk cloth, of Paris, of velvet, and of woven purses).[119] Like the guild for the weavers of silk head coverings, this guild appears to have taken shape at some point after 1280. The guild of makers of "draps de soye," velvet, and woven purses was the only silk-weaving guild for which yarn counts were stipulated for the warp—at least 1,900 warp yarns for silk looms warped with single yarn, and at least 1,800 warp yarns for silk looms warped with doubled yarn.[120] In order to understand how such counts were achieved, we need to delve into the warping process, which preceded the actual weaving process. This activity might have been carried out by specialized silk warpers, as was the case in fifteenth-century Florence (where many of the silk warpers were women), but it could also have been done by the weavers themselves, all of whom appear to have been men.[121]

In preparation for the dyeing process, the silk yarns had been reeled from bobbins onto reeling devices, which produced loose skeins that would absorb the dyes evenly. In preparation for the warping process, the yarns now needed to be wound again onto bobbins. The bobbins were then placed on a frame containing a series of upright or horizontal pegs that could hold the bobbins in place while the yarn was being pulled onto the warping frame.[122] In an illustration that we have from the silk industry in fifteenth-century Florence, the warper has threaded the silk yarns from twenty-two bobbins through a row of rings, which helped prevent the yarns from getting tangled during the warping process.[123] Behind the row of rings was the warping frame: an upside-down wooden "u" that was fitted with pairs of pegs on the left and right sides, with the pegs in each pair placed at exactly the same height;

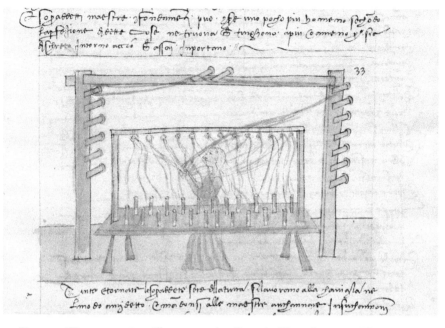

Figure 15. Woman warping silk on a warping frame in fifteenth-century Florence. From anonymous treatise on silk production, Florence, Biblioteca Medicea Laurenziana, Plut. 89 sup. Cod. 117, fol. 29r. Reproduced by permission of MiBACT (Ministero dei beni e delle activività culturale e del turismo).

additionally, moreover, there was one unpaired peg on the lower right side of the frame (fig. 15).

Holding all of the yarns in one hand, the warper began a process of zigzagging the yarns over all of the pegs. He or she began by making a knot at the end of the handful of yarns and looping that knot over the top peg on the left side of the frame. The yarns were then wrapped over and under two nearby pegs in the upper horizontal bar of the frame, then drawn over to the vertical bar on the right side, where they were looped over the top right peg; they were then drawn back to the second peg on the left, with the process continuing back and forth until the warper reached the second peg from the bottom on the right. From there, he or she may have wrapped the yarns around the bottom peg, to create a tail, or s/he may have simply reversed the process from the second-to-last peg, following a reverse path until s/he arrived at the two pegs on the top horizontal bar—where the yarns would be led over the right peg, rather than under it, and under the left peg, rather than over it; then the yarns would arrive again at the top left peg. One zigzag journey of the handful of yarns from the top left peg to the bottom right peg formed the complete length of the warp of the cloth.[124] One complete "turn" (a round-trip journey from top left to bottom right and then back again) constituted twice the length of the warp, and thus, when working with 22 bobbins, as the woman is doing in figure 15, a complete turn forms 44 precisely measured warp yarns. The two pegs on the top horizontal bar, which created the "cross" (yarns that alternatively went either over-under or under-over), helped maintain the order of the various clusters of threads. In order to achieve a warp with approximately 1,900 yarns, the warper in this figure would have needed to make 43 turns. If she were working with 20 bobbins, she would have needed to make 47 and a half turns.

In order to keep track of the number of turns that he or she had made, and thus of the number of yarns that he or she had created for the warp, the warper tied a cord, or ligature, around all of the warping yarns each time he or she turned the yarns around at the bottom of the frame.[125] These ligatures also enabled the weavers and guild regulators or mercers to easily check on the thread count of the warp before it went onto the loom.

The warping frame thus functioned as a system of measurement both for determining the ultimate length of the cloth to be woven and for easily counting the number of yarns that would constitute the warp on the loom. It was a device that was used in wool, linen, and silk cloth production in order to enforce guild standards for the length and thread counts of different types of cloth. Every town, and every type of cloth, had its own particular standards.[126] The minimum standards for Parisian silk cloth (1,800 doubled yarns or 1,900 single ones) would have resulted in pieces of silk cloth somewhere in the range of 55 centimeters wide. Both the approximate width and the legislated thread counts for Parisian silk cloth correspond to what we know about prescribed thread counts and widths for silk cloth that was produced in other major centers of silk production.[127]

The skill of the warper was critical for the final weaving process: by maintaining an even tension, choosing yarns of comparable thickness, and preventing the yarns from crossing each other, the warper played an extremely important role in the ultimate work of the weaver.[128] On an abstract level, such skills were the same for wool, linen, and silk warping, but because silk yarns had a much finer diameter than did the other two fibers, and because they were nearly friction-free, working with silk on the warping frame required its own specific skills. Nevertheless, because silk cloth was generally of smaller dimensions than wool cloth, the warping of a silk loom—at least of a silk loom with only one warp beam—usually took much less time than the warping of a wool loom: in fifteenth-century Florence, for instance, silk warpers usually completed their job in a single day. Wool warping, by contrast, could take up to fifteen days.[129]

Unlike the statutes for the makers of silk head coverings, the statutes for the guild of makers of "draps de soye," velvet, and woven purses assumed that the membership of the guild was predominantly male.[130] This assumption is supported by the evidence from the tax assessments, which reveal the names of seventeen men who were identified as makers of "draps de soye," velvet, and cloth of gold (cloth woven from both silk yarns and gold thread).[131] While seventeen weavers seems modest when we compare that group to the four hundred or so wool weavers in Paris, the size of this group compares favorably with the number of weavers who started new silk industries in towns of sixteenth-century Italy.[132] The male membership of this guild suggests that it was of higher status than the guilds of makers of silk head coverings or the makers of "tissuz de soie," which were almost exclusively female, and of the guild of makers of silk laces, which included both men and women. The assumption that this guild had an elevated status is also supported by the fact that it was one of the first guilds in Paris to require an entry exam in order to establish the competency of aspiring masters.[133]

One of the factors that contributed to the relatively elite status of the weavers of "draps de soye," velvet, and woven purses was the fact that they employed technically complex looms. Our clearest indication that some of these weavers worked with complex looms is the fact that some of them produced velvet—a piled textile that, in the Middle Ages, nearly always employed silk yarn to create the pile. The production process for velvet requires the use of two rotating beams for the warp threads: one to supply the ground warp threads, and one to supply the pile threads, which have to be released at a more rapid rate than the ground warp threads because they are woven over a set of fine metal rods, which form loops that are later cut to make the pile (figs. 16, 17, and 18). Most medieval looms had only one warp beam.[134] We know that some of the male weavers wove velvet because some of them are identified in the tax assessments as velvet weavers and because their guild was described as that of makers of "draps de soye" and velvet. The statutes for the guild did not mention the weaving of velvet, but they did mention looms with two warp beams.[135]

Figure 16. Velvet loom with two warp beams, at La Manufacture Prelle, Lyon, January 2014. Photo by author, reproduced by permission of Prelle Lyon.

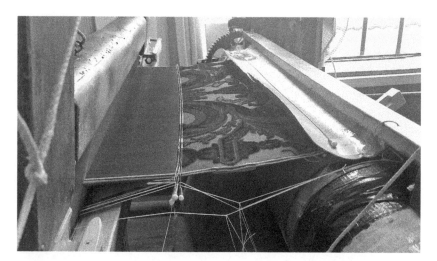

Figure 17. The use of metal rods to create the pile on cut velvet at La Manufacture Prelle, Lyon, January 2014. Late thirteenth-century velvet would have had a solid rather than a patterned pile, but the rods serve the same function in both types of velvet. Photo by author, reproduced by permission of Prelle Lyon.

The inclusion of velvet makers in the statutes for the makers of "draps de soye," velvet, and woven purses constitutes our earliest references to the fabrication of velvet anywhere in Europe—and it suggests that in this one area of silk textile production, the Parisian silk industry may have developed new techniques even before they appeared in Italy. In doing so, however, Parisian weavers would have employed a type of loom—one with two warp beams—that was already being used in Italy for the production of lampas weaves. Our earliest reference to a velvet of Italian provenance dates from 1311, and our earliest reference to velvet looms in Italy dates from 1345.[136]

In Paris, a velvet maker made an appearance in the earliest tax assessment of 1292, and we have a reference from 1278 to a purchase in Paris of a velvet cover for the headboard for the English king's bed.[137] By the 1290s, moreover, two major aristocrats in northern France purchased velvet items in Paris: in 1292 Count Robert II of Artois commissioned the production of twenty-seven luxurious saddles, which were to be decorated with embroidered coats of arms and silk velvet ("veluau de soie"), and in 1293 Count Guy of Flanders issued a receipt to the wealthy Parisian mercer Amauri of Amiens, who resided on the rue Troussevache, indicating that he owed Amauri 44 parisian livres for four pieces of velvet cloth that Amauri had delivered to the count.[138]

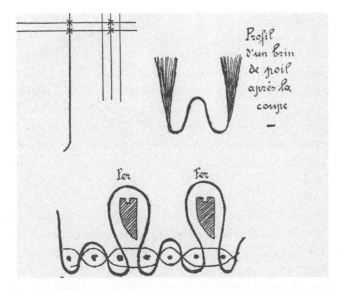

Figure 18. Cross section showing the difference between the path of ground warp yarns (represented by two undulating lines that go over and under the dots at the bottom of the image) and that of the pile warp yarns (represented by the darker undulating line that forms several small loops and two large loops), which travels over the iron rods, marked as "fer" on this drawing. After the pile warp has been woven over several rods, a sharp blade is run over the indentation in the rods to cut the warp yarn to make the pile (as shown in the upper right-hand part of the drawing). G. Gilonne, ed., *Dictionnaire pratique des tissus*, 235.

A year later, the record keepers for the Countess of Flanders recorded an expense of 54 livres for six pieces of velvet that had been purchased for her from Jehan of Lyon, who was probably a son or a grandson of the extremely prominent Parisian mercer Ymbert of Lyon.[139] Moreover, in 1302, when the French king's constable, Raoul of Nesle, died, he had numerous pieces of velvet cloth in his possession, several of which were striped and one of which was striped in gold.[140]

The commissioning of velvet-embellished saddles for Count Robert II of Artois is particularly significant because velvet makers who show up in the Paris tax assessments of the 1290s lived in neighborhoods that were also occupied by saddle makers.[141] Indeed, one of the velvet makers—Jehannot, the brother of Jehannot of Rieremont—was a very close neighbor of two of the saddle makers who were most frequently employed by Count Robert II of Artois: Gautier of Brussels and Renier du Tret (or "of Utrecht").[142] Multiple references to striped velvet and to velvet striped with gold in the postmortem inventory of Raoul of Nesle's possessions are also interesting because the Parisian silk that shows up in the English royal wardrobe accounts of the 1330s was striped, and we know that some of the silk weavers in Paris wove cloth of gold. In French account books of the period, the provenance of velvet was almost never identified. It seems reasonable to conclude, however, that all or most of the early velvet discussed here was made in Paris; certainly that must have been the case for the velvet that decorated Count Robert II of Artois's saddles.

The statutes for the guild of makers of "draps de soye," velvet, and woven purses never specifically define "draps de soye": the term may have encompassed both simple, monochrome, non-luxury silk weaves, such as *cendal* (which was often used as a lining material and was probably woven on looms that resembled those used to weave simple tabby-woven linens), and complex patterned weaves requiring the use of multiple draw cords or multiple pulleys and harnesses to raise differing combinations of warp threads. The standard number of pulleys and harnesses for horizontal looms for woolens was four.[143] Draw looms, by contrast, which were used for patterned silks, could have hundreds of pulleys, with each pair of pulleys facilitating the lifting of a distinct combination of warp threads.[144] There are no surviving archaeological remains of medieval draw looms, and our earliest visual evidence for draw loom designs dates from the fifteenth century.[145] Nevertheless, textile scholars assume that draw looms existed in thirteenth-century Italy, and we have a textual description dating from 1335 of a draw loom from Lucca.[146] We can surmise, moreover, that draw loom technology had arrived in northern France by 1304: in that year, Countess Mahaut of Artois commissioned the construction of a loom that included 200 pulleys.[147]

Although we have no material remains of silks that can be definitively linked to Parisian looms, and thus we cannot deduce what the silk looms were like, what we can determine from various written sources—including the Parisian tax assessments, the records of the English royal household, and the accounts of Countess Mahaut—is that, by the late thirteenth/early fourteenth century, Parisian silk cloth weavers were producing not only simple *cendal* but also small amounts of luxury silk cloth, velvet, and cloth of gold.[148] Moreover, by the early fourteenth century, if not before, some form of draw loom had reached northern France. In addition, the accounts of the court of Savoy indicate that silk cloth continued to be woven in Paris for at least a century.

But if silk cloth was woven in Paris for one hundred years, or even more, why is it that written references to silk cloth that was woven there are limited to a mere handful of aristocratic account books? One reason is that the household administrators who created these account books were inconsistent in the degree to which they took an interest in the provenance of textiles. Another has to do with the fact that velvet was one of the products of the Parisian luxury silk cloth industry, and velvet was almost never identified by provenance. Finally, the Parisian luxury silk cloth industry was modest in scale, and because of this its products may not have come to be known to a broad circle of consumers by clear identifying characteristics—such as selvedges of a particular color, as was the case with some of the products of the larger silk industries of Lucca and Venice.

Chapter 3

Immigrant Mercers and Silk Workers

In 1298 a Venetian named Rolant, whose profession was never identified in the sources but who may have been a mercer, was taxed on the rue Saint Merri, in a section of Paris that was occupied by a large number of Italians; his immediate neighbor on the tax list was a certain "Dame Oudart de Mont Gison." Rolant, who paid a substantial tax of 3 livres, 15 sous in 1298 (which was almost four times the average tax assessment), does not appear on the tax assessment of 1299. In his place, occupying the very same tax address that Rolant had occupied the previous year (the one right next to Dame Oudart), we find a certain silk weaver named Gautier the Burgundian, "maker of cloth of gold" (see fig. 21, VG near the bottom of the map). Gautier's tax of 20 sous, or 1 livre, was average for taxpayers overall, and significantly lower than that of Rolant of Venice, but it was the highest tax ever paid by any of the silk cloth weavers in the Parisian tax assessments.[1] The fact that Rolant and Gautier occupied precisely the same tax address in two consecutive years seems more than accidental. Indeed, it suggests that they may have shared a workshop in 1298. By the time the tax assessors showed up in 1299, however, Rolant had apparently moved to another address, leaving Gautier in the position of taxpaying head of household/workshop. A splitting up of the business assets may help explain why Gautier's 1299 tax payment was substantially less than Rolant's had been in 1298.

The possible business relationship between Gautier the Burgundian and Rolant of Venice—whose tax payment indicates that he must have been an entrepreneur rather than an artisan—provocatively suggests that immigrant entrepreneurs from the silk-making town of Venice may have participated in the introduction of luxury silk cloth production to Paris. It also demonstrates the limitations of the Parisian sources regarding the silk industry: the surviving sources allow us to formulate plausible hypotheses concerning connections between entrepreneurs and workers, but they never definitively illuminate working relationships.

*   *   *

Scholars have argued that the movement of silk technologies from one place to another in premodern societies was almost always accompanied by the migration of skilled artisans.[2] The principal goal of this chapter is to identify some of the immigrants who may have played a role in introducing new silk technologies to Paris. In the cases of throwsters and dyers, such identification is not possible because silk throwsters—and presumably silk dyers along with them—were already installed in Paris by the 1220s, long before the surviving Parisian tax assessments were compiled. We have a better chance of locating immigrant silk weavers because the first Parisian weavers of silk cloth seem to have become active at some point after 1280. For that reason, it seems likely that some of the earliest immigrant silk weavers who were active in Paris appeared in the tax assessments of 1292–1313.

Before we look for immigrant artisans, however, we need to look for immigrant entrepreneurs. Without the mediation of immigrant entrepreneurs who had business connections in both Paris and their regions of origin it seems unlikely that artisans of modest means would have relocated to Paris from centers of silk weaving in the Mediterranean basin. Silk artisans in centers of luxury silk production lived too far away from Paris to feel a spontaneous gravitational attraction to its working environment, and the industry for which they worked was too grounded in Mediterranean networks for them to risk, without some kind of encouragement, a move to unfamiliar territory where no silk cloth industry yet existed.

This chapter begins, therefore, with a discussion of mercers—the Parisian entrepreneurs who not only retailed silk textiles but also, in some cases, organized or oversaw silk production. In the first section I build the case that a particular subset of Parisian mercers organized part of the silk production process and oversaw the rest. In the second, I turn to a variety of source materials in an effort to locate mercers within that subset who had immigrated to Paris from the Mediterranean region. I then build the case that some of those mercers had production networks in Paris that included immigrant artisans from their hometowns or regions and that those immigrant artisans may well have played a central role in introducing silk technologies to Paris.

Mercers and the Organization of Silk Production in Paris

Written evidence for the organization of the Parisian silk textile industry occurs primarily in guild statutes, beginning with those that were first promulgated during and just after the reign of King Louis IX either by the royal provost of Paris, Étienne Boileau, or by his immediate successor, in the years between 1266 and 1275.[3] The guild statutes of medieval Paris never explicitly spelled out how an industry was organized. Rather, they tended to focus on issues such as minimum requirements for becoming a master or mistress or for completing an apprenticeship, minimum standards for the quality of raw materials to be used in the production process, limits on the numbers of apprentices or servants any one master or mistress could have in his or her workshop, and ways in which a craft could, or could not, be passed down through the family. Some statutes, moreover, addressed issues relating to fraud and theft.

Despite their opaque nature, however, the Parisian guild statutes do enable us to piece together a partial picture of the key participants in the production of silk textiles as well as the economic and power relationships among them. That picture suggests that mercers, who were the principal retailers of silk cloth and mercery goods in Paris, also took the lead in organizing and monitoring silk cloth production. Those sources also suggest that the organization of Parisian silk production differed, in certain details, from the organization found in the major Italian centers of silk production—Lucca, Florence, and Venice. In Venice, the weavers themselves apparently organized silk production. In late thirteenth- and early fourteenth-century Paris, fourteenth-century Lucca, and fifteenth-century Florence, by contrast, silk textiles were produced through a putting-out system, one in which silk entrepreneurs—mercers in Paris, *setaioli* in Italy—played a central role. Nevertheless, while the records from Lucca and Florence allow us to conclude that the *setaioli* owned the silk fiber through every stage of the production process, the sources for Paris do not allow us to draw the same conclusions. Indeed, it seems likely, as I will argue, that silk dyers and weavers in Paris were under the regulatory, but not the economic, control of the mercers.[4]

When the first set of Parisian guild statutes was compiled, between 1266 and 1275, the silk cloth industry did not yet exist there. Nevertheless, smaller silk textile goods—such as silk narrow ware and woven silk purses—were already in production, and the statutes for the mercers' guild suggest that the mercers already played a role in either commissioning those goods or creating them within their own workshops. Thus the statutes state that "no one of this craft is to mix together in the warp of silk narrow ware . . . or of any other work, linen or waste silk yarn and true silk yarn."[5] Similarly, "no one should commission nor buy [*faire faire ne acheter*] Saracen-style alms purses if those purses mix linen or cotton with silk."[6]

Aristocratic account books from the early fourteenth century and apprenticeship records from the early fifteenth affirm that mercers played exactly this kind of role in producing, commissioning, and ushering to completion small mercery goods: in 1304, for instance, an agent for Countess Mahaut of Artois purchased some gold and silver foil that was then "loaned" to the Parisian mercer Lando Belloni "to be worked" (meaning, apparently, that someone in Lando's workshop would turn the foil into gold thread and then work that thread into silk mercery goods).[7] Indeed, the countess's agent even went so far, on this occasion, as to purchase for Belloni a weaving blade and cards for tablet weaving.[8] Again in 1328 the same Lando Belloni (or "Lande Belon," as this immigrant from Lucca was referred to in French sources) "made" some narrow ware that was then embroidered by a goldsmith; and in 1322, the same Lando Belloni purchased some samite silk for Countess Mahaut and then either dyed it in his own workshop or had it dyed.[9] This pattern of mercer involvement in the production of mercery goods continued into the fifteenth century: sometime around 1400, a thirteen-year-old girl was apprenticed to a Parisian mercer and his wife to learn to weave "texus" (presumably silk narrow ware); in 1401, however, the girl decided to become a nun, so her guardians paid a fine to the mercers in question as compensation for the incomplete apprenticeship.[10]

In addition to suggesting that Parisian mercers were involved in the production of mercery goods, the original statutes from the period up to 1275 indicate that the mercers' guild enjoyed greater collective privileges than did the guilds of silk artisans. Thus, while mercers were allowed to elect their own guild officers, or jurors, and those elected jurors took their oath of office in the presence of the mercers themselves, the officers of most other silk guilds were appointed and they swore their oaths in front of the royal provost. One other silk guild—that of the ribbon makers—was allowed to elect its own officers but with the understanding—which was never mentioned in the case of the mercers—that the officers assumed their positions and continued to serve only "at the pleasure" of the royal provost of Paris; those officers, moreover, swore their oaths in the presence of the royal provost rather than in the presence of their fellow guild members.[11] Evidently, then, Étienne Boileau and his immediate successor recognized that there was a hierarchy among the mercery guilds and that the mercers were at the top of that hierarchy. This hierarchy was consistent with the fact that some of the mercers belonged to the most prominent bourgeois families of Paris—those whose men ended up governing the bourgeois community of the city by holding offices as provost of the merchants and as *échevins*.[12]

By 1275, we begin to discern that as a consequence of their social, political, and corporate prominence the mercers enjoyed ease of access to the royal provost, and as a result of that access they were able to convince him to promulgate statutes that protected their economic interests while restricting the behavior of silk artisans in other guilds. In the preface to a set of statutes that he passed in 1275, the royal provost indicated that the "community of mercers" came before him to lodge a complaint concerning the harm that silk throwsters (who had two guilds of their own) were causing them. Paraphrasing what the mercers had apparently said to him, the provost described the throwsters as virtual thieves who were purloining high-quality silk that belonged to the mercers:

> When some of the mercers of the city of Paris lend out their raw silk in order for it to be worked or thrown . . . the throwsters pawn it or sell it to Lombards or Jews, or they exchange with [the Lombards and Jews] the good silk that had been lent to them . . . for waste silk, which they then return in place of the good silk to the one who had lent it to them. . . .
>
> Moreover, after they have pawned or sold this good silk . . . when the one who lent it to them comes and demands his silk, they say that they have lost it and that they would voluntarily pay for its value, but that they have nothing with which to pay. Because of this, the ones who lend out the silk in order for it to be worked or thrown have [in the past] brought cause against the women in our presence, making complaints and demanding their silk. And the women repeat what they have already said, and they add that they have nothing with which to pay for the value [of the silk].[13]

Responding to this collective complaint from the mercers, the royal provost prohibited Jews and Lombards in Paris from taking raw or dyed silk fiber as a pledge for consumer loans. Additionally, after summoning all of the throwsters into his presence, the provost announced that, at the risk of being banished from the city, no throwster was to sell or pawn any of the silk that was loaned out to her for the throwing process, nor should any of them exchange good silk for bad. Any throwster who ignored the warning would have to remain outside the jurisdictional boundaries of the city until she had paid off her debt to the individual from whom she had taken the silk; if she reentered the municipal boundaries before paying off the debt, she would be placed in the pillory for two days.[14]

In northern French towns in the later thirteenth century banishment was a standard sanction for debtors—and it thus seems that the provost chose, at this point, to categorize throwsters who took silk fiber from mercers not as thieves but as debtors.[15] In 1324, statutes concerning the illicit sale or pawning of silk fiber indicated that those caught participating in such exchanges would be at the mercy or will of the king, "in body and possessions."[16] In most cases, this meant that throwsters who pawned fiber belonging to someone else could have their possessions seized to pay back the debt, or they could spend time in prison until they paid back their debts. It is unclear, however, if these punishments were limited to those who failed to repay their debts for the stolen fiber. We have no sources pointing to silk throwsters who were so punished, but we do know that one fifteenth-century linen spinner was imprisoned in the Châtelet of Paris for pawning linen fiber that was not hers and then failing to reimburse the owner of the fiber for his or her loss.[17]

The tension in the relationship between mercers and throwsters was a consequence of the fact that expensive fiber that belonged to the mercers, who were relatively wealthy, spent time in the homes, rooms, or workshops of throwsters, who, while not at the bottom of the economic hierarchy, were, like many other working Parisians, often in need of cash. Some of the problem apparently arose, moreover, when servants or apprentices working for the throwsters purloined silk fiber. We learn from a criminal case that came up in 1340 that some Parisian women—in this case, the wife of a sergeant working for the abbey of Saint-Martin-des-Champs—even specialized in reselling silk fiber that apprentices and other "ouvrières de soie" had stolen from their masters and mistresses.[18]

The problem of purloined silk fiber was exacerbated by the nature of silk fiber and by the fact that silk waste was, and is, a necessary by-product of the throwing process. While medieval silk entrepreneurs had a ballpark idea of how much silk waste was generated by the throwing process, the exact amount would depend, in any given case, on the particular qualities of the particular fiber with which the throwster was working. The impossibility of creating a surefire method of predicting how much good silk and how much waste silk the throwster should return to the mercer created an opportunity for some throwsters to enhance their incomes or pay off their consumer debts by exchanging small amounts of good silk for small amounts of waste silk.

The throwsters could also take advantage of various means of manipulating the perceived quantity of good silk that they returned to the mercers. This was possible because silk fiber was, and is, measured and priced by weight—and its weight can easily be manipulated by varying the moisture content of the fiber, by adding liquors, oil, urine, sugar water, or egg yolk to the fiber, by hiding the "waste" ends of silk filaments in the interior layers of skeins or bobbins of silk, or by mixing the waste parts of silk filaments into yarns containing good parts of the silk filaments.[19] Actual court records from the Châtelet are too spotty for us to determine how often cases were actually brought against throwsters, but we know from thirteenth-century Egyptian sources, from sixteenth-century Italian judicial records, and from a French merchants' manual of the seventeenth century that this kind of fiber loss was a frequent bone of contention between silk entrepreneurs and women who threw or wound silk.[20]

Fiber loss was also an issue in the workshops of women who wove silk head coverings. The original Parisian statutes for this guild, which were drawn up at some point between 1280 and 1300, stipulated that no member of the guild was to use any product that she had made or was about to make as a pledge for a loan taken from a Jewish, Lombard, or other moneylender; those who were caught doing so would pay a fine of 10 sous. It is not clear why the sanction, in this case, was lighter than that described for the throwsters.[21]

The mercers' claim that the throwsters stole silk fiber from them in order to pawn it or sell it, and the implication that the weavers of silk head coverings did the same, is indicative, as I elaborate in Chapter 5, that a significant portion of women silk workers participated in the Parisian market for credit, thus subjecting themselves to what may have been crippling cycles of indebtedness.[22] For now, however, our interest lies in what the regulations tell us about the organization of silk production: they reveal, in fact, that in many, or most, cases the mercers owned the fiber when it went out to the workshops or homes of throwsters and that they probably owned the silk fiber that went out to the workshops of weavers of silk head coverings as well. When these artisans completed the process of transforming the fiber, the finished yarn or the woven head coverings were returned to the mercers.[23]

By contrast, there is no evidence that the mercers owned the silk fiber as it passed through the workshops of silk dyers or of weavers who wove complex silks such as velvet. Thus, while statutes concerning the throwsters and makers of silk head coverings explicitly singled out the issue of women who used silk fiber that did not belong to them as pledge material for consumer loans, no such issue was ever raised in discussions of silk dyers, who were predominantly men, or of weavers who belonged to the guild of "Ouvriers de draps de soye . . . de veluyaus et de bourserie en lice," among whom the weavers of velvet and silk cloth were also predominantly men.[24] The silk dyers had no guild, so no complete set of statutes specifically addressed to them was ever drawn up. The "Ouvriers de draps de soye," however, had a guild for which the statutes were probably written down around the same time that the statutes for the weavers of silk head coverings were created. The statutes for the weavers of "draps de soye" and other complex silks make no mention of loan pledges.[25]

This is not to say, however, that the mercers exercised no control over silk dyers and male weavers of complex silk cloth. Indeed, it is clear that by the end of the first quarter of the fourteenth century they had the right to enforce guild regulations regarding quality control: in statutes that he promulgated in 1324, the royal provost of Paris put forward the idea that the mercers held policing powers over all aspects of mercery production, including dyeing and weaving. Once again, just as in 1275, the royal provost took his initiative in response to a request from the community of mercers, who had apparently described an urgent need for new regulations:

> To all who see this document, greetings from Jehan Loncle, guard of the *prêvoté* of Paris. The good men, the mercers of Paris, came before us and caused us to understand that in the sale and crafts of the said mercery several damaging misdeeds were being done by all of the common people from day to day due to the absence of convenient rules for the said crafts, and these were so great that if no remedy was put in place, grief and shame would ensue . . . and for this reason they asked us . . . to provide a convenient remedy.[26]

In subsequent paragraphs in this long set of statutes the royal provost forbade the use of silk fiber as a pledge for consumer loans—although this time he was more open-ended concerning the identity of those who engaged in these activities and he created harsher sanctions for the transgressors, placing them and their possessions at the mercy of the king.[27]

In his 1324 statutes concerning silk dyers and weavers, the royal provost focused on ways in which some of these artisans misrepresented the quality or quantity of silk fiber and the products derived from it: the dyers, by weighing the fiber down with liquors that they added to dye vats; the weavers, by mixing pure silk yarn with waste-silk yarn or with other fibers.[28] It appears, therefore, that whatever fraud the Parisian dyers or weavers might have engaged in (and their deceptions were hardly unique to the early fourteenth century),[29] their behavior was perceived as a problem of misrepresenting goods in the marketplace rather than one involving the sale or exchange of goods that did not belong to them. Moreover, nearly all of the sanctions for the dyers' and weavers' infractions involved simple fines rather than the threat of being placed at the mercy of the king. Only in the case of dyers who failed to use the expensive red dye known as *grano* was that sanction invoked.[30]

While the 1324 statutes leave open the possibility that, like throwsters and weavers of silk head coverings, dyers and weavers of "draps de soye" and other complex silk textiles sometimes used silk that did not belong to them as a pledge in consumer loans, the absence of any direct statement linking these artisans to illicit loans suggests, instead, that silk dyers and weavers of "draps de soye" worked on materials that they themselves owned during the production process—buying the materials from the mercers at the beginning of the process of transformation and then selling it back to the mercers when they were done.

Nevertheless, although there are no clear signs that the mercers maintained ownership of silk yarn that went out to the workshops of dyers and weavers of "draps de soye," this does not mean that the mercers ignored these stages of production altogether. Indeed, it is clear from the earliest statutes for Parisian mercers, which were compiled before 1275, and from aristocratic account books, that some mercers had narrow ware looms in their shops.[31] It thus seems possible that once the other silk-weaving crafts were introduced to Paris some mercers began to incorporate those weaving activities into their shops as well. Moreover, because they were the principal financial beneficiaries of the superior reputation of silk goods that were produced and sold in Paris, the mercers took care to establish high standards for all stages of silk production.

In the earliest statutes for the mercers those production standards were addressed to the mercers themselves.[32] In 1324, however, the mercers convinced the royal provost of Paris to give them broad disciplinary powers over all stages of production of silk textiles and other mercery goods. From then on, the four annually elected *prud'hommes* of the mercers' guild had the authority to visit "all of the places in Paris where the art of mercery is exercised or where mercery goods are made."[33] If they discovered any throwsters mixing good silk fiber with waste silk, throwsters or dyers weighing down silk fiber with liquors, weavers mixing good silk with waste silk, or embroiderers or weavers of narrow ware employing inferior metallic thread, such as gold thread of Lucca, the *prud'hommes* had the authority to see that the goods were destroyed and a fine imposed. The provost also stipulated that, if they perceived the need, the *prud'hommes* from the mercers' guild could bring with them during their visitations armed officers from the Châtelet.[34] This was not an empty threat: late medieval registers of Parisian civil court cases indicate that some artisans did, in fact, resist visitations from the sworn jurors of their guilds and that the jurors then turned to officers of the Châtelet in order to carry out their statutory visitations.[35]

The mercers, then, considered themselves the ultimate guarantors of the quality of Parisian silk textiles. During the first stage of production—that which produced the yarn itself—mercers maintained direct ownership over the raw material when it went out to the workshops of throwsters, and they seem to have maintained such ownership when the fiber went out to the workshops of veil weavers as well. Between the production of the yarn and the final marketing of "draps de soye" and other luxury cloth, however, there were a variety of possible relationships of production, relationships in which the category of "artisan" and that of "entrepreneur" could be blurred. In some cases, mercers like Lando Belloni supervised some forms of weaving and possibly some forms of dyeing within their own workshops.[36] In other cases, the mercers relinquished ownership of the fiber but maintained regulatory control of the process. This arrangement could suit the mercers' financial interests: by avoiding direct ownership of fiber as it underwent the processes of dyeing and complex weaving, the mercers transferred the burden of financial risk onto the shoulders of the artisans. The dyers were at risk because any error in the dyeing process could ruin a batch of silk, thus wasting both expensive dyes and valuable fiber;[37] the weavers of velvet and "draps de soye" were at risk because of the time lapse between the day when they purchased the silk yarn for a given piece of silk cloth and the day when they completed that cloth. A simple piece of *cendal* took several weeks to weave; more complex silks could take several months. During the intervening time, fluctuations in the silk textile markets could cause a weaver to lose money on his or her investment in the silk fiber.[38]

Although the mercers often avoided direct ownership of raw materials while they were being dyed or woven into velvet or "draps de soye," we learn from the statutes of 1324 that they nevertheless monitored the workmanship of all of the artisans who contributed to the creation of silk textiles in Paris. The technical knowledge of the mercers was thus crucial to the success of Parisian silk textile products. Since some of those mercers were immigrants to Paris from silk-making regions, it seems reasonable to assume that they may well have brought some of that technical knowledge with them when they moved to Paris.

The tax assessments reveal the presence in Paris of nearly 350 mercers.[39] Since the mercers were primarily male and relatively wealthy—paying an average tax, in 1297–1300, that was more than twice the overall average tax of just under one livre—nearly all of them would have shown up in the assessments and been identified by profession at least part of the time. We can thus assume that these numbers are relatively accurate. Not all mercers, however, were involved in the production and sale of luxury silk cloth. Those who were had to have sufficient capital, and they had to have easy access to suppliers of imported silk fiber, to artisans who produced silk yarn and cloth, and to retail consumers. The mercers of three neighborhoods in Paris fit all of these characteristics: those owning shops and probably residing along the rue Quincampoix (Q in fig. 19), those owning shops and probably residing on or around the rue Troussevache (T in fig. 19), and those who were taxed just below the rue Troussevache, in the area around the rue de la Buffeterie that was dominated by Italian (or "Lombard") merchants (L in fig. 19).[40]

The Troussevache mercery included 22 percent of the city's mercers.[41] In 1297–1300 these mercers paid an average tax that was over four and a half times the overall average tax; this indicates that they were the wealthiest group of mercers in Paris. Their numbers included six households of members of the prestigious Dammartin and Toussac families, whose men ended up serving as Parisian *échevins*.[42] Several other mercers in this neighborhood traveled in the same circles as the *échevin* families and were equally wealthy: on the rue Troussevache, Amauri of Amiens, Jehan of Lyon, Jehan le Roumain, Jehan Viel, Guillaume le Boursier, Marie Osane, and Jehan Tabarie the younger all sold silk products to aristocratic or royal households, as did

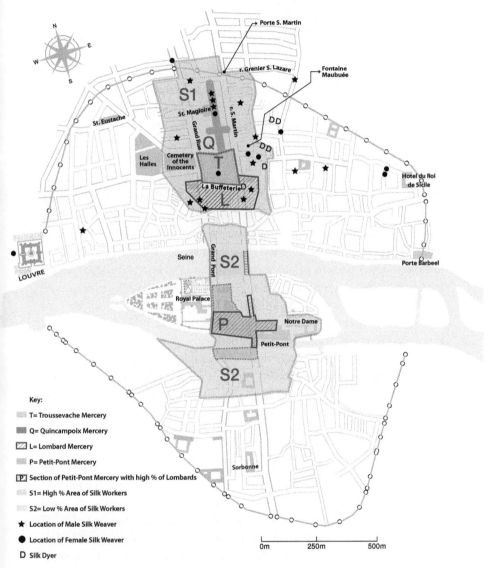

Key:

T= Troussevache Mercery

Q= Quincampoix Mercery

L= Lombard Mercery

P= Petit-Pont Mercery

P Section of Petit-Pont Mercery with high % of Lombards

S1= High % Area of Silk Workers

S2= Low % Area of Silk Workers

★ Location of Male Silk Weaver

● Location of Female Silk Weaver

D Silk Dyer

0m   250m   500m

Figure 19. Location of mercer neighborhoods and silk workers, Paris, c. 1300.
Adapted, in collaboration with author, by Eddie Peralta, Artworks, University of
California, Santa Barbara, from "Plan de la Ville de Paris sous Philippe-le-Bel dressé
par Albert Lenoir architecte d'après le travail de H. Géraud."

Geoffroi of Dammartin and Phelippe Anketin of the rue de la Courroierie and Jehan Tabarie the elder of the rue Guillaume Joce, which was also in the Troussevache mercery.[43] The Troussevache mercers Ymbert (or Imbert) of Lyon and Jacquet Tabarie, moreover, even gained positions as trusted furnishers and financiers of the royal administration.[44]

Extending northeast from the Troussevache mercery, the Quincampoix mercery included 28 percent of the mercers of Paris. In the years 1297–1300 these mercers paid an average tax that was twice the average Parisian tax but considerably less than the average tax of the mercers of the Troussevache area.[45] Like the Troussevache mercery, this street included a number of families whose men entered the ranks of the *échevins* and a number of mercers who did business with the highest aristocratic courts.[46] Many of the mercers of the Quincampoix mercery were as wealthy as those of the Troussevache area, but mixed among them was a greater proportion of modest mercers.

The Lombard neighborhood just below the Troussevache mercery included only 6 percent of the mercers of Paris.[47] However, these mercers were well placed, in terms of access to Italian suppliers and silk artisans: close to 10 percent of the male silk artisans (and close to 18 percent of the men who wove silk cloth) resided in the same neighborhood.[48] Moreover, with an average tax that was just over three times the overall average tax, the mercers in this neighborhood also had access to considerable capital. Two of the mercers in that neighborhood sold goods to the English royal court.[49] One of the mercers in the Lombard neighborhood, Jehan of Rueil, was an *échevin*; another, Jehan Marcel, may have been a member of the prominent *échevin* family that would come to include the famous provost of the merchants, Étienne Marcel.[50]

The section of Paris that I have labeled S1 in figure 19, which included the Troussevache, Quincampoix, and Lombard merceries, as well as a narrow, easily accessible band that wrapped around those three merceries, included 27 percent of the women who were identified in the tax assessments as silk throwsters and 30 percent of the men and women who were identified as "ouvrier/ouvrières de soie."[51] More significantly still, 44 percent of the women who were identified as weavers of silk cloth or head coverings, 67 percent of the silk dyers, and 76 percent of the men who were identified as makers of velvet, "draps de soye," or cloth of gold were located within that zone.[52]

A comparison of the characteristics of the mercers whose tax addresses were in the Troussevache, Quincampoix, and Lombard merceries with those of the one other Parisian neighborhood with a high concentration of mercers helps highlight the distinctiveness of those in the first group. Mercers owning shops and probably residing in the area around the Petit-Pont and on the Île-de-la-Cité (labeled P in fig. 19), who constituted 23.5 percent of the total number of mercers in the city, had easy access to Italian merchant-bankers who congregated on the Petit-Pont and the Cité. However, with an average tax that was approximately one-third of the overall average tax, those mercers do not seem to have had sufficient wealth to invest in silk production. Neither did they have easy access to silk workers: the zone labeled S2 in figure 19—which included the Petit-Pont mercery as well as a neighboring band that wrapped around it—included no silk cloth weavers or dyers and only 2 percent of the silk throwsters and 6 percent of the *ouvriers/ouvrières de soie*.[53] The evidence thus suggests that mercers in the Troussevache, Quincampoix, and Lombard merceries constituted the core of the Parisian entrepreneurs who managed silk cloth production in Paris. The question remains, however: did the mercers in these neighborhoods include immigrants who had moved to Paris from major centers of silk cloth production?

Immigrant Mercers

There were a lot of immigrants in late thirteenth-century Paris, and their numbers included immigrant mercers. Nevertheless, not all immigrant mercers originated in silk-producing regions. In order to determine which mercers —not to mention which silk workers—may have contributed to the origins and early development of the silk industry in Paris we need to begin with an inquiry into the foreign sources of imported luxury silk that reached Parisian consumers in the late thirteenth and early fourteenth centuries. Most of those silk textiles reached Paris through the mediation of international Italian merchants and merchant companies.

Royal and aristocratic account books from the period between c. 1270 and c. 1330, as well as material evidence from elite burials in Paris, point to several key areas of production of prestigious silks that ended up in Paris and northern France during those decades: Central Asia and China, which produced two distinct types of cloth of gold, known as "panni tartarici" or "drap tartaire," on the one hand, and "nach," or "nasi," on the other;[54] the Islamic eastern Mediterranean, most especially Asia Minor ("Turkey," which included Christian Armenia) and the Levant ("Outremer"); northern Italy, most especially Venice and Lucca; and the town of Montpellier in southern

France.[55] According to silk archaeologist Sophie Desrosiers, the town of Alès, which was just north of Montpellier, may belong on this list as well. Desrosiers has suggested that Alès may have been the place of origin of one of two distinct types of patterned silk, both of which were identified as "drap d'Areste" in northern French sources. Moreover, whether or not Alès was the place of origin of one type of *drap d'Areste*, it is clear that silk cloth was woven in that town.[56]

Although silk textiles from Iberia, Sicily, and the Greek Mediterranean had enjoyed considerable prestige in the twelfth century, references to them are relatively rare in late thirteenth- and early fourteenth-century French sources.[57] In the cases of Iberian and Greek silks, however, it would be going too far to argue that these textiles disappeared altogether from late thirteenth-century northern Europe. Desrosiers has argued that the original *drap d'Areste* was produced in Iberia, probably by North African weavers who immigrated to Iberia with the Almohads in the twelfth century, and her distribution map indicates that the Iberian *drap d'Areste* had a market in northern France.[58] Additionally, as Frédérique Lachaud has suggested, marriage connections that the French and English courts established with Iberia may have resulted in the importation of Iberian silks into France and England.[59] Papal inventories and French royal accounts also suggest that Byzantine and Greek silks were still making their way to the west in the late thirteenth and early fourteenth centuries.[60]

Three additional centers of late thirteenth-century silk production—southern Italy, Cologne, and Cyprus—may have been sources for low-prestige silk cloth that was marketed in Paris, but it would be difficult to track down those textiles, since low-prestige silks were almost never identified by place of origin. Documentary evidence indicates that silkworm cultivation (which was an extremely complicated process) was present in southern Italy by the tenth century, if not before, and that silk cloth production continued there after the brother of King Louis IX of France, Charles of Anjou, took over the kingdom of Sicily and southern Italy in 1266.[61] By 1260, Cologne was producing the simple silk textile called "cendal." It was also a center of production for very high prestige patterned narrow ware that was woven from silk and linen.[62] Cyprus was best known for its high-prestige silk embroideries, not for the weaving of silk (fig. 20).[63] Nevertheless, notarial records and a merchants' manual from the first half of the fourteenth century indicate that *cendal* was woven there as well.[64]

Central Asia, Asia Minor, the Levant, the former Byzantine empire, Lucca, Venice, Montpellier, Iberia, and possibly Alès: these were the centers

Figure 20. Grandson Antependium. This silk and gold textile was probably embroidered in Cyprus soon after the fall of Acre (the last crusader holdout) in 1291. Photo and permission courtesy of Bernisches Historisches Museum, Bern.

of silk production that supplied Paris with its prestigious silk textiles in the late thirteenth and early fourteenth centuries, and low-prestige silks from Cyprus, Cologne, and southern Italy may have been marketed in Paris as well. It seems significant, therefore, that the 341 mercers who show up in the Parisian tax assessments of 1292–1313 included individuals whose names identified them with nearly all of these centers of production, with the exceptions of Central Asia and Asia Minor.

Aristocratic, royal, and institutional records occasionally provide important information concerning the place of origin of immigrant mercers who resided in Paris. However, our principal evidence for Parisian mercers who may have migrated to Paris from other regions comes from surname evidence in the Parisian tax assessments: in some cases, individuals were identified as being "of" a particular town or region ("Marques of Lucca," "Gracien of Spain") or as having a particular regional identity ("Coluche the Lombard, "Gautier the Burgundian"). As discussed in Chapter 1, these toponymic surnames can sometimes be misleading. Nevertheless, since the use of surnames was a new phenomenon in late thirteenth-century Paris, and since regional surnames such as "the Lombard" referred to cultural differences, there is reason to believe that in most cases they provide us with accurate indicators of an individual's place of origin.[65] Unfortunately, however, only some taxpayers were identified with a surname, and not everyone who was given a surname had a toponymic surname. Generally the higher up the social hierarchy an individual was, the more likely it was that he or she would be identified with a surname; social hierarchy, however, was not a factor in determining who did, and who did not, have a topographic surname (table 1).

Despite the gaps and pitfalls in the surname evidence, the tax assessments, supplemented by account books and institutional sources, provide compelling evidence that the mercers and possible mercers of the Trousse vache, Quincampoix, and Lombard merceries included men, and probably some women, who had roots in a significant number of known silk-producing regions of the late thirteenth century: Lucca, Venice, Cyprus, the Levant, some part of the former Byzantine empire, and Montpellier. We can surmise that they were immigrants either because they had toponymic surnames indicative of origins in these places (in which case the immigrants may have been their immediate progenitors or spouses) or because other sources explicitly tell us that they were from those regions. Additionally, Iberia had one representative on the rue du Grenier-Saint-Lazare (or the rue du Guernier-de-Saint-Ladre), which

TABLE 1. SOCIAL HIERARCHY AND SURNAME EVIDENCE

	Mercers	Male Silk Cloth Weavers	Female Silk Cloth Weavers
Total number in tax assessments	341	17	9
Average tax payment (1297–1300) (s = sous; L = livres)	41 s (2 L)	5.6 s (.27 L)	2.8 s (.14 L)
Number/percentage identified with a surname	339 (99%)	12 (71%)	3 (33%)
Number/percentage identified with a topographic surname	160 (47%)	10 (59%)	2 (22%)

Note: Based on Appendix 2; Appendix 3, parts A and B.

was just a few meters from the rue Quincampoix, on the other side of the Porte-Saint-Martin (table 2).

In terms of sheer volume, Lucchese silks dominated the upper end of the silk market in the late thirteenth and early fourteenth centuries, so it makes sense that there were a number of Lucchese mercers in Paris.[66] Most Lucchese merchants in Paris were taxed as foreign Lombards, so, while they sold imported silk textiles, these merchants were unlikely to become officially involved in the local production of silk cloth, which fell under the purview of the mercers.[67] Between 1292 and 1313, however, three Lucchese merchants were identified in the tax assessments both as mercers and as "bourgeois of Paris"—individuals enjoying all of the rights, privileges, and obligations of members of the bourgeois community of Paris. Marques of Lucca and his widow, Mahaut, of the rue Troussevache, were always taxed among the bourgeois of Paris rather than as foreign Lombards.[68] Jehan Vanne, whose address was sometimes listed as the rue Troussevache and sometimes as the rue de la Buffeterie (soon to be renamed the rue des Lombards), was sometimes taxed as a Lombard and sometimes as a bourgeois of Paris. Twice he was identified as a mercer. Moreover, as I indicated in Chapter 1, he also joined the guild of hosiery makers.[69] A member of the prominent Bellardi Company of Lucca, Vanne sold a variety of textiles, including silks. In England, he also became a trusted officer of King Edward I.[70] His familial ties are also indicative of the ways in which Lucchese merchants began to put down permanent roots in Paris: Jehan's father-in-law, Jacques Bondos, who also appears to have been from Lucca, was a lay warden in the parish church of Saint-Jacques-de-la-Boucherie, and Bonvis Bondos, who was definitely from Lucca and probably

TABLE 2. PARISIAN MERCERS FROM SILK PRODUCING REGIONS, 1292–C. 1340

	Mercers Troussevache	Possible Mercers Troussevache	Mercers Quincampoix Mercery	Mercers Lombard Mercery	Mercers Petit-Pont Mercery	Total
Lucca	2[1]		1 (?)[2]	3[3]		5–6
Venice			1[4]	1 (?)[5]		1–2
Cyprus	1[6]	3 (?)[7]				1–4
Frankish Greece (?)	1–2[8]					1–2
Levant	2–3[9]		1[10]			3–4
Cologne, Germany	1[11]		1 (?)[12]			1–2
Iberia			1 (located near Quincampoix)[13]			1
Montpellier		1 (?)[14]				0–1
Southern Italy					1[15]	1
Total	7–9	0–4	3–5	3–4	1	14–23

1. Marques of Lucca and Jehan Vanne: Appendix 2, part A, nos. 43, 49; see also main text of this chapter, discussion preceding notes 68–71.

2. Coluche the Lombard: Appendix 2, part B, no. 5; see also main text of this chapter, discussion preceding note 78.

3. Bonvis Bondos; Lando and Ugolino Belloni: Appendix 2, part C, no. 5 (for Bonvis Bondos); see also main text of this chapter, discussion preceding notes 72–77.

4. Jacques/Jacquet of Venice: Appendix 2, part B, no. 35; see also main text of this chapter, discussion preceding note 85.

5. Rolant of Venice: Appendix 1, part A, no. 126; see also the first paragraph of this chapter.

6. Mahy de Lymesis: Appendix 1, part C, no. 19 (and Appendix 2, part A, no. 51). See also main text of this chapter, discussion preceding note 95.

7. Bertaut de Lymesi, Perronele de Lymesis, Thomas de Lymesi: Appendix 1, part C, nos. 17, 21, 23. See also also main text of this chapter, discussion preceding notes 91–95.

8. Jehan le Roumain; Eustache (or Huitace) la Roumainne, widow of Jehan le Roumain: Appendix 1, part C, nos. 32, 35 (and Appendix 2, part A, no. 9); see also main text of this chapter, discussion preceding notes 100–102.

9. Jehan Tabarie the elder (le viel), Jehan Tabarie the younger (le genne), Jacquet Tabarie (who may have been identical with Jehan Tabarie the Elder). While the French version of this surname did not include the preposition "de," Latin versions did. Appendix 1, part C, nos. 37–40 (and Appendix 2, part A, nos. 4, 41); see also main text of this chapter, discussion preceding notes 79–82.

10. Phelippe Tabarie: Appendix 1, part C, no. 41; see also main text of this chapter, discussion preceding notes 80 and 81.

11. Nicole of Cologne: Appendix 2, part A, no. 54; see also main text of this chapter, discussion preceding note 103.

12. Rogier of Germany: Appendix 2, part B, no. 88; see also main text of this chapter, discussion preceding note 104.

13. Gracien of Spain: Appendix 2, part E, no. 19; see also main text of this chapter, discussion preceding note 105.

14. Pierre of Montpellier: see main text of this chapter, discussion preceding note 88.

15. Jehan of Apulia: Appendix 2, part D, no. 32; see also main text of this chapter, discussion preceding note 108.

related to Jacques Bondos, bequeathed a house to the same parish.[71] Like Jehan Vanne, Bonvis Bondos was a mercer.[72]

Two other Lucchese mercers, Lando and Ugolino Belloni, were active in Paris in the second, third, and fourth decades of the fourteenth century. Lando's name emerges frequently as "Lande Belon" in French aristocratic account books, where we find him ushering silk narrow ware through the production process, overseeing the dyeing of silk cloth, and furnishing a variety of samites, velvets, *cendals*, and Mongol cloth of gold; in 1327, moreover, the French royal court sold him some of the silk textiles from the estate of Queen Clémence of Hungary. The fact that Lando was given such an opportunity indicates that he had a favorable relationship with the royal court.[73]

Lando and Ugolino never show up in the tax assessments of 1292–1313, but we know from a document of 1328 that Lando owned property in the Lombard mercery, on one of the two streets known as the Grand and Petit Marivaux.[74] There is good reason to believe that Ugolino owned property there as well.[75] We also know that by 1328 Lando was recognized as "bourgeois of Paris," and in the early 1340s the brothers (both identified as "bourgeois of Paris" by then) founded a chapel in honor of the image of the "Volto Santo," or Holy Face, of Lucca, in the Church of the Holy Sepulcher in Paris.[76] Like Jacques Bondos, both Lando and Ugolino Belloni put down roots in Paris, settling their families there and building ties with local religious institutions. Their Parisian descendants included a major furnisher to the court of Charles V and the wife of the *valet de chambre* of King Charles VI.[77] One other mercer of the Quincampoix mercery, Coluche the Lombard, may have been from Lucca, but it is also possible that he was from Venice, Milan, or some other town in northern Italy.[78]

After silks from Lucca, silks from the Mongol empire and the Levant, or "Outremer," seem to have enjoyed the greatest markets in late thirteenth-century northern France.[79] While no mercers from the Mongol empire appear among Parisian mercers, the Levant was represented by three, or possibly four, men with the surname Tabarie (or de Tabarie), which was the old French name for the town of Tiberias on the western shore of the Sea of Galilee. The Tabarie men (Jehan the elder, Jehan the younger, Phelippe, and possibly Jacquet) were probably all related to each other.[80] They resided both in the Troussevache and in the Quincampoix merceries and specialized in the sale of women's silk head coverings—"couvrechiefs," "barbettes," and wimples—which they sold to the Countesses of Artois, Flanders, and Hainaut, as well as to Queen Margaret of England.[81] One of them was also included on a list of Parisian merchants who were given privileges at the French court.[82] It seems very likely that these Tabarie men were from a crusader family that had relocated to France either after the fall of Tiberias in 1265 or after the fall of Acre in 1291. No other Parisian taxpayers were identified by this surname.

Aristocratic account books suggest that Venetian silks were the next in line after silks of the Levant, in terms of quantities that were consumed in northern France in the second half of the thirteenth century.[83] Like Lucca, Venice was well represented among the Lombard merchant companies of Paris.[84] However, only one Venetian—Jacquet of Venice, who resided on the rue Quincampoix and was taxed as a bourgeois of Paris—was ever identified as a mercer.[85] As I suggest later in the chapter, there is a possibility that, like Rolant of Venice, Jacquet was involved in the production of cloth of gold.[86]

Cloth of Aresta (*drap d'Areste*)—which, as already mentioned, could have come to Paris from either Iberia or Languedoc—shows up not only on a list of tariffs that were to be charged on goods sold in Paris but also on early fourteenth-century aristocratic and church inventories from Paris.[87] The Parisian tax assessments include no individuals from the towns of Alès or Montpellier who were explicitly identified as mercers. Nevertheless, one man from that region resided in the Troussevache mercery: Pierre of Montpellier, who was taxed as a goldsmith in 1297, lived on the rue de la Courroierie. Goldsmiths claimed the right to produce and sell mercery products that incorporated gold and silver materials—as was the case with cloth of gold and silks embroidered with gold or silver thread. For that reason, it is quite possible that Pierre was, in effect, a mercer.[88]

The Troussevache mercery included five individuals who were apparently from Cyprus. One of them, Jehan of Cyprus, was identified as an embroiderer rather than as a mercer.[89] With an annual above-average tax of 1.8 livres, Jehan paid the third highest tax of all of the embroiderers who appeared in the tax assessments. Given his financial standing and his membership in the embroiderers' guild, it seems possible that Jehan may have played an important role not only in selling imported Cypriot embroideries but also in introducing Cypriot embroidery methods to Paris.[90]

Jehan of Cyprus had four neighbors on the rue de la Courroierie who were identified as "of Lymesi" or "of Lymesis."[91] It might seem reasonable, at first glance, to assume that this toponymic surname referred to the village of Limesy, in Normandy. However, a closer look at the occupations of Parisians who were identified by that name indicates that at least half of them were involved in silk work.[92] It seems highly unlikely that at least 50 percent, and perhaps even more, of the Parisian residents who originated in a small Norman village would have ended up working with silk. Jehan of Cyprus's proximity on the rue de la Courroierie to four individuals from *Lymesis*, along with an apparent business association between Jehan and one of those four (Bertaut of Lymesi) that dated back to 1282, offer clues concerning the place of origin of Parisians from "Lymesis": the town of Limassol, on the south coast of Cyprus.[93] The toponym that we encounter in the Parisian tax assessments—"Lymesis," "Lymesus," and on occasion "Lymesi"—apparently represents the efforts of the Parisian tax assessors to capture in writing the Greek version of the town's name—*Lemesos*—that was reported to them orally.[94] The use of the Greek version of the name suggests that the individuals who identified with it may have traced their roots to the Greek, rather than the French, population of Cyprus.

Jehan of Cyprus's neighbors from Limassol included one goldsmith/ mercer and one goldsmith.[95] The juxtaposition of these three men—an embroiderer, a goldsmith/mercer, and a goldsmith—is significant, given the fact that Cypriot embroideries were made with gold thread and that Parisian guild statutes and aristocratic account books of the period frequently mention silk textiles decorated with *or de Chypre*—gold thread that either came from Cyprus or was produced according to standards that were associated with Cyprus.[96] A statute initiated by the Paris mercers' guild in 1324 stipulated that the gold thread used to decorate silk narrow ware in Paris had to be either "gold of Cyprus" or "gold of Paris"; the same statute forbade the use of "gold of Lucca."[97] While it is impossible to determine what characteristics the authors of the statute associated with the three types of gold thread, it seems likely that they were expressing a preference for metallic thread that used actual metal strips that were wrapped around a silk or linen core, as opposed to a cheaper kind of thread in which gilded animal membrane was wrapped around a silk or linen core. Surviving thirteenth-century embroideries that were probably produced in Cyprus and Paris employed the first kind of thread.[98] Woven silks from Lucca employed the second type.[99]

Another person in the Troussevache mercery who was probably from a Greek part of the Mediterranean was "Jehan le Roumain" ("Jehan, the person from the territory of the former Byzantine empire"). Jehan shows up twice in the household accounts of Eleanor of Castile, queen of England, as a vendor of head coverings and other mercery goods.[100] Jehan's name does not clarify for us whether he was born in Frankish Greece or merely spent a good deal of time there. Moreover, if he was in fact born in Frankish Greece, there is no way to determine whether his cultural identity was French or Greek, although it seems likely that he was descended from a French family that settled in Frankish Greece after the conquest of 1204 and then returned to France after the Greeks regained control of Byzantium in 1261.[101] After Jehan le Roumain died, his widow, Eustache (or Huitace) la Roumainne, began to pay taxes as a mercer.[102]

There were two mercers in the Troussevache and Quincampoix merceries whose surnames point to German origins. Nicole of Cologne, a widow who resided on the prestigious rue Troussevache, paid a very high tax of between 8 and 11.5 livres at a time when the average tax was about 1 livre, so it seems likely that she specialized in extremely valuable textiles—perhaps the high-prestige half-silk narrow ware from Cologne that survives in numerous European textile collections.[103] Rogier of Germany, on the rue Quincampoix, paid a tax that was about half the average tax—so his business was modest in scope.[104]

One mercer/belt maker whose surname suggests Iberian origins, Gracien of Spain, lived just a few meters outside the Quincampoix mercery, on the rue du Grenier-Saint-Lazare, which was just outside the walls of the city, on the other side of the Porte-Saint-Martin. Gracien and his son-in-law, who was also a mercer, paid a tax that was almost twice the average.[105] Although Gracien is the only mercer of Iberian origins who shows up in the tax assessments, one other Iberian who shows up on the same street was identified as a belt maker, which suggests that he, too, may have sold mercery goods.[106]

The cumulative evidence for Paris mercers who had roots or possible roots in silk-producing regions is impressive. In the period from 1292 to c. 1340 thirteen mercers whose principal taxpaying address was in or very near the Troussevache, Quincampoix, or Lombard mercery either are known to have originated in northern Italy or had surnames pointing to possible origins in seven different silk-weaving towns and regions—Lucca, Venice, Cyprus, Frankish Greece, the Levant, Iberia, and Cologne. Moreover, three additional men who were apparently from Cyprus, one apparently from Venice, and one apparently from Montpellier, all of them having tax addresses in the Troussevache, Quincampoix, or Lombard mercery, may have been mercers; and a "Lombard" mercer whose precise hometown is unknown was taxed on the rue Quincampoix.[107] Even if some of their surnames reflected the origins of progenitors rather than the origins of the mercers themselves, the evidence is still striking, especially when we note that the only mercer with a surname indicating Mediterranean origins who was not taxed in these three areas was Jehan of Apulia (*de Puille*), a mercer of modest means who was taxed in the Petit-Pont mercery.[108] Also striking is the fact that at least seven of these mercers conducted business with the most elite royal and aristocratic courts.[109] It seems, then, that silk-weaving regions were well represented among Parisian mercers who paid taxes in the most prestigious mercers' neighborhoods.

Immigrant Mercers and Silk Production

While nearly all of the Parisian mercers from silk-producing regions may have been involved in silk production, those who are of the greatest interest to us are the ones who had possible links with known Parisian silk workers from their native towns or regions. Also of interest are mercers whose taxpaying locations place them in close proximity to the taxpaying locations of known silk weavers: physical proximity was a key factor in the organization of Parisian luxury crafts.

The tax assessments point to possible production networks among silk workers and mercers from Venice, Cyprus, and Lucca. Additionally, the locations of Jacquet of Venice, who was a mercer, and Rolant of Venice, whose profession is never identified, suggest that they may have had working relations with three of the four weavers of Parisian cloth of gold who appear in the Parisian tax assessments.

The Venetians who appeared in the Parisian tax assessments included, in addition to Jacquet of Venice, an *ouvrière de soie* named Agnes of Venice and a weaver named Bertaut of Venice, who was identified as an "ovrier [ouvrier] de dras de soie."[110] The expression "ouvrière de soie" was used to describe silk throwsters, weavers of various silk textiles, makers of silk purses, and occasionally mercers, so we do not know the nature of the silk work that Agnes of Venice did.[111] However, Agnes's average tax of five sous was more substantial than that of most silk throwsters and weavers of silk narrow ware, so it appears that she had a relatively successful business.

Bertaut of Venice was one of the seventeen male silk weavers who show up in the tax assessments as producers of *draps de soye*, velvets, and cloth of gold. Both Bertaut of Venice and Agnes of Venice were located within a few blocks of Jacquet of Venice, although in opposite directions from Jacquet (Jacquet, Agnes, and Bertaut are represented by the three Vs near the top edge of zone S1 in fig. 21). It seems possible, therefore, that Jacquet of Venice

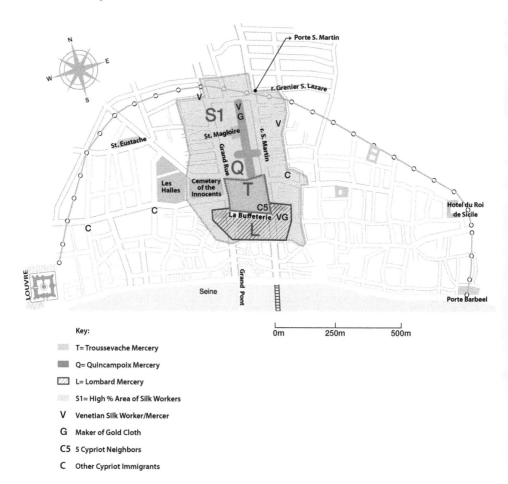

Key:

- ▨ T= Troussevache Mercery
- ▨ Q= Quincampoix Mercery
- ▨ L= Lombard Mercery
- ▨ S1= High % Area of Silk Workers
- **V** Venetian Silk Worker/Mercer
- **G** Maker of Gold Cloth
- **C5** 5 Cypriot Neighbors
- **C** Other Cypriot Immigrants

Figure 21. Clusters of foreign mercers and silk workers, Paris, c. 1300. Adapted, in collaboration with author, by Eddie Peralta, Artworks, University of California, Santa Barbara, from "Plan de la Ville de Paris sous Philippe-le-Bel dressé par Albert Lenoir architecte d'après le travail de H. Géraud."

had working relationships with both Agnes and Bertaut of Venice. This hypothesis appears even stronger when we look closely at Jacquet of Venice's particular location in 1292: in that year, he was taxed on the rue Quincampoix, near the end of the street as it approached the city walls. Separated from Jacquet by only one taxpayer was the taxpayer Guillaume du Vergier, whose occupation would be identified in 1299 as "maker of cloth of gold" (VG at the top center of fig. 21). Guillaume's brother Robert du Vergier, who was taxed alongside Guillaume in 1299, would be identified as a maker of cloth of gold in 1300.[112] This close physical juxtaposition of a Venetian mercer with two of the four men who were identified in the tax assessments as makers of cloth of gold may be a mere coincidence. However, when we take into consideration the fact that one other Venetian—Rolant of Venice—had occupied an address that was then taken over by a weaver of cloth of gold, the juxtaposition of Jacquet of Venice and the two weavers of cloth of gold takes on greater significance.

The nexus of silk workers and entrepreneurs from Cyprus was even more impressive. As I already mentioned, the embroiderer Jehan of Cyprus and four individuals from Limassol—including a mercer/goldsmith and a goldsmith—lived in the Troussevache mercery, on the rue de la Courroierie. This cluster of immigrants from Cyprus ("C5" in fig. 21) may have been involved with two silk workers who were also from Limassol—a woman weaver of silk narrow ware, named Perrenele, who lived near the Porte-Saint-Honoré on the rue des Poulies, and an *ouvrière de soie* named Marguerite, who lived below Les Halles, on the rue Tirechape (two Cs on the left half of fig. 21).[113] Although the residences or workshops of these two silk workers were not particularly close to the rue de la Courroierie, they were certainly within walking distance: the rue des Poulies was around 700 meters away, and the rue Tirechape was around 450 meters away. Another worker from Limassol, whose profession is not identified, lived just two blocks from the rue de la Courroierie, in a section of Paris (zone "S1" in fig. 21) that had a high concentration of silk workers, so this may have been yet another member of the nexus of Cypriot silk workers and entrepreneurs centered on the rue de la Courroierie.[114] All eight of the Cypriots who show up in the Parisian tax assessments either sold silk, worked with it, or lived in a neighborhood where a high percentage of residents sold or worked with silk.

The final silk nexus involving immigrant mercers is that surrounding Jehan Vanne and Bonvis Bondos, who were both from Lucca and probably related to each other by marriage: Jehan Vanne was the son-in-law of Jacques Bondos, who was probably the father, or another relation, of Bonvis Bondos.[115] Jacques and Bonvis Bondos owned two adjacent properties on the south side of the rue de la Buffeterie, and it appears that Jacques owned a third property on the north side of the street as well.[116] Bonvis Bondos's tax address was always listed on the south side of the street, while Jacques Bondos usually paid taxes on the north side of the street, along with his sons-in-law, including, in 1300, Jehan Vanne.[117]

In addition to being a mercer and a member of the Bellardi Company, Jehan Vanne also became a member of the Parisian guild of hosiery makers at some point in the late thirteenth century, probably because he wanted to get involved as an entrepreneur.[118] Hosiery, at this time, could be made of silk, linen, or wool.[119] Over twenty additional hosiery makers, moreover, resided on or very near the rue de la Buffeterie, and at least one of those artisans was clearly Italian.[120] It seems probable, moreover, given their location in the principal Lombard zone of Paris, that some of the other hosiery makers on the rue de la Buffeterie were Italian as well. Several other Italian hosiery makers were located in the Lombard zone on the Île-de-la-Cité.[121]

The tax assessors identified Jacques Bondos's property as the terminal point of a particular segment of the south side of the rue de la Buffeterie.[122] Because Jacques's property marked a terminal point for the tax assessors and Bonvis's property immediately preceded it, we can safely conclude that any taxpayers who were listed on that block after Bonvis Bondos resided or worked in one of the two properties belonging to Jacques or Bonvis Bondos. These tenants of Bonvis or Jacques Bondos included a gold beater, who would have been involved in the making of gold thread for silk textiles, and an Italian who was identified as a mangler—someone who worked with a cloth press in order to enhance the sheen of a textile after it had been woven.[123] Mangles were used on both wool and linen, but in a property associated with a mercer, it is likely that the resident mangler would have practiced his craft to finish certain silks, such as *cendal*.[124]

Although we cannot link Bonvis Bondos or Jehan Vanne directly to any silk weavers, we know that Bonvis definitely had ties to a gold beater and a mangler who was an immigrant from Italy. Jehan Vanne, moreover, who was a member of the hosiery guild, resided in close proximity to a number of hosiery makers, including at least one who was an immigrant from Italy. It thus appears that this cluster of entrepreneurs from Lucca was involved in some kind of silk production. As I mentioned earlier in this chapter, moreover, we have clear evidence that Lando Belloni, another Parisian entrepreneur from Lucca, supervised the production of silk narrow ware and oversaw the dyeing of silk cloth.

The evidence thus suggests that the mercers of Paris were the principal organizers of silk production there and that their numbers included individuals from nearly every silk-producing region of Europe and the Mediterranean. Some of the mercers from Venice, Cyprus, and Lucca, moreover, appear to have had links with silk workers, including a few from Venice, Cyprus, and an unidentified part of Italy. It is highly probable that some of these immigrant mercers played a role in convincing some of the immigrant silk workers from their places of origin to move to Paris and that those workers, as well as some of the immigrant mercers, played a role in introducing new silk technologies to Paris.

While mercers and entrepreneurs from towns and regions that produced silk cloth would have played an important role in convincing artisans to move to Paris, it is also likely that incentives for moving to Paris came from even higher up. No surviving documentation enables us to substantiate this hypothesis for late thirteenth-century Paris. Nevertheless, the entire history of the spread of silk cloth production in premodern western Europe points to a repeated pattern of intervention on the part of rulers and magistrates. In 1147, after capturing the Greek towns of Thebes, Corinth, and Athens, King Roger II of Sicily compelled Jewish silk workers from those towns to move to Palermo, Sicily, thus either initiating or vastly improving the royal silk workshops there.[125] In the 1230s, the city of Bologna created incentives that enticed a number of Milanese silk weavers into moving to Bologna. In 1314, moreover, Bologna, Venice, and Florence created incentives to attract Lucchese silk weavers who had to leave their hometown in the wake of a political upheaval.[126] Similarly, at some point between 1301 and 1309, King Charles II of Naples attempted to bring a silk industry to Naples.[127] Ruler intervention became even more frequent in the fifteenth century, when, in fact, we can point not only to Italian examples but also to that of the French king: in 1466 King Louis XI decided to lend his support to the nascent silk industry of Lyon, but when the merchants of Lyon reacted negatively he decided, in 1470, to move the Lyon industry to Tours, where he compelled the merchant community to lend its financial support. Significantly, nearly all of the silk workers who were brought to Tours were Italian. By 1480 there were twenty-four Italians and one Greek working in the silk industry of Tours.[128] The Greek man—"Jacques Cathacalo, tireur d'or, trait de la nacion de Grece"— was a gold beater and gold wire maker.[129] Gold beating, gold strip production, and the spinning of gold strips into gold thread were ancient arts, extending back in France to at least the sixth century.[130] Nevertheless, a number of sources from fifteenth- and sixteenth-century Italy indicate that the production of gold thread was a tricky art, one that sometimes sent rulers and entrepreneurs out on hunting expeditions to find gold beaters with the requisite skills.[131] It seems significant, moreover, that this particular maker of gold wire was Greek, given the evidence from thirteenth-century Paris that silk workers from Cyprus, who were probably Greek as well, may have been involved in the production of gold thread.

To be sure, Renaissance rulers were more conscious of economic policy than were those of the late thirteenth century. Nevertheless, a French royal example from the early fourteenth century suggests that members of the French court were already conscious of the positive role that they could play in stimulating new forms of business and industry. In 1318 Queen Jeanne of Burgundy enticed ten of the most elite wool weavers of Paris to relocate to the town of Gray, in Burgundy, in order to start a new wool industry there. The contract between the queen's agents and the wool weavers indicated that she would provide housing and land where the weavers could set up tentering frames, that she intended to construct and to maintain at her own expense two fulling mills, and that the weavers' moving expenses would be covered by both a gift of 500 livres and an interest-free loan of 1,000 livres, to be paid off over a ten-year period. In their broad outlines, these financial inducements resemble those of fifteenth-century contracts that Italian rulers and urban magistrates offered to silk workers in order to convince them to start up new industries in new towns.[132]

While we cannot point to a contract between the royal court and the immigrant silk workers of Paris, thirteenth- and fourteenth-century evidence certainly suggests that Parisian silk weavers and entrepreneurs were in close contact with the French royal court. As I point out in Chapter 4, the statutes for the guild of makers of "draps de soye" and velvet stipulated that members of the guild who were working for members of the royal household were exempt from guild regulations prohibiting working at night. Similar statutes come up in the regulations for only a few other Parisian guilds—such as that of the goldsmiths.[133] And as I have already indicated, the mercers Lando Belloni of Lucca and Jehan Tabarie enjoyed favorable relations with the royal court. Significantly, moreover, all of the known individuals who owned pieces of silk cloth that was woven in Paris were related by blood or by marriage to the French king: in 1317 Queen Jeanne of Burgundy, the wife of King Philip V of France, wore an embroidered cape made with cloth of gold of Paris during her coronation at Reims.[134] In the 1320s Edward II of England, who had married Isabel, the daughter of King Philip IV of France, in 1308, owned a piece of silk made in Paris; and Blanche of Namur, queen of Sweden, who was a distant cousin of the Capetian kings, owned a piece of Parisian silk at the time of her death in 1363/64.[135] It seems likely that Edward came into possession of his Parisian silk at the time of his marriage to Isabel and that Blanche's silk followed her to Sweden at the time of her marriage in 1335. Even at the end of the century, our one clear reference to a piece of Parisian silk cloth comes from the accounts of a relative of the French king— Count Amadeus VIII of Savoy, whose mother was related to the Valois royal line.[136] Amadeus's agents, however, had purchased this piece of silk cloth from a merchant from Lyon, so his possession of the Parisian silk does not seem to have arisen from his connections with the French court.

Instigation from the royal household may well help explain how silk mercers and weavers of luxury silk cloth came to settle in Paris in the last third of the thirteenth century, but it does not explain how the industry actually took root and persisted for at least a hundred years. The successful implantation of the new industry depended on the transmission of imported technological knowledge from one generation of silk workers to the next. The social relations that gave rise to such transmission would have taken shape within household workshops, where women and men who were masters or mistresses trained their spouses, children, and apprentices in the technical skills of their trade.

The Parisian guild statutes for all of the silk professions and crafts, both those written before 1275 and those, such as the statutes for the two guilds of silk cloth weavers, that were written after 1280, included regulations for taking on apprentices.[137] None of those guilds, moreover, prohibited the transmission of guild status from husbands to wives or from parents to children, and some explicitly exempted children of masters and mistresses from the limitations placed on the number of apprentices a master or mistress could have.[138] As I indicate in Chapter 4, familial transmission of workshops was legally encouraged by Parisian inheritance laws, which favored spouses as principal heirs and children (both male and female) as secondary heirs, with equal partition of inherited goods among all heirs of the same degree of kinship.

Since Paris did not have a central repository for notarized contracts until the end of the fifteenth century, we lack evidence, especially for the thirteenth and fourteenth centuries, concerning the actual practice of apprenticeship in Paris. To be sure, the guild regulations do mention apprentices, but the statutes focus primarily on the minimal length of time that apprentices had to remain in service: there is no language whatsoever concerning the conveyance of skills. There was no logical relationship, moreover, between the minimal number of years required of apprentices and the difficulty of the tasks that they needed to master: the minimal amount of time for an apprenticeship under a silk throwster, for instance, was seven years, while apprentice weavers of "draps de soye" and velvet served a minimum of only six years, and there was no minimal requirement at all for apprentices who trained with mercers.[139] These asymmetrical requirements suggest that long periods of service were designed not only to assure proper conveyance of skills but also to enhance the economic advantage of masters and mistresses, who, in the last years of apprenticeships, could benefit financially from the unpaid labor of apprentices who had already learned their craft.[140]

Apprenticeship contracts from other French towns in this period do include language specifying that masters or mistresses were expected to teach apprentices the skills of the craft; and Parisian court cases from the late fourteenth and fifteenth centuries indicate that Parisian contracts contained similar language.[141] Nevertheless, not every apprenticeship was designed to create a professional equal of the master or mistress under whom the apprentice served. Indeed, many artisans who completed their apprenticeships never managed to set up their own workshops and gain the status of master or mistress of the trade.[142] In some cases, moreover, apprentices trained with entrepreneurs or artisans in well-remunerated professions but for the purpose of learning a much less lucrative craft. Such was the case, for instance, at some point around 1400, when Guillemete, the thirteen-year-old daughter of a certain Jehan Fachu, was apprenticed to the wife of a mercer in order to learn to weave narrow ware.[143]

We have no direct evidence concerning apprentices who served in the shops and workshops of late thirteenth-century and early fourteenth-century Parisian mercers and silk weavers. For that reason, we have no idea how many apprentices in the silk trades went on, in those decades, to become skilled masters or mistresses themselves. The sources do indicate, however—if only through fragmentary evidence in the tax assessments—that Parisian mercers and artisans passed their skills and workshops on to their spouses and heirs. Among the Parisian mercers who had migrated to Paris from Mediterranean centers of silk production, at least two—Jehan Tabarie the younger and Jehan le Roumain—had wives who paid taxes as mercers after their husbands died.[144] The Tabarie men also passed their business knowledge down through the generations: from father to son, and possibly on to grandsons as well.[145] Such seems to have been the case as well with Jacques and Bonvis Bondos: both were probably mercers, and Jacques was probably the father of Bonvis.[146] The tax assessments do not enable us to say anything meaningful about the passing on of family workshops and artisan skill among immigrant silk weavers, but it seems reasonable to assume that such transmission took place. Moreover, the fact that two weavers of cloth of gold—Guillaume and Robert du Vergier—were brothers who lived side by side suggests that they learned the craft together, perhaps from a parent.[147]

It was primarily through the household workshop that medieval artisans and entrepreneurs conveyed their skills to their peers and to the next generation, and the fragmentary evidence suggests that such was the case among immigrant mercers and silk weavers in Paris. Men and women with knowledge of silk production immigrated to Paris, bringing their families with them or marrying Parisians once they arrived. They set up workshops and began to train their spouses, their children, and—in some cases—their apprentices to practice the skills that they had learned in silk-producing towns in various parts of the Mediterranean.

While much of the technological knowledge that contributed to the growth of the luxury silk cloth industry of Paris probably arrived there through the mediation of immigrant mercers and artisans from northern Italy, the social relations of silk production changed considerably once the industry took root in northern French soil. This was especially true in the case of women. In both Italy and Paris, women played a major role in the production of silk. Only in Paris, however, were women able to gain positions as managers of silk production and as artisans working in positions of high-status labor. We turn, now, to an analysis of women's roles in the Parisian silk industry.

Chapter 4

Gender, Work, and the Parisian Silk Industry

In 1294, during a series of shopping trips in Paris, Dame Marie du Val, a favored agent of the Countess of Flanders, bought mercery goods from a number of prominent mercers, including two whom we have already encountered: Jehan Tabarie and Mahy of Arras. Marie also exchanged money with a number of women artisans and entrepreneurs who were involved in the silk industry. To one "poor woman who throws silk" Marie gave alms of 16 sous; to an anonymous woman who "weaves purses" she paid close to three and a half livres, or 70 sous, for four lengths of "tissu" (probably tablet woven narrow ware), four purses, and a looped cord for holding keys. She also bought a few purses from a woman named Alice the purse maker, and she spent almost five livres on head coverings that she purchased from Marie Osane, a Beguine who was one of the ten wealthiest mercers in Paris. From a gold beater named Odeline Courson, who, like Marie Osane, lived on the prestigious rue Quincampoix, Marie du Val bought over 94 livres' worth of gold strips, gold foil, and luxury belts.[1]

These encounters with Parisian silk women from every rung of the social and economic ladder are illustrative of the apparent contradictions that need to be addressed and explained in this chapter. On the one hand, throwsters, and other silk women who worked in predominantly female crafts, tended to earn modest incomes, and for that reason some of them were subject to impoverishment. On the other hand, the Parisian silk industry offered extraordinary opportunities for women, even in professions that, in towns in northern Italy, were often exclusively male. As I will argue, moreover, even Parisian silk mistresses who occupied the lowliest of silk professions were better off than most other working women in high and late medieval society. Indeed, gendered relationships in the Parisian silk industry differed not only from such relationships in Italian silk industries but also from those in other textile industries in northern France and the Low Countries.

*   *   *

In Paris, as elsewhere, women predominated among silk workers.[2] The tax assessments of 1292–1313 reveal the names of 47 artisan men and 187 artisan women whose profession linked them to the various stages in the production of silk cloth (see table 3).[3] If we add in the makers of silk narrow ware, where the number of men who were identified in the tax assessments came closer to equaling the number of women, the total numbers of silk artisans comes to 90 men and 241 women. In the tax assessments, then, women constituted 73 percent of those who participated in artisanal activities that contributed to the making of silk cloth or narrow ware. However, since women artisans were far more underrepresented in the tax assessments than were men, it seems likely that there were somewhere around 1,418 Parisian women who contributed to the production of silk cloth and narrow ware and that they constituted at least 80 percent of the artisans who participated in the activities that were necessary for the production of those textiles (table 3).[4]

Women predominated among Parisian silk workers. Conversely, silk work predominated among forms of employment for Parisian women. In the tax assessment of 1300, for instance, silk workers and mercers constituted 26 percent of the women whose profession was listed in an unambiguous fashion ("Marie Osane, merciere"; "Marie qui file soie"), and they constituted 15 percent of the larger group of women that included both those with clearly identified professions and those for whom a professional name might have been a mere surname rather than an actual professional identity ("Marie la Merciere").[5] No other craft or profession came close to employing this many women. The next largest form of women's employment—that of street peddler, or *regratière*—provided employment in 1300 for 13 percent of the women who had an unambiguous professional identity and 10 percent of the larger group that included those who were identified both unambiguously and ambiguously with professional names.[6]

Despite their numerical dominance among silk workers, however, and despite the enormous importance of silk work as a form of employment for

TABLE 3. SILK MEN AND WOMEN WHO APPEAR IN THE PARISIAN TAX ASSESSMENTS
OF 1292, 1296–1300, 1313

	Men	*Women*
Throwsters	0	93 + est. 66 *ouvrières de soie* who were throwsters = 159
Dyers	5	1
Weavers of veils and those who "carie soie"	0	9 + estimated 9 *ouvrières de soie* who were silk cloth weavers = 18
Weavers of "draps de soye," velvet, and cloth of gold	17 + estimated 2 additional ouvriers de soie = 19	0
Gold beaters	23	1
Gold spinners	0	8
Total for silk cloth	47	187
Weavers of narrow ware ("tissu de soie")	2 (?)	22 + c. 19 *ouvrières de soie* who wove "tissu de soie" = 41
Weavers of ribbons and laces	41	13
Total including both cloth and narrow ware	90 (around 25%? of total number of male silk artisans)	241 (around 17% of total number of female silk artisans)
Percentage of silk workers in the tax assessments	27%	73%
Estimated total number in Paris population	360	1,418
Estimated percentage of male/female silk artisans	20%	80%

Note: Many individuals appeared more than once in the tax assessments, but I have counted each of them only once. See this chapter's notes 3 and 4 for explanations of these numbers.

women, silk women had less status and less wealth than their male counterparts. And this, too, fits a broader pattern, one that was nicely analyzed by Jordan Goodman in an article on gender, labor, and silk work in Renaissance and early modern Florence.[7] Goodman observed that while the fifteenth through the seventeenth centuries saw major changes in the percentages of male and female silk weavers, the overall gendered distribution of labor status remained the same: men predominated in positions of high-status labor while women predominated in positions of low-status labor. Throughout those centuries, all of the Florentine *setaioli*, who organized production, were apparently men.[8] Moreover, at the top of the income hierarchy among silk artisans in Florence, all of the dyers were men. Among silk weavers, however, there were marked changes. In the fifteenth century, when the Florentine industry specialized in complex silk weaves, such as cut velvet, men, who did all of the complex weaving, predominated among silk weavers. By the seventeenth century, however, after Florence's silk industry had shifted over to the large-scale production of simpler, less expensive silk cloth, including taffeta and satin, women constituted the majority of silk cloth weavers. Among the producers of the yarn itself, men tended to predominate as throwsters in fifteenth-century Florence, running complex, expensive throwing machines that could do the work of dozens, if not hundreds, of hand throwsters; all of the winding, by contrast, which was done by hand on far simpler instruments of production, was done by women (Fig. 22; and see fig. 12 in Chapter 2).[9]

Goodman highlighted four characteristics that determined the status of a particular category of silk work in Renaissance and early modern Florence: income and the way in which it was distributed, technological complexity, the requisite level of skill, and the visibility of the finished product.[10] My own analysis of gendered patterns in the Parisian silk industry of the late thirteenth and early fourteenth centuries constitutes a modified version of Goodman's categories. In late thirteenth- and early fourteenth-century Paris, I argue, we can identify five elements that contributed to the status of a given category of silk work: the first three—income level, skill, and the complexity (and thus expense) of tools of production—resemble categories highlighted by Goodman. The fourth element, which is a modification of Goodman's idea of visibility, entailed distinction: the distinctive identity of a given product in local and international markets and the degree to which the producer him- or herself came into contact with the distinctive consumers for whom the textiles were produced. The fifth element, which I am adding to Goodman's list, entailed autonomy—both the degree to which members of a particular guild or craft group were able to exercise collective autonomy, or self-governance, and the degree to which the members of a particular craft worked independently on tools and materials that they themselves owned.[11]

Taking these five markers of status into consideration, it is easy to draw the conclusion that in late thirteenth- and early fourteenth-century Paris, as in fifteenth- through seventeenth-century Florence, male silk workers predominated in high-status silk crafts while female silk workers predominated

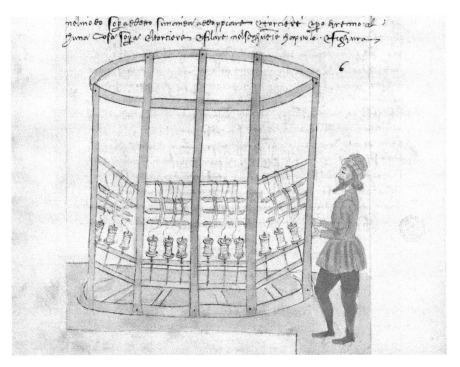

Figure 22. Man operating a silk-throwing machine in fifteenth-century Florence. From anonymous treatise on silk production, Florence, Biblioteca Medicea Laurenziana, Plut. 89 sup. Cod. 117, fol. 7v. Reproduced by permission of MiBACT (Ministero dei beni e delle activitá culturale e del turismo).

in low-status silk crafts. In the first section of this chapter I discuss the evidence supporting this point, emphasizing the five markers of labor status. In the second and third sections of the chapter, however, I shift the perspective, comparing and contrasting the status of Parisian silk women (especially those who were the mistresses of their own workshops) with the status of other working women, both in and outside of Paris. Looked at from this perspective, Parisian silk women appear to have had extremely high status. For a variety of important reasons, and in a number of important ways, gendered patterns in the medieval Parisian silk industry differed significantly from those of Renaissance and early modern Florence (and probably medieval Lucca as well), and Parisian silk work offered women a variety of unusual opportunities. Hence, even the lowliest of Parisian silk crafts had some level of status and even the most elite of silk crafts and professions was within women's reach. Indeed, it turns out that in Paris, if not in Florence and

Lucca, at least some women gained access to nearly every silk craft or profession. Moreover, women constituted a very significant portion of the high-status entrepreneurs who organized silk production, and some of the women in that group attained extremely elevated positions within their profession. In the fourth section of this chapter I will attempt to explain why Parisian silk work was able to offer these opportunities to women. Differences between women's opportunities in the silk industry of Paris and women's opportunities in the silk industries of Florence and Lucca can be largely explained through an examination of differences between northern French and northern Italian inheritance systems. But our discussion will also need to explain the degree to which the Parisian silk industry offered women unusual opportunities in a northern French context.

In the concluding section of the chapter I return to the issue of silk women and poverty, highlighting the sharp differences in economic and social status between silk women who owned and managed their own workshops and those who did not.

The Gendered Hierarchy of Parisian Silk Work

The seven Parisian tax assessments that were compiled between 1292 and 1313 indicate that, with the exception of the level of management, which was carried out by mercers, every stage in the production of Parisian silk textiles involved two different groups with two differently gendered constitutions. In the production of gold and silk thread, the gold beaters, who created metallic foil and metallic strips for making gold or silver thread and who sold the finished metallic thread to consumers, were predominantly male; gold spinners, by contrast, who wound metallic strips or gilded animal membrane around a fiber core, were all women.[12] In the production of silk yarn, winding and throwing were carried out exclusively by women, while the dyeing of those yarns was carried out by a small group that was predominantly male (see tables 4 and 5). The gendered constitution of the silk throwsters differed significantly from that of the throwsters of fifteenth-century Florence largely because there were no mechanized silk-throwing machines in late medieval Paris, thus the capital investment that was required in order to open a workshop was much more modest.

The weaving of Parisian silk narrow ware also broke down into two differently gendered groups. The guild statutes for the makers of "tissuz de

TABLE 4. AVERAGE TAXES OF PREDOMINANTLY MALE AND PREDOMINANTLY FEMALE
SILK CRAFTS AND PROFESSIONS

Predominantly Female Silk Artisans	Average Tax 1297–1300: < 5 sous	Average Tax 1297–1300: 5–19 sous	Average Tax 1297–1300: > 20 sous
Throwsters (93W/0M)	4.1 sous		
Gold spinners (8W/0M)	3.1 sous		
Weavers of "tissu/z" (22W/2M?)	3.2 sous		
Weavers of veils and those who "carie soie" (9W/0M)	2.8 sous		
Ouvrier/es de soie (113W/5M)	4.8 sous		
Predominantly Male Silk Artisans			
Dyers (1W/5M)		8.5 sous	
Gold beaters (1W/23M)		14.5 sous	
Weavers of ribbons and laces (13W/41M)		9.1 sous (average tax for women: 11.4 sous)	
Weavers of "draps de soye," velvet, cloth of gold (0W/17M)		5.6 sous	
Mercer-Entrepreneurs (45W/296M)			40.7 sous (average tax for women: 40.8 sous)

Note: W = number of women in all 7 tax assessments; M = number of men in all 7 tax assessments.

TABLE 5. AVERAGE TAXES OF COMPARABLE MALE AND FEMALE CRAFTS

	Predominantly Male	*Predominantly Female*
Yarn production	(Dyers): 8.5 sous	(Throwsters): 4.1 sous
Gold thread production	(Beaters): 14.5 sous	(Spinners): 3.1 sous
Narrow ware production	(Weavers of ribbons and laces) 9.1 sous	(Weavers of "tissu/z") 3.2 sous
Cloth production	("Draps de soye," velvet, cloth of gold) 5.6 sous	(Veils, "carie soie") 2.8 sous

soie" assumed that these weavers were usually women; the tax assessments affirm that assumption.[13] By contrast, the makers of ribbons and laces ("laceurs de fil et de soie"; also known as "dorelotiers") were described in masculine terms in the guild statutes, and the tax assessments confirm that most of these artisans were men (see tables 4 and 5).[14] Unfortunately, nothing in the guild statutes or anywhere else in the sources enables us to determine how the work of these two groups differed.

There were also two differently gendered groups of weavers of silk cloth. All seventeen of the makers of "draps de soye," velvet, and cloth of gold who appeared in the tax assessments were male and the guild statutes for the weavers of "draps de soye" and velvet referred to the guild members using masculine nouns and pronouns.[15] By contrast, the guild statutes for the weavers of silk veils used feminine nouns and pronouns, and all nine of the identifiable taxpayers who produced silk veils or who were described as "qui carie soie" were women.[16] There are good reasons for believing that "qui carie soie" referred to weaving; I am assuming that, much like the women who wove silk veils, these women wove unpatterned, monochrome silks.[17]

At the top of the hierarchy of production, the retail-entrepreneurs known as mercers, some of whom organized silk production, were predominantly male. Two hundred ninety-six different men were identified in the tax assessments as mercers; 45 women were so identified.

As Table 4 makes clear, in the tax assessments of 1297–1300, which are the most comparable to each other in terms of numbers of people who were taxed and the average tax that was paid, the average tax for the membership of all of the silk crafts in which women predominated was under 5 sous, and thus nearly all of those artisans fell into the lowest taxation category, that of the *menu peuple*. By contrast, the average tax of the membership of all of the silk artisan groups in which men predominated fell into a middling range that was between 5 and 19 sous. The artisans in this middling group tended to pay a tax that was less than the overall average tax of 20 sous, or 1 livre, but their taxation level earned them a place among those who were labeled as *gros* rather than as *menu*.[18] This middling economic status was common for high-status artisans. In 1300, for instance, the wool weavers paid an average tax of 12.2 sous.[19] At the very top of the silk hierarchy, the mercers paid an above-average tax of 40.7 sous, which was slightly more than twice the overall average tax in the 1297–1300 tax assessments. Significantly, within the craft groups that were predominantly male, even the average taxes paid by the women were considerably higher than those of the members of the female craft groups.

The income differences between artisan groups that were predominantly male and those that were predominantly female emerge in an especially striking manner when we compare the average taxes of the differently gendered groups that contributed to the same material object or to comparable material objects: gold beaters and gold spinners, who contributed to two different stages in the making of gold thread; throwsters and dyers, who did the same in the making of silk yarn; weavers of narrow ware called "tissuz" or "tissu" and weavers of ribbons and laces; male weavers of "draps de soye," velvet, and cloth of gold and female weavers of veils and those who "carie soie." In three of the four categories, the average tax of the predominantly male group was more than twice that of the women's group; and the average tax of the members of the predominantly male group in the fourth category was exactly twice that of the women's group.

The evidence from the Countess of Flanders's account book, which tells us that her agent Marie du Val gave alms to a poor silk throwster, provides corroborating evidence that the incomes of a number of women in predominantly female silk crafts were near the bottom of the economic hierarchy.[20] Such evidence is bolstered, moreover, by the guild statutes, where we find both throwsters and women weavers of silk head coverings being accused of pawning off or selling silk fiber that had been entrusted to them to spin or weave.[21] We find no such accusations against the predominantly male guilds that participated in the silk industry. These discussions of silk women's involvement with pawnbrokers suggest that many silk women were drawn into destructive cycles of consumer debt, presumably because there were times when their incomes did not match their expenses.[22]

But income level was only one marker of the lower status of women's silk work. The women's guilds also stand out for their lower skill level and for the fact that opening a workshop required less capital investment than was the case, at least, for the male silk weavers and for silk dyers. The statutes for the three predominantly female silk guilds that centered on the two main stages in the production of silk cloth—throwing silk yarn and weaving silk veils—commenced with the statement that the craft was open to anyone who was willing to obey the rules of the guild.[23] The statutes for the guild for makers of silk head coverings added the qualifier "as long as she knows how to practice the craft well and loyally." The statutes for women who made the narrow ware known as "tissu/z de soie" indicated that women could not become mistresses until they had practiced the craft for a year and a day because they needed to acquire the requisite skills, but there was no mention of any kind of test concerning that skill.[24]

The statutes for the male guild of weavers of "draps de soye" and velvet, by contrast, specified that skilled knowledge was a prerequisite to becoming a master in the guild, and for that reason, prospective masters were to be examined by the guardians of the craft. Prospective members also had to pay an entrance fee to the king and to the guardians of the craft; the fee thus created a barrier for prospective members who were without means:

> Whoever wants to be a master in the said craft needs to know how to carry out every aspect of the craft, by himself, without counsel or aid from anyone, and he must be examined by the guardians of the craft. And if he is found to be competent, as indicated above, he must buy the said craft from the king or from his lieutenant, in whichever jurisdiction he may reside within the territory of the Châtelet of Paris. And he will pay 20 sous to the king and 10 sous to the said guardians of the craft for their trouble.[25]

The requirement of an entry exam for the makers of "draps de soye," velvet, and woven purses constituted one of the first such requirements among all of the craft guilds of Paris.[26] None of the other silk guilds was so explicit about the need for expertise.

In addition to meeting the guild's standards of expertise and paying an entrance fee, some or all of the weavers in the predominantly male guild of silk cloth weavers also needed to acquire looms that were more expensive than the looms employed by women silk weavers. At least some of the male silk weavers had looms for weaving velvet, which required two warp beams—one to release the ground warp yarn and one to release the pile yarns, which had to be released at a much more rapid rate than the ground warp yarns because the pile yarns were woven over metal bars in order to create the pile (figs. 16–18 in Chapter 2).[27]

Additionally, there is reason to believe that some of the male silk weavers were working on draw looms, which needed hundreds of pulleys and harnesses in order to create patterned weaves. In any case, as indicated in Chapter 2, account book evidence suggests that draw looms had reached northern France by 1304, when Countess Mahaut of Artois commissioned the construction of a loom with 200 pulleys.[28]

Women silk weavers in Paris—and in Florence—employed simpler equipment requiring much less capital investment. The weavers of silk head coverings needed only a simple loom with a single warp beam, a single cloth beam at the other end, and two to four pedals that were attached to two to four pulleys and shafts to lift up the warp (fig. 23). The same was probably true as well of those who "carie soie."

There was also a hierarchy of investment among those who produced silk yarn. Silk dyers, most of whom were male, needed to invest in multiple dye vats as well as a vat for cooking the gummy sericin off of the raw silk fiber; and they needed a sealed chamber where the fumes from burning sulfur could slowly bleach some of the silk fiber until it was white. Most of the dyers' vats had to have some kind of furnace underneath so that the cooking or dye bath could be heated (figs. 10–11 in Chapter 2).[29] By contrast, silk throwsters, all of whom were women, needed only reeling and winding wheels, bobbins, frames for holding skeins and bobbins, and some kind of spindle or spindle wheel (fig. 12 in Chapter 2). These tools of production, most of them made of wood, were much less costly than the iron or copper vats and furnaces that constituted the dyers' equipment.

We have no way of knowing whether or not there was a hierarchy of investment among narrow ware weavers because we do not know the nature of the weaving practices that distinguished the two groups. One of the groups probably used a box loom for making tabby-woven ribbons and the other probably used weaving frames for tablet weaving, along with wooden tablets and weaving swords (figs. 24–25).

In any case, the equipment that was necessary for the weaving of narrow ware was less costly than that which was required for either of the groups of silk cloth weavers. For that reason, it is difficult to explain why the average tax of the predominantly male ribbon weavers was considerably higher than that of the weavers of "draps de soye," velvet and cloth of gold, and why the

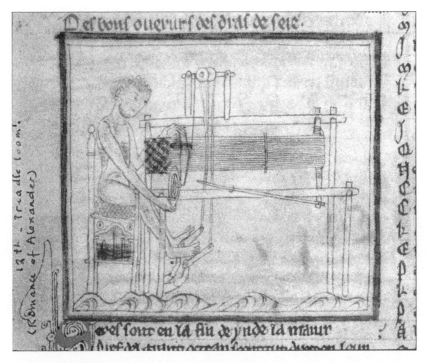

Figure 23. Man at a loom. The weaver sits at a simple tabby-weave loom, with a warp beam opposite him (on the right side of the image) and a cloth beam immediately in front of him. At the weaver's feet are two pedals that attach to two cords that run up to two pulleys and then down to two shafts with heddles, through which the warp yarns have been threaded. Stepping on a pedal causes one of the two shafts to rise, thereby raising half of the warp yarns and creating the shed through which the weft shuttle can be passed. From Eustache of Kent, Romance of Alexander, France, twelfth century C.E.. Trinity College Library, Cambridge, ms. O.9.34, f. 32v. Photo credit: Visual Arts Library/Art Resource, NY.

average tax of the weavers of "tissuz de soie," who were nearly all women, was higher than the average tax of the weavers of silk head coverings, all of whom were women. The explanation may lie in the fact that the Parisian silk cloth industry was relatively young at the time that the tax assessments were compiled: if the weavers of silk cloth and veils had only recently set up their ateliers, they may still have been encumbered by business debts; the tax assessors may have taken those business debts into consideration when they calculated the tax payments of the weavers of silk cloth and silk head coverings.

*   *   *

Figure 24. Manuscript illumination depicting Arachne weaving narrow ware on a box loom. The Hague, Koninklijke Bibliotheek, 74 G 27, Christine de Pisan, *L'Epistre d'Othea* (Auvergne?, c. 1450–1475), fol. 59v. Photo courtesy of Koninklijke Bibliotheek.

In addition to a gendered income hierarchy, a gendered hierarchy of skill, and a gendered hierarchy of capital investment, there was also a gendered hierarchy involving the distinctiveness of the product, at least in so far as the weaving of veils and "draps de soye" was concerned. While silk veils from Paris, which were woven by women, apparently entered the market anonymously, with no effort to identify their place of origin, luxury silk cloth from Paris, which was woven by men, had an identity that sometimes linked it to its place of origin, much like luxury cloth from Lucca, Venice, "Turkey," and the Mongol empire. Thus we find references to "silk cloth of Paris" or "cloth of gold of Paris" not only in royal and aristocratic account books recording original purchases but also in the postmortem inventory of Blanche of Namur, queen of Sweden. Particularly significant is the fact that Queen Blanche's piece of Parisian silk retained its identity months, or even years, after it was purchased.[30]

Figure 25. The Virgin Mary engaged in the process of tablet weaving. The Hague, Koninklijke Bibliotheek, KB 76 F 21 (book of hours, 1400–1410), fol. 14r. Photo courtesy of Koninklijke Bibliotheek.

The prestige of Parisian luxury silk must have rubbed off on the male silk weavers: in much the same way that we identify wines or cheeses by their place of origin, it seems that some luxury silk cloth from Paris had distinctive characteristics that were attributed to the skilled creators of that cloth. The statutes for the makers of "draps de soye" and velvet suggest, moreover, that the distinctiveness of these weavers also entailed relatively close relations with elite consumers. The statutes specified, for example, that only those weavers who were working for "the king, the queen or the heirs of France" were allowed to work on Sundays, holidays, and at night. Similarly, the members of that same guild who worked in the houses of "very noble princes" were exempt from the regulation stipulating that guild members had to work in the houses or ateliers of masters in the guild.[31] None of the statutes for any of the other silk guilds mentioned this kind of proximity to aristocratic and royal consumers. The one other guild for which similar exemptions applied was that of the goldsmiths, who were near the top of the status and income hierarchy among Parisian artisans. According to the *Livre des métiers*, goldsmiths who were working for "the king, the queen, their children, their siblings or the bishop" were exempt from the regulation stating that goldsmiths were not to work at night.[32]

One final indicator of status or distinction involved autonomy, both in the form of collective self-governance and in the form of economic independence. Overall, independent self-governance was not a characteristic of the Parisian craft guilds, which emerged not as a consequence of artisanal or bourgeois autonomy but as an expression of royal power and jurisdiction. The original statutes of the Parisian guilds, which were gathered together in the *Livre des métiers* between 1266 and 1275, were created at the instigation of the royal provost of Paris, who was a royal officer. The provost exercised ultimate jurisdiction over the guilds and had the last word on the creation and enforcement of rules governing the crafts. Some guilds were also under the authority of members of the royal household—as was the case with the bakers, who were subject to the authority of the king's pantler.[33] Despite the subordinate status of all of the guilds, however, some of them were granted more opportunities for collective self-governance than were others.

Among the silk guilds, the group that was granted the greatest degree of collective self-governance was the community of mercers, whose membership included a number of individuals whose families included members of the *échevinage*.[34] In a manner that was extremely unusual within the guild statutes of the *Livre des métiers*, the statutes for the mercers' guild specified that the mercers themselves elected the four *prud'hommes* who enforced the rules of the guild and that those elected *prud'hommes* subsequently took an oath to uphold the rules of the guild in the presence of the mercers themselves rather than in the presence of the officers of the Châtelet:

> The four *prud'hommes* will be elected by the community of the craft and will be led in front of you [the members of the guild of mercers] to swear on the relics of saints that they will keep watch over the craft well and loyally, and that they will [go before] the provost or come when he summons them in order to report all of the transgressions and infractions that they find among the members of the craft.[35]

As discussed in Chapter 3, moreover, the provost also promulgated new statutes in response to requests that came from the mercers, and in 1324 the provost granted the *prud'hommes* of the mercers the right to exercise policing authority over all crafts that created mercery goods.

The statutes for one other guild of predominantly male silk workers— that of the ribbon makers—also indicated that the *prud'hommes* were elected but without indicating who did the electing or that the *prud'hommes* took their oath in the presence of the guild members. Indeed, the statute describing that election stipulated that while the guild membership may have had the right to elect its jurors, the actual swearing into office of those jurors was subject to the good graces of the provost: after the members of the ribbon makers' guild elected their jurors, the statute proclaimed, "the provost of Paris installs [those jurors into office] and hosts them at his pleasure."[36] In other words, if the elected jurors of the guild did not meet the provost's approval they would not assume office; and if at any point the jurors fell out of the provost's favor, they would lose their office.

The statutes for the silk women's guilds went even further in denying self-governing autonomy to the guild membership. None of the statutes for any of the three women's guilds that contributed to silk cloth production mentioned the election of jurors, and the statutes for two of those guilds mentioned that the jurors were hosted and put in place at the pleasure of the provost.[37] The statutes for the two guilds of silk throwsters (who were nearly all women), moreover, mention only *prud'hommes* as jurors, but it seems that at least part of the time the oversight duties of those guilds were carried out by male and female jurors working together: the fifth statute for the guild of throwsters using small spindles indicated that apprenticeship contracts needed to be signed in the presence of both the "masters" and two or three "preudesfames" of the guild, and a later marginal note to the statutes for that guild indicates that in 1309 two men and two women served as the "mestres de ce mestier."[38] Only in the case of the guild of weavers of silk head coverings, however, do we find that women from the guild were expected, from the beginning, to constitute the entire panel of jurors.[39]

In addition to exercising far less collective self-governance than was the case for the predominantly male mercers' and ribbon makers' guilds, many female silk workers also exercised less economic autonomy within their workshops than was the case for male silk workers. As discussed in Chapter 3, the only references that the mercers ever made to the possible loss of fiber that belonged to them as entrepreneurs concerned throwsters, whom they suspected of sometimes selling or pawning off silk fiber that belonged to the mercers. Similar statutes concerning the women who wove silk head coverings indicated that these women also pawned fiber that did not belong to them—but the statutes do not specify who did own the fiber. The statutes relating to this problem indicate that throwsters and weavers of silk head coverings worked on raw materials that did not belong to them. Conversely, the absence of such statutes concerning silk dyers and the weavers of "draps de soye" and velvet suggests that these artisans—who were predominantly male—probably worked on materials that they themselves owned.

No matter how we measure work status then—income level, skill, capital investment, distinctive and recognizable identity of the product and those who made it, autonomy of guild governance, or economic independence of the workshop—the women's silk crafts in Paris were clearly of lower status than were the silk crafts in which men predominated.

That said, however, we need to take into consideration the fact that silk women in Paris actually achieved levels of income and work status that were extremely unusual for medieval women. Largely because women had greater inheritance rights in northern Europe than in towns of northern Italy, significant differences emerge when we compare the status, wealth, and independence of Parisian silk women with the status, wealth, and independence of Florentine women in the silk industry. But even in comparison to other working women in Paris and in other western European towns north of the Alps, the silk women of Paris stand out. In the three sections that follow, I describe and attempt to explain the relatively high status of Parisian silk women relative to other working women. In the section that immediately follows this one, I compare the status of Parisian silk women who were at the bottom of the silk hierarchy—those in craft groups that were predominantly female—with the status of other working women. I then turn, in the next section, to a discussion of the Parisian silk women who gained access to, and prominence within, silk crafts and businesses that were dominated by men. I then attempt to explain, in the penultimate section of the chapter, the legal and cultural context that enabled Parisian silk women to achieve unusual levels of economic and work status.

The Status of Women in Predominantly Female Silk Guilds vis-à-vis Other Working Women

The first section of this chapter opened with a discussion of the average taxes paid by silk women in predominantly female craft groups relative to the average taxes that were paid by men and women who participated in silk crafts that were dominated by men. That analysis highlighted the fact that silk crafts that were predominantly female were decidedly lower in status than were silk crafts with a predominantly male membership. But if we shift our analysis to a comparison of Parisian women's silk crafts with other forms of women's work, the resulting picture looks quite different. We can begin with the fact that, in the Parisian tax assessments, women in the Parisian silk industry constituted the largest group of women for whom a profession was identified. That number even holds up if we focus only on silk women who participated in the relatively low-status silk activities where women tended to predominate: in the 1300 tax assessment the total number of silk throwsters, *ouvrières de soie*, makers of *tissu/z de soie*, women who "carie soie," and spinners of gold thread comes to 87; the next largest group of working women in that tax assessment consisted of women street peddlers, or *regratières*, who constituted a group of 49–75 women.[40]

There are two possible explanations for the predominance of silk women in the tax assessments: either silk women in Paris outnumbered women in every other category of work, or the size of their wealth tended to exceed that of most other working women, and thus a higher proportion of silk women appeared in the tax assessments. There is good reason to believe that the second explanation is more accurate. First, some 60 percent of Parisian heads of household were too poor to appear in the tax assessments,[41] and female heads of household were more likely to fall into the category of people who were too poor to pay taxes than were men. Second, it is clear that some working women, like wool spinners, were severely underrepresented in the tax assessments—even more so than was the case for silk women.

The Parisian tax assessments point to the presence there of approximately 400 wool weavers. If each weaver who was taxed as the head of an atelier worked at a loom with a second weaver who was not taxed, and if those two weavers relied on the labor of a separate group of warpers, 400 taxed wool weavers would have relied on the labor of approximately 4,800 wool spinners. If, however, the 400 taxed wool weavers included both of the weavers at each loom, and if they did their own warping, they would have relied on the labor of approximately 1,600 wool spinners. In any case, whether the wool weavers of Paris generated work for 4,800 or 1,600 spinners, it is clear that those spinners were nearly invisible, as far as the Parisian tax assessors were concerned: only 10 wool spinners show up in the Parisian tax assessments.[42]

Some wool was spun in the countryside[43] or by married women who never showed up in the tax assessments. Nevertheless, we gain the impression from scattered miracle stories, court cases, and statutes that quite a number of Parisian women—both married and unmarried—combed, carded, and spun wool.[44] Those same sources suggest, however, that the working conditions for wool spinners were different from those of silk throwsters. Wool spinners and combers, it would seem, were often trained and employed by drapers, dyers, or weavers rather than working out of their own workshops and training their own apprentices.[45] Wool spinners could easily work at home, but their labor remained marginal and few of them could accumulate capital by benefiting from the labor of apprentices and employees.

It thus seems that the principal explanations for the near invisibility of wool spinners in the tax assessments are their relative poverty, the simplicity of their tools of production, and their absorption into the workshops of more prosperous artisans, many of whom were men.[46] Viewed in relationship to the nearly invisible wool spinners of Paris, the taxpaying silk throwsters of Paris—whose average tax of four sous was actually two times larger than the minimum tax of two sous—look relatively prosperous and independent.

The third element that I considered in comparing silk groups in which women predominated to silk groups in which men predominated was capital investment. That discussion made clear that women's capital investment was more modest than men's. But again, if we compare these same silk women with other working women, our perspective on their capital investment changes. The fact that so many of these silk women show up in the tax

assessments suggests that they not only had better incomes than the 60 percent of Parisian heads of household who never showed up in the tax assessments but also had more capital resources than those other female heads of
household. Most of those resources would have been tied up in the tools of
their trade: reeling wheels, spindles, bobbins, frames for holding bobbins and
skeins, and possibly spindle wheels, in the case of the throwsters; horizontal
treadle looms, in the case of the weavers of silk veils; weaving frames or box
looms, in the case of the weavers of silk narrow ware. Moreover, because
these women took on apprentices—and indeed, all of the silk women except
the weavers of silk veils were allowed to take on more than one apprentice
(and the weavers of silk veils could have two apprentices if one of them was
a relative)—they needed to invest in sufficient equipment to keep not only
themselves but also those apprentices occupied.[47] Taking on apprentices,
moreover, enhanced the income of the mistresses in these crafts. By putting
others to work, mistresses in the predominantly female silk trades were able
to move beyond mere subsistence, accumulating capital by drawing income
from the labor of other women. Such was certainly the case with Michelette
la Chambellande, a single or widowed maker of silk narrow ware who, in
1409, paid a fine to the Châtelet because she had taken on three apprentices,
which was one more than her guild allowed.[48] This ability for some mistresses
to move ahead, presumably by putting others to work, stands out in sharp
relief when we examine some of the silk women whose tax payments were
considerably higher than the average tax payment within their crafts: while
the average tax for *ouvrières de soie*, between 1297 and 1300, was 4.8 sous,
Dame Marie la Coquesse and Marie of Lagny each paid 20 sous, and Aalis
of Saint Joce paid 24 sous. And while the average tax for silk throwsters was
4 sous, Dame Isabel d'Oroër paid 48 sous.[49] By contrast, wool spinners, as I
have already mentioned, were frequently trained in the workshops of more
elite artisans or entrepreneurs, such as drapers and dyers, so they lacked the
opportunity to put others to work.

Further evidence of silk women's ability to invest in multiple tools of
production comes from the fact that the tax assessors associated some silk
women with multiple silk activities. In the tax assessments of 1296, 1299, and
1300, for instance, Isabel of Glatigni was identified first as a silk dyer, then as
an *ouvrière de soie*, and finally as a silk throwster.[50] I suspect that Isabel may
point to a broader pattern among the *ouvrières de soie*, whose average tax
assessment of 4.8 sous was higher than the average tax of all other silk groups

in which women predominated (see table 4). Given their relatively high tax rates, it seems likely that the *ouvrières de soie* were labeled with this umbrella term precisely because the apprentices and workers in their ateliers engaged in more than one silk activity.

A fourth aspect of work status that we examined in the first section of this chapter had to do with the distinctiveness of the product and the proximity that such products could help foster between producers and elite consumers. Among silk cloth weavers, only the men who wove "draps de soye," velvet, and cloth of gold had such status. However, when we move into the territory of smaller mercery goods and silk yarn—areas in which women predominated—we find a number of products that retained their "made in Paris" identity. Silk yarn that had been thrown in Paris shows up in the late fourteenth-century accounts of the Count and Countess of Savoy and in a fifteenth-century trade manual from London, which tells us that, in fact, the silk yarn of Paris garnered a higher price than that of London.[51] Silk and gold purses that were made in Paris show up in a bundle of goods that were confiscated from some merchants in Aix-en-Provence in 1343.[52] And narrow ware that had been made in Paris shows up in the 1290 accounts of Eleanor of Castile, queen of England; in an early fourteenth-century account book from Naples; in a late fourteenth-century inventory from the Church of the Holy Sepulcher in Paris; and in the late fourteenth-century accounts of the courts of Savoy and Burgundy.[53] Producing these mercery items could also bring the women who made them into contact with aristocratic consumers. As we have already seen, in 1294 two women purse makers sold purses and other mercery goods to an agent for the Countess of Flanders. Similarly, in 1311 Aliz of Basoches, "ouvrière de soie," made belts for Countess Mahaut of Artois and for her daughter Jeanne; and in 1314 Marguerite the purse maker was paid 32 sous for two purses that were purchased "in [Countess Mahaut's] presence."[54] In 1375 Berbalaut la tissiere, who made narrow ware, sold some of it to agents for the Duke of Burgundy.[55]

The final category of work status that we examined in the first section had to do with autonomy and self-governance. Although the women's silk guilds in Paris had less autonomy than did the men's silk guilds, we need to analyze the Parisian silk guilds not only in relationship to men's guilds but also in relationship to other women's work organizations. Viewed through that lens, the Parisian silk guilds stand out, since Paris was one of only three cities in western Europe that had guilds that were exclusively, or almost exclusively, female.[56] In Paris, all of the predominantly female guilds for which the statutes described members with feminine nouns involved some kind of silk work: four of the female guilds involved silk throwing or weaving, another involved the weaving or embroidering of silk alms purses, and another (which we will examine in more detail in Chapter 5) involved the confection of gold and silk hats.[57] Two additional guilds, for which the statutes described members with masculine (or both masculine and feminine) nouns but which had a majority of women members, also involved goods that were made out of silk.[58]

The position of sworn jurors for the female guilds opened up a rare opportunity for medieval women to hold public office. Even if the women jurors had to work alongside male jurors, these positions nevertheless enabled some Parisian silk women to gain recognition as trusted leaders in their crafts and to assume public positions with sworn duties and responsibilities. In the case of the guild of weavers of silk head coverings, the women jurors carried out their responsibilities without the interference of male jurors.

Additionally, as Tanya Stabler Miller has pointed out, at least two of these women's guilds had some kind of confraternity.[59] We know almost nothing about the activities of these confraternities, but their mere existence offers intriguing evidence that even outside of the religious sphere, women in medieval towns were sometimes able to constitute all-female communities of mutual support and conviviality.

Silk Women in Predominantly Male Spheres

Paris was unusual not only because it had a number of silk guilds that were predominantly female and many of the single women and widows who worked in those crafts were actually wealthy enough to be taxed but also because a number of women gained positions, and even prominence, in silk crafts and guilds that were predominantly male. Isabel of Glatigni, for instance, was identified in the tax assessment of 1296 as a silk dyer, and in 1298 Gile la Male-Vie, the widow of the mercer Symon Male-Vie, was identified as a gold beater (in 1313, however, Gile was again, like her deceased husband, identified as a mercer).[60] As indicated in the discussion at the beginning of the chapter, moreover, a second woman gold beater—Odeline Courson—was one of the most prominent furnishers in an account of purchases that were made for the Countess of Flanders in 1294.

The most prominent women in the silk industry were the women mercers. Forty-five of them show up in the tax assessments, paying an average tax, in the years 1297–1300, of 40.8 sous, which was slightly higher than the average tax for the mercers overall. In the tax assessments of 1292–1313, women mercers constituted 13.2 percent of the mercers who paid taxes in those years, which was slightly higher than women's overall representation in the seven tax assessments, which was 13.1 percent.[61] The fact that women mercers paid a higher average tax than the men and that they were more strongly represented in the tax assessments than were women overall is already surprising, since their average tax was almost double the average tax of all taxpayers, and the percentage of women within a profession tended to decline as the income level rose.[62] But this is only the first surprise: among the more elite mercers, those who resided in the three wealthiest mercery neighborhoods—Troussevache, Quincampoix, and Lombard—women mercers constituted 15 percent of the taxpayers, and their average tax in 1297–1300 was 55 sous.[63] Moving even higher up the social and economic scale among the mercers, we find two women—the Beguine Marie Osane, who never married, and the widow Nicole of Cologne—among the elite group of twelve mercers who paid taxes that were greater than 11 livres (2,640 deniers) at least once between 1297 and 1300. These two women thus constituted 16.7 percent of the very highest economic stratum of mercers.[64]

The fact that women mercers were overrepresented in the wealthiest mercer neighborhoods and among the very wealthiest of mercers suggests that some of them must have organized silk production. Indeed, we know that was the case for the mercer Jehanne du Faut, whose surviving testament indicates that she bequeathed a house in the Parisian Beguinage to one of her silk throwsters and several other rent-bearing properties to her silk factor—the agent who could conduct business in Jehanne's name.[65]

As the example of Marie Osane suggests, women mercers also emerged as important furnishers to aristocratic households. Such was the case as well with the widow of Amauri of Amiens, who sold over 375 livres' worth of silk textiles to the Count of Artois in 1299.[66] Women mercers continued to appear in aristocratic and royal account books well into the fourteenth century. We find several women among the prominent mercers who held stalls in the gallery of the royal palace on the Île-de-la-Cité in the 1370s.[67] And in the 1360s and 1370s Martine la Thierry emerged as one of the most important mercers in Paris. We find Martine in the accounts of the kings of France and Navarre, the Count of Savoy, and the Dukes of Anjou and Burgundy.[68]

Between 1375 and 1378, Martine sold more than 2,000 francs' worth of silk textiles to the Duke of Anjou, and her only rival in the duke's accounts was Dino Rapondi, the banker and merchant from Lucca who had risen to prominence as a major furnisher for the Duke of Burgundy.[69] In 1370 Martine was the sole outfitter of silk textiles for ten galley ships that King Charles V sent to Pope Urban V.[70] In 1377, moreover, after Martine provided him with over 670 francs' worth of silk textiles for a bedroom set, King Charles ordered the agents who were collecting an extraordinary tax for his war effort to use part of the money to reimburse Martine.[71] Martine thus provides us with an extremely telling example of the ways in which private consumption of luxury goods could impinge upon matters of state and the central role that women furnishers could play in such matters.

Martine la Thierry was not alone among Parisian women in achieving extraordinary levels of success as a furnisher for royal and aristocratic households. Indeed, she fits into a broader pattern of prominent women furnishers who rose to the top of their professions in thirteenth-and fourteenth-century Paris. Beginning around 1278 and continuing for the next fifty years, two women linen merchants dominated the international market for luxury linens from Paris, selling their wares to the kings of England and France, shipping goods to the pope in Avignon, and provisioning the Countess of Artois. For at least six months in 1316 the Parisian draper Isabel of Tremblay held a near monopoly on the sale of luxury woolens to the French royal household. Between 1299 and 1307 a spice dealer named Peronnelle held the title of "king's spice dealer." Two other women held the title of "purveyor of the king's gloves" in the 1370s and 1380s, and another held the title of "king's tapestry dealer."[72]

While there were also women merchants in Ghent, and some women mercers in London did business with the royal court, those women did not, as far as I know, gain these levels of prominence as furnishers, and we find virtually no such merchant women in northern Italy.[73] How, then, do we explain the relative status, prosperity, and prominence of Parisian silk women and of Parisian merchant women?

Explaining the High Status of Parisian Silk Women

This chapter opened with a discussion of the silk industry of Florence, where, as was the case in Paris, women predominated numerically. Nevertheless, unlike the silk women of Paris, those of Florence tended to remain at the bottom levels of the silk industry. As far as I know, no women ever emerged as silk entrepreneurs in Florence, and dyeing was pretty much an all-male activity as well.[74]

Several legal contexts help explain the ability of Parisian silk women to enter into entrepreneurial and artisanal arenas that were off limits to Florentine silk women. First, in Florence, from 1325 on, succession law dictated that, in the absence of explicit testamentary bequests, daughters who had already received their dowry were excluded from both their paternal and their maternal inheritance if they had any male relatives, and widows were expected to draw on those same dowries in order to survive.[75] In Paris, by contrast, much as was the case in other northern towns at this time, customary law fostered complete parity among all heirs of the same degree of kinship—even to the point of overriding testamentary gifts—and that legal system was much more favorable to widows as well.

According to Parisian customary law, surviving spouses were to receive one-half of all of the conquests that a couple had made during a marriage.[76] Additionally, widows were guaranteed a dower, which either conformed to the stipulations of a prenuptial agreement or, in the absence of such an agreement, consisted of the usufruct of one-half of the property—both inherited and acquired—that the husband brought into the marriage, plus one-half of any direct inheritance that came to her husband during the course of the marriage.[77] Moreover, if adult children still lived with their parents when one of those parents died, the surviving spouse—whether the widow or the widower—was to be recognized as the head of the family company, because, as the civil court of the *échevins* of Paris deliberated in 1293, "li pere, ou la mere, sunt chief d'ostel." As long as the children remained with that parent, any acquisitions that they made belonged to the parent.[78] Within a year or so after the death of one parent, surviving spouses and their adult children often split up their common property, with the widow or widower taking one half and the children equally dividing the other half. The Parisian tax assessments indicate that when such a division took place, more often than not it was the widow who remained with the original family business while the children moved on.[79]

In Paris, legal custom and local practice thus resulted in a large number of widows taking over the businesses or ateliers that had once been run either by their husbands or by the married couple.[80] Moreover, because Parisian custom, and those who interpreted it, strictly adhered to the principle that all heirs of the same degree of kinship should divide an inheritance equally, and because Parisian inheritance favored immediate descendants over ascendants, unmarried adult daughters had as much access to familial wealth as did unmarried adult sons.[81] In practice, sons were more likely to take over family businesses than were daughters,[82] but this statistical pattern was, in all likelihood, a consequence of the fact that daughters tended to separate from the natal household at a younger age than their brothers did, in order to marry. Daughters—and sons—who had separated from the communal natal household were given a "dot" that was considered an equal share of the value of the common property at the time that the share was handed over to them; henceforth, they had no further claim on the communal property of the household—but they were still eligible for their share of the lineage property of their fathers and mothers or other relations.[83]

Despite the fact that sons were more likely than daughters to take control of family businesses, there were still a considerable number of daughters who assumed such control.[84] Moreover, it is clear that the French capital produced some outstanding never-married businesswomen, such as the mercer Marie Osane.[85] It is also clear that many, many wives, even those of the most prominent *échevins*, worked—sometimes in the same business or craft as that of their husbands (as was the case with the mercer Mahy of Arras and his wife), sometimes in retail fields or crafts that were complementary to those of their husbands (as was the case with the linen merchant Geneviève la Fouacière, whose husband was a mercer), and sometimes in areas that were completely distinct from those of their husbands (as in the cases of six women moneylenders or money changers who were married to a draper, a gold beater, a tavern keeper, an armorer, and a spice dealer).[86]

Working single and widowed women in thirteenth- and fourteenth-century Paris also benefited from relatively liberal guild statutes. One Parisian guild—that of the makers of Saracen tapestries—prohibited widows from taking over the husband's atelier, and a few others prevented widows from taking on apprentices.[87] But we have to wonder how effective these prohibitions were: in the 1370s, in any case, a woman named Perronnelle of Crepon was the king's tapestry furnisher.[88]

Among the silk guilds, the only restriction on women's work was that of the guild of weavers of "draps de soye," velvet and woven purses, which simply stated that a widow who married a man who was not a member of the guild had to be a weaver herself if she wanted to maintain her workshop. This was no stricter than the rule for male masters in the guild, who were also expected to be able to practice the craft themselves and thus to pass the competency exam.

Parisian women also benefited from the right to appear in court on their own, and although there were restrictions on married women's independence in court, the Parisian bourgeois court tended to interpret those restrictions in ways that offered married women opportunities to engage in legal actions on their own. Customary law usually required that a wife appear in court along with her husband and that he guarantee any contracts involving his wife; however, husbands could authorize their wives to alienate property on their own and to appear in court alone.[89] Moreover, Parisian courts were perfectly capable of recognizing that in some circumstances—as when a husband was away from Paris for an extended period of time—it was necessary to grant the wife authority to appear in court alone, even without the husband's consent.[90] Parisian judges, moreover, rejected attempts to render contracts invalid because wives had entered into them without their husband's consent.[91] Thirteenth- and fourteenth-century married women in Paris may not have been as free as were those of Douai and Ghent to appear on their own in court, but they were far freer than were Frenchwomen of the sixteenth century, who had to contend with a whole series of royal acts that raised women's age of majority, hindered their use of property, placed all children under the patriarchal authority of their fathers, and put pressure on married women to make contracts only with their husband's consent. Similarly, thirteenth- and fourteenth-century Parisian women seem to have enjoyed greater privileges in craft guilds than was the case in the early modern period. We find, for instance, that in 1600, the Parisian guild of ribbon makers ruled that daughters of members of the trade could work as apprentices, but they had to cease practicing the craft if they married men who were not members. No such restrictions had existed in the thirteenth century.[92]

Surviving civil court records from late medieval Paris indicate, moreover, that, at least in the case of those who were single or widowed, Parisian working women were considered completely capable of representing themselves in court and signing legal contracts on their own. In 1397, for instance, Jehanne of Saint Fiacre, a maker of the silk narrow ware known as "tissu/z de soie," made a written contract with a certain Robert Aussouart in which she promised to take on Robert's cousin Jehannete as an apprentice for three years in exchange for a fee of 12 livres tournois, half of which would come to Jehanne at the end of the contracted apprenticeship. When the girl failed to complete the apprenticeship, Jehanne of Saint Fiacre pressed charges against Robert

Aussouart in the court of the Châtelet and was then granted the right to collect damages with interest.[93] In 1399, the provost of Paris paid Jehannette la Riche, a maker of silk and gold narrow ware ("orfrois"), the apprenticeship fee for a girl whose grandmother had died and whose parents had disappeared.[94] In 1409 Michelette la Chambellande, another weaver of silk narrow ware ("tisseuse"), paid a fine to the Châtelet because she had taken on three apprentices, which was one more than the guild statutes allowed.[95] One has to wonder what happened to all of these independent makers of silk narrow ware in the early modern period: in the Parisian notarial records of the sixteenth century, nearly all of the makers of *tissu/z de soie* were men.[96]

Another institutional circumstance that helped create favorable conditions, in late thirteenth-century Paris, for silk women who were either single or widowed was the strength, there, of the movement of semireligious women known as Beguines. As Tanya Stabler Miller has demonstrated, the landscape of Paris was dotted with small communities of independent Beguines, many of whom were involved in silk work.[97] And as the testament of the wealthy Beguine mercer Jehanne du Faut makes clear, the bonds among Beguines could cross social and economic divisions, thereby mitigating some of the disadvantages that fell upon women who had no familial inheritance to draw upon. Jehanne du Faut bequeathed a house in the Parisian Beguinage to a silk throwster, and she designated as her principal heir a woman named Beatrice la Grande who had worked as her "factor" ("Beatrice dicta la grant factor et impensor").[98]

Factors worked as agents and go-betweens for entrepreneurs. They clearly fell into the category of professionals rather than manual laborers, and indeed, as the example of Francesco Balducci Pegolotti suggests, factors for major international Italian banking companies could acquire a great deal of technical knowledge about the international world of commerce.[99] Nevertheless, as we learn from the testament of a young factor from Siena, written in Paris in 1300, the income levels of factors could be modest, and they sometimes fell into dire straits: in his testament the young man declared that he had come to Paris to work as a salaried factor for the well-known Sienese Gallerani banking company; lacking property of his own, owing money to the company, and fearing that he was on his deathbed, he implored one of the partners in the company to give him a decent burial.[100] Further evidence of the precarious finances of factors comes from a Parisian court case: in 1362, when the Lucchese merchant Andrea Simonetti, who resided in Paris, claimed that his deceased landlord's nephew had assumed possession of a large quantity of expensive commercial goods that belonged to Simonetti, his adversary responded in court that Simonetti was a mere factor for a large Lucchese firm, and thus he could not possibly have owned such a valuable inventory.[101]

What Jehanne du Faut's testament thus suggests is that the emotional bonds among Beguines helped dissolve some of the hierarchical divisions that created barriers between silk workers and factors of modest means, on the one hand, and wealthy entrepreneurs, on the other. Moreover, those bonds even encouraged some wealthy women to pass their wealth on to their modestly endowed employees. The testament also tells us that the community of mercers included women who managed the production of silk.

Nondiscriminatory legal customs and guild regulations help explain why women had access to all parts of the economy, but they take us only so far in trying to explain why Paris came to be one of only three medieval towns in northern Europe that had formalized guilds that were exclusively or predominantly female, or why some women mercers in Paris, along with other wealthy Parisian merchant women, rose to the pinnacles of their professions.

If we look more broadly at other medieval and early modern towns that had all-female guilds, or where women merchants rose to great heights, it becomes clear that the textile trades, especially those involving linen and silk, often offered extraordinary opportunities for women. In the three medieval towns that had all-female guilds—Paris, Cologne, and Rouen—those guilds all involved some aspect of silk or linen production. In Paris all eight of the female guilds or guilds with a majority of female members involved silk production or the production of luxury items that were made with silk.[102] In Rouen and Cologne the predominantly female guilds were concentrated entirely within the silk and linen industries.[103]

In the area of entrepreneurship, textile trades seem to have offered the best opportunities for both medieval and early modern women. Again, silk and linen often offered the greatest opportunities, but in a few towns—such as Douai—a considerable percentage of highly placed wool merchants were women.[104] At the level of entrepreneurship, there seems to have been a shared cultural perception—at least in large swaths of northern France and the Low Countries—that women could contribute particular skills when it came to managing textile production and distinguishing various qualities of textile materials and products.

Finally, as Daryl Hafter has pointed out in her discussion of early modern Rouen, the fact that a given town was under royal control rather than being governed by merchant-*échevins* could also foster an environment in which women merchants thrived.[105] Part of this difference had to do with who passed the guild statutes: in Paris the provost, who was a royal officer, did so; in many other towns the *échevins*, who often controlled the wool industry, did so. That difference may well explain why guild statutes in Paris did not tend to restrict women's access to predominantly male activities, as was the case in towns such as Ghent.[106]

Parisian women entrepreneurs from prominent families also benefited from the fact that the men in their families could count on lucrative opportunities working for the royal administration. These men tended to diversify their working activities, devoting part of their time to retail businesses—especially the sale of wool, silk, and other luxury goods—and part of their time to carrying out public administrative responsibilities. A number of the administrative positions that the men attained were extremely lucrative—and they were completely out of reach for the women in these families.[107] As far as elite bourgeois Parisian men were concerned, then, the fact that the women in their families and social circles sometimes exercised more influence in the marketplace than they did was hardly a threat to their masculinity or authority—because the really serious prestige and wealth were to be found in the exclusively male realm of high-level public office and administration.[108]

Poor Silk Women

Parisian silk women, then, tended to be better-off than most other working women: mistresses in the artisanal silk crafts had their own workshops where they could profit from the labor of others, and at the top of the hierarchy there were a number of very prominent women mercers. Nevertheless, the "pavre feme ki file soie" to whom Marie du Val gave alms in 1294 was not the only poor silk woman in Paris. In taking into account the reasons why some silk women were wealthy enough to show up in the tax assessments and others were poor enough to accept alms, we need to remember that the structure of guilds and the distribution of wealth meant that for every master or mistress in a craft there were a considerable number of apprentices and workers who could never hope to own their own workshops.

We catch glimpses of marginalized silk women who could never hope to manage their own workshops in court records from fourteenth-century Paris. The household servant and petty thief Marion du Val, for instance, who was imprisoned at the Châtelet in 1389 after stealing some jewelry from her employer, seems to have started out as an apprentice or worker in the workshop of a maker of silk purses and religious vestments; and Perrete d'Arencourt, a silk throwster, apparently augmented her working income through petty theft as well.[109] It seems unlikely that either of these women harbored any hope of ever rising to the level of mistress of her craft. If they had, they would have been more careful to guard their reputations as honest women— not in the sexual sense but in the commercial sense. The desperate acts of theft on the part of these two women indicate that there were some silk women who remained, throughout their lives, at the bottom of the economic and social hierarchy. In Chapter 5, which looks at the relationships between Parisian silk women and Jewish and foreign Lombard residents of Paris, we will examine one of the most essential economic instruments that contributed to the survival of poor silk women: pawnbroking.

Chapter 5

Jews, Foreign Lombards, and Parisian Silk Women

The earliest collection of Parisian guild statutes, which was compiled between 1266 and 1275, included, in the statutes for women who made gold and silk hats, a rule indicating that if mistresses (or masters) in the guild wanted to send their apprentices out to be trained in the households or ateliers of "Jews, workers or mercers," those mistresses and masters needed to ensure that the wives of the masters of the households in question knew how to practice the trade.[1] The statute raises tantalizing questions about the nature of Jewish-Christian interactions in late thirteenth-century Parisian silk textile workshops. We will return to it in the second part of this chapter.

*   *   *

As a commodity, primary material, and object of exchange, silk created social relations among people with differing geographical origins and religious backgrounds. Chapter 3 attempted to ferret out the evidence concerning silk workers and mercers from the Mediterranean basin who immigrated to Paris, thereby diversifying the Parisian bourgeois community and helping to launch the fledgling silk cloth industry there. This chapter analyzes evidence concerning relations that arose between Parisian silk workers, on the one hand, and two groups that were considered outsiders to Parisian bourgeois society but whose members, nevertheless, had a relatively strong presence in Paris at the end of the thirteenth century: Jews and foreign Lombard moneylenders.

We have already encountered Jewish and Lombard moneylenders in two guild statutes that were promulgated in Paris in the last quarter of the thirteenth century in order to prevent female silk workers—throwsters and weavers of silk head coverings—from selling or pawning silk fiber that did not belong to them.[2] The assumption in both statutes was that Jewish and Lombard moneylenders or merchants constituted the two groups with whom these women were most likely to put up pledges of silk fiber in order to borrow money. In the second half of the thirteenth century this assumption made sense, for at least two reasons: by the mid-thirteenth century, Jews and a particular subset of foreign Lombards constituted the two groups that specialized in pawnbroking in towns north of the Alps, and both groups included individuals who worked with (and thus could assess the quality of) silk fiber.[3] I argue in the first section of this chapter, however, that during the thirteenth century Parisian silk women who needed to borrow money would have been more inclined—if they had a reasonable choice—to do business with Jewish moneylenders rather than Lombard moneylenders. My argument builds on the scholarship of Joseph Shatzmiller, Gérard Nahon, and William C. Jordan, who have pointed out that Jewish moneylenders engaged in a high percentage of loans to modest borrowers, including women, and that, at least before the expulsion of the Jewish population of France in 1306, they offered better loan terms than did their Christian peers.[4] I add to the previous discussion the hypothesis that a perception of sexual danger would have played an important role in discouraging single women from borrowing from Lombard moneylenders.

In the second part of the chapter I turn to other relations that developed, in the second half of the thirteenth century, between Parisian silk workers and Jews, including those who made silk and gold hats. Despite the fact that French Jews filled a specialized niche in the credit market, I argue, they engaged in other economic activities as well. In Paris, Jewish women—and possibly some men—participated in the artisanal production of silk textile products, and the statute for the makers of gold hats suggests that some of these Jewish women actually trained Christian apprentices. The evidence concerning Jewish women's artisanal activity in Paris provides a new perspective on the economic activities of northern European Jews at this time: historians are well aware that throughout the Mediterranean world Jews were often involved in silk production. Scattered evidence suggests, moreover, that for reasons relating to internal needs of the Jewish community, some medieval French Jewish women probably produced luxurious embroideries. Nevertheless, no one has considered the possibility that northern European Jews may have engaged in textile production. By elucidating what we can know or surmise about religious objects and clothing items that were employed by the Jewish community, and by examining contacts between northern French and Mediterranean Jews at this time, I attempt to explain how Parisian Jews might have come to be involved in silk textile production.

In the third and final section of the chapter I explain and describe the transformations that these patterns underwent over the course of the fourteenth century. During that time period, the French king cracked down on both Jews and foreign Lombards, especially those who engaged in moneylending. French Jews were subjected to two cycles of expulsion and return, followed by one final expulsion in 1394. Thus there were periods in the fourteenth century when no Jews resided in Paris, and even when they did reside there, their numbers were greatly reduced and, given the financial burdens that they bore vis-à-vis the royal court, their loan terms may not have been as good as they had been in the thirteenth century. After the expulsion of 1306, moreover, it seems unlikely that Jewish women would have resumed their relationships with Christian apprentices.

After the middle of the thirteenth century, Italian merchants and moneylenders in France were also subjected to increasingly repressive royal policies. As a result of these developments, the Parisian credit market underwent significant transformations over the course of the fourteenth century. I thus attempt, in this final section of the chapter, to tease out evidence concerning sources of credit that remained available for female borrowers of modest means over the course of the fourteenth century and in the fifteenth as well.

Jewish and Lombard Moneylending in Thirteenth-Century Paris

By the end of the thirteenth century, credit played a ubiquitous role in the medieval economy.[5] In Paris, as elsewhere, people who had money found ways to lend it out, despite declarations by Christian leaders condemning the practice of charging interest on loans. Some local entrepreneurs who engaged in commercial or money-changing activities, for instance, also offered the occasional loan on the side. Such was the case with a number of Parisian *échevins*, who loaned money both to the king and to prominent notables.[6] Nevertheless, by the second half of the thirteenth century, Jews and a particular subset of foreign Lombards had come to be perceived as specialists in the French market for consumer credit. Both groups extended credit to a wide range of borrowers, but it appears that they gravitated toward different economic niches: Lombard moneylenders extended more loans to individuals and institutions at the high end of the social and economic scale, while Jewish moneylenders extended more loans to those at the bottom of the social scale.[7] The emergence of these differing niches was the consequence of relatively recent events.

Unlike specialized Lombard moneylenders, who did not become active north of the Alps until the end of the twelfth century, Jews had been lending money in West Francia and the French kingdom since at least the tenth century.[8] In the early eleventh century, a period when they could not rely on effective royal or seigneurial backing to insure the security of their loans, Jewish moneylenders in the French royal domain and its surrounding counties often engaged in pawnbroking because, unlike loans that relied on contracts, those that were extended against physical pledges provided the lender with a guaranteed return on the loan even if the borrower defaulted.[9]

During the prosperous twelfth century, however, when increasingly effective royal and seigneurial protection helped guarantee Jewish loans, and when the Capetian kings had not yet begun a century-long cycle of arbitrary seizures of Jewish property and expulsions of Jews, French and Francophone Jewish moneylenders expanded their commercial and moneylending activities to include written contractual arrangements. Their clients included not only territorial princes but also prominent religious institutions, such as the abbey of Saint Denis.[10] Documents of practice suggest, however, that by the late 1240s Jewish lending had become increasingly marginalized and that pawn loans had once again gained prominence. Thus by the 1240s, if not before, French Jewish moneylenders were specializing in the kinds of loans that were especially attractive to workers of modest means, including single women artisans.

The decline and marginalization of medieval French Jewry in general, and of French Jewish moneylending in particular, began in 1180–1182, when King Philip Augustus first seized Jewish property and subsequently expelled all of the Jews from his domain.[11] Although the king's domain was extremely limited in 1182, this first expulsion nevertheless had a profound effect on the French Jewish community. Philip Augustus invited the Jews of his domain, including those of Paris, to return in 1198. William C. Jordan has argued convincingly, however, that many French Jews remained in neighboring Francophone jurisdictions, such as Normandy and Champagne.[12]

This first royal expulsion and return, along with several subsequent events in thirteenth-century Paris, had a profound effect on the Parisian

Jewry.[13] A community that had consisted of over 2,000 inhabitants before 1180 had shrunk, by 1296, to 82 households, which probably included around 300–330 men, women, and children.[14] Those Jews who did return to Paris in 1198 were not able to buy back or repossess their former properties on the Île-de-la Cité, so from then on Parisian Jews were concentrated on five streets of the right bank and on the Petit-Pont, which joined the Île-de-la-Cité to the left bank (fig. 26).[15] Thus, since the Île-de-la-Cité would never include very many silk workers, the first cycle of expulsion and return increased the potential for direct contacts between Jewish moneylenders—and artisans— and Christian silk workers on the right bank of Paris.

French Jewish moneylenders suffered a second major blow in 1223, when King Louis VIII declared that all debtors who had outstanding Jewish loans had three years to pay back the loans, they were only responsible for repaying the principal, and that principal would go to the king or to other lords who exercised direct lordship over Jews rather than to the Jewish lenders who had extended the loans in the first place.[16] In one fell swoop, then, the king negated the single most important source of income for French Jews, wiped out most of their capital, brought money into his own coffers, and won the support of French Christians who owed money to Jewish moneylenders. Louis VIII did not prohibit Jews from taking interest on future loans—but one wonders how they managed to raise the capital in order to make those loans. Indeed, the fact that the king invited Lombard moneylenders to come to Paris for the first time in 1225 suggests that he was well aware that his seizure of Jewish assets in 1223 precipitated a crisis in the Parisian credit market.[17]

In 1227 King Louis IX basically repeated his father's seizure of 1223, claiming for himself the principal on all loans that Jews had made in the previous four years.[18] The following year, moreover, he declared that Jews were no longer allowed to charge "usury" on loans, and in 1230 he defined "usury" as any interest collected on a loan. After he took his crusader vow in 1244, moreover, Louis IX apparently redoubled his efforts to stamp out French Jewish moneylending.[19]

Two sets of documentary sources, which provide narrow windows on Jewish lending in Capetian lands during the 1230s and 1240s, suggest that these royal actions had a profound effect on Jewish lending. Several Parisian charters from the 1230s suggest, as Aryeh Graboïs has argued, that at least some Parisian Jews responded to the new restrictive atmosphere by disguising loans as payments for landed property, which remained, nevertheless, in the

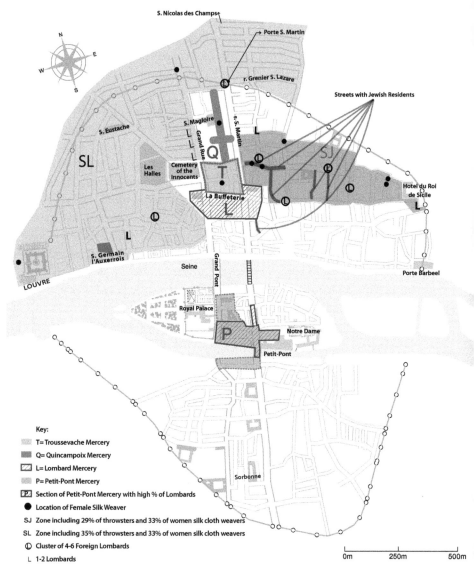

Figure 26. Jewish, Lombard, and silk-working neighborhoods, Paris, c. 1300.
Adapted, in collaboration with author, by Eddie Peralta, Artworks, University of
California, Santa Barbara, from "Plan de la Ville de Paris sous Philippe-le-Bel dressé
par Albert Lenoir architecte d'après le travail de H. Géraud."

hands of the "seller."[20] More revealing still are the inquests that King Louis IX conducted in 1247–1248 in order to investigate corruption among his administrators. Since Jewish loans were now considered illegal, such corruption included efforts to enforce Jewish loans. According to William C. Jordan, the inquests from Picardy, just north of the Île-de-France, indicate that after 1245 Jewish moneylenders were forced to replace "straight" loans with pawn loans. In some areas of that region, moreover, Jewish lending collapsed altogether after individual moneylenders took flight in order to avoid the legal consequences of their continued lending activities.[21] Narrative sources suggest, however, that in Paris Jewish moneylending continued right up to the expulsion of 1306.[22]

Louis IX's inquests from 1247–1248 also suggest that by the 1240s—if not before—Jewish lenders in Capetian lands were specializing in loans to modest borrowers. In his examinations of the inquests from Touraine, Anjou, Normandy, Maine, Artois, and lower Languedoc, Gérard Nahon found that 37 percent of borrowers on Jewish loans were from small villages. Among both rural and urban loans, moreover, Nahon found that over two-thirds of the transactions involved original loans of less than 5 livres.[23] The inquests from Picardy affirm this general pattern.[24] By the 1240s, Nahon and Jordan suggest, French Jewish moneylenders had become specialists in modest loans, loans that helped village peasants, widows, and presumably spinsters survive from one week to another.[25] Late thirteenth- and early fourteenth-century evidence from Montpellier appears to indicate that Jewish lenders also specialized in modest loans in that town.[26] There is good reason to believe, moreover, that because of the increasingly hostile atmosphere in which they operated, Jewish moneylenders offered better terms on their loans than did Christian lenders in order to attract clients. A number of Christian and Jewish observers noted that Jewish loans had fairer terms.[27]

A very high percentage of northern French Jews who engaged in moneylending, moreover, were women: in the 1247–1248 inquests examined by Nahon and Jordan, women constituted between 26 and 50 percent of the Jews who extended loans.[28] Evidence from Vitry-le-François, in northeastern France, suggests, moreover, that that pattern continued to the end of the century: a royal list of Jewish lenders from that town indicates that between c. 1280 and 1300, 37 percent of Jewish moneylenders (21 out of the 57) were women.[29] William C. Jordan found, moreover, that Christian women who needed to borrow money often did business with female lenders within the Jewish community.[30]

Unfortunately, other than a few charters from Paris in the 1230s (which concern a single loan), we have no documentary evidence that enables us to analyze or quantify lending patterns among Parisian Jews: none of the royal inquests of 1247–1248 survives for the French capital, and the Parisian tax assessments, which offer only scanty evidence concerning the professions of Jewish taxpayers, include no evidence concerning Parisian Jews who engaged in moneylending. The tax assessments do suggest, however, that Jewish moneylenders in the French capital had only modest amounts of capital to draw upon: in 1297 the average tax of Parisian Jews was just slightly above the overall average tax of 1 livre, and the highest tax paid by any Parisian Jew—15 livres—was only half the average tax paid by foreign Lombards from the moneylending town of Piacenza.[31]

While the documentary sources remain relatively silent concerning Jewish moneylending activities in Paris, several narrative sources indicate that Jewish lending in late twelfth- and thirteenth-century Paris resembled that of other parts of the Capetian realm. In his discussion of King Philip Augustus's decision to cancel Jewish debts in 1180, the king's biographer, Rigord, painted a disapproving picture of wealthy Parisian Jews who imprisoned in their homes Christian debtors who had defaulted on their loan payments (Rigord failed to mention, however, that such private confinement of debtors, which originated in Greek and Roman law, was widely practiced in France at the time).[32] Similarly, a number of narrative accounts concerning the alleged Parisian host desecration of 1290 indicated that the Jewish man who perpetrated the desecration was a moneylender. That man, the narratives claimed, had offered to redeem the clothing that a poor Christian woman had pawned to him if she would bring him a consecrated host as payment for her loan.[33] One final Parisian source, the chronicle of Geoffrey of Paris, looked favorably on Jewish moneylending, lamenting, after the expulsion of 1306, that poor Christians were going to suffer as a result of this royal act:

All the poor complain, for the Jews were much milder
In the conduct of their business than the Christians are now;
These demand guarantees and mortgages, pledges, too, and take
    everything
Until they have stripped men quite bare . . . but had the Jews remained
In the kingdom of France, Christians would have had
Much succour that is theirs no longer.[34]

Documentary evidence thus suggests that Jewish moneylenders in various parts of thirteenth-century northern France specialized in modest pawn loans and that many of them were women whose lending activities met the needs of women borrowers. Narrative sources, moreover, enable us to conclude that in Paris at that time Jewish moneylenders were also serving the needs of modest borrowers, including women of limited means. We have no direct evidence that Jewish women in Paris acted as moneylenders in the thirteenth century, but the patterns from neighboring regions and from late fourteenth-century Paris indicate that that must have been the case.

Jewish residential patterns in late thirteenth-century Paris probably played an important role in encouraging a good number of silk women to seek loans from Jewish lenders. Four of the six streets where Jews clustered— the rue Neuve Saint Merri, the rue Frank Mourier, the Court-Robert-de-Paris, and the rue des Jardins—were right in the middle of a section of Paris (zone SJ on fig. 26) that had a high percentage of women silk workers: 29 percent of throwsters, 33 percent of women who wove silk cloth or head coverings, 37.5 percent of women who spun gold thread, 46 percent of women who made *tissu/z de soie*, and 22 percent of the *ouvrières de soie*.[35] That same section of Paris also included a sprinkling of foreign Lombards, some of whom might have been moneylenders as well (fig. 26); their average tax of 6.2 livres was more modest than that of the foreign Lombards in the major Lombard zone around the rue de la Buffeterie but considerably higher than that of Jewish taxpayers.[36]

Nevertheless, differences in the composition of Jewish and foreign Lombard households probably encouraged silk women to do business with Jewish lenders rather than foreign Lombard lenders: while the Jews of Paris tended to reside with their nuclear families, Lombard merchants and moneylenders often took up temporary residence in Paris in all-male, or nearly all-male, households. The tax assessments highlight this difference: while the numbers of Jewish and foreign Lombard taxpaying units were nearly equal (86 Lombard and 82 Jewish units in 1297), their gendered composition was strikingly different. No women appear on the 1297 list of Lombard taxpayers, but 14 women are mentioned on the Jewish list, where they appear as independent taxpayers, as wives, and as daughters.[37]

The nearly exclusive male presence among the foreign Lombard taxpayers was a consequence of a major pattern in their temporary, or semipermanent, form of migration. While many foreign Lombards came to reside in Paris for years, or even decades at a time, and while they often worked in partnership with their brothers and nephews, they tended to leave their wives, sisters, and mothers behind in Italy.[38] Indeed, Lombards who did bring their wives to Paris—or who ended up marrying Frenchwomen—often crossed over into the status of bourgeois of Paris, giving up citizenship status in their towns of origin.[39]

Given what we know about gender and Jewish moneylending—that Christian women in need of credit frequently did business with Jewish women who offered credit—we have to conclude that the masculine nature of foreign Lombard households and businesses in Paris must have played a major role in inhibiting silk women from borrowing money from foreign Lombards. Indeed, this gendered characteristic of Lombard households and businesses suggests that we should expand William C. Jordan's insightful arguments about the anomie that Christian borrowers must have felt when they crossed the threshold into Jewish neighborhoods or Jewish places of business: single and widowed women who crossed the threshold into Lombard places of business or into Lombard neighborhoods must have experienced an equal, or possibly greater, sense of alienation.[40]

Certainly these were not exclusively male spaces, since Lombard businessmen employed women as domestic servants and a sprinkling of silk workers actually resided in the Lombard zone. Moreover, as we learn from the tax assessments, some foreign Lombards set up temporary households with female lovers in Paris: the assessment of 1292 identified one Lombard on the Île-de-la-Cité as "Jacques le lombart, qui a la fille à Amelot la bele" (Jacques the Lombard, who had a daughter with Amelot la bele).[41] Amelot was not the only Parisian woman to be impregnated by a foreign Lombard. Court records point to at least one such woman in the fourteenth century and another in the fifteenth—and since there are very few surviving court records from medieval Paris, we can assume that there must have been a number of others.

Such pregnancies, as the fourteenth-century court case indicates, could be disastrous for both the woman and her offspring. In 1389 Colette Phelipe, a Parisian domestic servant who had moved to Paris from Caen, was imprisoned in the Châtelet after allowing her fifteenth-month-old daughter to be left at Notre Dame Cathedral, which had a nursery for abandoned babies. At the time that she became pregnant, Colette had been working as a domestic servant for a household of Italian men who occupied a house in the Lombard zone on the right bank. After the baby was born, the father—an Italian named Athevrien—helped Colette out for a while, setting the child up with a wet nurse who lived outside of Paris. Subsequently, however, Athevrien left

Paris, leaving Colette to fend for herself. In the meantime, moreover, Colette was dismissed from her job. A man from Geneva then set Colette up in a rented room where she spun wool, and where he apparently sought sexual favors from time to time, but her situation remained precarious. When her daughter's wet nurse showed up on her doorstep wanting to return the infant and collect her unpaid wages, Colette, who had no money and no idea how she might support both herself and the child, panicked. When a woman who was probably a procuress suggested that the baby could be left at the nursery at Notre Dame, Colette passively accepted the advice, allowing the other woman to take her daughter to the cathedral. Colette was subsequently arrested and probably executed.[42]

As Colette's story suggests, many single Parisian women must have experienced the residences, business establishments, and neighborhoods of foreign Lombard men as spaces that vibrated with male sexual energy. And indeed, not all of that sexual energy came to be relieved through consensual relationships: a surviving fragmentary criminal record from the abbey of Saint-Martin-des-Champs suggests that Lombards residing in Paris may have been overrepresented among perpetrators of sexual aggression. In that document, which includes cases from 1332 to 1357, Lombard men were the suspects in half of the cases (two out of four) involving accusations of rape.[43]

Silk women who needed to borrow money and to avoid unwanted pregnancies were much safer turning to Jewish lenders than to foreign Lombard lenders. Even if they had to borrow from a Jewish man, rather than a Jewish woman, female borrowers could nearly always rest assured that the Jewish man in question was well established within a nuclear family that was somewhere nearby. Christian women who needed to borrow money may have confronted a variety of anxieties when they entered the interior business spaces of Jewish moneylenders, but it is highly unlikely that fear of sexual danger constituted one of those anxieties.

But what about the silk women who did not reside in the section of Paris that included the major Jewish streets? Where did they go when they needed to borrow money? Some of those women may well have turned to Lombard moneylenders, some of whom lived in close proximity to them. To gain a full picture of Lombard lending patterns that were available to these silk women, we need to back up, to the third decade of the thirteenth century.

In their pioneering studies of the market for credit in the medieval Low Countries, Georges Bigwood and Raymond De Roover argued that, in the high and late Middle Ages, northern Italian merchants and entrepreneurs who resided temporarily in areas north of the Alps consisted of two main groups: members of large-scale international merchant-banking companies, such as the Bellardi of Lucca, the Tolomei and Gran Tavola of Siena, and the Anguissola and Scotti of Piacenza (all of which had representatives in late thirteenth-century Paris), and individuals or members of small family companies, primarily from the Piedmont towns of Alba, Asti, and Piacenza, who were invited into specific political jurisdictions for a number of years in order to practice pawnbroking.[44] The first group, whose companies imported luxury goods from the East and exported northern French and Flemish woolens, became a prominent presence at the Champagne Fairs in the twelfth century and often got involved in large-scale international banking as well, serving both kings and popes. The second group did not show up north of the Alps until the end of the twelfth century.[45]

In Bruges, the separate category of juridically defined Lombard pawnbrokers (who were sometimes labeled Cahorsins as well) seems to have had a continuous presence from the late thirteenth century until the end of the fifteenth. Indeed, because they specialized in pawnbroking they possessed a large warehouse, which could still be found on late sixteenth-century maps of Bruges.[46]

For France, we have evidence of royal charters granting protection to Lombard pawnbrokers in the early thirteenth century and again in the last quarter of the fourteenth.[47] In the intervening years, however, while we catch glimpses of Lombards and Lombard companies (including at least one family of lenders from Asti) that extended consumer loans in and around Paris, and of foreign Lombard moneylenders who had to pay fines for practicing "usury" in France, it is difficult to determine how much Lombard pawnbroking actually took place in Paris.[48]

Our earliest evidence concerning the presence in France of specialized Lombard pawnbrokers comes from a charter that King Louis VIII issued in 1225, when he invited Lombards from the Piedmont town of Asti to come reside in Paris for five years; in exchange for royal protection, the beneficiaries of the charter had to make an annual payment of 50 sous (2.5 livres) per household. The charter implied, moreover, that pawnbroking was to be the main economic activity of this group: it specified that the beneficiaries of the charter had the right to sell pawn pledges that had been left in their care for over one year.[49]

According to Robert-Henri Bautier, by the end of the thirteenth century and the beginning of the fourteenth, Lombards from Piacenza and Siena had emerged as the most important Italian moneylenders in France.[50] We catch glimpses of some of their lending activities, but the sources reveal less than a handful of pawn loans, which constituted the most important form of credit for borrowers who had few assets and were thus high credit risks for conventional loans.[51]

While moneylenders from Piacenza appear to have played an extremely important role in the French and Parisian credit markets overall, it is unclear if they loaned money to single women of modest means. Part of the reason had to do with the urban geography of Paris: foreign Lombards from Piacenza clustered in the masculinized Lombard zone that stretched across the rue de la Buffeterie, from the area around the church of Saint Opportune to the area around the church of Saint Merri (fig. 26).[52] Nearly all of the silk women who had relatively easy access to this Lombard zone had easy access as well to Jewish lenders, or to foreign Lombards who were more integrated with the broader Parisian population.

Foreign Lombards from Piacenza were also extremely wealthy, paying an average tax, in the years 1297–1300, of over 30 livres. With tax assessments ranging between 42 livres and 142 livres, moreover, Gandoufle of Arcelles (or Gandolfo di Arcelli), who was from Piacenza, often paid the highest tax of anyone in Paris.[53] Thus, as we might expect, the clients of these wealthy moneylenders included some of the most powerful aristocrats and institutions in Paris and its region. We learn from the last will and testament of Gandolfo that his clients included several members of the royal family and court, the towns of Rouen, Dreux, Poissy, and Pontoise, and several religious institutions.[54]

With only Gandolfo's testament to work with, and no written documentation indicating whether or not some lenders from Piacenza engaged in pawnbroking, it is difficult to determine how far down the economic scale these lenders were willing to go when they extended loans to individual borrowers. In his testament, Gandolfo attempted to make peace with his creator by restoring his ill-gotten gains to the people who had borrowed money from him. Seven of those restitutions were as small as one livre. Assuming that those restitutions covered only the interest that he had charged on loans and that his interest rate was between 20 and 25 percent, the original loans seem to have been in the modest range of four to five livres. Nevertheless, most of the borrowers to whom Gandolfo extended these restitutions had substantial means to draw upon—and the financial circumstances of the others are simply not known to us. Three of the seven borrowers to whom Gandolfo made restitutions of one livre were Parisian *échevins*, one was the powerful butchers' guild, and one was the abbey of Yverneaux. It is also significant, for our purposes, that Gandolfo's list of over fifty borrowers to whom he wished to make restitution did not include any women.[55]

An early fourteenth-century account of the prominent Gallerani merchant-banking firm of Siena, which concerned 243 delinquent Parisian loans dating from c. 1302 to 1305, offers a more complete picture of modest Parisian borrowers, including widows. With three exceptions, all involving pledges of valuable items made with precious materials, these were outright loans rather than pawn loans.[56] It appears that for that reason the lenders often insisted that the principal borrowers take out their loans in conjunction with co-borrowers, who would be obliged to assume responsibility for payments if the principal borrower defaulted.[57] In the cases of widowed or single women who were the principal borrowers, nearly all did so in conjunction with male co-borrowers or guarantors. This was true for fourteen loans.[58] Only one loan concerned a woman who borrowed alone, and that woman, "Damma Alucca," a neighbor of the Gallerani bankers on the rue de la Calandre on the Île-de-la-Cité, was apparently extremely wealthy: her original loan had been for almost 600 livres.[59] Two other women seem to have borrowed as a pair, without the assistance of any men. Those two women represent the only case, in this record of 243 loans, in which women who were not from the neighborhood ventured into the Gallerani banking office without the accompaniment of a man.[60] This pattern suggests that single silk women—whose main social contacts were often with other women—may have had trouble taking out outright loans, as opposed to pawn loans. Unfortunately, while we know that specialized Lombard pawnbrokers were granted permission to offer loans in Paris in the 1220s and again beginning in 1378, and while we know that they continued to exercise their trade in neighboring regions, evidence concerning their actual lending activities in thirteenth- and fourteenth-century Paris is lacking.[61]

While Parisian geography suggests that many Parisian silk women had easy access to Jewish lenders, there were neighborhoods, nevertheless, where silk women had better access to foreign Lombards than to Jewish lenders. Around a third of the women working in female-dominated silk crafts (including 35 percent of the throwsters and 35 percent of the *ouvrières de soie*) resided in a large stretch of the Right Bank that wrapped around Les Halles and extended to areas beyond the city walls and north of the Porte-Saint-Martin (zone SL on fig. 26).[62] Those neighborhoods, which encompassed the parishes of Saint-Germain-l'Auxerrois, Saint Eustache, and Saint-Nicolas-des-Champs, included no Jews and a light sprinkling of foreign Lombards. Most of the foreign Lombards in the parish of Saint-Germain-l'Auxerrois were prominent bankers who also worked as financial officers for the king. Their average tax—21.4 livres—was extremely high and for that reason it seems unlikely that they would have made loans to modest artisan women.[63] In the parishes of Saint Eustache and Saint-Nicolas-des-Champs, by contrast, each of which had around 3–4 Lombard taxpaying units, the average tax paid by the foreign Lombards was just over 5 livres, which suggests that their resources were much more modest than those of the Lombards of Piacenza and of the parish of Saint-Germain-l'Auxerrois but substantially larger than those of Jewish taxpayers.[64] These Lombards were also more integrated into the Parisian community than were those of the area around the rue de la Buffeterie: in the parish of Saint Eustache, the Lombards resided on three different streets. In the parish of Saint-Nicolas-des-Champs, the four Lombard taxpaying units (which included three members of the Tolomei banking company of Siena) clustered outside of the walls, close to the Porte-Saint-Martin.[65] The relatively modest wealth of the Lombards of the parishes of Saint Eustache and Saint-Nicolas-des-Champs, the absence of Jews in those neighborhoods, and the fact that those Lombards rubbed shoulders with neighboring Parisians all suggest that if any of these Lombards engaged in moneylending, they may well have attracted the business of silk women in their neighborhoods. Even so, some of the silk women in these parishes may have chosen to cross over to the other side of the Right Bank in order to borrow from Jewish lenders: the records concerning the delinquent debts owed to the Gallerani indicate that modest individuals from Paris and its region were often willing to travel considerable distances in order to borrow money.[66]

While our knowledge about the actual lending practices of Lombard moneylenders in late thirteenth-century Paris is extremely limited, the broader context for Lombard and Jewish lenders does help us pose some reasonable hypotheses: given the opportunity, thirteenth-century Parisian silk women, especially those who were single, probably preferred to borrow from Jewish moneylenders when they were in need of cash. Some silk women in the parishes of Saint-Germain-l'Auxerrois, Saint Eustache, and Saint-Nicolas-des-Champs, however, may have borrowed from foreign Lombard lenders. The urban geography of Paris, Lombard lending patterns, and their own fears of sexual danger would have contributed to these women's choices. Another factor that could draw particular borrowers to particular lenders would have been the relationship that developed between apprentices and those who trained them, a topic addressed in the next section.

Parisian Jews and the Production of Silk Textile Goods

As I mentioned at the beginning of this chapter, the Parisian guild statutes of 1266–1275 included, in the statutes for "Fesserresse de chappeaux d'or et d'euvres a IIII pertuis" (Women who make gold hats and items with four openings), a rule indicating that if masters or mistresses in this guild wanted to send their apprentices to someone else's workshop to be trained, they needed to ensure that the wives in those households were actually skilled in the craft. The text reads: "No men or women should send their apprentices or workers to the homes [or workshops] of Jews, workers, or mercers, if the wives [of those Jews, workers, or mercers] do not know the craft."[67]

The first statute for this guild describes the hats as "chapiaux d'orfreis," thereby indicating that the hats were embroidered or woven with gold thread.[68] Silk is never explicitly mentioned in the statutes, but its use is taken for granted. Indeed, silk was the fiber of choice when working with gold thread or with pearls, and these statutes indicate that all of these hats were decorated with gold thread and some were decorated with pearls.[69] Apparently, then, the statutes concern the construction of embroidered or woven silk and gold hats, often decorated with pearls—much like some hats that Countess Mahaut of Artois purchased from the Parisian mercer Jehan le Viel in 1308.[70] The authors of the statutes took for granted not only that some Jewish women were skilled in this area of production but also that Christian guild masters and mistresses would seek them out as skilled teachers of Christian apprentices. We can well imagine that some of those Jewish mistresses and Christian apprentices developed relationships of mutual trust and understanding—as was the case, at least some of the time, when Christian women worked as wet nurses in Jewish households.[71]

This association of Jews with hat making receives some reinforcement from the Parisian tax assessments, where the only Jewish taxpayers who were identified with artisanal crafts were a jeweler and a man who was identified as either a maker or retailer of hats: in 1292 he was described as "Cressin, who wears the hats" (*qui porte les chaperons*) and in 1296 he was

Figure 27. Illumination, from the beginning of the book of Judges, showing two Hebrew men wearing peaked gold-colored hats. Illuminated Bible, Paris, last third of the thirteenth century. Department of Special Collections, Davidson Library, University of California, Santa Barbara, BS 75 1250 (unfoliated). Photo by Tony Mastres, Photographic Services, University of California, Santa Barbara.

identified as "Cressin the hat maker" or "Cressin the hat retailer" (*Cressin le chaperonnier*).[72]

It seems significant that the only two Parisian Jews whose crafts were identified were a jeweler—who would have specialized in making Jewish engagement rings, for instance—and a hat maker, who probably specialized in retailing or making "Jewish hats."[73] But for our purposes, it is even more significant that Christian guild masters and mistresses would choose to send their female apprentices to train in the homes of Jewish women who were experts at making silk and gold embroidered hats. Apparently this was a skill for which some Jewish women had gained some renown, perhaps because their talents were needed to make the peaked or funnel-shaped hats that were worn by Jewish men. Artistic representations often indicate that these hats were yellow or gold in color (fig. 27). Moreover, we find that in the late fourteenth century a major furnisher of hats for the royal court of Navarre was a Jewish man named Jacob the hat maker (*toquero*) of Saragossa, who made hats from cloth of gold decorated with gold braid.[74]

There are several additional hints suggesting that Parisian Jews might have been involved in the production of silk textiles. Among the Jews who appear in the tax assessment of 1292 we find a man named "Lyon, Fillesoie."[75] The surname or professional name "Fillesoie" points to a possible familial or personal association with silk throwing; since no other men are ever identified as silk throwsters in the Parisian tax assessments, I am inclined to conclude that the name was indicative of a familial surname rather than a personal professional identity.[76] Along similar lines, one woman who had converted to Christianity from Judaism was identified in one tax assessment as a silk throwster and in another as a maker of hair or head ornaments (she was identified as a "coiffriere").[77] One other woman, the daughter of a convert from Judaism, was a member of the embroiderers' guild, which specialized in the confection of silk and gold embroideries.[78]

Another woman with roots in the Jewish community, Jehanne the Convert, apparently married the son of mercers and practiced the mercery trade as well. As far as we can tell, Jehanne the Convert's husband—Jehan Hardi—was the son of Estienne and Mahaut Hardi, mercers who had resided on the rue Quincampoix, which constituted one of the most important mercery neighborhoods in Paris.[79] Estienne and Mahaut Hardi do not appear in the one assessment that was created after 1300 (that of 1313); in their place we find, on the rue Quincampoix, "Jehanne the convert and her husband Jehan Hardi," who paid a very high tax of 15 livres.[80] Jehan Hardi, it would seem, was the son of Estienne and Mahaut.

Jehanne the Convert's 1313 tax entry is interesting for two reasons. First, it gives Jehanne priority over her husband. Paris tax assessors usually listed only one member of each household, and because men were assumed to be the breadwinners, husbands were almost always listed alone. In this case, however, not only did the assessors list Jehanne along with her husband, but by listing her first they credited her with the bulk of the responsibility for paying the tax. The second interesting aspect of this entry is the exponential difference between the level of the taxes that Estienne and Mahaut Hardi had paid between 1297 and 1300 and the tax that Jehanne and her husband paid in 1313: the highest tax that Estienne and Mahaut ever paid in a single year, 42 sous (or 2.1 livres), was slightly more than twice the average tax for the years 1297–1300.[81] The tax that Jehanne and her husband paid in 1313, however, was over seven times the average tax for that year.[82]

The size of Jehanne's tax assessment and the priority that the assessors gave her within the household suggest that the business of Jehanne and her husband was much more successful than that of the couple who appear to have been her in-laws and that Jehanne herself was largely responsible for that success. The fact that Jehan and Jehanne owned a stall in the new "Halle" of Paris indicates that they were involved in either the silk- or belt-making business, and belt making was closely related to mercery. Their probable relationship with Estienne and Mahaut Hardi suggests that they were mercers.[83]

How are we to interpret this cluster of evidence concerning Parisian Jews, along with Parisians who had converted to Christianity from Judaism, who worked with silk? Does the evidence point to a larger pattern within the Jewish community? Perhaps not in all cases: some of these women, especially some of the Jewish converts, may have ended up doing silk work because silk work was a major source of employment for Parisian women. Nevertheless, the guild statute concerning gold hats, the apparent surname "Fillesoie," and Jehanne the Convert's extraordinary business success seem to point to deeper relations between French Jews and silk textile production.

Several patterns of Jewish consumption probably generated a need for some Jewish women to develop skills as silk embroiderers. We learn from a description of the twelfth-century Parisian Jewish scholar Jacob Tam, for instance, that he wore embroidered silk garments.[84] There is good reason to believe, as well, that Torah curtains would have been made of embroidered silk: mosaic evidence from the sixth century of the Christian era indicates that Torah curtains were already being decorated at that time, and the oldest surviving Torah curtain from Europe—which dates from the late sixteenth century—is a silk textile decorated with appliqué and embroidery.[85] There is also scattered evidence that Jewish women in Egypt worked as embroiderers—probably because there, too, their skills met the sartorial and ceremonial needs of the local community.[86]

When considering the evidence concerning Jehanne the Convert, who was apparently a mercer, our analysis needs to move beyond the sphere of local consumption within the Jewish community. Jehanne increased the income of her husband's family by a factor of 350 percent. It seems likely, therefore, that she brought her skills as a mercer into her marriage and it is likely, as well, that she developed those skills even before she converted to Christianity. If that was the case, we need to ask how and why a Parisian Jewish woman might have had special skills in the mercery trade.

No previous scholarly discussion of the economic activities of northern French Jews provides us with any clues concerning Jehanne's skills as a mercer or concerning Lyon Fillesoie's surname. However there are hints that northern French Jews were aware of textile technologies. One commentary by the influential French rabbinic scholar Rashi, for instance, who flourished in Champagne in the second half of the eleventh century, provides us with our earliest western European reference to a horizontal pedal loom—the loom, apparently introduced to the west from somewhere in the Mediterranean basin, that would enable the explosive success of the northern French and Flemish wool industries in the twelfth century.[87] Moreover, if we look beyond northern France, to the Mediterranean basin, we encounter a broader Jewish context that helps us make sense of Lyon Fillesoie's surname and of Jehanne the Convert's apparent skills as a mercer. For, unlike Jews of northern France and Germany, those of the Mediterranean basin had a long history of expertise in the production of silk cloth.

Sources concerning Jewish involvement in silk production in Egypt date back to at least the sixth century, and there is intriguing, if ambiguous, evidence from third- or fourth-century Byzantium as well.[88] In the twelfth century, moreover, Jewish silk dyers and weavers were active in Egypt, and we know that Jewish silk workers were forcibly transported from Thebes, Corinth, and Athens to Sicily by the Norman king Roger II.[89] Around 1170, moreover, Benjamin of Tudela noted the presence of substantial numbers of Jewish silk workers in Thebes, Thessalonica, and Constantinople, and while visiting the Holy Land he observed that the Jewish community of Jerusalem (which included around two hundred individuals) had a monopoly on dyeing and that there were isolated Jewish dyers in Jaffa and Bethlehem.[90] We also know that there were Jewish silk artisans in Iberia and southern Italy and possibly in Montpellier as well.[91] In the last decades of the fourteenth century, moreover, a Jewish woman from Pamplona named Dueña Encave, who was a mercer-embroiderer, became a prominent furnisher for the royal household of Navarre.[92]

Does it make sense to propose that Jews in Paris may have had contact with some of these Mediterranean Jews or that perhaps some of the Jews in Paris had actually migrated to the French capital from Jewish centers of textile production in the Mediterranean? Indeed it does. Twelfth- and thirteenth-century sources offer scattered evidence concerning contacts between northern French Jews and the Jewish communities of Iberia and the Middle East, along with several examples of Jewish migration from the Mediterranean basin to northern France. There were two thirteenth-century migrations of Jews from France to the Holy Land, in 1211 and again in 1258; and we know that those migrants continued to maintain contact with their coreligionists in Europe.[93] The Parisian tax assessments suggest, moreover, that after the fall of Acre in 1291, at which time the important Jewish community there was destroyed, at least one Jewish family moved back to Paris: the assessment of 1292 includes a physician named Lyon of Acre, along with his son and wife.[94]

French and Iberian Jews also had substantial contact with each other, with movement in both directions. The most notable twelfth-century example of such contact is that of Abraham ben Ezra, a prominent biblical commentator and translator of scientific works from Arabic into Hebrew, who was born somewhere in Iberia around 1089. Abraham is known to have visited or resided in Toledo, Cordoba, and Lucena. Around 1140, however, he left Iberia for good, traveling first to Rome, where he wrote at least one biblical commentary and consulted ancient Hebrew texts belonging to Jewish scholars there. From Rome, he traveled to centers of Jewish learning in Salerno, North Africa, Egypt, and Lucca. Finally, after visiting several centers of Jewish scholarship in Languedoc, Abraham ended up in Rouen, where he translated a number of important texts from Arabic and Judeo-Arabic into Hebrew. He also corresponded with, and probably met, the well-known Parisian scholar Jacob Tam.[95]

Contacts and travels between northern French and Iberian centers of Jewish learning continued into the thirteenth century. Jonah, a relative of the well-known Catalan religious leader Nachmanides (1194–1270), attended school in northern France, and Rabbi Moses of Coucy, who had studied in Paris, went on a preaching tour in Iberia in 1236.[96] Moreover, a royal list of Jewish moneylenders who were active in Vitry-le-François between 1280 and 1300 listed one woman who was identified as "Heloise, the wife of the Spaniard" (*Hauuys, la femme l'Espagnol*).[97]

It seems likely, then, that some French Jewish women of the twelfth and thirteenth centuries developed skills as silk embroiderers. Evidence pointing to contacts between the northern French Jewish community and those of the Mediterranean basin suggests, moreover, that some Mediterranean Jews with skills as silk workers or as silk entrepreneurs may well have migrated to Paris or that Parisian Jews picked up such skills during their travels in the Mediterranean.

Changing Circumstances in the Fourteenth Century

If, in the thirteenth century, women silk workers easily borrowed money from Jewish moneylenders, and possibly from Lombard moneylenders as well, and if their numbers included Jewish textile workers and entrepreneurs, the same was not necessarily true in the fourteenth century, when royal repression of both the Jewish and the foreign Lombard communities brought about major transformations.

For the Jews of France, the long thirteenth century came to an end in 1306, when King Philip the Fair ordered the expulsion of all of the Jews of his kingdom. Since the kingdom now encompassed a much larger territory than had been the case in 1182, the size of the affected Jewish community was much larger: William C. Jordan has estimated that between 100,000 and 150,000 Jews were sent into exile in 1306. The exiles were allowed to take some travel money and the clothing on their backs, but otherwise they were compelled to leave behind all of their assets, including their business inventories and records. The numbers, and poverty, of these exiles placed enormous pressure on both the Jewish and the Christian communities where they settled—in northern Spain, Provence, Savoy, Hainault, Flanders, and Germany—leading to new waves of anti-Jewish sentiment and violence in the early fourteenth century.[98]

In 1315, King Louis X issued a charter inviting Jews to resettle in France for twelve years. A few Jews did return, but we do not know much about their numbers; nor is it clear exactly when they left again: it seems, in fact, that a number of them left France at least five years before the charter expired in 1327.[99] Between 1327 and 1361, there were virtually no Jews in France. Then, in 1361, King John II issued a charter inviting Jews to return to his kingdom. In Paris, the new Jewish community, which did not really take off until the 1370s, came to include around a dozen households, a synagogue, and a cemetery, all of them centered around the rue des Rosiers.[100] In 1394, King Charles VI ordered the final medieval expulsion of Jews from France.

The recall charters of 1315 and 1361 mentioned artisanal activity within Jewish communities, but there is no direct evidence from the fourteenth century for Jewish involvement in the training of Christian apprentices.[101] It is certainly possible, however, that some Jewish women in France continued to produce silk embroideries in order to meet the internal needs of the Jewish community.

Of Jewish credit operations in fourteenth-century Paris we can be more certain since, once again, moneylending constituted an important part of Jewish income, and both charters of recall allowed for the practice. The charter of 1315 explicitly allowed for interest rates of 2 pennies (deniers) per livre per week (or 43 percent per annum); it repeated, moreover, older prohibitions against accepting liturgical objects as pawn pledges, thus implying that other forms of pawnbroking were legitimate. The charter of 1361 allowed for an even higher interest rate of 4 pennies per livre per week (or 86 percent per annum), but it was decreased again to 2 pennies per week in 1365.[102] These upper limits were higher than those defined for Lombard moneylenders in the fourteenth century, but they do not necessarily mean that all Jewish lenders demanded these high rates. We know of at least one case, in fact, in which a Jewish lender asked for only one penny per livre per week—which meant that his rates were comparable to those that were allowed for Lombard lenders.[103]

For the period between 1361 and 1394, we can delve into the actual practice of Jewish lending. Drawing on notarial records from Dijon, Roger Kohn found that the majority of Jewish loans from the period 1361–1394 were of modest size, and they were extended, for the most part, to agricultural workers (*vignerons*) and artisans.[104] Kohn also found evidence of pawnbroking—which could involve not only modest borrowers but also the Duke of Burgundy himself—and of Jewish women participating in lending.[105] Kohn estimated, moreover, that despite the limited size of the Jewish community in Dijon, Jewish lenders provided loans for some 28 percent of the residents of the town, which consisted of approximately 2,400 households, and that they loaned extensively to rural borrowers as well.[106]

While we do not know anything about the statistical patterns of Jewish lending in Paris between 1361 and 1394, we do know that one prominent Jewish lender there was a widow named Precieuse and that she accepted pawn pledges of jewelry, goldware, and silverware from the Duke of Berry.[107] Parisian criminal records from the year 1389–1390 indicate, moreover, that petty thieves pawned stolen items to Parisian Jews and that the police lingered around the Parisian Jewry hoping to arrest such thieves before they offloaded their stolen goods to pawnbrokers, who were not held responsible for accepting stolen goods as pledges.[108] A document recorded by the Parlement of Paris in 1379 indicates, moreover, that Parisian Jews were accepting pawn pledges of used clothing; for that reason the king's officers wanted Jewish lenders to pay the membership fee for the guild of sellers of used clothing ("mestier de freperie"). The leader of the Jewish community responded that moneylenders should not have to pay such a fee, even if they accepted used clothing as pawn pledges and later sold it; but he conceded that another group of Jewish residents in Paris, who specialized in the sale of used clothing, should indeed pay the fee. This evidence suggests that Jewish pawnbrokers in

Paris were generating an overstock of unredeemed pledges of used clothing and there thus arose a need for some Jews to specialize in the resale of that clothing.[109]

Two court cases from around this time help illuminate the relations that could emerge, during the last decade of Jewish residence in medieval Paris, between Jewish moneylenders in Paris and their female clients. One of those documents affirms William C. Jordan's suggestion that debt played a powerful role in creating animosity toward Jews. The other, however, suggests that the relationship of lender and borrower sometimes played a role in creating a bond of trust.[110] In the first case, Jehan Jozeau, a guard who worked for the Châtelet, confessed in court in 1403 that he had once stolen back some clothing that his wife had pawned to a Jewish pawnbroker in Paris. Presumably the theft occurred during the Maillotin antitax revolt of 1382, when a great deal of violence came to be directed against Jewish and foreign Lombard moneylenders; if that was indeed the case, Jehan's wife must have pawned her clothing in 1381 or 1382.[111]

The second case concerns a single woman named Jehanette de l'Hopital, a poor linen vendor who was accused, around 1380 or 1381, of attempting to practice sorcery. According to the royal letter of remission that pardoned her of this presumed crime, Jehanette, who was originally from Lyon but now lived in Paris, sought out the Parisian business address of a Jewish moneylender and physician named Bonjour in order to borrow some money. During her meeting with Bonjour, the letter claimed, Jehanette also asked him for something to cure a headache, but Bonjour put off prescribing a remedy, wishing to see a sample of her urine so that he could make the proper diagnosis. After examining the urine, Bonjour told Jehanette that she was very much in love, and she affirmed that that was indeed the case, but her lover, who had once led her to believe that they would get married, was now backing out of the relationship. Bonjour then told Jehanette to bring him one of her belts. After placing some kind of love potion inside the belt, he instructed Jehanette that she should wear it, with the herbal potion on top of her stomach, whenever she was with her lover. Despite these efforts, the lover ended up marrying another woman instead, and Jehanette was subsequently thrown into prison for practicing sorcery.[112]

We might want to doubt some of the details of this narrative, because, in seeking the king's pardon, Jehanette would have depicted her own actions and motivations in the best light. It thus seems possible that she invented the story about the loan in order to suggest that she had had no intention, when she originally sought out Bonjour, of attempting to use a love potion in order to win back the affection of her lover. Nevertheless, the story presents a plausible picture of a Christian woman who placed her trust in a Jewish physician who also engaged in moneylending.

The cumulative evidence thus suggests that while the numbers of Jews in France were limited, in the years between 1315 and 1327 and again between 1361 and 1394, the patterns of Jewish lending resembled, for the most part, those of thirteenth-century France; and indeed, it is in the evidence from the latter period that we finally catch glimpses of poor and modest women who borrowed money from Jewish lenders in Paris and of at least one Parisian Jewish woman who acted as a moneylender. But where did people turn for loans in the years when no Jews resided in France—between 1306 and 1315, and again between 1327 and 1361, and after 1394?

Lombard moneylenders offered one alternative. But they, too, experienced royal repression in the late thirteenth and fourteenth centuries. Of course, unlike Jews, Lombard moneylenders could ride out difficult times in France by drawing on resources from home, and when things got really bad, they could simply return to Italy—if, that is, they had not been incarcerated.[113] Nevertheless, between the early and later fourteenth century there were significant shifts in the geographical origins of Lombard lenders and entrepreneurs who were active in France, and there seem to have been some important shifts in business organization as well. While a variety of international factors contributed to this shifting landscape, French royal policies certainly played a role.

Although it was King Louis VIII who first invited specialized Lombard pawnbrokers to begin practicing their trade in the French kingdom in 1225, royal repression eventually followed: in 1269 and again in 1274 Louis IX and Philip III ordered the expulsion of all Lombard, Cahorsin, and foreign "usurers" from France.[114] Under King Philip IV (1284–1314), moreover, combined policies of heavy taxation, forced and "voluntary" loans, fines, arrests, and extortion created an environment in which the resources of many Italian entrepreneurs and moneylenders in France declined sharply.[115]

Philip IV set the stage for his successors, who perceived in Italian merchants and moneylenders easy sources of badly needed revenue to cover their mounting expenses, especially those related to armed skirmishes both before and during the Hundred Years' War. In 1324, Italians in France paid a subsidy for the war in Gascony.[116] In 1330, Lombard moneylenders were arrested and had to put up bond.[117] In 1331, and again in 1347, the king declared that all debtors who owed money to Lombard moneylenders were obliged to repay only the principal on their loans, and their loan payments would go to the king rather than to the Lombard lenders.[118] In 1341 all Florentines in France had to contribute to a royal subsidy.[119] The list of such measures goes on and on.

There is no question that foreign Lombard moneylenders residing in France suffered as a result of these royal measures. During an inquest into the status and activities of Lombards in France, carried out by royal officers between 1309 and 1311, a number of Italian merchants and moneylenders described resources that had diminished drastically over the previous several years: the former receiver of Champagne, whose resources had once amounted to 2,000 livres, reported a total household value of 200–300 livres, all of it coming from his wife's assets; concerning a prominent moneylender from the town of Asti in the Piedmont, witnesses reported resources that had declined from 30,000 livres to 6,000. Some respondents indicated that they had sent resources back to Italy or that they had given up moneylending altogether, becoming, in one case, a tavern keeper, and, in another, a yarn merchant.[120] In the final years of the thirteenth century and the first two decades of the fourteenth, moreover, a number of major Italian merchant-banking companies, including most of those from Siena, collapsed. The causes were multiple and international, but there is no question that the business climate in France did not help matters. After the collapse, most merchant elites from Siena gave up international banking altogether.[121]

By the end of the fourteenth century, then, the French landscape of Italian merchants, bankers, and pawnbrokers had shifted. In Paris, the high-end market for consumer credit came to be dominated not by specialized pawnbrokers from the Piedmont or by Sienese bankers but by prominent furnishers for royal and aristocratic courts, most of whom were from Lucca or Florence and many of whom now married Frenchwomen, becoming, along with their descendants, permanent members of the Parisian bourgeois community.[122] After 1378, when the king issued a charter granting them permission to settle in France for fifteen years, three foreign pawnbrokers from the Garetti family of Asti also settled in Paris (most likely without their wives)—but they hardly seem to have dominated the scene.[123] The sources suggest, instead, that in the second half of the fourteenth century a plethora of Parisian artisans, lawyers, merchants, money changers, and priests also operated as lenders and pawnbrokers and that at least some of the married and assimilated Italians worked alongside their wives as pawnbrokers, serving a broad spectrum of borrowers.[124]

The household accounts of Jean, Duke of Berry, reveal not only that he pawned precious objects to his furnishers from Lucca, Florence, and Genoa, as well as to the Jewish pawnbroker Precieuse, but also that he purchased numerous items on credit from butchers, fishmongers, poulterers, drapers, and tapestry makers. Additionally, he pawned almost 40,000 francs' worth of precious gemstones to a goldsmith and a significant amount of jewelry to Renault Pizdoë, a money changer from a family of Parisian *échevins*.[125]

Most revealing of the types of credit that would have been available to women who worked as silk throwsters and weavers is the postmortem inventory of Barthelemy Castaing—who was evidently of Italian origin—and his wife, Agnes, which was compiled soon after Barthelemy's death in 1349.[126] Barthelemy, who had probably come to Paris from Florence or Genoa, was identified in his postmortem inventory as a spice dealer.[127] He resided on the Grand Rue (or the rue Saint Denis), in the Lombard section of the Right Bank that stretched across the rue de la Buffeterie. The inventory of Barthelemy's and Agnes's effects reveals that they worked not only as spice dealers but also as money changers, deposit bankers, and pawnbrokers. Mixed among their personal possessions, the compilers of the inventory found numerous items that Barthelemy and Agnes were holding as pawn pledges. Some of the items—like a tapestry depicting the "Kings of Cologne" (i.e., the three kings of the Christmas story)—must have been of considerable value. Others—"an old corset, for a girl"; "half of an old red coat, for a woman"—had clearly been pledged by people near the bottom of the economic hierarchy.[128] Of great interest to us is the fact that Barthelemy's wife sometimes participated in his lending business, especially, it would seem, when women clients borrowed on their own: the compilers of the inventory indicated that a woman named Agnes la Cousturiere had borrowed 100 gold florins from Barthelemy and Agnes. Also of interest is the presence, among the pawned items, of linen yarn, which was probably pawned by linen spinners.[129]

The evidence concerning Barthelemy Castaing suggests that some of the Parisian Lombards who married locally and assimilated into French society assumed business practices that differed from those of the foreign Lombards of the late thirteenth and early fourteenth centuries: rather than working in exclusively male environments, with brothers, uncles, and nephews, at least some of the assimilated Italians placed the nuclear household at the center of their business, working alongside their wives. Moreover, the example of Agnes la Cousturiere suggests that the presence of a working wife could help attract women clients. It seems, moreover, that Barthelemy Castaing was not alone, among assimilated Italians, in working in partnership with his wife: a sentence issued by the Parisian Parlement in 1319 indicates that Jehanne, the wife of Furquin of Lucca, handled some of the couple's financial affairs: it was Jehanne who had deposited some of the couple's money with a certain Denise the Money Changer, who now refused to return the deposit. The court ruled in favor of the couple.[130]

It is not possible, given the fragmentary nature of the surviving records, to paint a complete picture of the credit market in fourteenth-century Paris. Nevertheless, we can draw some conclusions. First, during the periods when Jews were in residence they continued to play a vital role in the local economy by providing credit for the most marginal of borrowers. And second, even though Jewish lenders were absent much of the time, and would be permanently absent after 1394, and even though foreign Lombard moneylenders and entrepreneurs in France suffered a variety of setbacks, credit for modest borrowers—especially in the form of pawn loans—continued to be made available. A variety of part-time and professional lenders extended credit to modest borrowers; indeed, many of the informal lenders of the late fourteenth century probably looked a lot like informal lenders of the late thirteenth. The one noticeable change in the credit market has to do with the assimilation of Italian entrepreneurs into the bourgeois population of Paris. As Italian entrepreneurs began to marry Frenchwomen and gain the status of "bourgeois of Paris," their business practices began to look a lot like those of other Parisians, who were accustomed to working side by side as married couples. Given their expertise in the area of finance, however, many of these assimilated Italians continued to work as bankers and lenders. There is no way of knowing if, between 1327 and 1361, and again after 1394, the Italian lenders who had assimilated into Parisian bourgeois society were able, or willing, to meet the full load of demands from modest borrowers, including single women silk workers, who had once turned to Jewish pawnbrokers when they were strapped for cash, but it appears that they responded to at least some of those demands.

Conclusion

In January 1397 a merchant from Lyon sold three ells of red, green, and purple "silk of Paris" to agents working for the Count of Savoy.[1] While the purchase indicates that the count's agents tended to operate within commercial zones that were external to Paris and the Île-de-France, it also points to the prestigious quality of the silk itself, which managed to retain its Parisian identity even as it traveled from Paris to Lyon and then on to the county of Savoy.

The Paris that produced this piece of silk was even more resplendent as a center of luxury production and consumption than it had been toward the end of the thirteenth century. Despite the numerous crises of the fourteenth century—the massive mortality brought about by several waves of the Black Death, beginning with that of 1348; the tumult of the early years of the Hundred Years' War, which brought marauding troops to the suburbs of Paris in 1346 and again between 1356 and 1360; and popular revolts against corrupt leadership and excessive taxation in 1358 and 1382—Paris remained a residence of choice for France's aristocratic and clerical elites. Indeed, by 1400 there were even more elite private residences in Paris than there had been in 1300, and the occupants of those residences ushered in a new era of conspicuous consumption. That consumption gave rise, between c. 1380 and 1407, to some of the greatest artistic and literary accomplishments of the French Middle Ages, as well as to some of the most sumptuous clothing and textiles.[2]

At the forefront of the new era of personal luxury and artistic patronage stood the royal household of Charles VI and his queen, Isabeau of Bavaria, as well as the households of the princes of the blood—most notably the king's younger brother, Louis, Duke of Orléans; the king's cousin John the Fearless, Duke of Burgundy; and the king's uncle John, Duke of Berry.[3] The taste for beautiful works of art, clothing, and furnishings trickled down to lower levels of the social hierarchy as well. Thus the luxury crafts of Paris—including, apparently, the craft of weaving fine silk cloth—continued to flourish at the end of the fourteenth century and in the early years of the fifteenth.

Although most of the Parisian architecture of the early years of Charles VI's reign is now gone, we know that the art patronage of that era often began with a flurry of construction—new private residences were built on both sides of the Seine, and older residences were enlarged and renovated. The tower of Duke John the Fearless of Burgundy, on the rue Étienne Marcel—a mere remnant of the residence that once occupied the space—and the Sainte-Chapelle at the royal château of Vincennes just southeast of Paris offer fragmentary reminders of the residential splendor that took shape during those years.[4] Each of the new, or newly expanded, residences needed to be furnished, hung with tapestries, decorated with satin bedroom sets, and, in many cases, filled with books. Much of that work was financed by the flow of new, and more regular, forms of taxation, which had arisen as a result of the ongoing war with Flanders and England.[5] We have already seen one example of such use of public funds in Charles VI's command ordering his tax collectors to reimburse the Parisian mercer Martine la Thierry for silk textiles that she had sold to the king.[6] We know, as well, that significant portions of the household accounts of the queen and of the princes of the blood were financed by taxes that were originally instituted in the thirteenth century as war aids but were now simply major components of public finance.[7]

In the field of manuscript illumination, Paris saw, in the period between 1380 and 1407, the extraordinary work of the Dutch miniaturists known as the Limbourg brothers, who illuminated the *Très riches heures* of the Duke of Berry. Other masters of the art of manuscript illumination included the Boucicaut master and the master of Christine de Pisan's *City of Ladies*.[8] In the finely detailed miniatures of these artists we can trace the evolution of fashion, the sumptuous nature of the silk textiles that were then in vogue, and the growing importance of marking one's clothing with personal mottoes and emblematic devices. One miniature in a copy of the *Dialogues* that Pierre Salmon wrote for Charles VI depicts the king dressed in black, which was his emblematic color of the moment. His velvet clothing is embroidered with his then favored motto—"Jamais"—as well as with a golden "tiger" wearing a crown, which was also one of his personal emblems. His red satin bed set is embroidered with a second golden "tiger" and with yet another of his personal emblems—branches of the broom plant.[9]

In earlier years Charles had favored an emblematic motto that he borrowed from his uncle Louis II, Duke of Bourbon: the word "Esperance," usually depicted on a blue belt or on a representation of a blue belt. Charles's association with this motto has led some textile historians to suggest that a piece of brocaded red, blue, and gold striped velvet, which constitutes the back of a chasuble now in the Musées des Tissus in Lyon, may have been produced in Paris for Charles VI. Its woven pattern depicts pods of the broom plant and blue belts containing the motto "Esperance" (fig. 28).[10]

The king was not the only consumer to commission such elaborate textiles. Indeed, as Susan Crane has suggested, this was an era of "talking garments"; making the garments talk required the labor of Parisian embroiderers, whose numbers must have soared in these years.[11] The background textiles for these embroidered garments were almost always silks or silk velvets; the floss of choice was gold thread, complemented by various colors of silk. In 1394–1395 Queen Isabeau purchased, for 56 livres, a piece of vermillion velvet embroidered with gold songbirds and white roses; and in 1403 she purchased, for 80 livres each, several pieces of black velvet decorated with an embroidered design depicting intertwined sprigs of her husband's and her own emblematic flowers: the king's broom plant and her own pimpernel.[12] Portraits of the queen in the books presented to her by Christine de Pisan give us an idea of what some of the embroidered velvets must have looked like.[13] Along similar lines, as we learn from both account books and visual representations, John the Fearless, Duke of Burgundy, had his velvet clothing and satin bedroom sets embroidered with his own personal emblems: oak leaves and the motto "il me tarde," for instance.[14] We know that most of the embroiderers for these "talking" garments resided in Paris; would that we could know where the velvets and satins were actually woven.

As it turned out, the years between 1382 and 1407 did not mark the beginning of a new age of prosperity for the French capital; rather, they constituted the eye of a horrifically destructive storm, one whose fury returned in 1407. Ill winds had already begun to blow in 1392, when the young King Charles VI experienced his first episode of temporary insanity. As those episodes increased in length and frequency, it rapidly became clear that Charles was incapable of ruling. Among those who took charge of administering the realm, two princes of the blood—the king's brother Louis of Orléans and his cousin Duke John the Fearless of Burgundy—began to jockey for control. John the Fearless was the favorite with the Parisian populace because he advocated the limitation of state power and the reduction of taxes.

After John the Fearless masterminded Louis of Orléans's assassination in 1407, civil war broke out between those who aligned with John's Burgundian

Figure 28. Back of a chasuble, made of silk and gold brocaded velvet. The brocade depicts sprigs of broom plant as well as blue belts inscribed with the motto "Esperance." Italy (or possibly France), 1380–1422. Musée des tissus/Musée des arts décoratifs, Lyon, MT 25688. © Lyon, MTMAD–Pierre Verrier.

party and those who aligned with the party of the royal court, which came to be known as the Armagnacs. For the next thirteen years, Paris was wracked by the violent conflict between these rival parties and their allies. Several times in that period, most especially during the insurrection of the Cabociens in 1413 and that of the Capeluches in 1418, the conflict erupted into widespread mob violence. According to one chronicler, the violence that swept through the streets of Paris during a single twenty-four-hour period in June 1418 took the lives of 1,600 people.[15]

While daily life in Paris fell into a vortex for over a decade after the assassination of 1407, order seemed to return in 1420 when the city was handed over to English rule. Nevertheless, the new order did not bring a return of prosperity. Indeed, the war that continued to rage between the English and the French caused major disruptions in the flow of goods to Paris, thereby sparking skyrocketing costs for basic commodities. And in the meantime, the bottom fell out of the luxury market, since only one elite consumer—the English king's regent, John, Duke of Bedford—came to reside in Paris. By the early 1420s, scholars have estimated, nearly half of the population had left town.[16]

The restoration of French control in 1436, and the eventual end of the Hundred Years' War in 1457, hardly brought relief to Paris's economic woes, since the newly triumphant French king chose not to return to the capital. Earlier experience of anti-Armagnac hostility had instilled in Charles VII a considerable amount of distrust of the Parisian people, so he established his court in the Loire valley, visiting the French capital, after 1436, only occasionally. His son Louis XI followed suit.[17]

The king's absence did not go unnoticed. Again and again in the 1440s the anonymous author of the "Journal of a Bourgeois of Paris" (who was probably a canon at Notre Dame) complained that there was no news of the king, the queen, or "any other lord" coming "to Paris or to any place within 200 leagues of Paris—and still their administrators tax us continuously!"[18] Secular elites, moreover, were not the only ones who stayed away: by 1500, three-quarters of the bishops who had once maintained Parisian residences had abandoned the French capital. Paris's economy, and the luxury crafts that had once constituted a major part of that economy, thus continued to stagnate.[19] Prosperity would not return until the early sixteenth century, when King Francis I moved the royal court back to Paris.

In the meantime, it was the Loire valley that experienced much of the economic rebound after the end of the long war between France and

England. In 1460 the king established an armor industry in Tours to make Italian-style armor. Its early artisans included at least one Italian and one Spaniard—and Louis XI would later recruit at least a dozen more master artisans from Milan.[20] As noted in Chapter 3, moreover, Louis XI also gave his support, in 1470, to a new silk industry in Tours. Much like the Parisian silk industry of the late thirteenth century, the new silk industry in Tours relied on the immigration of skilled artisans from the Mediterranean region: weavers from Italy and a man from Greece who made gold thread.[21]

At some point between 1397, when the Count of Savoy's agent purchased a piece of Parisian silk, and 1467, when King Louis XI commanded all of the Parisian guilds to organize themselves for the city's defense, silk cloth production apparently ceased to exist in Paris. The list of guilds in the 1467 *ordonnance* included wool and linen weavers, silk dyers, and makers of luxury belts and purses, but there is no mention there of weavers of silk cloth, velvet, or cloth of gold.[22] A tariff list from Strasbourg dating from the second half of the fifteenth century does mention "Paris silk," but the entry appears to concern silk yarn from Paris rather than silk cloth.[23]

It is impossible for us to know precisely when, between 1397 and 1467, the Parisian luxury silk cloth industry ceased to exist. We may be tempted to point to the absence of silk weavers in the Parisian tax assessments of the 1420s and thus conclude that the industry had already disappeared by then, but those tax assessments were extremely limited in terms of the numbers of Parisians who were assessed and the numbers for whom professions were identified, so we cannot interpret their silence in any conclusive way.[24] Nor does the silence of early fifteenth-century aristocratic account books provide us with conclusive evidence: after all, during the one-hundred-year period when Paris did have a silk cloth industry, that industry must have produced far more finished textiles than the extant account books would lead us to believe. Parisian silk, it would seem, was sometimes sold without any indication of provenance. Indeed, as I have already mentioned, in the case of velvet, provenance was almost never mentioned.

Though we have no idea how many pieces of silk the Parisian silk cloth industry produced, we do know that that industry persisted from the 1290s to at least the 1390s and that it disappeared at some point before 1467. It is easy to understand why it disappeared: throughout the fifteenth century, from the outset of civil strife in 1407 through the era of English occupation and French recovery, French and English ruling elites stayed away from the French capital. As France began to recover from the long years of war and civil strife, the royal court sponsored new industries—including a new silk cloth industry—but in doing so the court favored the Loire valley rather than Paris. Silk yarn—and probably small mercery goods as well—continued to be produced in Paris. In the absence of royal, aristocratic, and episcopal courts, however, the local market could no longer sustain a luxury silk cloth industry.

In addition to the important role played by immigrants in enhancing the skilled labor pool for the new armor and silk industries of late medieval France, two additional medieval phenomena that we have examined in these pages persisted, or at least reemerged, in early modern Paris and in other parts of France as well: the prominence of women in the luxury clothing and silk industries, and the importance of all-female guilds. In the seventeenth and eighteenth centuries a number of prominent women who sold luxury textiles and luxury textile products established themselves in the gallery of the Palais de Justice in Paris, and in the eighteenth century we find them as well on the newly fashionable rue Saint Honoré.[25] Writing about eighteenth-century Paris, Jennifer Jones has observed that "from seamstresses and linen drapers to female hairdressers and *marchandes de modes*, women played an important role in the Parisian fashion trade." Along parallel lines, Cynthia Truant has underscored the importance of all-female guilds—especially those in the linen and clothing trades—in providing single women of seventeenth- and eighteenth-century Paris with employment and in allowing collective self-determination for some working women.[26] Concerning eighteenth-century Tours, moreover, Célia Drouault has argued that women predominated among silk workers and that silk work provided single women with a level of economic independence that they might not have otherwise experienced.[27] All of those gendered patterns, I would argue, had precedents, and perhaps even roots, in the luxury silk industries of thirteenth-century Paris.

Appendix 1. Mediterranean Immigrants Paying Taxes as "Bourgeois of Paris" or Included on Parisian Guild Lists

A. Italians

	Name	Place-name	Profession	Tax Range (in deniers)	Street	Year/Folio[1]	Parish/Quête[2]
1	Master Donnadieu	Lombart	physician (mire)[3]	936–1,488	rue de la Boucherie	1296 f. 28v 1299 f. 216	Par. S. Séverin, 1
2	Master Guillaume	le Lombart		432	rue de la Boucherie	1299 f. 216	Par. S. Séverin, 1
3	Master Pierre	le Lombart		240	rue des Boucheries	1296 f. 35v	Par. S. Médard
4	Dame Agnes	la Lombarde		18	rue Perdue	1313 f. 45	Par. S.-Geneviève-du-Mont, 1
5	Agnes	la Lombarde		36	place Maubert or rue Garlande	1292 f. 74v	Par. S.-Geneviève-du-Mont, 2
6	Agnes	la Lombarde		120	rue Frépillon	1296 f. 9	Par. S.-Nicolas-des-Champs, 1
7	Amiot	le Lombart	broker	108	rue des Estuves	1313 f. 18	Par. S.-Nicolas-des-Champs, 1
8	Aubert	le Lombart		240	Cloister S. Benoît	1296 f. 34v	Par. S. Benoît (list of those who died)
9	Aubertin	le Lombart	mint worker or money changer	96	?	1298 f. 150v	Par. S. Merri; list of mint workers or money changers

Appendix 1 (continued)

A. Italians (continued)

	Name	Place-name	Profession	Tax Range (in deniers)	Street	Year/Folio[1]	Parish/Quête[2]
10	Bans	Lombart	armorer	60	rue S. Séverin or Petit-Pont	1292 f. 67	Par. S. Séverin, 2
11	Barbe	le Lombart	broker	144	rue de Mibray	1300 f. 260v	Par. S. Merri, 1
12	Batille	le Lombart	mint worker or money changer	108	?	1298 f. 151	Par. S. Paul (or S. Pôl), list of money changers/minters
13	Bertaut	le Lombart		96	Grand Rue	1298 f. 104	Par. S. Eustache (or Huitace), 4
14	Bertelemi	le Lombart		840	bourg S. Marcel	1292 f. 77v	Par. S. Marcel
15	Binde	le Lombart		720	port Notre Dame	1313 f. 35v	Par. S. Landry
16	Binde	le Lombart	mint worker or money changer	72	?	1299 f. 228v 1300 f. 299v	Par. S. Merri, list of mint workers or money changers
17	Bocassin	Lombart	money changer	360	rue de la Pierre-au-let	1313 f. 26v	Par. S.-Jacques-de-la-Boucherie, 3
18	Bonne Aventure	Lombart	stocking/hosiery maker	120–240	rue de la Calandre	1296 Piton 128[4] 1298 Piton 139 1299 f. 11 LdM 115[5]	Par. S.-Germain-le-Vieux
19	Cambin Lupperel	Lombart		108	rue de la Barre or Cloister S. Merri	1313 f. 20	Par. S. Merri, 3

20	Chenel de Pistoire	Lombart	stocking/hosiery maker			LdM 116	
21	Chevissant	le Lombart		576	rue de la Calandre	1292 f. 62v	Par. S.-Germain-le-Vieux
22	Clarent	le Lombart		360	rue aux Fèves	1313 f. 37v	Par. S. Martin
23	Colin	le Lombart	porter	24	rue des Ecoliers de S. Denis	1298 f. 145v	Par. S.-André-des-Arts
24	Coluche	le Lombart	mangler	432	rue de la Courroierie	1299 f. 194 1300 f. 267v	Par. S.-Jacques-de-la-Boucherie, 3
25	Coluche	le Lombart	mercer	600–900	rue Quincampoix	1299 Piton, 141[6] 1300 f. 253	Par. S. Josse
26	Conrad	le Lombart		0–900	rue des Prouvoires	1296 f. 7c 1297 f. 43 1298 f. 103 1299 f. 165v 1300 f. 244v	Par. S. Eustache (or Huitace), 1(1296), 2
27	Conrad	le Lombart		48	rue S. Jacques	1297 f. 90v	Par. S. Séverin, 3
28	Courradin (et ses compaignons de vin)	le Lombart		2,160	cloister S. Merri	1313 f. 20	Par. S. Merri, 3
29	Dine	le Lombart	tavern keeper	96	rue S. Martin	1296 f. 17	Par. S.-Jacques-de-la-Boucherie, 1

Appendix 1 (continued)

A. Italians (continued)

	Name	Place-name	Profession	Tax Range (in deniers)	Street	Year/Folio[1]	Parish/Quête[2]
30	Emeline	la Lombarde	maker of Saracen alms purses			Depping,[7] 383	
31	Ermengart	la Lombarde	embroiderer			Depping, 380	
32	Estienne	le Lombart	broker	192	rue de la Çavaterie	1299 f. 211	Par. S.-Germain-le-Vieux
33	Figuelin	le Lombart	horse broker	192	rue des Arcis	1300 f. 270	Par. S.-Jacques-de-la-Boucherie, 3
34	Franchequin	le Lombart	mint worker or money changer	72	?	1299 f. 228v 1300 f. 299v	Par. S. Merri, list of mint workers or money changers
35	François	le Lombart		108	rue de la Harpe, Carrefour S. Séverin, or Grand Rue	1313 f. 42	Par. S. Séverin, 3
36	François	le Lombart	tavern keeper	432	rue Bourc-Tybourt	1300 f.282	Par. S. Paul (or S. Pôl), 2
37	Frassequin	le Lombart		288	rue de Mibray	1313 f. 19	Par. S. Merri, 1
38	Gabriel	le Lombart	horse broker	6–144	rue de la Buffeterie/rue S.	1296 f. 18v 1299 f. 194	Par. S.-Jacques-de-la-Boucherie, 3

	Name		Occupation	Amount	Location	Date	Parish
39	Garde	le Lombart		192	rue de la Calandre	1292 f. 62v	Par. S.-Germain-le-Vieux
40	Gautier	le Lombart	barber	72	parvis Notre Dame	1299 f. 214	Par. S. Christophe
41	Girart	Lombart	broker	36	rue Neuve S. Merri	1300 f. 264	Par. S. Merri, 3
42	Gerbaut	le Lombart		696	rue Perrin Gascelin	1296 f. 5	Par. S.-Germain-l'Auxerrois, 5
43	Gracien	le Lombart		216	outside the walls, Bourg of the Temple	1292, f. 77v	
44	Gracieux	le Lombart	mint worker or money changer	96	?	1297 f. 93v	Par. S. Merri, list of mint workers or money changers
45	Grégoire	le Lombart	broker	72–144	le Grant Marivas	1299 f. 194v / 1300 f. 270v	Par. S.-Jacques-de-la-Boucherie, 3
46	Grifon	le Lombart		24	?	1292 f. 49	Par. S. Gervais, 2
47	Guerin	le Lombart		36	rue de la Barillerie	1292 f. 60	Par. S. Barthélemy
48	Guérin	le Lombart	tavern keeper	60	rue S. Christophe	1300 f. 288	Par. S. Christophe
49	Guiart	Lombart	armorer	96	rue du Petit-Pont or S. Séverin	1292 67	Par. S. Séverin, 2
50	Guillaume	le Lombart		240–288	rue du Four	1296 f. 7 / 1297 f. 42v	Par. S. Eustache (or Huitace), 1

Appendix I (continued)

A. Italians (continued)

	Name	Place-name	Profession	Tax Range (in deniers)	Street	Year/Folio[1]	Parish/Quête[2]
51	Guillaume	Lombart		12	near the Porte Barbéel	1292 f. 47	Par. S. Gervais, 2
52	Guines	le Lombart	tavern keeper	432	rue de la Calandre	1313 f. 38	Par. S.-Germain-le-Vieux
53	Henri	le Lombart	tavern keeper	216	rue aux Fèves	1300 f. 286	Par. S.-Germain-le-Vieux
54	Jacquemin	le Lombart		120	cloister S. Merri	1296 f. 15	Par. S. Merri, 2
55	Jacquemin Guy	le Lombart		4,320	rue de la Calandre	1313 f. 38	Par. S.-Germain-le-Vieux
56	Jacques	le Lombart	goldsmith	240	rue de la Barillerie	1300 f. 284	Par. S.-Pierre-des-Arcis
57	Jacques	le Lombart	spice dealer	900	rue de la Calandre	1300 f. 285v	Par. S.-Germain-le-Vieux
58	Jacques	le Lombart	tavern keeper	696	rue de la Boucherie	1297 f. 63 / 1297 f. 95v	Par. S. Séverin, 1 (and list of those who died)
59	Jacques	le Lombart	spice dealer	72	rue Jehan Pain-Moulet	1313 f. 19v	Par. S. Merri, 1
60	Jacques	Lombart	dyer	18	rue des Arcis	1313 f. 26v	Par. S.-Jacques-de-la-Boucherie, 3
61	Jaquemin	le Lombart		216	rue des Gravilliers	1292 f. 29	Par. S.-Nicolas-des-Champs, 1
62	Jehan	le Lombart		24	rue des Estuves (09)	1297 f. 77v	Par. S.-Nicolas-des-Champs, 2

#	Name		Occupation	Number	Street	Date references	Parish
63	Jehan	le Lombart	tavern keeper	360–576	rue S. Geneviève	1296 f. 32 1297 f. 66 1299 f. 225 1300 f. 296	Par. S.-Geneviève-du-Mont
64	Jehan Vanne (belart) (lucais)	Lombart	mercer, stocking maker	696–14,400	rue de la Buffeterie or rue Troussevache	1296 f. 17v 1297 Piton, 132 1299 Piton, 143 1300 Piton, 149 1300 267v 1313 f. 26v LdM 115	Par. S.-Jacques-de-la-Boucherie, 1, or list of Lombards
65	Jehanne	la Lombarde	street peddler (*regratier*)	36	rue S.-André-des-Arts or S.-Germain-des-Prés	1299 f. 219v	Par. S.-André-des-Arts
66	Jehanne/Jehannette	la Lombarde		72–96	rue Mau-Destour	1298 f. 105 1299 f. 170 1300 f. 248	Par. S. Eustache (or Huitace), 4
67	Jehannette	la Lombarde	maker of Saracen alms purses			Depping, 384	
68	Jehanne	la Lombarde		12	ruelle Sans Chief (?)	1292 f. 32	Par. S. Merri, 1
69	Lappe	le Lombart		90	Court-Robert-de-Paris	1313 f. 20v	Par. S. Merri, 3

Appendix I (continued)

A. Italians (continued)

	Name	Place-name	Profession	Tax Range (in deniers)	Street	Year/Folio[1]	Parish/Quête[2]
70	Lappe (and his brothers)	le Lombart		3,600	rue de la Porte Nicolas Arrode, outside the walls	1313 f. 7	Par. S. Eustache (or Huitace), 1
71	Lorence	la Lombarde		24	rue S. Martin	1292 f. 37v	Par. S. Merri, 4
72	Maheut	la Lombarde		36	rue S. Honoré, outside the walls	1292 f. 4v	Par. S.-Germain-l'Auxerrois, 1
73	Mainfroi	le Lombart	maker of mail coats	240	rue de la Hyaumerie	1300 f. 269v	Par. S.-Jacques-de-la-Boucherie, 2
74	Marguerite	la lombarde	360	rue Viez du Temple	1313, f. 29v	Par. S. Gervais, 3	
75	Marguerite	la Lombarde		24	rue S. Cosme	1300, f. 293	Par. S. Benoît, 1
76	Marie	la Lombarde		288	rue S. Martin (?)	1292 f. 38	Par. S. Merri, 4
77	Martin	le Lombart	tooth puller	108	rue de la Çavaterie	1313, f. 38	Par. S.-Germain-le-Vieux
78	Meilleur	le Lombart	tavern keeper	108	rue Neuve S. Merri	1313 f. 20	Par. S. Merri, 2
79	Mellin[8]	Lombart	armorer	180	rue de Milbray	1313 f. 19	Par. S. Merri, 1

80	Nicolas	le Lombart	quilter/maker of padded clothing and cushions	144	rue de la Calandre	1300 f. 285v	Par. S.-Germain-le-Vieux
81	Nicoluche (and his companions, from Siena)	le Lombart		5,400	rue des Petits Souliers or rue de la Tableterie or rue S. Opportune	1313 f. 13v	Par. S. Opportune
82	Othebonne	le Lombart		360	rue de la Chanvrerie	1296 f. 11	Par. S. Eustache (or Huitace), 2
83	Pagan	le Lombart		3,600	rue de Mibray	1313 f. 19	Par. S. Merri, 1
84	Pasquier	le Lombart	stocking/hosiery maker	96	rue de la Buffeterie	1299 f. 191 1300 f. 267v LdM 115	Par. S.-Jacques-de-la-Boucherie, 1
85	Perruche	le Lombart	armorer	24	rue S. Merri	1300 f. 260v	Par. S. Merri, 1
86	Philippe	le Lombart	brass beater	24	rue du Temple	1299 f. 187 1300 f. 263v	Par. S. Merri, 3
87	Pierre	le Lombart	broker	36	rue Geoffroi l'Angevin	1300 f. 263	Par. S. Merri, 3
88	Pilous	le Lombart	broker	24	cloister S. Merri	1300 f. 262v	Par. S. Merri, 2
89	Plesin	le Lombart	cordovan leather worker	144	rue de la Buffeterie (?)	1300 f. 267v	Par. S.-Jacques-de-la-Boucherie, 1

Appendix 1 (continued)

A. Italians (continued)

	Name	Place-name	Profession	Tax Range (in deniers)	Street	Year/Folio[1]	Parish/Quête[2]
90	Poge	le Lombart	armorer	108–1,200	rue de la Çavaterie	1296 Piton, 128 1297 Piton, 134 1299 Piton, 145 1300 Piton, 151 1300 f. 285	Par. S. Martial
91	Pouche	le Lombart		720	rue S. Martin, outside the walls	1313 f. 16v	Par. S.-Nicolas-des-Champs, 1
92	Raimbaud/Rimbaut	le Lombart		900	rue de la Chanvrerie	1298 f. 105 1299 f. 170 1300 f. 248	Par. S. Eustache (or Huitace), 4
93	Renuche (and his brothers)	le Lombart		1,800	rue de la Coçonnerie	1313 f. 011	Par. S. Eustache (or Huitace), 4
94	Regnier	le Lombart	tavern keeper	240	rue aux Fèves	1300 f. 286	Par. S.-Germain-le-Vieux
95	Rique	le Lombart	tavern keeper	1,440–1,488	rue S. Christophe	1292 f. 65 1299 f. 213v 1300 f. 288v	Par. S. Christophe
96	Richart	le Lombart	furrier	72	rue du Temple	1297 f. 50v	Par. S. Merri, 3
97	Richart	le Lombart	furrier	900	rue S. Martin	1298 f. 113	Par. S.-Jacques-de-la-Boucherie

		le Lombart				
98	Rogier (and companions)	le Lombart	cordovan leather worker	120–240	rue de la Viez-Monnaie or de la Buffeterie	1297 f. 53v 1298 Piton, 137 1299 Piton, 143 1299 f. 193 (listed here but taxed as a Lombard)	Par. S.-Jacques-de-la-Boucherie, 2
99	Rolant	le Lombart	broker	36	rue de la Harengerie	1299 f. 160v	Par. S.-Germain-l'Auxerrois, 5
100	Roulant	le Lombart	broker	12	le Petit Marivas	1292 f. 42	Par. S.-Jacques-de-la-Boucherie, 2
101	Saintisme	le Lombart	broker	36	rue des Arcis	1300 f. 270	Par. S.-Jacques-de-la-Boucherie, 3
102	Secotin	le Lombart		720	rue Sac-a-lie	1313 f. 41v	Par. S. Séverin, 2
103	Senebaut/Sanebaut	le Lombart	tavern keeper	96–168	rue Garlande	1296 f. 28v 1297 f. 62v 1299 f. 215 1300 f. 289	Par. S. Séverin, 1
104	Sequin	le Lombart	tavern keeper	324	rue de la Calandre	1313 f. 38	Par. S.-Germain-le-Vieux
105	Tane	le Lombart	stocking/hosiery maker	108–192	rue de la Calandre	1296 Piton, 128 1298 Piton, 139 1299 f. 211 1300 f. 285v LdM p. 115	Par. S.-Germain-le-Vieux

Appendix I (continued)

A. Italians (continued)

	Name	Place-name	Profession	Tax Range (in deniers)	Street	Year/Folio[1]	Parish/Quête[2]
106	Thomas	le Lombart	host of messengers	72	rue des Arcis	1313 f. 26v	Par. S.-Jacques-de-la-Boucherie, 3
107	Master Ernoul	de Luques		60	Grand Rue	1292 f. 22v	Par. S.-Leu-S.-Gilles
108	Jehan	de Luques		12	rue des Poulies	1292 f. 56	Par. S. Paul (or S. Pôl), 1
109	Mahaut (widow of Marques)	de Luques		144	rue Troussevache	1300 f. 268	Par. S.-Jacques-de-la-Boucherie, 1
110	Marques	de Luques	mercer	24–240	rue Troussevache	1292 f. 40 1296 f. 17v 1298 f. 113v 1299 f. 191v 1300 f. 301v	Par. S.-Jacques-de-la-Boucherie, 1
111	Thierry Bouche Fol	de Luques		720	rue Neuve S. Merri	1313 f. 21	Par. S. Merri, 4
112	Eudeline	de Pavie	maker of Saracen alms purses			Depping, 384	
113	Robert	de Pavie	clerk/cleric		rue du Temple	1300 f. 263v	Par. S. Merri, 3
114	Robert	de Pavie		24–36	porte du Temple	1297 f. 99v 1299 f. 180v	Par. S.-Nicolas-des-Champs, 2

	Name		Occupation		Street	Reference	Parish
115	Agnes	de Venyse	silk worker	24–96	rue Mau-Conseil	1299 f. 167 / 1300 f. 245v	Par. S. Eustache (or Huitace), 3
116	Benoît	de Venise		36	rue du Chevet S.-Denis-de-la-Chartre	1292 f. 63v	Par. S.-Denis-de-la-Chartre
117	Bertaut	de Venise	silk weaver	44	rue des Petits Champs	1313 f. 21v	Par. S. Merri, 6
118	Gautier	de Venise		48–144	rue S.-Germain-l'Auxerrois	1292 f. 13v / 1296 f. 34	Par. S.-Germain-l'Auxerrois, 6, list of the dead
119	Girart	de Venise	servant of the *marchands d'eau*	12–96	rue S. Martin/ rue Amauri-le-Roissi	1292 f. 39v / 1298 f. 113 / 1299 f. 190v	Par. S.-Jacques-de-la-Boucherie, 1
120	Girart	de Venyse	cook	72	rue des Arcis	1300 f. 270v	Par. S.-Jacques-de-la-Boucherie, 3
121	Jacques/Jacquet	de Venise	belt maker/mercer	0–144	rue Quincampoix	1297 f. 53 / 1298 f. 114 / 1299 f. 192	Par. S.-Jacques-de-la-Boucherie, 1
122	Jacques[9]	de Venyse		240	rue Quincampoix	1292 f. 31	Par. S.-Nicolas-des-Champs, 2
123	Robert	de Venise		22	rue Perrin Gascelin	1313 f. 6v	Par. S.-Germain-l'Auxerrois, 5
124	Robert	de Venise	goldsmith	60–120	rue S.-Germain-l'Auxerrois	1297 f. 71 / 1298 f. 101 / 1299 f. 161	Par. S.-Germain-l'Auxerrois, 6

Appendix 1 (continued)

A. Italians (continued)

	Name	Place-name	Profession	Tax Range (in deniers)	Street	Year/Folio[1]	Parish/Quête[2]
125	Robert[10]	de Venyse	goldsmith	120	rue aux Lavandières	1300 f. 236v	Par. S.-Germain-l'Auxerrois, 4
126	Rolant	de Venise		240–900	rue S. Merri, rue de la Buffeterie	1292 f. 1 (Lombard section) 1296 f. 17 1296 Piton, 125 1297 Piton, 130 1298 f. 110v	Par. S. Merri, 2; Par. S.-Jacques-de-la-Boucherie, 1
127	Rolant	de Venyse		24	rue Jehan le Comte	1300 f. 270	Par. S.-Jacques-de-la-Boucherie, 2

B. Iberians

	Name	Place-name	Profession	Tax range (in deniers)	Street	Year/Folio	Parish/Quête
1	Anciau	d'Arragon	cabinet/chest maker	168	Grand Rue	1297 f. 40v	Par. S.-Germain-l'Auxerrois, 5
2	Guillaume	d'Arragon	fuller	12–72	rue du Viez Cimetière S. Jehan	1292 f. 48 1297 f. 84 1298 f. 117v	Par. S. Gervais, 2–3

3	Guillaume	d'Arragon	cook (1297–1300)	12–96	rue Garlande/S. Julien	1292 f. 67 1297 f. 89v 1298 f. 144 1299 f. 216 1300 f. 289v Depping, 357n. 3	Par. S. Séverin, 1
4	Guillaume	d'Arragon	parchment maker	24–120	rue des Blancs Manteaux	1297 f. 85v 1298 f. 139v 1299 f. 203v 1300 f. 279	Par. S.-Jehan-en-Grève, 3
5	Henri	d'Arragon	valet sword maker			Depping, 367	
6	Jehan	d'Arragon	barber	24	rue S.-André-des-Arts/S. Germain-des-Prés	1299 f. 219v 1313 f. 41	Par. S.-André-des-Arts/S. Severin, 1
7	Jehan	d'Arragon	cook	12–144	r. Garlande (1292) rue S. Jacques/ Petit-Pont	1292 f. 66v 1297 f. 62v 1299 f. 215 1300 f. 289	Par. S. Séverin, 1
8	Jehan	d'Arragon	cabinet/chest maker	72	rue de Mibray	1313 f. 19	Par. S. Merri, 1
9	Jehan	d'Arragon, the younger	cook	44		1313 f. 40v	Par. S. Séverin, 1
10	Nicolas	d'Arragon	locksmith	36	rue des Anglais	1298 f. 148	Par. S.-Geneviève-du-Mont, 2

Appendix 1 (continued)

B. Iberians (continued)

	Name	Place-name	Profession	Tax Range (in deniers)	Street	Year/Folio	Parish/Quête
11	Phelippe	d'Arragon	saddle maker	576	Grand Rue	1297 f. 53	Par. S.-Jacques-de-la-Boucherie, 2
12	Pierre	d'Arragon	felt/blanket maker	360	Grand Rue	1296 f. 17v 1297 f. 53 1298 f. 114	Par. S.-Jacques-de-la-Boucherie, 2
13	Pierre	d'Arragon	metal worker (1299)	24	Grand Rue, outside the walls	1292 f. 21v 1299 f. 170	Par. S. Sauveur
14	Pierre	d'Arragon	valet sword maker			Depping, 368	
15	Raoul	d'Arragon	furrier	24	rue de la Draperie, Grand Pont, Pelleterie or Planche Mibray	1298 f. 137	Par. S.-Jacques-de-la-Boucherie, 5
16	Richart	d'Arragon	cabinet/chest maker	84–1,080	Grand Rue	1296 f. 4v 1298 f. 100v 1299 f. 160 1300 f. 239 1313 f. 6	Par. S.-Germain-l'Auxerrois, 5
17	Aubin	d'Espaingne	entertainer (jongleur)	24–36	rue aux Jongleurs	1298 f. 132 1299 f. 180v	Par. S.-Nicolas-des-Champs, 2

	Name	Surname	Occupation	Amount	Location	Date references	Parish
18	Aubin	d'Espaingne	entertainer (*jongleur*)	36	rue aux Jongleurs	1299 f. 175	Par. S. Josse, 7
19	Gautier	d'Espaingne		120–1,620	rue or ponceau de Bièvre	1292 f. 74v, 1297 f. 65v	Par. S.-Geneviève-du-Mont, 1–2
20	Gracien	d'Espaingne	mercer/belt maker[11]	240–432	rue du Grenier S. Lazare (or Guernier de S. Ladre)	1292 f. 28, 1296 f. 13v, 1297 f. 47, 1298 f. 108, 1299 f. 177v, 1300 f. 255	Par. S.-Nicolas-des-Champs, 1
21	Guillaume	d'Espaingne	cordovan leather worker	36	rue S.-Germain-l'Auxerrois	1313 f. 3	Par. S.-Germain-l'Auxerrois, 3
22	Guillaume	d'Espaingne		84	Grand Rue	1292 f. 023	Par. S.-Leu-S.-Gilles
23	Guillot	d'Espaingne	cordovan leather worker	36–72	rue S.-Germain-l'Auxerrois	1298 f. 125, 1299 f. 155v, 1300 f. 234v	Par. S.-Germain-l'Auxerrois, 3
24	Jehan	d'Espaingne, or l'Espaignol	"sergent a cheval" (1300)	360–600	rue du Temple, outside the walls	1296 f. 10v, 1297 f. 48v, 1298 f. 109v, 1299 f. 182, 1300 f. 259v	Par. S.-Nicolas-des-Champs, 3
25	Jehanne (1292) Dame Jehanne	d'Espaingne	bath house servant or proprietor (1299–1300)	24–96	rue Sans Chief or Grand Rue, outside the walls	1292 f. 27v, 1297 f. 76v, 1298 f. 130v, 1299 f. 177, 1300 f. 254v	Par. S.-Nicolas-des-Champs, 1

Appendix 1 (continued)

B. Iberians (continued)

	Name	Place-name	Profession	Tax Range (in deniers)	Street	Year/Folio	Parish/Quête
26	Jehannete	l'Espaignole	embroiderer		Porte Baudéer	Depping, 379	Par. S. Paul (or S. Pôl)
27	Michiel	d'Espaingne/ l'Espaingnol	belt maker (1300)	36–84	rue du Grenier S. Lazare (or Guernier de S. Ladre)	1296 f. 13v 1298 f. 131 1299 f. 178 1300 f. 255v	Par. S.-Nicolas-des-Champs, 1
28	Michel	d'Espaingne	tailor	24	rue de la Clé or rue de la Huchette	1300 f. 290	Par. S. Séverin, 2
29	Robin	d'Espaigne	grain merchant (1298–1300)	72–96	ruelle aux Foins	1296 f. 2v 1297 f. 38v 1298 f. 98v 1299 f. 155v 1300 f. 234v	Par. S.-Germain-l'Auxerrois, 3
30	Guillaume	Navarre[12]	weaver (1297–1300)	24–120	rue de la Bretonnerie or rue des Blancs Manteaux	1292 f. 58 1297 f. 86v 1298 f. 119v, 141 1299 f. 205v 1300 f. 281v	Par. S. Paul (or S. Pôl), 2
31	Maitre Jehan	le Navarrois	physician (mire)	168	Grand Rue	1292 f. 22v	Par. S.-Leu-S.-Gilles

	Name	Place-name	Profession	Tax (in deniers)	Street	Year/Folio	Parish
32	Robert	de Navarre (1299) navarre	weaver (1299–1300)	24–36	rue des Blancs Manteaux, rue du Puit or rue des Singes	1292 f. 58 1299 f. 206 1300 f. 281v	Par. S. Paul (or S. Pôl), 2
33	Roger	de Navarre Navarre	gardener (courtillier) (1297)	24–60	?	1292 f. 15v 1297 f. 71v 1300 f. 241	Par. S. Eustache (or Huitace), 1
34	Sanse	de Navarre	messenger	18	rue S. Merri	1313 f. 20	Par. S. Merri, 2

C. Other Mediterranean Immigrants

	Name	Place-name	Profession	Tax (in deniers)	Street	Year/Folio	Parish
1	Aaliz	d'Acre		72	rue de la Porte Baudéer outside the walls	1292 f. 59	Par. S. Paul (or S. Pôl), 3
2	Dame Agnes	d'Acre		316–672	Place S. Michiel	1292 f. 60 1296 f. 25v 1297 f. 60 1298 f. 121 1299 f. 208v 1300 f. 283v	Par. S. Barthélemy
3	Amendant[13]	d'Acre		96	rue Franc Morier	1292 f. 78 1296 f. 36v 1297 f. 96	Lists of Jewish taxpayers

Appendix 1 (continued)

C. Other Mediterranean Immigrants (continued)

	Name	Place-name	Profession	Tax (in deniers)	Street	Year/Folio	Parish
4	Maitre Estienne	d'Acre		36	Place S. Michiel	1292 f. 60	Par. S. Barthélémy
5	Guillaume	d'Acre	tavern keeper	120	rue de la Mortellerie	1299 f. 205	Par. S. Paul (or S. Pôl), 1
6	Jehan	d'Acre	pardon seeker	216		1313 f. 42	Par. S. Séverin, 3
7	(Sire) Jehan	d'Acre	tavern keeper	432–1,392	Place S.-Denis-de-la-Chartre	1292 f. 63v 1296 f. 27 1297 f. 61 1298 f. 122v 1299 f. 212 1300 f. 286v 1313 f. 36v	Par. S.-Denis-de-la-Chartre
8	Lorenz	d'Acre	measurer of salt	84–144	rue S.-Germain-l'Auxerrois	1300 f. 236v 1313 f. 4v	Par. S.-Germain-l'Auxerrois, 4
9	Lyon (and his wife)	d'Acre	physician (*mire*)	60		1292 f. 78	List of Jewish taxpayers
10	Marguerite	d'Acre		432	rue du Chantre	1296 f. 1	Par. S.-Germain-l'Auxerrois, 1
11	Marguerite	d'Acre		72	rue S. Paul (or S. Pôl)	1299 f. 208 1300 f. 283	Par. S. Paul (or S. Pôl), 3
12	Mahy	d'Acre or	cordovan leather	216–240	rue de la Calandre	1297 f. 61	Par. S.-Germain-le-Vieux

13	Thomas	d'Acre	metal worker	36		1313 f. 31	Par. S.-Jehan-en-Grève
14	Hue	de Babiloine (Cairo, Egypt)		24	rue Guérin Boucel	1292 f. 27v	Par. S.-Nicolas-des-Champs, 1
15	Agnes	de Cypre		36	rue des Estuves	1313 f. 18	Par. S.-Nicolas-des-Champs, 2
16	Jehan	de Chypre	embroiderer	300–432	rue de la Courroierie	1292 f. 40 1296 f. 17 1297 f. 52v 1298 f. 113v 1299 f. 191v 1300 f. 267v Depping, 380	Par. S.-Jacques-de-la-Boucherie, 1
17	Bertaut	de Lymesi (Limassol, Cyprus)		480	rue de la Courroierie	1292 f. 40	Par. S.-Jacques-de-la-Boucherie, 1
18	Jehan	de Lymesi/Lymesis		12–60	rue de la Petite Bouclerie/rue Guillaume Espaulart	1292 f. 37 1300 f. 264v	Par. S. Merri, 4
19	Mahy	de Lymesis	mercer/goldsmith	60–240	rue de la Courroierie	1292 f. 40 1296 f. 17 1297 f. 52v 1298 f. 113v 1299 f. 191v 1300 f. 267v	Par. S.-Jacques-de-la-Boucherie, 1

Appendix 1 (continued)

C. Other Mediterranean Immigrants (continued)

	Name	Place-name	Profession	Tax (in deniers)	Street	Year/Folio	Parish
20	Marguerite	de Limesus	silk worker	36	rue Tirechape	1313 f. 3v	Par. S.-Germain-l'Auxuerrois, 3
21	Peronele	de Lymesis		144	rue de la Courroierie	1296 f. 17	Par. S.-Jacques-de-la-Boucherie, 1
22	Perrenele	de Lymesis	weaver of silk narrow ware (*tissuz*)	24	rue des Poulies	1298 f. 124v	Par. S.-Germain-l'Auxerrois, 2
23	Thomas	de Lymesi/Lymesis	goldsmith	36–60	rue de la Courroierie	1292 f. 40 1296 f. 17 1297 f. 52v 1299 f. 191v	Par. S.-Jacques-de-la-Boucherie, 1
24	Bertaut	d'Outremer	money changer	144–360	rue de la Pelleterie	1297 f. 60 1298 f. 121 1299 f. 209 1300 f. 284	Par. S. Barthélémy
25	Guillaume	d'Outremer		432–2,760	rue aux Lavandières or rue Jehan Lointier	1296 f. 4 1297 f. 40v 1298 f. 99v, 100 1299 f. 159 1300 f. 226v	Par. S.-Germain-l'Auxerrois, 4

26	Henri	d'Outremer	draper	576–2,160	rue de la Croix du Tiroir	1297 f. 39 1298 f. 98v 1299 f. 156 1300 f. 235 1313 f. 3v	Par. S. Germain-l'Auxerrois, 3
27	Jacques	d'Outremer		1,080	rue Perrin Gascelin	1313 f. 6v	Par. S.-Germain-l'Auxerrois, 5
28	Raoul	d'Outremer	baker	144–216	rue de la Juiverie	1297 f. 60 1298 f. 121v 1299 f. 210 1300 f. 285	Par. S. Martial
29	Robert	d'Outremer	tavern keeper	204–1,008	Place de Grève or rue S. Jehan	1292 f. 52 1296 f. 22 1297 f. 57v 1300 f. 277	Par. S. Jehan-en-Grève
30	Bertaut	le Roumain		36		1300 f. 297v	Par. Notre-Dame-des-Champs
31	Eudeline	la Roumainne		36	rue Agnes la Bouchière	1297 f. 79	Par. S. Merri, 2
32	Eustache[14] (or Huitace)	la Roumainne	mercer	240–432	rue Troussevache	1296 f. 17v 1298 f. 113v 1299 f. 191v 1300 f. 268	Par. S.-Jacques-de-la-Boucherie, 1

Appendix 1 (continued)

C. Other Mediterranean Immigrants (continued)

	Name	Place-name	Profession	Tax (in deniers)	Street	Year/Folio	Parish
33	Guibert	le Roumain		240	rue du Chevet S.-Denis-de-la-Chartre	1296 f. 27 1298 f. 122v 1299 f. 212 1300 f. 286v 1313 f. 36	Par. S.-Denis-de-la-Chartre
34	Guillaume	le Roumain		12	rue Guillaume Bourdon	1292 f. 8	Par. S.-Germain-l'Auxerrois, 3
35	Jehan	le Roumain		432	rue Troussevache	1292 f. 40v	Par. S.-Jacques-de-la-Boucherie, 1
36	Symon	le Roumain		60–432	Grand Rue	1292 f. 20 1298 f. 104 1299 f. 218	Par. S. Eustache (or Huitace), 2
37	Adeline	Tabarie (widow of Jehan Tabarie le genne)	mercer	288–432	rue Troussevache	1298 f. 113v 1299 f. 191v	Par. S.-Jacques-de-la-Boucherie, 1
38	Jacquet	Tabarie (of Tiberias)		2,880	rue Troussevache	1313 f. 25	Par. S.-Jacques-de-la-Boucherie, 1

39	Jehan	Tabarie le viel (the older)	mercer	696–816	rue Guillaume Joce; rue Troussevache (in 1300)	1292 f. 40v 1296 f. 17v 1297 f. 53 1298 f. 113v 1299 f. 192 1300 f. 268	Par. S.-Jacques-de-la-Boucherie, 1
40	Jehan	Tabarie le genne (the younger)		360–576	rue Troussevache	1292 f. 40v 1296 f. 17v 1297 f. 52v	Par. S.-Jacques-de-la-Boucherie
41	Phelippe	Tabarie	merchant of wimples	96	rue de Bière	1300 f. 266	Par. S. Merri, 4
42	Jehan	de Thunes/Tunes (of Tunis)	tavern keeper	216	rue S. Christophe	1299 f. 214 1313 f. 39	Par. S.-Geneviève-des-Ardents
43	Jehan	de Tunes		192		1292 f. 72	Par. S. Hilaire
44	Jehan	de Tunes		24	rue de la Tanerie or ruelle de la Triperie	1292 f. 45 1297 f. 83	Par. S.-Jacques-de-la-Boucherie, 4
45	Jehan	de Tunes	glassworker	12	rue de la Barre	1292 f. 52v	Par. S.-Jehan-en-Grève
46	Nicolas	de Tunes	carpenter	24	rue du Fauconnier	1300 f. 280v	Par. S. Paul (or S. Pôl), 1

Appendix 1 (continued)

C. Other Mediterranean Immigrants (continued)

	Name	Place-name	Profession	Tax (in deniers)	Street	Year/Folio	Parish
47	Pierre	de Tunes	restaurateur (bufetier)	72–216	rue de la Poterne S. Paul (or S.Pôl)/ Porte Baudéer, outside the walls	1292 f. 59v 1296 f. 25v 1297 f. 60v 1298 f. 120v 1299 f. 207v 1300 f. 283v	Par. S. Paul (or S. Pôl), 3
48	Jacques Mahoumet		(weaver)[15]	30	rue des Rosiers	1313 f. 30v	Par. S. Gervais, 4
49	Jehan Mahommet		harness maker	12–216	Grand Rue, or Petit/Grant Marivas	1292 f. 41v 1296 f. 19 1297 f. 53 1298 f. 114 1299 f. 192 1300 f. 268v	Par. S.-Jacques-de-la-Boucherie, 2
50	Simon Mahommet		weaver	60	rue du Puits or des Blancs Manteaux or des Singes	1292 f. 58 1313 f. 34 Depping, 403	Par. S. Paul (or S. Pôl), 4

1. Folio number references are to folio numbers in the original manuscripts of the seven Parisian tax assessments (1292, 1296, 1297, 1298, 1299, 1300, 1313). For the 1292 tax assessment readers can consult the 1991 revised edition of Géraud, and for the 1296, 1297, and 1313 assessments, readers can consult Michaëlsson's editions; all four of these editions provide folio numbers in the margins. The assessments of 1298–1300 remain unpublished in AN KK 283.

2. For the purposes of the tax assessments, larger parishes were divided into different "quêtes." I give the numbers of the quêtes in the last column because they are useful for narrowing down the physical location of taxpayers. For a map of the various parishes and quêtes in 1300, see Bourlet and Bethe, "Création des plans," 163. This map is also available on the Alpage website: http://alpage.huma-num.fr/documents/Illustration_colloque/BOURLET_Paroisses_1300.pdf (accessed September 9, 2015).

3. Professional identities were inconsistently reported from one tax assessment to another. For the sake of brevity in this appendix, I have indicated only that a given taxpayer or guild member was associated with a profession at least once in the tax assessments or guild statutes, but I have not indicated the precise tax year(s) or guild statute for each taxpayer's known professional identity.

4. Piton = Piton, *Les lombards*, 124–156. This is an edition of the sections of the 1296–1300 tax assessments that taxed foreign Lombards as a separate group. A number of Italian immigrants were taxed both as "bourgeois of Paris" and as foreign Lombards, but I have tracked down foreign Lombard listings only for individuals who are discussed in various chapters of this book.

5. LdM = *Livre des métiers*, ed. Lespinasse and Bonnardot.

6. Listed with the Lombards in 1299 but described as "mercer bourgeois."

7. Depping = Depping, ed., *Réglemens*.

8. Possibly identical with Andri, or Andri Melin, armorer, who was taxed as a foreign Lombard in 1296 and 1298–1300: Piton, 125, 137, 143, 150.

9. Possibly the same as the Jacques de Venyse in entry no. 121.

10. Possibly same as the Robert de Venise in entry no. 124.

11. In 1297 Gracien was identified as a "corratier" (broker), but this may be a scribal error for "corroier" (belt maker). He was identified as a belt maker in 1299 and 1300.

12. Two taxpayers are identified as "of Navarre" in one tax assessment but as "Navarre" (without the preposition) in another. For this reason, I am including all individuals identified with the simple surname "Navarre."

13. Son of Lyon d'Acre: Appendix 1, part C, no. 9.

14. Widow of Jehan le Roumain: Appendix 1, part C, no. 35.

15. Bautier, "Une opération de décentralisation industrielle," 661. See also Chapter 1, discussion preceding note 105.

Appendix 2. Mercers in the Parisian Tax Assessments, Arranged by Neighborhood

A. Mercers in the Troussevache Neighborhood

	Forename	Surname	Tax Range 1292–1300 (in deniers)	Tax 1313 (in deniers)	Average Tax 1297–1300 (in deniers)	Street	Year/Folio[1]	Parish/Quête[2]
1	Adam	d'Amiens	1,488	NA	1,488	rue Troussevache	1300 f. 268	Par. S.-Jacques-de-la-Boucherie, I
2	Adam	le Harengier	600–744	NA	648	rue de la Courroierie (1298), rue Amauri de Roissy (1296, 1299, 1300)	1296 f. 17 1298 f. 113v 1299 f. 191v 1300 f. 267v	Par. S.-Jacques-de-la-Boucherie, I
3	Adam[3]	Mauregart	NA	5,760	NA	rue Auberi-le-Bouchier	1313 f. 13v	Par. S.-Jacques-de-la-Boucherie, I
4	Adeline	(femme Jehan Tabarie)[4]	288–432	NA	360	rue Troussevache	1298 f. 113v 1299 f. 191v	Par. S.-Jacques-de-la-Boucherie, I
5	Adeline	du Port	216–240	NA	232	rue de la Courroierie	1296 f. 17, 1298 f. 113v 1299 f. 191 1300 f. 267v	Par. S.-Jacques-de-la-Boucherie, I
6	Dame Agnes	des Granches	744	NA	744	rue Troussevache	1299 f. 191v	Par. S.-Jacques-de-la-Boucherie, I
7	Amauri	d'Amiens	2,640	NA	NA	rue Troussevache	1296 f. 17v	Par. S.-Jacques-de-la-Boucherie, I

8	Ameline	du Val[5]	1,200–1,488	NA	1,488	rue Troussevache	1296 f. 17v 1300 f. 268	Par. S.-Jacques-de-la-Boucherie, 1
9	Eustache[6] (or Huitace)	la Roumainne	432–432	NA	432	rue Troussevache	1298 f. 113v 1299 f. 191v	Par. S.-Jacques-de-la-Boucherie, 1
10	Gautier	Hualle	NA	144	NA	rue Auberi-le-Bouchier	1313 f. 013v	Par. S.-Leu-S.-Gilles
11	Gautier	la Chievre	432–432	NA	432	rue Auberi-le-Bouchier (1297–1300), rue de la Courroierie (1296)	1296 f. 17 1297 f. 46 1298 f. 106 1299 f. 173 1300 f. 251	Par. S.-Jacques-de-la-Boucherie, 1; S.-Leu-S.-Gilles
12	Gautier	le Creus	300	NA	NA	rue Troussevache	1296 f. 17v	Par. S.-Jacques-de-la-Boucherie, 1
13	Geoffroi	de Dammartin	2,160–2,760	NA	2,760	rue de la Courroierie	1296 f. 17 1300 f. 267v	Par. S.-Jacques-de-la-Boucherie, 1
14	Girart	de Lyons	240	NA	240	rue Troussevache	1300 f. 268	Par. S.-Jacques-de-la-Boucherie, 1
15	Gilles	Toussac	696–1,104	NA	978	rue Troussevache	1296 f. 17v 1297 f. 52v 1298 f. 113v 1299 f. 191v 1300 f. 268	Par. S.-Jacques-de-la-Boucherie, 1
16	Guarnot	de Lyons	1,800–3,840	NA	3,840	rue Guillaume Joce	1296 f. 17v 1299 f. 192	Par. S.-Jacques-de-la-Boucherie, 1

Appendix 2 (continued)

A. Mercers in the Troussevache Neighborhood (continued)

	Forename	Surname	Tax Range 1292–1300 (in deniers)	Tax 1313 (in deniers)	Average Tax 1297–1300 (in deniers)	Street	Year/Folio[1]	Parish/Quête[2]
17	Guillaume	de Lyons	1,800–2,160	NA	2,130	rue Troussevache	1296 f. 17v / 1298 f. 113v / 1299 f. 191v / 1300 f. 268[7]	Par. S.-Jacques-de-la-Boucherie, 1
18	Guillaume	de Sans	840–1,008	NA	936	rue Troussevache	1296 f. 17v / 1298 f. 113v / 1299 f. 191v / 1300 f. 268	Par. S.-Jacques-de-la-Boucherie, 1
19	Guillaume	du Pont de l'Arche	NA	1,080	NA	rue Auberi-le-Bouchier	1313 f. 14	Par. S.-Leu-S.-Gilles
20	Guillaume	Feret	NA	1,800	NA	rue Auberi-le-Bouchier or rue S. Denis	1313 f. 23	Par. S. Merri, 7
21	Guillaume	la Souriz	NA	216	NA	rue Auberi-le-Bouchier	1313 f. 13v	Par. S.-Leu-S.-Gilles
22	Guillaume	le Boursier	744–1,104	NA	744	rue Troussevache	1296 f. 17v / 1298 f. 113v / 1299 f. 191v	Par. S.-Jacques-de-la-Boucherie, 1

23	Guillaume	le Rebours	NA	2,160	NA	rue Auberi-le-Bouchier	1313 f. 13v	Par. S.-Leu-S.-Gilles
24	Henri	de Cormeilles	600	NA	600	rue Troussevache	1298 f. 113v	Par. S.-Jacques-de-la-Boucherie, 1
25	Imbert (or Ymbert)	de Lyons	2,400–8,160	NA	6,000	rue Troussevache	1296 f. 17v / 1299 f. 191v / 1300 f. 268	Par. S.-Jacques-de-la-Boucherie, 1
26	Imbert (or Ymbert)	le Noir	960	NA	NA	rue de la Courroierie	1296 f. 17	Par. S.-Jacques-de-la-Boucherie, 1
27	Jacques, Jacquemin	Bone-Foi	20–192	NA	144	rue Auberi-le-Bouchier	1297 f. 46 / 1298 f. 106 / 1299 f. 173	Par. S.-Leu-S.-Gilles
28	Jacques	de Cormeilles	600–744	1,800	648	rue Troussevache	1298 f. 113v / 1299 f. 191v / 1300 f. 268 / 1313 f. 24v	Par. S.-Jacques-de-la-Boucherie, 1
29	Jacques	de la Porte	24	NA	24	rue S. Martin near S. Merri	1298 f. 135v	Par. S.-Jacques-de-la-Boucherie, 1
30	Jacques	de Sans	96	NA	96	rue de la Courroierie	1300 f. 268	Par. S.-Jacques-le-la-Boucherie, 1
31	Jacques	le Potier	432–432	NA	432	rue Troussevache	1298 f. 113v / 1299 f. 191v / 1300 f. 268	Par. S.-Jacques-de-la-Boucherie, 1

Appendix 2 (continued)

A. Mercers in the Troussevache Neighborhood (continued)

	Forename	Surname	Tax Range 1292–1300 (in deniers)	Tax 1313 (in deniers)	Average Tax 1297–1300 (in deniers)	Street	Year/Folio[1]	Parish/Quête[2]
32	Jehan	Cordelier	NA	1,440	NA	rue Auberi-le-Bouchier	1313 f. 14	Par. S.-Leu-S.-Gilles
33	Jehan	de Beuse-Ville	NA	216	NA	Grand Rue, near rue de la Buffeterie	1313 f. 24v	Par. S.-Jacques-de-la-Boucherie, 1
34	Jehan	de Laigny	240	NA	NA	rue Troussevache	1296 f. 34v	Par. S.-Jacques-de-la-Boucherie, list of the dead
35	Jehan	de Laon	144–600	NA	300	rue Troussevache	1296 f. 17v / 1297 f. 52v / 1298 f. 113v / 1299 f. 191v / 1300 f. 268	Par. S.-Jacques-de-la-Boucherie, 1
36	Jehan	d'Esne	NA	720	NA	rue Auberi-le-Bouchier	1313 f. 13v	Par. S.-Leu-S.-Gilles
37	Jehan	d'Estreinqueville	NA	2,160	NA	rue Auberi-le-Bouchier	1313 f. 13v	Par. S.-Leu-S.-Gilles
38	Jehan	du Perche, du Porche	120–216	NA	120	rue Troussevache	1296 f. 17v / 1298 f. 113v	Par. S.-Jacques-de-la-Boucherie, 1

39	Jehan	le Begues	NA	1,800	NA	rue Auberi-le-Bouchier	1313 f. 13v	Par. S.-Leu-S.-Gilles
40	Jehan	l'Espicier	NA	1,440	NA	rue Troussevache	1313 25	Par. S.-Jacques-de-la-Boucherie, 1
41	Jehan	Tabarie le viel	816	NA	816	rue Guillaume Joce; rue Troussevache[8]	1292 f. 40v 1299 f. 192 1300 f. 268	Par. S.-Jacques-de-la-Boucherie, 1
42	Jehan	Tonsac, Toussac	1,104–1,800	2,520	1,464	rue de la Courroierie	1298 f. 113v 1299 f. 191 1300 f. 267v 1313 f. 24v	Par. S.-Jacques-de-la-Boucherie, 1
43	Jehan	Vanne[9]	696–3000	14,400	1728	rue de la Buffeterie/ rue Troussevache	1296 f. 17v 1297 Piton, 132 1299 Piton, 143 1300 Piton, 149 1300 f. 267v 1313 f. 26v	Par. S.-Jacques-de-la-Boucherie, 1, 3
44	Jehan	Viel	1,104–2,100		1,629	rue Troussevache	1296 f. 17v 1297 f. 52v 1298 f. 113v 1299 f. 191v 1300 f. 268	Par. S.-Jacques-de-la-Boucherie, 1
45	Jehanne	du Fanc, du Faut	696–744	NA	744	rue Troussevache	1296 f. 17 1298 f. 113v 1299 f. 191v 1300 f. 268	Par. S.-Jacques-de-la-Boucherie, 1

Appendix 2 (continued)

A. Mercers in the Troussevache Neighborhood (continued)

	Forename	Surname	Tax Range 1292–1300 (in deniers)	Tax 1313 (in deniers)	Average Tax 1297–1300 (in deniers)	Street	Year/Folio[1]	Parish/Quête[2]
46	Julienne	de Saint Germain	744	NA	744	rue de la Courroierie	1299 f. 191v	Par. S.-Jacques-de-la-Boucherie, 1
47	Marie	la Beguine, Osane	2,160–2,760	NA	2,680	rue Troussevache	1292 f. 40v[10] / 1296 f. 17v / 1298 f. 113v / 1299 f. 191v / 1300 f. 268	Par. S.-Jacques-de-la-Boucherie, 1
48	Marie	Toussac	1,800–1,800	NA	1,800	rue de la Courroierie (1300), rue Amauri de Roissy (1298)	1298 f. 113v / 1299 f. 191v / 1300 f. 267v	Par. S.-Jacques-de-la-Boucherie, 1
49	Marques	de Luques	192	NA	192	rue Troussevache	1299 f. 191v	Par. S.-Jacques-de-la-Boucherie, 1
50	Martin	Viel	960–1,488	NA	1,194	rue Troussevache	1296 f. 17v / 1297 f. 52v / 1298 f. 113v / 1299 f. 191v / 1300 f. 268	Par. S.-Jacques-de-la-Boucherie, 1
51	Mahy	de Lymesi; de Lymesis	72–72	NA	72	rue de la Courroierie	1299 f. 191v / 1300 f. 267v	Par. S.-Jacques-de-la-Boucherie, 1

52	Mahy	Viel, le boursier	480–900	NA	717	rue Troussevache	1296 f. 17v 1298 f. 113v 1299 f. 191v 1299 f. 230 (list of the dead) 1300[11] f. 268	Par. S.-Jacques-de-la-Boucherie, 1
53	Michiel	Toussac	1,440–1,800	NA	1,592	rue Troussevache	1296 f. 17v 1298 f. 113v 1299 f. 191v 1300 f. 268	Par. S.-Jacques-de-la-Boucherie, 1
54	Nicole	de Couloingne	1,920–2,760	NA	2,200	rue Troussevache	1292 f. 40v 1296 f. 17v 1297 f. 52v 1299 f. 191v 1300 f. 268	Par. S.-Jacques-de-la-Boucherie, 1
55	Phelippe	Anquetin (or Anketin)	1,020–2,880	NA	2,720	rue de la Courroierie	1296 f. 17 1298 f. 113v 1299 f. 191 1300 f. 267v	Par. S.-Jacques-de-la-Boucherie, 1
56	Pierre	de Fribois	96	NA	96	rue Guillaume Joce	1299 f. 191v	Par. S.-Jacques-de-la-Boucherie, 1
57	Pierre	de Lyons	840–1,800	NA	1,592	rue Troussevache	1296 f. 17v 1298 f. 113v 1299 f. 191v 1300 f. 268	Par. S.-Jacques-de-la-Boucherie, 1

Appendix 2 (continued)

A. Mercers in the Troussevache Neighborhood (continued)

	Forename	Surname	Tax Range 1292–1300 (in deniers)	Tax 1313 (in deniers)	Average Tax 1297–1300 (in deniers)	Street	Year/Folio[1]	Parish/Quête[2]
58	Pierre	de Sens	1,104–1,200	NA	1,168	rue Troussevache	1298 f. 113v 1299 f. 19rv 1300 f. 268	Par. S.-Jacques-de-la-Boucherie, I
59	Pierre	Gervaise	NA	180	NA	rue de la Courroierie	1313 f. 24v	Par. S.-Jacques-de-la-Boucherie, I
60	Pierre[12]	le Normant	120	NA	NA	rue Troussevache	1296 f. 17v	Par. S.-Jacques-de-la-Boucherie, I
61	Pierre	le Picart	NA	720	NA	rue Auberi-le-Bouchier	1313 f. 13v	Par. S.-Leu-S.-Gilles
62	Pierre	Viel	1,200	NA	1,200	rue Troussevache	1300 f. 268	Par. S.-Jacques-de-la-Boucherie, I
63	Raoul	Creteville	NA	288	NA	rue Auberi-le-Bouchier	1313 f. 14	Par. S.-Leu-S.-Gilles
64	Richart		432	NA	432	rue de la Courroierie	1299 f. 191	Par. S.-Jacques-de-la-Boucherie, I
65	Richart	de la Saunerie	744–744	NA	744	rue Guillaume Joce	1299 f. 19rv 1300 f. 268	Par. S.-Jacques-de-la-Boucherie, I

66	Richart	des Polies	3,360–3,360	NA	3,360	rue de la Courroierie	1299 f. 191 1300 f. 267v	Par. S.-Jacques-de-la-Boucherie, 1
67	Richart	l'Anglois	NA	216	NA	rue Auberi-le-Bouchier	1313 f. 13v	Par. S.-Leu-S.-Gilles
68	Robert	la Chiare, la Chievre	696–2,100	NA	1,212	rue Auberi-le-Bouchier	1296 f. 17 1297 f. 52 1298 f. 113 1299 f. 190v 1300 f. 267	Par. S.-Jacques-de-la-Boucherie, 1
69	Robert	la Vache	432	NA	432	rue Troussevache	1300 f. 268	Par. S.-Jacques-de-la-Boucherie, 1
70	Robert	l'Ointier	240	720	240	rue de la Courroierie	1300 f. 267v 1313 f. 24v	Par. S.-Jacques-de-la-Boucherie, 1
71	Rogier	de Peronne	192–240	NA	204	rue Troussevache	1297 f. 52v 1298 f. 113v 1299 f. 191v 1300 f. 268	Par. S.-Jacques-de-la-Boucherie, 1
72	Symon	de Chato	240–240	NA	240	rue de la Courroierie	1296 f. 17 1299 f. 191 1300 f. 267v	Par. S.-Jacques-de-la-Boucherie, 1
73	Thibaut	d'Estampes	744	NA	744	rue Troussevache	1299 f. 191v	Par. S.-Jacques-de-la-Boucherie, 1
74	Thibaut	des Planches	0	NA	NA	rue Troussevache	1300 f. 268	Par. S.-Jacques-de-la-Boucherie, 1

Appendix 2 (continued)

A. Mercers in the Troussevache Neighborhood (continued)

	Forename	Surname	Street	Tax Range 1292–1300 (in deniers)	Tax 1313 (in deniers)	Average Tax 1297–1300 (in deniers)	Year/Folio[1]	Parish/Quête[2]
75	Thibaut	le Picart	rue Auberi-le-Bouchier	NA	216	NA	1313 f. 24v	Par. S.-Jacques-de-la-Boucherie, 1
76	Thomas	de Chanevieres	rue de la Courroierie	1,440–1,920	NA	1,860	1296 f. 17 1299 f. 191 1300 f. 267v	Par. S.-Jacques-de-la-Boucherie, 1

76 mercers = 22.3% of total number of mercers in the Paris tax assessments (341).
Average tax 1297–1300: 1,125 deniers = 93.75 sous = 4.7 livres.

B. Mercers in the Quincampoix Neighborhood

	Forename	Surname	Street	Tax Range 1292–1300 (in deniers)	Tax 1313 (in deniers)	Average Tax 1297–1300 (in deniers)	Year/Folio	Parish/Quête
1	Agnes	de Saint Germain	rue Quincampoix	72	NA	72	1299 f. 182	Par. S.-Nicolas-des-Champs, 2
2	Ameline	de la Porte	rue Quincampoix	NA	72	NA	1313 f. 23	Par. S. Merri, 7
3	Baudoin	Viel	rue Quincampoix	480–744	NA	744	1296 f. 10 1299 f. 181v 1300 f. 259	Par. S.-Nicolas-des-Champs, 2

4	Bertaut	de Fosséz	36	NA	NA	rue Quincampoix	1292 f. 38	Par. S. Merri, 4
5	Coluche	le Lombart	600–900	NA	750	rue Quincampoix; rue Où l'en Cuist les Oës	1299 f. 227 / 1300 f. 253	Par. S.-Leu-S.-Gilles/ Par. S. Josse
6	Estienne	de Dammartin	600	NA	NA	rue Quincampoix	1292 f. 38v	Par. S. Merri, 4
7	Estienne	d'Esparnon	432	NA	432	rue Quincampoix	1300 f. 266v	Par. S. Merri, 4
8	Estienne	du Mesnil	96	NA	96	rue Quincampoix	1297 f. 51v	Par. S. Merri, 4
9	Estienne[13]	Hardi	240–432	NA	336	rue Quincampoix	1297 f. 51v / 1298 f. 112v / 1299 f. 230	Par. S. Merri, 4 / Par. S. Merri, list of the dead
10	Estienne	Hauville	NA	180	NA	rue Quincampoix	1313 f. 18v	Par. S.-Nicolas-des-Champs, 2
11	Eustache (or Huitace)	a la Pellete, a la Pilete	1,008–1,104	NA	1056	rue Quincampoix	1298 f. 114 / 1299 f. 192	Par. S.-Jacques-de-la-Boucherie, 1
12	Evrart	le Noir	504–1,440	NA	808	rue Quincampoix	1292 f. 38 / 1297 f. 51v / 1298 f. 112v / 1300 f. 266	Par. S. Merri, 4
13	Gautier	d'Argentueil	600	NA	600	rue Quincampoix	1298 f. 107	Par. S. Josse
14	Gautier	Monfort	240	NA	240	rue Quincampoix	1297 f. 46v	Par. S. Josse
15	Geoffroi	Morise	NA	180	NA	rue Quincampoix	1313 f. 18v	Par. S.-Nicolas-des-Champs, 2

Appendix 2 (continued)

B. Mercers in the Quincampoix Neighborhood (continued)

	Forename	Surname	Tax Range 1292–1300 (in deniers)	Tax 1313 (in deniers)	Average Tax 1297–1300 (in deniers)	Street	Year/Folio	Parish/Quête
16	Dame Gile	de Mesons	NA	720	NA	rue Quincampoix	1313 f. 23	Par. S. Merri, 7
17	Gile	la Male-Vie	NA	3,600	NA	rue Quincampoix	1313 f. 23	Par. S. Merri, 7
18	Gilles	de Pierre-Frite	NA	180	NA	rue Quincampoix	1313 f. 18v	Par. S.-Nicolas-des-Champs, 2
19	Gilles	de Rece	72	NA	72	rue Quincampoix	1298 f. 109	Par. S.-Nicolas-des-Champs, 2
20	Guiart	Girart	NA	504	NA	rue Quincampoix	1313 f. 23	Par. S. Merri, 7
21	Guillaume	Cotart, Courtart	96–120	NA	108	rue Quincampoix	1298 f. 109 1299 f. 182	Par. S.-Nicolas-des-Champs, 2
22	Guillaume	de Courbeul	216	NA	216	rue Quincampoix	1297 f. 51v	Par. S. Merri, 4
23	Guillaume	le Povre	36	NA	NA	rue Quincampoix	1292 f. 38v	Par. S. Merri, 4
24	Guillaume	le Telier	900	NA	900	rue Quincampoix	1298 f. 114	Par. S.-Jacques-de-la-Boucherie, 1
25	Haoÿs[14]	de Dammartin	336–432	4,320	384	rue Quincampoix	1297 f. 51v 1298 f. 112v 1299 f. 190	Par. S. Merri, 4, 7

213

26	Henri	de l'Estanc	288–432	720	324	rue Quincampoix	1297 f. 53 1298 f. 114 1299 f. 192 1300 f. 268 1313 f. 25	Par. S.-Jacques-de-la-Boucherie, 1
27	Hue	de Saint Ligier	NA	180	NA	rue Quincampoix	1313 f. 18v	Par. S.-Nicolas-des-Champs, 2
28	Imbert	de la Quarriere	96–360	NA	264	rue Quincampoix	1297 f. 51v 1298 f. 112v 1299 f. 192	Par. S. Merri, 4; Par. S.-Jacques-de-la-Boucherie, 1
29	Isabel[15]	de Cambrai	192	NA	192	rue Quincampoix	1298 f. 112v	Par. S. Merri, 4
30	Jacqueline	la Vivienne	72	NA	72	rue Quincampoix	1300 f. 266v	Par. S. Merri, 4
31	Jacques	Buisson/du Buisson	240–360	NA	280	rue Quincampoix	1296 f. 17v 1297 f. 53 1298 f. 114 1300 f. 268v	Par. S.-Jacques-de-la-Boucherie, 1
32	Jacques	d'Arenci	216–216	108	216	rue Quincampoix	1298 f. 114 1299 f. 192 1300 f. 266v 1313 f. 23	Par. S.-Jacques-de-la-Boucherie, 1; Par. S. Merri, 4, 7
33	Jacques	de Peronne	NA	144	NA	rue Quincampoix	1313 f. 23	Par. S. Merri, 7
34	Jacques	de Verdun	900	7,200	900	rue Quincampoix	1298 f. 114 1313 f. 23	Par. S.-Jacques-de-la-Boucherie, 1; Par. S. Merri, 7

Appendix 2 (continued)

B. Mercers in the Quincampoix Neighborhood (continued)

	Forename	Surname	Tax Range 1292–1300 (in deniers)	Tax 1313 (in deniers)	Average Tax 1297–1300 (in deniers)	Street	Year/Folio	Parish/Quête
35	Jacquet	de Venyse	0	NA	NA	rue Quincampoix	1299 f. 192	Par. S.-Jacques-de-la-Boucherie, 1
36	Jehan	de Biaumont	240–240	1,440	240	rue Quincampoix (1299, 1313), rue de la Courroierie (1300)	1299 f. 189v, 1300 f. 267v, 1313 f. 18v	Par. S. Merri, 4; Par. S.-Jacques-de-la-Boucherie, 1; Par. S.-Nicolas-des-Champs, 2
37	Jehan	de Chartre	NA	720	NA	rue Quincampoix	1313 f. 18v	Par. S.-Nicolas-des-Champs, 2
38	Jehan	de Dammartin	240–432	3,600	324	rue Quincampoix (1297–1300), rue de la Courroierie (1313)	1292 f. 38, 1297 f. 51v, 1298 f. 112v, 1299 f. 190, 1300 f. 266v, 1313 f. 25	Par. S. Merri, 4; Par. S.-Jacques-de-la-Boucherie, 1
39	Jehan	de Meudon	432–432	540	432	rue Quincampoix	1297 f. 51v, 1299 f. 189v, 1300 f. 266v, 1313 f. 23	Par. S. Merri, 4, 7

						rue		
40	Jehan, Jehannot	de Montleheri	48–96	NA	72	rue Quincampoix	1298 f. 135 1300 f. 266v	Par. S. Merri, 4
41	Jehan	de Morlieus	NA	72	NA	rue Quincampoix	1313 f. 18v	Par. S.-Nicolas-des-Champs, 2
42	Jehan	de Succy	NA	360	NA	rue Quincampoix	1313 f. 23	Par. S. Merri 7
43	Jehan	de Valenton	168	NA	168	rue Quincampoix	1298 f. 109	Par. S.-Nicolas-des-Champs, 2
44	Jehan	de Ville-Parisie	NA	144	NA	rue Quincampoix	1313 f. 23	Par. S. Merri, 7
45	Jehan	d'Esparnon	3,720–3,840	21,600	3,840	rue Quincampoix	1296 f. 10v 1299 f. 18v 1300 f. 259 1313 f. 18v	Par. S.-Nicolas-des-Champs, 2
46	Jehan	d'Yvri	72	NA	72	rue de Bière	1300 f. 266	Par. S. Merri, 4
47	Jehan	Girart	NA	360	NA	rue Quincampoix	1313 f. 23	Par. S. Merri, 7
48	Jehan	la Berbiz	NA	360	NA	rue Quincampoix	1313 f. 18v	Par. S.-Nicolas-des-Champs, 2
49	Jehan	Lavé	360	NA	NA	rue Quincampoix	1296 f. 16	Par. S. Merri, 4
50	Jehan	le Pellier	1,680, 2,400–2,760	7,200	2,640	rue Quincampoix	1292 f. 38v 1297 f. 51v 1299 f. 189v 1300 f. 266v 1313 f. 23	Par. S. Merri, 4. 7

Appendix 2 (continued)

B. Mercers in the Quincampoix Neighborhood (continued)

	Forename	Surname	Tax Range 1292–1300 (in deniers)	Tax 1313 (in deniers)	Average Tax 1297–1300 (in deniers)	Street	Year/Folio	Parish/Quête
51	Jehan	le Petit, de Biaumont	240	NA	240	rue Quincampoix	1297 f. 51v	Par. S. Merri, 4
52	Jehan	Pasquier	240–240	NA	240	rue Quincampoix	1296 f. 17v 1298 f. 114 1300 f. 268v	Par. S.-Jacques-de-la-Boucherie, 1
53	Jehan	Poret	NA	2,160	NA	rue Quincampoix	1313 f. 23	Par. S. Merri, 7
54	Jehanne	de Boismeigue	288	NA	288	rue Quincampoix	1300 f. 259v	Par. S.-Nicolas-des-Champs, 2
55	Jehanne	de Saint Martin	192	NA	192	rue Quincampoix	1298 f. 109	Par. S.-Nicolas-des-Champs, 2
56	Jehanne	la Liniere	NA	1,800	NA	rue Quincampoix	1313 f. 25	Par. S.-Jacques-de-la-Boucherie, 1
57	Jehanne	l'Amee	NA	72	NA	rue Quincampoix	1313 f. 18v	Par. S.-Nicolas-des-Champs, 2
58	Jehan	de Meudon	360	NA	NA	rue Quincampoix	1292 f. 38v	Par. S. Merri, 4
59	Jehan	de Peronne	480	NA	NA	rue Quincampoix	1292 f. 38v	Par. S. Merri, 4

60	Joce	de Monci	432	NA	432	rue Quincampoix	1298 f. 112v	Par. S. Merri, 4
61	Lorenz	de Biaumont	300	720	300	rue Quincampoix	1300 f. 259 / 1313 f. 18v	Par. S.-Nicolas-des-Champs, 2
62	Lyedot	de Reins	NA	18	NA	rue Quincampoix	1313 f. 18v	Par. S.-Nicolas-des-Champs, 2
63	Dame Mahaut[16]	la Hardie	336	NA	336	rue Quincampoix	1299 f. 190 / 1300 f. 266v	Par. S. Merri, 4
64	Marguerite	de Troies	144	NA	144	rue Quincampoix	1300 f. 266v	Par. S. Merri, 4
65	Martin	de Bondies	336–360	NA	348	rue Quincampoix	1298 f. 112v / 1300 f. 266v	Par. S. Merri, 4
66	Mahy	d'Arraz	NA	7,200	NA	rue Quincampoix	1313 f. 23	Par. S. Merri, 7
67	Michiel	de la Quarriere	432–504	NA	468	rue Quincampoix	1299 f. 18v / 1300 f. 259	Par. S.-Nicolas-des-Champs, 2
68	Michiel	de Pavelli	168	NA	168	rue Quincampoix	1300 f. 268v	Par. S.-Jacques-de-la-Boucherie, 1
69	Nicolas	d'Amiens	1,200–1,260	NA	1,230	rue Quincampoix	1298 f. 112v / 1300 f. 266v	Par. S. Merri, 4
70	Nicolas	de Flori	84	NA	84	rue Quincampoix	1298 f. 107	Par. S. Josse
71	Nicolas	Derbi	48	NA	48	rue de Bière	1299 f. 189v	Par. S. Merri, 4
72	Nicolas	le Petit	NA	7,200	NA	rue Quincampoix	1313 f. 25	Par. S.-Jacques-de-la-Boucherie, 1

Appendix 2 (continued)

B. Mercers in the Quincampoix Neighborhood (continued)

	Forename	Surname	Tax Range 1292–1300 (in deniers)	Tax 1313 (in deniers)	Average Tax 1297–1300 (in deniers)	Street	Year/Folio	Parish/Quête
73	Olivier	Chief-de-fer	2,160–2,760	NA	2480	rue Quincampoix	1298 f. 114 1299 f. 192 1300 f. 268v	Par. S.-Jacques-de-la-Boucherie, 1
74	Perrenele	de Valenton	120–216	NA	168	rue Quincampoix	1299 f. 181v 1300 f. 259	Par. S.-Nicolas-des-Champs, 2
75	Phelippe	d'Esparnon	288	360	288	rue Quincampoix	1299 f. 189v 1313 f. 23	Par. S. Merri, 4, 7
76	Pierre	de Saint Germain	192	NA	192	rue Quincampoix	1300 f. 266v	Par. S. Merri, 4
77	Pierre	de Taverni	96–144	360	120	rue Quincampoix	1298 f. 109 1299 f. 182 1313 f. 18v	Par. S.-Nicolas-des-Champs, 2
78	Pierre	Evrart	NA	360	NA	rue Quincampoix	1313 f. 18v	Par. S.-Nicolas-des-Champs, 2
79	Pierre	le Pellier	1,200	NA	NA	rue Quincampoix	1292 f. 38	Par. S. Merri, 4
80	Raoul	de Bondies	192	1,080	192	rue Quincampoix	1298 f. 112v 1313 f. 23	Par. S. Merri, 4, 7

81	Raoul	de Crovile	168–240	NA	240	rue Quincampoix (1300), rue Auberi-le-Bouchier (1296)	1296 f. 17 / 1300 f. 268v	Par. S.-Jacques-de-la-Boucherie, 1
82	Raoul	de la Quarriere	432–576	NA	504	rue Quincampoix	1298 f. 114 / 1297 f. 53	Par. S.-Jacques-de-la-Boucherie, 1
83	Raoul	la Mouche	192	NA	192	rue Quincampoix	1299 f. 190	Par. S. Merri, 4
84	Raoul	le Boursier	NA	1,440	NA	rue Quincampoix	1313 f. 18v	Par. S.-Nicolas-des-Champs, 2
85	Richart	Loquet	NA	540	NA	rue Quincampoix	1313 f. 23	Par. S. Merri, 7
86	Robert	de Lusebrat	192	NA	NA	rue Quincampoix	1296 f. 17v	Par. S.-Jacques-de-la-Boucherie, 1
87	Robert	de Moncy	NA	3,600	NA	rue Quincampoix	1313 f. 23	Par. S. Merri, 7
88	Rogier	d'Alemengne	120	NA	120	rue Quincampoix	1297 f. 51v	Par. S. Merri, 4
89	Rogier	de Prouvinz	72	NA	72	rue Quincampoix	1300 f. 266vPar. S. Merri, 4	
90	Symon	Asce	240–288	NA	264	rue Quincampoix	1296 f. 17v / 1298 f. 150v	Par. S.-Jacques-de-la-Boucherie, 1; Par. S. Merri
91	Symon	de Vitri	600–600	NA	600	rue Quincampoix	1299 f. 18v / 1300 f. 259	Par. S.-Nicolas-des-Champs, 2
92	Symon	Piquet	NA	360	NA	rue Quincampoix	1313 f. 18v	Par. S.-Nicolas-des-Champs, 2

Appendix 2 (continued)

B. Mercers in the Quincampoix Neighborhood (continued)

	Forename	Surname	Tax Range 1292–1300 (in deniers)	Tax 1313 (in deniers)	Average Tax 1297–1300 (in deniers)	Street	Year/Folio	Parish/Quête
93	Symon	d'Esparnon	840	NA	NA	rue Quincampoix	1292 f. 38v	Par. S. Merri, 4
94	Symon	Male-Vie	840	NA	NA	rue Quincampoix	1292 f. 38	Par. S. Merri, 4
95	Thibaut	de Flori	1,800–2,760	NA	2,200	rue Quincampoix	1297 f. 46v 1298 f. 107 1299 f. 175	Par. S. Josse
96	Thomas	d'Esparnon	360–960	NA	360	rue Quincampoix	1292 f. 38v 1299 f. 189v 1300 f. 266vPar. S. Merri, 4	
97	Yve	le Breton	NA	720	NA	rue Quincampoix	1313 f. 23	Par. S. Merri, 7

97 mercers = 28.4% of the total number of mercers in the Paris tax assessments (341).
Average tax 1297–1300: 497.6 deniers = 41.5 sous = 2.1 livres.

C. Mercers in the Lombard Neighborhood

	Forename	Surname	Tax Range 1292–1300 (in deniers)	Tax in 1313 (in deniers)	Average Tax 1297–1300 (in deniers)	Street	Year/Folio	Parish/Quête
1	Adam	le Tainturier	1,200	NA	1,200	Grand Rue, cloister S. Opportune	1300 f. 250	Par. S. Opportune

2	Agnes	(femme Guillaume Cousin)	144	NA	144	rue S. Opportune	1300 f. 250	Par. S. Opportune
3	Alain	le Ber	NA	360	NA	rue S. Opportune	1313 f. 4	Par. S.-Germain-l'Auxerrois, 4
4	Baudoin	de Sessons, de Soissons	936–1,200	NA	1,086	rue de la Viez Monnaie	1297 f. 54 1298 f. 115 1299 f. 194 1300 f. 270	Par. S.-Jacques-de-la-Boucherie, 3
5	Bonvis	Bondon (or Bondos)	2100	NA	2,100	rue de la Buffeterie	1299 f. 194	Par. S.-Jacques-de-la-Boucherie, 3
6	Gilbert	du Hommet	24	NA	24	rue des Arcis	1300 f. 270	Par. S.-Jacques-de-la-Boucherie, 3
7	Guillaume	de Saint Marcel	696–744	NA	720	ruelle de la Barre (1297), rue S. Opportune (1300)	1297 f. 46 1300 f. 236	Par. S. Opportune
8	Jehan	Cousin	420–744	NA	582	rue S. Opportune	1298 f. 106 1300 f. 250	Par. S. Opportune
9	Jehan	de Rueil	1,488–1,620	NA	1,521	rue de la Savonnerie (1300), rue de la Viez Monnaie (1299)	1297 f. 53v 1298 f. 114v 1299 f. 193 1300 f. 269	Par. S.-Jacques-de-la-Boucherie, 2

Appendix 2 (continued)

C. Mercers in the Lombard Neighborhood (continued)

	Forename	Surname	Tax Range 1292–1300 (in deniers)	Tax 1313 (in deniers)	Average Tax 1297–1300 (in deniers)	Street	Year/Folio	Parish/Quête
10	Jehan	la Vache	432	NA	NA	rue de la Viez Monnaie	1296 f. 18v	Par. S.-Jacques-de-la-Boucherie, 3
11	Jehan	le Normant	900	NA	900	cloister S. Opportune, Grand Rue	1299 f. 172	Par. S. Opportune
12	Jehan	le Picart	288–432	NA	360	ruelle de la Barre (1297), rue des Petits Souliers (1298), rue de la Tableterie (1296)	1296 f. 12 / 1297 f. 46 / 1298 f. 106	Par. S. Opportune
13	Jehan	de Saint Marcel	NA	180	NA	rue S. Opportune	1313 f. 4	Par. S.-Germain-l'Auxerrois, 4
14	Jehan	le Seelleur	NA	2,160	NA	rue de la Hanterie, rue de la Tableterie	1313 f. 5v	Par. S.-Germain-l'Auxerrois, 5
15	Jehan	Quatre Sens	192–240	NA	240	Tableterie, ruelle de la Barre	1296 f. 12 / 1297 f. 46	Par. S. Opportune
16	Jehan	Marcel	3,600	NA	NA	cloister S. Merri	1292 f. 34	Par. S. Merri, 2
17	Nicolas	Casteillon	24	NA	24	rue S. Opportune	1298 f. 129	Par. S. Opportune

	Forename	Surname	Tax Range 1292–1300 (in deniers)	Tax 1313 (in deniers)	Average Tax 1297–1300 (in deniers)	Street	Year/Folio	Parish/Quête
18	Nicolas	le Tainturier	NA	360	NA	rue des Petits Souliers	1313 f. 13v	Par. S. Opportune
19	Simon	de Petit-Pont	744–816	NA	780	rue S. Opportune	1298 f. 106 1300 f. 250	Par. S. Opportune
20	Thibaut	de Seineville	NA	1,440	NA	rue des Petits Souliers or de la Tableterie or S. Opportune	1313 f. 13	Par. S. Opportune

20 mercers = 6% of the total number of mercers in the Parisian tax assessments (341).

Average tax 1297–1300: 745 deniers = 62 sous = 3.1 livres.

D. Mercers in the Petit-Pont Neighborhood

Forename	Surname	Tax Range 1292–1300 (in deniers)	Tax 1313 (in deniers)	Average Tax 1297–1300 (in deniers)	Street	Year/Folio	Parish/Quête
Aalis	de Mons	96	NA	96	rue des Marmosez	1297 f. 61v	Par. S.-Pierre-aux-Boeufs
Adam	Faguee (and his widow)[17]	408	NA	NA	rue du Petit-Pont	1296 f. 28v 1296 f. 34v	Par. S. Séverin, 2
André	le Bourguignon	36	NA	36	rue Berthe	1299 f. 217v	Par. S. Séverin, 2
Auberée	de Rouen	NA	144	NA	rue de la Huchette	1313 f. 41v	Par. S. Séverin, 2
Baudet	le François	24–144	144	144	rue de la Huchette (1292), rue Serpente (1292), Petit-Pont (1299)	1292 f. 68v 1299 f. 210v	Par. S. Séverin, 2

Appendix 2 (continued)

D. Mercers in the Petit-Pont Neighborhood (continued)

	Forename	Surname	Tax Range 1292–1300 (in deniers)	Tax 1313 (in deniers)	Average Tax 1297–1300 (in deniers)	Street	Year/Folio	Parish/Quête
6	Baudet	le Picart	36–72	NA	54	rue du Petit-Pont	1297 f. 89v 1299 f. 216v	Par. S. Séverin, 2
7	Baudoin	le Picart	24	NA	NA	rue S. Séverin, rue du Petit-Pont	1292 f. 67v	Par. S. Séverin, 2
8	Estienne	de Montereul	192	NA	NA	rue de la rivière Jehan-le-Cras	1292 f. 60v	Par. S. Barthelémy
9	Flandrine	d'Amiens	96–120	NA	108	rue de la Calandre (1298, 1299), rue du Marché Palu (1299)	1298 f. 122 1299 f. 210v	Par. S.-Germain-le-Vieux
10	Foursinet		96	NA	96	Petit-Pont, rue S. Jacques	1299 f. 215	Par. S. Séverin, 1
11	Gautier	de Petit-Pont	24	NA	24	Petit-Pont, rue S. Jacques	1299 f. 215	Par. S. Séverin, 1
12	Geoffroi	Buhure	NA	360	NA	Petit-Pont	1313 f. 40v	Par. S. Séverin, 2
13	Geoffroi	le Normant	36	NA	36	rue Hébert-aux-Broches	1299 f. 217v	Par. S. Séverin, 2

14	Geoffroi	de Rains	24–72	NA	24	rue du Petit-Pont	1296 f. 28v / 1297 f. 89v	Par. S. Séverin, 2
15	Geoffroi	le Borgne	72	NA	72	Petit-Pont, rue S. Jacques	1299 f. 215	Par. S. Séverin, 1
16	Guillaume	a la Pilete	NA	1,080	NA	rue de la Calandre	1313 f. 38v	Par. S.-Germain-le-Vieux
17	Guillaume	de Nichole	216–432	432	228	rue du Petit-Pont (1296, 1299, 1300), rue de la Calandre (1313)	1296 f. 28v / 1299 f. 210v / 1300 f. 285v / 1313 f. 38v	Par. S. Séverin, 2; S.-Germain-le-Vieux
18	Guillaume	de Saint Omer	72	NA	72	rue du Petit-Pont	1299 f. 216v	Par. S. Séverin, 2
19	Guillaume	Domont	72	NA	72	rue Neuve Notre Dame	1299 f. 214	Par. S. Christophe
20	Guillaume	le Boisteus	NA	360	NA	rue de la Çavaterie	1313 f. 37v	Par. S. Martial
21	Guillaume	le Bourguignon	NA	144	NA	rue de la Huchette	1313 f. 41v	Par. S. Séverin, 2
22	Guillaume	le Clerc	72	NA	NA	rue de la Pelleterie	1296 f. 20	Par. S.-Jacques-de-la-Boucherie, 5
23	Guillaume	le Normant	840	NA	NA	rue de la rivière Jehan-le-Cras	1292 f. 60v	Par. S. Barthelémy
24	Henri	Fessart (mari a la coronee)	NA	32	NA	ruelle des Planches Mibray	1313 f. 36v	Par. S.-Denis-de-la-Chartre

Appendix 2 (continued)

D. Mercers in the Petit-Pont Neighborhood (continued)

	Forename	Surname	Tax Range 1292–1300 (in deniers)	Tax 1313 (in deniers)	Average Tax 1297–1300 (in deniers)	Street	Year/Folio	Parish/Quête
25	Hue	l'Englais, l'Englois	60–84	NA	72	rue devant la Cour le Roi (1300), rue de la Pelleterie (1297), Draperie (1297)	1297 f. 83 1300 f. 283v	Par. S.-Jacques-de-la-Boucherie, 5
26	Jacques	de Balemont	NA	108	NA	rue de la Çavaterie	1313 f. 37v	Par. S. Martial
27	Jehan	Bourc-l'abbé	24–96	NA	60	rue Hébert-aux-Broches (1298), Petit-Pont (1299)	1298 f. 145 1299 f. 210v	Par. S. Séverin, 2
28	Jehan	Caleboudré	48	NA	48	rue du Petit-Pont	1297 f. 89v	Par. S. Séverin, 2
29	Jehan	Charmentré, de Charmentré	108–168	NA	168	rue du Petit-Pont	1296 f. 28v 1299 f. 210v	Par. S. Séverin, 2
30	Jehan	de Biset	36–96	NA	66	rue de l'Orberie (1297), rue de la Calandre (1297), rue devant la Cour le Roi (1298)	1297 f. 87v 1298 f. 121	Par. S. Barthélemy
31	Jehan	de l'Espine	96	NA	96	rue de la Pelleterie	1297 f. 55v	Par. S.-Jacques-de-la-Boucherie, 5

32	Jehan	de Puille	24	NA	24	Petit-Pont	1299 f. 210v	Par. S.-Germain-le-Vieux
33	Jehan	Fo-vis	24	NA	24	rue Berthe	1298 f. 144v	Par. S. Séverin, 2
34	Jehan	le Flamenc	84–192	432	138	rue de la Pelleterie (1297–1300), rue de la Calandre (1313)	1297 f. 60 1298 f. 121 1299 f. 209 1300 f. 284 1313 f. 38v	Par. S. Barthélémy; S.-Germain-le-Vieux
35	Jehan	le Galais	24–36	NA	32	rue Hébert-aux-Broches (1298, 1299), rue de la Clé (1300), rue de la Huchette (1300)	1298 f. 145 1299 f. 217v 1300 f. 290v	Par. S. Séverin, 2
36	Jehan	le Picart	72	NA	72	rue de la Pelleterie	1298 f. 121	Par. S. Barthelémy
37	Jehan	Soufflet	72	NA	72	rue du Petit-Pont	1299 f. 216v	Par. S. Séverin, 2
38	Jehan	Vent-de-Bise	72–96	NA	84	rue devant la Cour le Roi	1296 f. 20 1299 f. 208v 1300 f. 283v	Par. S.-Jacques-de-la-Boucherie, 5; S. Barthelémy
39	Jehanne	Faguee	192	NA	192	rue S. Jacques, Petit-Pont	1299 f. 215	Par. S. Séverin, 1
40	Jehanne	fille Marie la merciere	24	NA	NA	Cité near S. Christolphe	1292 f. 065	Par. S. Christophe
41	Jehanne	la Hongresse	NA	72	NA	rue aux Oublaiers	1313 f. 40	Par. S. Madeleine

Appendix 2 (continued)

D. Mercers in the Petit-Pont Neighborhood (continued)

	Forename	Surname	Tax Range 1292–1300 (in deniers)	Tax 1313 (in deniers)	Average Tax 1297–1300 (in deniers)	Street	Year/Folio	Parish/Quête
42	Jehanne	la Mestresse	24	NA	24	parvis Notre Dame	1299 f. 214	Par. S. Christophe
43	Jehan	le Galois	36	NA	NA	rue de la Huchette or rue Serpente	1292 f. 68v	Par. S. Séverin, 2
44	Marguerite	d'Orliens	24	NA	24	Petit-Pont or rue S. Jacques	1299 f. 215	Par. S. Séverin, 1
45	Marguerite	la Picarde	120	NA	NA	rue Neuve Notre Dame	1292 f. 65v	Par. S. Christophe
46	Marie	la merciere	24	NA	NA	near S. Christolphe	1292 f. 65	Par. S. Christophe
47	Maron	de Monz	432	NA	432	rue S.-Pierre-aux-Boeufs	1299 f. 213	Par. S.-Pierre-aux-Boeufs
48	Michiel	le Normant	36	NA	36	rue du Petit-Pont	1299 f. 216v	Par. S. Séverin, 2
49	Nicolas	Chauçon	84	NA	84	rue Neuve Notre Dame	1300 f. 288v	Par. S.-Geneviève-des-Ardents
50	Nicolas	de Saint-Leu-d'Eserenz	NA	72	NA	rue de la Calandre	1313 f. 38v	Par. S.-Germain-le-Vieux
51	Nicolas	du Liege	72	NA	72	rue de la Pelleterie	1299 f. 196v	Par. S.-Jacques-de-la-Boucherie, 5

52	Nicolas	Genne	264	NA	NA	rue du Petit-Pont	1296 f. 28v	Par. S. Séverin, 2
53	Oudin	du Palés	36	NA	36	Petit-Pont, rue S. Jacques	1299 f. 215	Par. S. Séverin, 1
54	Perrenelle	l'Esmeraude	192	NA	192	rue de la Viez Draperie	1298 f. 121v	Par. S.-Pierre-des-Arcis
55	Perrot	Tout-gris	NA	576	NA	rue Neuve Notre Dame	1313 f. 39	Par. S.-Geneviève-des-Ardents
56	Phelippe	Montereul, de Moutereul	120–240	NA	NA	rue de la rivière Jehan-le-Cras (1292), Viez Draperie (1296)	1292 f. 60v, 1296 f. 26	Par. S. Barthélémy
57	Pierre	Chartain	72–72	72	72	rue devant la Cour le Roi (1297, 1298), rue de la Pelleterie (1313)	1297 f. 60, 1298 f. 121, 1313 f. 37v	Par. S. Barthélémy
58	Pierre	de Wirmes	NA	108	NA	Petit-Pont	1313 f. 40v	Par. S. Séverin, 2
59	Pierre	l'Aguillier	24–36	NA	30	rue de la Pelleterie	1299 f. 209, 1300 f. 284	Par. S. Barthélémy
60	Raoul	de Saint Germain	168	NA	168	Petit-Pont, rue S. Jacques	1299 f. 215	Par. S. Séverin, 1
61	Raoul	le Breton	24	NA	24	rue devant la Cour le Roi	1298 f. 142	Par. S. Barthélémy
62	Renart	de Crespi	192	NA	192	Petit-Pont, rue du Marché Palu	1298 f. 122	Par. S.-Germain-le-Vieux

Appendix 2 (continued)

D. Mercers in the Petit-Pont Neighborhood (continued)

	Forename	Surname	Tax Range 1292–1300 (in deniers)	Tax 1313 (in deniers)	Average Tax 1297–1300 (in deniers)	Street	Year/Folio	Parish/Quête
63	Renart	le mercier	72	NA	72	Petit-Pont	1299 f. 210v	Par. S.-Germain-le-Vieux
64	Renaut	l'Englais	24	NA	24	Petit-Pont, rue S. Jacques	1299 f. 215	Par. S. Séverin, 1
65	Richart	a la Tache	48	NA	NA	list of the dead	1296 f. 34v	Par. S. Barthélémy
66	Richart	de Maante	24–96	NA	64	rue de la Pelleterie (1298, 1299), rue Gervaise Laurent (1300)	1298 f. 116 1299 f. 196v 1300 f. 284v	Par. S.-Jacques-de-la-Boucherie, 5; S.-Pierre-des-Arcis
67	Richart	le Normant	36	NA	36	Grand Pont, rue de la Pelleterie, ruelle des Planches Mibray, Draperie	1298 f. 137	Par. S.-Jacques-de-la-Boucherie, 5
68	Richart	l'Englais	48	72	48	rue S. Jacques and Petit-Pont (1299)	1299 f. 215 1313 f. 41v	Par. S. Séverin, 1
69	Robert	l'Eschicouart	60	NA	60	rue devant la Cour le Roi	1300 f. 283v	Par. S. Barthélémy

70	Robert	Rualant	NA	18	NA	rue de la Huchette	1313 f. 41v	Par. S. Séverin, 1
71	Robin	de Saint Leu	NA	18	NA	rue de la Huchette	1313 f. 41v	Par. S. Séverin, 2
72	Robin	du Bourc-l'abbé	NA	18	NA	rue de la Huchette	1313 f. 41v	Par. S. Séverin, 2
73	Robin	l'Anglois	NA	18	NA	rue de la Huchette	1313 f. 41v	Par. S. Séverin, 2
74	Symon	l'Englais	696	NA	NA	rue du Petit-Pont	1296 f. 28v	Par. S. Séverin, 2
75	Thomas	Gascoing	168	NA	168	rue Neuve Notre Dame	1297 f. 62v	Par. S.-Geneviève-des-Ardents
76	Thomas	Gibet	NA	432	NA	rue de la Calandre	1313 f. 38v	Par. S.-Germain-le-Vieux
77	Thomas	l'Englais	216	NA	216	Petit-Pont	1299 f. 210v	Par. S.-Germain-le-Vieux
78	Thomas	l'Escuelier	168	NA	NA	rue Neuve Notre Dame	1296 f. 28	Par. S.-Geneviève-des-Ardents
79	xxx	Fourtin	36	NA	36	parvis Notre Dame, ruelle des Chambres l'Evêque	1299 f. 214	Par. S. Christophe
80	Yve	le Breton	24–24	18	24	rue Hébert-aux-Broches (1298), rue Bertes (1313), rue du Petit-Pont (1299)	1298 f. 145 / 1299 f. 216v / 1313 f. 41v	Par. S. Séverin, 2

80 mercers = 23.5% of total number of mercers in the Paris tax assessments (341).
Average tax 1297–1300: 87 deniers = 7.2 sous = 36 livre.

Appendix 2 (continued)

E. Mercers Residing in Sections of Paris Other than the Trousservache, Quincampoix, Lombard, and Petit-Pont Neighborhoods

	Forename	Surname	Tax Range 1292–1300 (in deniers)	Tax in 1313 (in deniers)	Average Tax 1297–1300 (in deniers)	Street	Year/Folio	Parish/Quête
1	Aalis	de Meulun	72		72	rue Viez du Temple	1300 f. 275v	Par. S. Gervais, 4
2	Aalis	du Mur	432	NA	432	rue Nicolas Arrode	1298 f. 101v	Par. S. Eustache (or Huitace), 1
3	Agnes	Toussac	240	NA	240	rue S. Benoît	1299 f. 221	Par. S. Benoît, 1
4	Alain	l'Englois	24	NA	24	rue du Vieux Cimetière S. Jehan	1297 f. 85	Par. S.-Jehan-en-Grève, 2
5	anonymous	wife (or widow) of Pierre de la Court	96	NA	96	rue des Poulies	1298 f. 97v	Par. S.-Germain-l'Auxerrois, 2
6	Bertaut	a la Male	36	NA	36	rue S. Martin, outside the walls	1299 f. 175v	Par. S. Laurent
7	Blanche	de Soissons	240	NA	240	rue S. Honoré	1300 f. 234	Par. S.-Germain-l'Auxerrois, 3
8	Denise	de Compigne	24	NA	24	rue Cul-de-Sac-le-Grand	1298 f. 133v	Par. S. Merri, 3

				NA				
9	Estienne	Rose	576–744	NA	660	Grand Rue (1297); near Porte S. Denis (1298)	1296 f. 8v / 1297 f. 44 / 1298 f. 104v	Par. S. Eustache (or Huitace), 2 and 4
10	Eustache (or Huitace)	le Piquart	72	NA	72	rue au Fuerre	1300 f. 247v	Par. S. Eustache (or Huitace), 4
11	Gautier	l'Englais	24	NA	24	rue aux Porées	1298 f. 144v	Par. S. Séverin, 1
12	Geneviève	la Paonniere	360	NA	360	rue Neuve S. Merri	1298 f. 112	Par. S. Merri, 4
13	Geoffroi		24	NA	24	rue de la Truanderie	1298 f. 128	Par. S. Eustache (or Huitace), 3
14	Geoffroi	le Blezois	24	NA	24	rue du Bourc-l'Abbé	1299 f. 74	Par. S.-Leu-S.-Gilles
15	Geoffroi	le Breton	24	NA	24	rue de Guerneles	1300 f. 242	Par. S. Eustache (or Huitace), 1
16	Geoffroi	l'Englais	96	NA	96	rue Roland l'Avenier	1298 f. 100	Par. S.-Germain-l'Auxerrois, 4
17	Geoffroi	Milet	NA	72	NA	rue au Lyon	1313 f. 12v	Par. S. Sauveur
18	Girart	Foriz, Souriz	192–240	NA	208	rue de la Charronnerie	1297 f. 45v / 1298 f. 105v / 1299 f. 171v	Par. S. Innocents
19	Gracien	d'Espaingne	432	NA	432	rue du Grenier S. Lazare (or Guernier de S. Ladre)	1298 f. 108	Par. S.-Nicolas-des Champs, 1

Appendix 2 (continued)

E. Mercers Residing in Sections of Paris Other than the Troussevache, Quincampoix, Lombard, and Petit-Pont Neighborhoods (continued)

	Forename	Surname	Tax Range 1292–1300 (in deniers)	Tax 1313 (in deniers)	Average Tax 1297–1300 (in deniers)	Street	Year/Folio	Parish/Quête
20	Guillaume	a la Main	96–144	NA	112	rue au Lyon	1298 f. 105v / 1299 f. 170v / 1300 f. 249	Par. S. Sauveur
21	Guillaume	de Saint Omer	36	NA	36	rue de la Boucherie	1299 f. 225	Par. S.-Geneviève-du-Mont
22	Guillaume	du Vergier	24	NA	24	rue de Biau-bourc	1300 f. 262v	Par. S. Merri; 3
23	Guillaume	le Normant	36–840	NA	312	Cité (1292); rue S. Honoré (1297, 1298)	1292 f. 60v / 1297 f. 69 / 1298 f. 124v	Par. S. Barthelémy, Par. S.-Germain-l'Auxerrois
24	Guillaume	Longue-espée	24–36	NA	30	rue du Temple, outside the walls	1300 f. 256 / 1299 f. 178v	Par. S.-Nicolas-des-Champs, 1
25	Guillaume	Piquete	NA	36	NA	rue de Tire-Vit	1313 f. 12v	Par. S. Sauveur
26	Isabel	d'Orliens	432	NA	432	rue Thibautodé	1298 f. 100	Par. S.-Germain-l'Auxerrois, 4
27	Jacques	de Courceles	72–144	NA	96	Grand Rue	1297 f. 44 / 1298 f. 104 / 1299 f. 168 /	Par. S. Eustache (or Huitace), 4

28	Jacques	de la Porte	36	NA	NA	Grand Rue	1292 f. 20	Par. S. Eustache (or Huitace), 2
29	Jehan	(son-in-law of Gracien d'Espaingne)	432	NA	432	rue du Grenier S. Lazare (or Guernier de S. Ladre)	1298 f. 108	S.-Nicolas-des-Champs, 1
30	Jehan	Anfroi	240	NA	NA	rue au Fuerre	1296 f. 8	Par. S. Eustache (or Huitace), 2
31	Jehan	Asce	360	NA	360	list of the dead	1298 f. 150v	Par. S. Merri
32	Jehan	Boc	144	NA	144	rue S. Sauveur	1298 f. 105v	Par. S. Sauveur
33	Jehan	de Compigne	48	NA	48	rue Mauconseil	1300 f. 245v	Par. S. Eustache (or Huitace), 3
34	Jehan	des Moes, des Noes	24–30	NA	26	rue du Temple, outside the walls	1297 f. 77 / 1298 f. 131 / 1299 f. 178v	Par. S.-Nicolas-des-Champs, 1
35	Jehan	d'Estampes	168–192	NA	180	rue des Escoufles	1299 f. 200 / 1300 f. 276v	Par. S. Gervais, 4
36	Jehan	Kalboudre	42	NA	42	rue de Montmorency	1298 f. 130v	Par. S.-Nicolas-des-Champs, 1
37	Jehan	le Hongre	24	NA	24	rue du Temple	1300 f. 263v	Par. S. Merri, 3
38	Jehan	le Juenne	NA	144	NA	Grand Rue, outside the walls	1313 f. 12	Par. S. Sauveur

Appendix 2 (continued)

E. *Mercers Residing in Sections of Paris Other than the Troussevache, Quincampoix, Lombard, and Petit-Pont Neighborhoods (continued)*

	Forename	Surname	Tax Range 1292–1300 (in deniers)	Tax 1313 (in deniers)	Average Tax 1297–1300 (in deniers)	Street	Year/Folio	Parish/Quête
39	Jehan	le Loorrain	336–600	NA	448	Cemetery of S. Eustache (or S. Huitace)	1298 f. 105, 1299 f. 169v, 1300 f. 248	Par. S. Eustache (or Huitace), 4
40	Jehan	Maillart	24	NA	24	rue de Tire-Vit	1299 f. 171	Par. S. Sauveur
41	Jehan	Quatre-sous	0			near porte de Monmartre	1300 f. 241	Par. S. Eustache (or Huitace), 1
42	Jehan	le Bellenc, le Bellene	24–72	NA	60	rue au Fuerre	1292 f. 20v, 1299 f. 169, 1300 f. 247v	Par. S. Eustache (or Huitace), 2
43	Jehan	Maquet	36	NA	NA	rue des Prouvoirs	1292 f. 17	Par. S. Eustache (or Huitace), 1
44	Jehan	Viel		144		Grand Rue, outside the walls	1313 f. 12	Par. S. Sauveur
45	Laurent	Amiot	36	NA	36	rue de la Coçonnerie	1299 f. 168	Par. S. Eustache (or Huitace), 4
46	Michiel	d'Amiens	3,840	NA	NA	rue de la Ferronnerie	1292 f. 9v	Par. S.-Germain-l'Auxerrois, 4

47	Nicaise	de Soissons	144–168	NA	152	rue au Lyon	1298 f. 105v 1299 f. 170v 1300 f. 249	Par. S. Sauveur
48	Nicolas	de Henaut	NA	2,160	NA	Grand Rue; ruelle S. Gilles	1313 f. 14	Par. S.-Leu-S.-Gilles
49	Pierre	Choyn	24–24	NA	24	near S. Eustache (or S. Huitace)	1299 f. 163 1300 f. 241v	Par. S. Eustache (or Huitace), 1
50	Pierre	de Louvres	24	NA	24	rue Pavée S. Sauveur	1297 f. 74	Par. S. Sauveur
51	Pierre	de Prouvence	24	NA	24	rue du Bourc-l'Abbé	1299 f. 174	Par. S.-Leu-S.-Gilles
52	Pierre	de Vitri	336–600	NA	456	rue Simon le Franc	1298 f. 112 1299 f. 187v 1300 f. 264	Par. S. Merri, 3
53	Pierre	le Greffier	192	NA	192	Grand Rue, outside the walls	1297 f. 45	Par. S. Sauveur
54	Raoul	Vire	NA	72	NA	rue Pavée S. Sauveur	1313 f. 12v	Par. S. Sauveur
55	Richart	Ameloin	NA	19	NA	rue S. Martin	1313 f. 15	Par. S. Josse
56	Richart	le Chandelier	288–312	NA	300	Grand Rue, outside the walls	1299 f. 170v 1300 f. 249	Par. S. Sauveur
57	Robert	de la Mote	696–744	NA	728	Grand Rue	1297 f. 44 1299 f. 168 1300 f. 246v	S. Eustache (or Huitace), 4

Appendix 2 (continued)

E. Mercers Residing in Sections of Paris Other than the Troussevache, Quincampoix, Lombard, and Petit-Pont Neighborhoods (continued)

	Forename	Surname	Tax Range 1292–1300 (in deniers)	Tax 1313 (in deniers)	Average Tax 1297–1300 (in deniers)	Street	Year/Folio	Parish/Quête
58	Robert	de Presemont	96–120	NA	112	rue au Lyon	1298 f. 105v 1299 f. 170v 1300 f. 249	Par. S. Sauveur
59	Robert	le Biau	36	NA	36	rue au Fuerre	1299 f. 169	Par. S. Eustache (or Huitace), 4
60	Robert	le Normant	24	NA	24	rue de la Verrerie	1298 f. 139	Par. S.-Jehan-en-Grève, 2
61	Rogier	Guerart	72–576	NA	312	rue de la Saunerie (1297, 1298), in front of the Châtelet (1300), ruelle au Poisson (1297)	1297 f. 41v 1298 f. 101v 1300 f. 272	Par. S.-Germain-l'Auxerrois, 6
62	Rogier	le Picart, le Piquart	36–60	NA	48	rue au Fuerre	1299 f. 169 1300 f. 247v	Par. S. Eustache (or Huitace), 4
63	Rogier	l'Englais	36	NA	36	rue Cul-de-Sac-le-Grand	1299 f. 186	Par. S. Merri, 3
64	Rogier	l'Englais	24	NA	24	rue du Bourc-l'Abbé	1299 f. 174	Par. S.-Leu-S.-Gilles

65	Rogier	l'Englais	36	NA	NA	rue au Fuerre	1292 f. 20v	Par. S. Eustache (or Huitace), 2
66	Symon	Cornet	36	NA	36	in front of the Châtelet	1300 f. 272	Par. S.-Jacques-de-la-Boucherie, 4
67	Symon	de Monci	432	NA	432	rue S. Martin	1298 f. 112v	Par. S. Merri, 4
68	Thibaut	de Moy	192	NA	192	rue de la Charronnerie	1297 f. 45v	Par. S. Innocents

68 = 19.9% of total number of mercers in the Paris tax assessments (341).

Average tax 1297–1300: 165.6 deniers = 13.8 sous = .7 livre.

1. Folio number references are to folio numbers in the original manuscripts of the 7 Parisian tax assessments (1292, 1296, 1297, 1298, 1299, 1300, 1313). For the 1292 tax assessment readers can consult the 1991 revised edition of Géraud, and for the 1296, 1297, and 1313 assessments, readers can consult Michaëlsson's editions: all four of these editions provide folio numbers in the margins. The assessments of 1298–1300 remain unpublished in AN KK 283.

2. For the purposes of the tax assessments, larger parishes were divided into different "quêtes." I provide the numbers of the quêtes because they are useful for narrowing down the physical location of taxpayers. For a map of the various parishes and quêtes in 1300, see Bourlet and Bethe, "Création des plans," 163. This map is also available on the Alpage website: http://alpage.huma-num.fr/documents/Illustration_colloque/BOURLET_Paroisses_1300.pdf (accessed September 9, 2015).

3. It was Adam's widow Alés who was taxed, but he was the one who was identified as a mercer.

4. Adeline's husband, Jehan Tabarie the younger (le genne), had been taxed on the rue Troussevache in 1292: 1292, f. 40v. He was a mercer, but the tax assessment did not identify him as such: see Chapter 3, notes 80 and 81.

Appendix 2 (continued)

5. In 1296 Ameline was simply identified as "La femme Richart du Val, mercier" (with the professional title in the masculine); in 1300 she was identified with her own name and the profession was in the feminine.

6. Eustache was the widow of Jehan le Roumain, who appeared in the tax assessment of 1292 (p. 91) but was not identified there as a mercer. However, account book evidence indicates that he was indeed a mercer (see Chapter 3, note 100).

7. In 1300 it was Guillaume's unnamed widow who was taxed, as a mercer.

8. Between 1299 and 1300 Jehan Tabarie the elder apparently moved to the house on the rue Troussevache that had formerly belonged to his son, Jehan Tabarie the younger, and to his daughter-in-law, Adeline, both of whom had apparently died by then. We know that Jehan the younger was a mercer, but he was never taxed as such. On his widow, see note 4 to this Appendix.

9. In 1300 Vanne was taxed both as a Lombard and as a bourgeois of Paris, for a total of 12.5 livres, or 3,000 deniers. He was identified as a mercer in 1299 and 1300.

10. In 1292 Marie was identified as "Marie, fille Osane."

11. In 1300 it was Mahy's unnamed widow who was taxed, as a mercer (merciere).

12. It was Pierre's widow who was taxed in 1296, but he was the one identified as a mercer.

13. Husband of Mahaut la Hardie: Appendix 2, part B, no. 63.

14. Taxed with her son-in law and one other person in 1313.

15. There were many possible ways to spell "Isabel"; I have used this one throughout the appendices for the sake of consistency.

16. Widow of Estienne Hardi: Appendix 2, part B, no. 9. In 1299 she was listed simply as "la fame feu Estienne Hardi."

17. Adam Faguee's widow was taxed, unnamed, on fol. 28v, but he was listed as the mercer; in that same year Adam was taxed among the dead of his parish on fol. 34v. Jehanne Faguee, who was probably the same widow, was taxed as a mercer in 1299: Appendix 2, part D, no. 39.

Appendix 3. Silk Weavers in the Parisian Tax Assessments

A. Male Cloth Weavers (Makers of "Draps de Soye," Velvet, and Cloth of Gold)

	Forename	Surname	Profession	Tax (in deniers)	Average Tax 1297–1300 (in deniers)	Street	Year/Folio[1]	Parish/Quête[2]	Location on Fig. 19 (S1/S2)	Location on Fig. 26 (SL/SJ)
1	Bertaut	de Venise	ovrier de dras de soie	44	NA	rue des Petits Champs	1313 f. 21v	Par. S. Merri, 6	S1	
2	Daniau	le Breton	ovrier de dras de saye	72	NA	rue du Franc Mourier	1313 f. 32	Par. S.-Jehan-en-Grève, 3		SJ
3	Gautier	le Bourguignon	qui fet dras dor	240	240	rue S. Merri	1299 f. 184v	Par. S. Merri, 2	S1	
4	Gautier	de Miremont	qui fet le veluiau	30 / 24	27	Grand Rue	1297 f. 8tv / 1299 f. 192	Par. S.-Jacques-de-la-Boucherie, 2	S1	
5	Guerin	le Breton	qui fair dras de soye	18	NA	rue Quincampoix	1313 f. 25	Par. S.-Jacques-de-la-Boucherie, 1	S1	
6	Guillaume		feseeur de dras de soye	0	NA	rue de la Coçonnerie	1313 f. 11v	Par. S. Eustache (or Huitace), 4	S1	SL
7	Guillaume	le Breton	qui fait dras de soie	36	36	rue et ruelle S. Bon	1298 f. 132v	Par. S. Merri, 1	S1	

Appendix 3 (continued)

A. Male Cloth Weavers (Makers of "Draps de Soye," Velvet, and Cloth of Gold) (continued)

	Forename	Surname	Profession	Tax (in deniers)	Average Tax 1297–1300 (in deniers)	Street	Year/Folio[1]	Parish/Quête[2]	Location on Fig. 19 (S1/S2)	Location on Fig. 26 (SL/SJ)
8	Guillaume[3]	du Vergier	qui fet dras dor	96	96	rue Quincampoix	1299 f. 18v	Par. S.-Nicolas-des-Champs, 2	S1	
9	Henri	le Breton	qui fait dras de soie	36	36	rue Baille-Hoë	1298 f. 133	Par. S. Merri, 2	S1	
10	Jehan[4]	de Croisetes	qui fet dras de soie	24	24	rue du Fossé-S.-Germain	1299 f. 154	Par. S.-Germain-l'Auxerrois, 2	SL	
11	Jehan	de Fontenay	ovier de dras de soie	36	NA	rue Symon-le-Franc	1313 f. 21v	Par. S. Merri, 6	S1	SJ
12	Jehan	de Liramont (Riremont?)	qui fait veluau	168	168	rue de la Harengerie	1298 f. 101	Par. S.-Germain-l'Auxerrois, 5	S1	SL
13	Jehannot	brother of Jehannot de Rieremont	qui fet veluet	36	NA	rue de la Harengerie(?)	1292 f. 12v	Par. S.-Germain-l'Auxerrois, 5	S1	SL
14	Nicolas		qui fet dras de soie	36	36	rue Où l'en cuist les Oës	1299 f. 174v	Par. S.-Leu-S.-Gilles	S1	SL

	Forename	Surname	Profession	Tax (in deniers)	Average Tax 1297–1300 (in deniers)	Street of Residence	Year/Folio	Parish/Quête	Location on Fig. 19 (S1/S2)	Location on Fig. 26 (SL/SJ)
15	Noel		qui fet dras dor	24	24	rue Agnes la Bouchière	1300 f. 261v	Par. S. Merri, 2		SJ
16	Robert	du Vergier	qui fet dras dor	24	24	rue Quincampoix	1300 f. 259	Par. S.-Nicolas-des-Champs, 2	S1	
17	Raoul		le tesserrant de soie	24	24	rue du Temple, outside the walls	1300 f. 259v	Par. S.-Nicolas-des-Champs, 3		

Average tax 1297–1300: 66.8 deniers = 5.6 sous.

13/17 located in S1 = 76%.

0/17 located in S2 = 0%.

B. Women Cloth Weavers (Makers of Silk Head Coverings and Women Who "Carie Soie")

	Forename	Surname	Profession	Tax (in deniers)	Average Tax 1297–1300 (in deniers)	Street of Residence	Year/Folio	Parish/Quête	Location on Fig. 19 (S1/S2)	Location on Fig. 26 (SL/SJ)
1	Aalis		Qui fet cuevrechies de soie	24	NA	rue Neuve S. Merri	1292 f. 37	Par. S. Merri, 4	S1	SJ
2	Aveline		Qui karie soie	48/36	42	rue Quincampoix	1298 f. 135 1299 f. 190	Par. S. Merri, 4	S1	
3	Bienvenue		Qui fet cuevrechies de soie	36	36	rue des Rosiers	1299 f. 199v	Par. S. Gervais, 4		SJ

Appendix 3 (continued)

B. Women Cloth Weavers (Makers of Silk Head Coverings and Women Who "Carie Soie") (continued)

	Forename	Surname	Profession	Tax (in deniers)	Average Tax 1297–1300 (in deniers)	Street	Year/Folio[1]	Parish/Quête[2]	Location on Fig. 19 (S1/S2)	Location on Fig. 26 (SL/SJ)
4	Edeline		qui carie soie	24	24	rue du Temple, outside the walls	1300 f. 263v	Par. S. Merri, 3		SL
5	Erembourc		Qui fet cuevrechies de soie	24	24	rue Froit-Mantel	1299 f. 152v	Par. S.-Germain-l'Auxerrois, 1		SL
6	Houdee	de Fossez	Qui fet cuevrechies de soie	36	36	Grand Rue, outside the walls	1299 f. 177	Par. S.-Nicolas-des-Champs, 1		SL
7	Jehanne	Malfouee	Qui carie soie	36	36	rue Guillaume Joce	1299 f. 191v	Par. S.-Jacques-de-la-Boucherie, 1	S1	
8	Julienne		Qui fet couvrechies de soye	180	NA	rue des Rosiers	1313 f. 30v	Par. S. Gervais, 4		SJ
9	Lorence	d'Argent-ueil	Qui quarrie soie	36	36	rue Neuve S. Merri	1300 f. 265	Par. S. Merri, 4	S1	

Average tax 1297–1300: 33.4 deniers = 2.8 sous.
4/9 located in S1 = 44%; 0/9 located in S2 = 0%.

245

C. Weavers of "Tissulz de Soie"

	Forename	Surname	Tax (in deniers)	Average Tax 1297–1300 (in deniers)	Street of Residence	Year/Folio	Parish/Quête	Location on Fig. 19 (S1/S2)	Location on Fig. 26 (SL/SJ)
1	Aalis		18	NA	rue Geoffroi l'Angevin	1313 f. 22v	Par. S. Merri, 7		SJ
2	Aalis	d'Arches	0	NA	Court-Robert-de-Paris	1300 f. 304	Par. S. Merri, list of the dead	S1	SJ
3	Ade	de Saint Lo	24	24	Foulerie?	1300 f. 280v	Par. S. Paul (or S. Pôl), 1		
4	Agnes	de Biauvez	24	24	rue des Escoufles	1299 f. 200	Par. S. Gervais, 4		SJ
5	Climence	de Gornai	36	36	rue des Petits Champs	1297 f. 80v	Par. S. Merri, 4	S1	
6	Estienne		24	24	rue Espaulart	1298 f. 134v	Par. S. Merri, 3	S1	SJ
7	Estienne	de Fresnes	48	48	rue S. Martin	1300 f. 253	Par. S. Laurent		
8	Isabelot		24	24	rue Viez du Temple	1297 f. 87	Par. S. Paul (or S. Pôl), 2		SJ
9	Jacqueline	la Violete	24	24	rue de Biau-Bourc	1300 f. 263	Par. S. Merri, 3	S1	
10	Jehanne		24	24	rue des Arcis?	1298 f. 136	Par. S.-Jacques-de-la-Boucherie, 3	S1	
11	Liesse		36	36	rue de Tiron	1298 f. 141v	Par. S. Paul (or S. Pôl), 2		SJ
12	Marguerite		24	NA	rue de la Bretonnerie	1292 f. 54v	Par. S.-Jehan-en-Grève, 3		SJ

Appendix 3 (continued)

C. Weavers of "Tissulz de Soie" (continued)

	Forename	Surname	Tax (in deniers)	Average Tax 1297–1300 (in deniers)	Street of Residence	Year/Folio	Parish/Quête	Location on Fig. 19 (S1/S2)	Location on Fig. 26 (SL/SJ)
13	Marguerite		24	24	rue des Rosiers	1298 f. 138	Par. S. Gervais, 4		SJ
14	Marguerite	d'Andainne	24	24	rue Geoffroi l'Angevin	1299 f. 186	Par. S. Merri, 3		SJ
15	Marie		24	24	rue Vernueil	1298 f. 127	Par. S. Eustache (or Huitace), 1		SL
16	Marie	d'Arraz	24	24	rue des Prescheurs	1299 f. 169v	Par. S. Eustache (or Huitace), 4		SL
17	Marie	la Beguine	240	240	rue de la Bretonnerie	1300 f. 279	Par. S. Jehan-en-Grève, 3		SJ
18	Marie	la Toutainne	36	36	rue Quincampoix	1300 f. 259	Par. S.-Nicolas-des-Champs, 2	S1	
19	Marote	de Laigni	24	24	rue de la Bretonnerie	1297 f. 8v	Par. S.-Jehan-en-Grève, 3		SJ
20	Pentecoust		12	NA	rue Col-de-Bacon	1292 f. 6v	Par. S.-Germain-l'Auxerrois, 2		SL
21	Perrenele	de Lymesis	24	24	rue des Poulies	1298 f. 124v	Par. S.-Germain-l'Auxerrois, 2		SL

22	Perrenele		30	30	rue du Cimetière S. Nicolas	1298 f. 13v	Par. S.-Nicolas-des-Champs, 1	
23	Sedile	de Meleun	24	24	rue Pierre Sarrazin	1300 f. 293	Par. S. Benoît, 1	
24	Supplice		24	24	rue des Petits Champs	1300 f. 265v	Par. S. Merri, 4	S1

All of the weavers listed are women except, possibly, the two named "Estienne."

Average tax 1297–1300: 38 deniers = 3.2 sous.

7/24 located in S1 = 29%; 0/24 located in S2 = 0%.

11/24 located in SJ = 46%; 4/24 located in SL = 17%.

D. Weavers of Ribbons and Laces: "Dorelotiers," Makers of "Lacets de Soie"

Forename	Surname	Profession	Tax (in deniers)	Average Tax 1297–1300 (in deniers)	Street	Year/Folio	Parish/Quête	Location on Fig. 19 (S1/S2)	Location on Fig. 26 (SL/SJ)
1	Aalis		la dorelotiere	24	24		1298 f. 126v	Par. S. Eustache (or Huitace), 1		SL
2	Alain		le dorelotier	24	NA	rue Guérin-Boucel	1292 f. 27v	Par. S.-Nicolas-des-Champs, 1		
3	Ameline		qui fet laz	24	NA	rue Geoffroi l'Angevin	1292 f. 35v	Par. S. Merri, 3		SJ

Appendix 3 (continued)

D. Weavers of Ribbons and Laces: "Dorelotiers," Makers of "Lacets de Soie" (continued)

	Forename	Surname	Profession	Tax (in deniers)	Average Tax 1297–1300 (in deniers)	Street	Year/Folio	Parish/Quête	Location on Fig. 19 (S1/S2)	Location on Fig. 26 (SL/SJ)
4	Ameline	la Panetiere	fet laz de soie	72	72	rue de Biau-Bourc	1300 f. 263	Par. S. Merri, 3	S1	SJ
5	Edeline		fet les laz	12	NA	rue Geoffroi l'Angevin	1292 f. 35	Par. S. Merri, 3		SJ
6	Geoffroi		le dorelotier	36	NA	la rue Percée	1292 f. 22	Par. S. Sauveur		
7	Gile		qui fet laz de soie	84	NA	rue de la Hyaumerie	1296 f. 18v	Par. S.-Jacques-de-la-Boucherie, 2	S1	
8	Guiart		qui fait laz a chapiaus	36	36	rue Geoffroi l'Angevin	1300 f. 263	Par. S. Merri, 3		SJ
9	Guillaume	de Corbueil	dorelotier	192 192 192 144 1080	176	rue Quincampoix	1292 f. 38 1298 f. 112v 1299 f. 181v 1300 f. 259 1313 f. 18v	Par. S. Merri, 4	S1	

No	First name	Surname	Occupation			Location	References	Parish		SL
10	Guillaume	des Isles	dorelotier	24 24 42 60	37.5	Grand Rue, outside the walls	1297 f. 76 1298 f. 130v 1299 f. 177 1300 f. 254v 1300 f. 305	Par. S.-Nicolas-des-champs, 1		SL
11	Guillaume		le dorelotier	1104	NA	rue de la Chanverrie	1292 f. 20	Par. S. Eustache (or Huitace), 2		SL
12	Guillaume		le dorelotier	96	NA	rue Saint Sauveur	1296 f. 11v	Par. S. Sauveur		
13	Guillaume		le dorelotier	360	NA	corner of la Coçonnerie	1313 f. 11	Par. S. Eustache (or Huitace), 4	S1	SL
14	Hermant		le dorelotier	144 144 144 144	144	Grand Rue, outside the walls	1292 f. 21v 1296 f. 11v 1297 f. 45 1298 f. 105	Par. S. Sauveur		SL
15	Huchon		le dorelotier	24	NA	Grand Rue, outside the walls	1292 f. 26	Par. S. Laurent		
16	Hue		le dorelotier	24	NA	rue S. Sauveur	1292 f. 21v 1300 f. 305	Par. S. Sauveur		
17	Hue		le dorelotier	36	36	rue Darne-Estat	1297 f. 76 1298 f. 130	Par. S. Laurent		

Appendix 3 (continued)

D. Weavers of Ribbons and Laces: "Dorelotiers," Makers of "Lacets de Soie" (continued)

	Forename	Surname	Profession	Tax (in deniers)	Average Tax 1297–1300 (in deniers)	Street	Year/Folio	Parish/Quête	Location on Fig. 19 (S1/S2)	Location on Fig. 26 (SL/SJ)
18	Jacques	Rigolet	dorelotier	72 36	54	rue au Lyon	1298 f. 105v 1299 f. 170v	Par. S. Sauveur		SL
19	Jehan	Bon Baron	dorelotier	24	24	rue au Lyon	1298 f. 129	Par. S. Sauveur		SL
20	Jehan		le dorelotier	84	84	rue S. Martin	1300 f. 253	Par. Laurent		
21	Jehan		le dorelotier	24	24	Grant or Petit Marivas	1300 f. 270v	Par. S.-Jacques-de-la-Boucherie, 3	S1	
22	Jehan	le Picart	dorelotier	96	96	rue de Hue-Leu	1298 f. 107v	Par. S. Laurent		
23	Jehan		le dorelotier	24	NA	rue du Bourc-l'Abbé	1292 f. 24	Par. S.-Leu-S.-Gilles		SL
24	Jehanne		qui fet laz de soie	24		rue S. Honoré, outside the walls	1300 f. 231	Par. S.-Germain-l'Auxerrois, 1		SL

25	Jehanne		la dorelotier	24	24	Grand Rue, outside the walls	1298 f. 128v 1299 f. 170v 1300 f. 248v	Par. S. Sauveur		SL
26	Jehannette	la Fourniere	fet laz	36	36	la Hyaumerie	1300 f. 269v	Par. S.-Jacques-de-la-Boucherie, 2	Si	
27	Lorence	d'Arraz	qui fet laz a chapiaus	24	24	Grand Rue, between rue au Fuerre and la Truanderie	1299 f. 168	Par. S. Eustache (or Huitace), 4	Si	SL
28	Mahaut	de Serains/de Serains	qui fet les laz	48 36	42	rue aux Jongleurs	1299 f. 175 1300 f. 253	Par. S. Josse	Si	
29	Mahaut		qui fait lacets	24	NA	rue Cul-de-Sac	1292 f. 35	Par. S. Merri, 3		
30	Marie		la dorelotier	696 696 744 744 744	732	rue de la Chanverrie	1296 f. 11 1297 f. 45 1298 f. 105 1299 f. 170 1300 f. 248	Par. S. Eustache (or Huitace), 4	Si	SL
31	Nicolas		le dorelotier	36	NA	rue du Grenier S. Lazare (or Guernier de S. Ladre)	1313 f. 16v	Par. S.-Nicolas-des-Champs, 1		SL
32	Perronnele		la laciere	24	NA	rue Neuve S. Merri	1292 f. 35v	Par. S. Merri, 3	Possibly Si	Possibly SJ

Appendix 3 (continued)

D. Weavers of Ribbons and Laces: "Dorelotiers," Makers of "Lacets de Soie" (continued)

	Forename	Surname	Profession	Tax (in deniers)	Average Tax 1297–1300 (in deniers)	Street	Year/Folio	Parish/Quête	Location on Fig. 19 (S1/S2)	Location on Fig. 26 (SL/SJ)
33	Pierre	de Barevile	dorelotier	48	48	rue Auberi-le-Bouchier	1300 f. 251	Par. S.-Leu-S.-Gilles	S1	
34	Pierre	de Taverni	dorelotier	240	240	rue Quincampoix	1300 f. 259	Par. S.-Nicolas-des-Champs, 2	S1	
35	Raoul	le Cordier	qui fait lacets	0	NA	rue du Bourc-l'Abbé	1300 f. 303[7]	Par. S.-Leu-S.-Gilles		SL
36	Raoul		le dorelotier	24	24	rue du Temple, outside the walls	1297 f. 77	Par. S.-Nicolas-des-Champs, 1		
37	Raoul		le dorelotier	72	NA	Grand Rue, outside the walls	1313 f. 15v	Par. S. Laurent		
38	Richart		le dorelotier	24	24	rue Sans Chief	1297 f. 86	Par. S. Paul (or S. Pôl), 1		
39	Richart		le dorelotier	84 180	84	Grand Rue, outside the walls	1299 f. 177 1313 f. 16	Par. S.-Nicolas-des-Champs, 1		SL

40	Richart		le dorelotier	18	NA	Grand Rue, outside the walls	1313 f. 16	Par. S.-Nicolas-des-Champs, 1		SL
41	Richart		le dorelotier	24 36	30	rue S. Martin, outside the walls	1299 f. 177 1300 f. 254v	Par. S.-Nicolas-des-Champs, 1		SL
42	Richart		le laceur	72	72	Grand Rue (Sellerie)	1300 f. 268v	Par. S.-Jacques-de-la-Boucherie, 2	S1	
43	Richeut		fet les laz	60	NA	rue de la Courroierie	1292 f. 40	Par. S.-Jacques-de-la-Boucherie, 1	S1	
44	Richeut		la lacerresse	120	NA	near rue Auberi-le-Bouchier	1292 f. 39v	Par. S.-Jacques-de-la-Boucherie, 1	S1	
45	Robert	Bon Baton	dorelotier	60	60	rue Quincampoix	1300 f. 268v	Par. S.-Jacques-de-la-Boucherie, 1	S1	
46	Robert		le dorelotier	48	NA	rue au Lyon	1292 f. 22v	Par. S. Sauveur		SL
47	Robert		le dorelotier	12 24	24	rue Pavée	1292 f. 22 1299 f. 171	Par. S. Sauveur		SL
48	Robert		le dorelotier	96 96 96 72	88	rue Quincampoix	1296 f. 13 1297 f. 46v 1298 f. 107 1299 f. 175	Par. S. Josse	S1	
49	Robin	Billart	le dorelotier	60	60	rue Frépillon	1300 f. 256	Par. S.-Nicolas-des-Champs, 1		

Appendix 3 (continued)

D. Weavers of Ribbons and Laces: "Dorelotiers," Makers of "Lacets de Soie" (continued)

	Forename	Surname	Profession	Tax (in deniers)	Average Tax 1297–1300 (in deniers)	Street	Year/Folio	Parish/Quête	Location on Fig. 19 (S1/S2)	Location on Fig. 26 (SL/SJ)
50	Salemon		le dorelotier	96 24	24	Grand Rue, outside the walls	1292 f. 27 1297 f. 76	Par. S.-Nicolas-des-Champs, 1		SL
51	Symon	Muriel	dorelotier	66	NA	rue de. Néele	1313 f. 8v	Par. S. Eustache (or Huitace), 1		SL
52	Thomas	Baron	dorelotier	0	NA	list of the dead	1313 f. 48v	?		
53	Thomas		le dorelotier	240 900 900	900	Grand Rue	1292 f. 20 1298 f. 104 1299 f. 168	Par. S. Eustache (or Huitace), 2, 4	S1	SL
54	Thomas		le dorelotier	36 24	24	rue Pavée	1292 f. 22 1297 f. 74	Par. S. Sauveur		SL

Weavers of ribbons and laces (13F/41M):
Average tax 1297–1300: 109 deniers = 9 sous.
17–18/54 in S1 = 31–33%; 0 in S2 = 0%.

1. Folio number references are to folio numbers in the original manuscripts of the 7 Parisian tax assessments (1292, 1296, 1297, 1298, 1299, 1300, 1313). For the 1292 tax assessment readers can consult the 1991 revised edition of Géraud, and for the 1296, 1297, and 1313 assessments, readers can consult Michaëlsson's editions: all four of these editions provide folio numbers in the margins. The assessments of 1298–1300 remain unpublished in AN KK 283.

2. For the purposes of the tax assessments, larger parishes were divided into different "quêtes." I give the numbers of the quêtes because they are useful for narrowing down the physical location of taxpayers. For a map of the various parishes and quêtes in 1300, see Bourlet and Bethe, "Création des plans," 163. This map is also available on the Alpage website: http://alpage.huma-num.fr/documents/Illustration_colloque/BOURLET_Paroisses_1300.pdf (accessed September 9, 2015).

3. Identified in 1299 as the brother of Robert du Vergier, who was also a silk weaver. He (and his brother) were also close neighbors of Jacquet de Venyse; see main text of Chapter 3, discussion preceding note 112.

4. Identified as an "ouvrier de soie" in 1298 and 1299.

5. Second listing in 1300 is the list of those who died. In 1299, and for the first listing in 1300, Guillaume was not given a surname, but the address was the same as the 1297 and 1298 listings.

6. 1300 entry is on the list of the dead.

7. List of the dead.

Appendix 4. Silk Throwsters in the Parisian Tax Assessments

	Forename	Surname	Tax (in deniers)	Average Tax 1297–1300 (in deniers)	Street	Year/Folio[1]	Parish/Quête[2]	Location on Fig. 19 (S1/S2)	Location on Fig. 26 (SL/SJ)
1	Aalis		24	24	rue des Escouffles	1298 f. 138	Par. S. Gervais, 4		SJ
2	Dame Aalis		48	48	rue S. Martin	1300 f. 265v	Par. S. Merri, 4	S1	SJ
3	Aalis	de Louviaus	60	60	rue de la Petite Bouclerie	1297 f. 80v	Par. S. Merri, 4	S1	SJ
4	Aalis	de Louviers	24	24	rue Jehan Tyson	1299 f. 154v	Par. S.-Germain-l'Auxerrois, 2		SL
5	Aalis	la Sarradine	18	NA	rue Symon le Franc	1313 f. 21v	Par. S. Merri, 6		SJ
6	Ade	de Senliz	0	NA	rue de Richebourc	1300 f. 231v	Par. S.-Germain-l'Auxerrois, 1		SL
7	Adeline	de Domont	36	36	rue Espaulart	1300 f. 264v	Par. S. Merri, 3	S1	SJ
8	Adeline	la Beguine	24	24	porte du Temple	1300 f. 258	Par. S.-Nicolas-des-Champs, 2		SL
9	Agnes	de Pertes/Portes	96	96	rue des Petits Champs	1299 f. 189 / 1300 f. 265v	Par. S. Merri, 4	S1	

10	Agnes	la Paumiere (or no surname)	12 48 36	48	rue Geoffroi l'Angevin	1292 f. 35 1298 f. 134 1313 f. 22v	Par. S. Merri, 3		SJ
11	Dame Agnes	la Sonneite	120	120	rue de Frépillon	1297 f. 47v	Par. S.-Nicolas-des-Champs, 1		
12	Aleinete		22	NA	rue de Richebourc	1313 f. 1v	Par. S.-Germain-l'Auxerrois, 1		SL
13	Ameline		36	36	rue Quincampoix	1300 f. 266v	Par. S. Merri, 4	Si	
14	Ameline		72	72		1299 f. 164v 1300 f. 243	Par. S. Eustache (or Huitace), 1		SL
15	Ameline		24	NA	rue Neuve S.Merri	1292 f. 35v	Par. S. Merri, 3	Si	SJ
16	Ameline		24	24	rue de Biau-bourc	1298 f. 133v	Par. S. Merri, 3	Si	
17	Ameline	de Corbuel	48	48	rue du Temple	1298 f. 134 1299 f. 187	Par. S. Merri, 3		SJ
18	Ameline	de Macy	72	72	rue d'Averon	1298 f. 98	Par. S.-Germain-l'Auxerrois, 2		SL
19	Ameline	la Beguine	72	72	rue Pierre Sarrazin	1299 f. 221	Par. S. Benoît, 1		
20	Ameline	la Pourverse	36	36	rue Jehan Tyson	1300 f. 233v	Par. S.-Germain-l'Auxerrois, 2		SL

Appendix 4 (continued)

	Forename	Surname	Tax (in deniers)	Average Tax 1297–1300 (in deniers)	Street	Year/Folio[1]	Parish/Quête[2]	Location on Fig. 19 (S1/S2)	Location on Fig. 26 (SL/SJ)
21	Ameline	l'Aguerrie	36	36	rue des Cordeliers	1299 f. 220v	Par. S. Cosme		
22	Amelot (or Emelot)		24	NA	rue du Perron	1292 f. 76v	Bourg S.-Germain-des-Prés		
23	anonymous		24	24	rue de la Petite Bouclerie	1299 f. 188v	Par. S. Merri, 4	S1	SJ
24	Avice		24	24	rue des Escoufles	1298 f. 138	Par. S. Gervais, 4		SJ
25	Avicette		24	24	rue du Temple, outside the walls	1298 f. 109v 1299 f. 182v	Par. S.-Nicolas-des-Champs, 3		SL
26	Basile/Basilette	la Beguine	48 36	42	rue Quincampoix	1299 f. 181v 1300 f. 259	Par. S.-Nicolas-des-Champs, 2	S1	
27	Climence	de Plailly	24	24	rue des Petits Champs	1299 f. 188v	Par. S. Merri, 4	S1	
28	Colette		36	36	rue des Blancs Manteaux	1300 f. 279	Par. S.-Jehan-en-Grève, 3		SJ
29	Erembourc	la Bourgoigne	18	NA	ruelle des Planches Mibray?	1313 f. 36v	Par. S.-Denis-de-la-Chartre	S2	

30	Ermenjart	de Chevreuse	72	72	rue Raoul Roissel	1299 f. 165 1300 f. 243v	Par. S. Eustache (or Huitace), 1		SL
31	Eustache (or Huitace)		24	24	rue des Petits Champs	1298 f. 135	Par. S. Merri, 4	Si	
32	Geneviève		24	24	rue des Augustins, outside the walls	1297 f. 71v	Par. S. Eustache (or Huitace), 1		
33	Geneviève	de Meudon	24	24	rue de la Petite Bouclerie	1297 f. 79v 1298 f. 133v	Par. S. Merri, 3	Si	SJ
34	Gile		24	24	rue Symon le Franc	1300 f. 264v	Par. S. Merri, 3	Si	SJ
35	Gile	de Galardon	72	72	rue des Cordeliers	1299 f. 220v	Par. S. Cosme		
36	Gile	de Louvres	24	24	rue Où l'en Cuist les Oës	1299 f. 174v	Par. S.-Leu-S.-Gilles	Si	SL
37	Gile	de Saint Denys	60	60	rue S. Martin, outside the walls	1300 f. 255	Par. S.-Nicolas-des-Champs, 1		SL
38	Guillemete		24	NA	rue de Frépillon	1292 f. 28v	Par. S.-Nicolas-des-Champs, 1		
39	Houdée		24	24	rue S. Martin	1298 f. 135	Par. S. Merri, 4	Si	SJ
40	Houdée		24	24	rue du Cimetière S. Nicolas	1300 f. 257	Par. S.-Nicolas-des-Champs, 1		
41	Isabel[3]		24 36	30	near Porte au Coquilliers	1299 f. 164v 1300 f. 243v	Par. S. Eustache (or Huitace), 1		SL

Appendix 4 (continued)

	Forename	Surname	Tax (in deniers)	Average Tax 1297–1300 (in deniers)	Street	Year/Folio[1]	Parish/Quête[2]	Location on Fig. 19 (S1/S2)	Location on Fig. 26 (SL/SJ)
42	Isabel		24	24	rue et ruelle S.Bon	1298 f. 132v	Par. S. Merri, 1	S1	
43	Isabel		36	36	rue de Frépillon	1297 f. 77	Par. S.-Nicolas-des-Champs, 1		
44	Isabel		60	60	rue des Gravilliers	1297 f. 77	Par. S.-Nicolas-des-Champs, 1		SL
45	Isabel		24	24	rue de Néelle	1300 f. 242v	Par. S. Eustache (or Huitace), 1		SL
46	Isabel	de Crespi	24 36	30	rue Chapon	1299 f. 179v 1300 f. 257	Par. S.-Nicolas-des-Champs, 1		SL
47	Dame Isabel	de Glatigni	36	36	rue Geoffroi l'Angevin	1300 f. 263	Par. S. Merri, 3		SJ
48	Isabel	de Lymueil	144	144	rue des Cordeliers	1299 f. 220v	Par. S. Cosme		
49	Dame Isabel	d'Oroër	480 504 744	576	rue du Temple	1297 f. 79v 1298 f. IIIv 1300 f. 263v	Par. S. Merri, 3		

50	Isabel	la Beguine	24	24	rue de Richebourc	1300 f. 231v	Par. S.-Germain-l'Auxerrois, 1		SL
51	Isabel	la Buschiere	24	24	rue des Gravilliers	1300 f. 256v	Par. S.-Nicolas-des-Champs, 1		SL
52	Isabel	la Rousse	36	36	rue du Bourc-l'Abbé	1299 f. 174	Par. S.-Leu-S.-Gilles	Sr	SL
53	Jehanne		24	24	rue d'Averon	1298 f. 124v	Par. S.-Germain-l'Auxerrois, 2		SL
54	Jehanne	(la Beguine)	60 / 24 / 18	42	rue du Temple	1297 f. 79v / 1298 f. 134 / 1313 f. 20v	Par. S. Merri, 3		SJ
55	Jehanne		24	24	rue de Frépillon	1300 f. 256v	Par. S.-Nicolas-des-Champs, 1		
56	Jehanne		108	NA	rue de la Croix du Tiroir	1313 f. 2	Par. S.-Germain-l'Auxerrois, 2		SL
57	Jehanne	Broche	24	24	rue Geoffroi l'Angevin	1298 f. 133v	Par. S. Merri, 3		SJ
58	Jehanne	de Bondies	24	24	rue Nicolas Arrode, outside walls	1297 f. 71v	Par. S. Eustache (or Huitace), 1		SL
59	Jehanne	Gorjon	120	NA	rue des Gravilliers	1296 f. 9v	Par. S.-Nicolas-des-Champs, 1		SL
60	Jehanne	la Beguine	24	24	rue des Cordeliers	1297 f. 91	Par. S. Cosme		

Appendix 4 (continued)

	Forename	Surname	Tax (in deniers)	Average Tax 1297–1300 (in deniers)	Street	Year/Folio[1]	Parish/Quête[2]	Location on Fig. 19 (S1/S2)	Location on Fig. 26 (SL/SJ)
61	Jehanne	la Cointe	24	24	Rue Traversaine	1299 f. 164v 1300 f. 243v	Par. S. Eustache (or Huitace), 2		SL
62	Jehanne	la converte/la coiffiere	72	72	rue du Temple	1298 f. 111v 1300 f. 304v	Par. S. Merri, 3		SJ
63	Jehanne	la Cordiere	24	24	Grand Rue, outside the walls	1300 f. 248v	Par. S. Sauveur		SL
64	Jehannette		24	24	rue Quincampoix	1297 f. 78	Par. S.-Nicolas-des-Champs, 2	S1	
65	Jehannette	la Boiteuse	36	36	rue des Cordeliers	1299 f. 220v	Par. S. Cosme		
66	Jehannette	la Parcheminiere	36	36	rue S. Martin	1300 f. 265v	Par. S. Merri, 4	S1	SJ
67	Juliane		72	NA	rue du Temple	1313 f. 20v	Par. S. Merri, 3		SJ
68	Julienne	la Françoise	24	24	rue du Grenier S. Lazare (or Guernier S. Ladre)	1299 f. 178	Par. S.-Nicolas-des-Champs, 1		SL

69	Juliote			24	Porte Monmartre	1298 f. 126v	Par. S. Eustache (or Huitace), 1		SL
70	Dame Lorence	la Beguine	24	24	rue de la Petite Bouclerie	1299 f. 188v	Par. S. Merri, 4	S1	SJ
71	Lorence		24	24	rue du Temple	1299 f. 186v	Par. S. Merri, 4		SJ
72	Lorence	de Lyle	36	36	rue de la Mortellerie	1299 f. 198	Par. S. Gervais, 2		
73	Liesse		42	42	rue Pastourelle	1298 f. 109v	Par. S.-Nicolas-des-Champs, 3		
74	Mahaut[4]	la Beguine	96 72	84	rue des Cordeliers	1297 f. 64v 1300 f. 292v	Par. S. Cosme		
75	Mahaut	aus Cholez[5]	192	192	rue des Cordeliers	1299 f. 220v 1300 f. 292v	Par. S. Cosme		
76	Mahaut		24	NA	rue du Bourc-l'Abbé	1292 f. 24	Par. S.-Leu-S.-Gilles	S1	SL
77	Marguerot		12	NA	rue Symon le Franc	1292 f. 29v	Par. S.-Nicolas-des-Champs, 2	S1	SJ
78	Marie	de Gatinais	24	24	rue Pavée	1299 f. 224	Par. S.-Geneviève-du-Mont, 1	S2	
79	Nicole		72	72	near rue du Four	1299 f. 164 1300 f. 243	Par. S. Eustache (or S. Huitace), 1		SL

Appendix 4 (continued)

	Forename	Surname	Tax (in deniers)	Average Tax 1297–1300 (in deniers)	Street	Year/Folio[1]	Parish/Quête[2]	Location on Fig. 19 (S1/S2)	Location on Fig. 26 (SL/SJ)
80	Nicole	l'Aumosniere	36	36	rue du Temple	1299 f.187	Par. S. Merri, 3		SJ
81	Odierne		36	36	rue Espaulart	1299 f. 188	Par. S. Merri, 3	S1	SJ
82	Perrenele		24	34	rue de Biau-bourc	1298 f. 133v	Par. S. Merri, 3	S1	SJ
83	Richeut	de Duigny	36	36	rue du Cimetière S. Nicolas	1299 f. 179v	Par. S.-Nicolas-des-Champs, 1		
84	Roberge		24	24	rue S. Denis, outside the walls	1300 f. 254v	Par. S.-Nicolas-des-Champs, 1		SL
85	Roberge		24	24	rue de la Plastriere	1300 f. 242	Par. S. Eustache (or Huitace), 1		SL
86	Sebile		36	36	rue du Cimetière S. Nicolas	1300 f. 257	Par. S.-Nicolas-des-Champs, 1		
87	Sedile		24 / 36	30	rue des Blancs Manteaux	1298 f. 139v / 1300 f. 256v	Par. S.-Jehan-en-Grève, 3		SJ
88	Sedile	de Sans	30 / 36	33	rue des Gravilliers	1299 f. 179 / 1300 f. 256v	Par. S.-Nicolas-des-Champs, 1		SL
89	Sedile	l'Engleiche	24 / 96	60	rue des Gravilliers	1297 f. 77 / 1300 f. 256v	Par. S.-Nicolas-des-Champs, 1		SL

90	Sevestre		24	24	rue du Clos Bruneau	1300 f. 297	Par. S.-Geneviève-du-Mont, 2	
91	Thiece		30	NA	rue de Champ-Fleuri	1313 f. 1v	Par. S.-Germain-l'Auxerrois, 1	SL
92	Thomasse[6]	du Vergier	72	72	rue Quincampoix	1298 f. 109	Par. S.-Nicolas-des-Champs, 2	S1
93	Thomasse	la Beguine	120 / 96	108	rue des Cordeliers	1297 f. 64v / 1300 f. 292v	Par. S. Cosme	

Average tax 1297–1300: 49.3 deniers = 4.1 sous.
Throwsters residing in S1 = 25/93 = 27%.
Throwsters residing in S2 = 2/93 = 2%.
Throwsters residing in SJ = 27/93 = 29%.
Throwsters residing in SL = 33/93 = 35%.

1. Folio number references are to folio numbers in the original manuscripts of the 7 Parisian tax assessments (1292, 1296, 1297, 1298, 1299, 1300, 1313). For the 1292 tax assessment readers can consult the 1991 revised edition of Géraud, and for the 1296, 1297, and 1313 assessments, readers can consult Michaëlsson's editions: all four of these editions provide folio numbers in the margins. The assessments of 1298–1300 remain unpublished in AN KK 283.

2. For the purposes of the tax assessments, larger parishes were divided into different "quêtes." I give the numbers of the quêtes because they are useful for narrowing down the physical location of taxpayers. For a map of the various parishes and quêtes in 1300, see Bourlet and Bethe, "Création des plans," 163. This map is also available on the Alpage website: http://alpage.huma-num.fr/documents/Illustration_colloque/BOURLET_Paroisses_1300.pdf (accessed September 9, 2015).

3. Variations on this name include Ysabel, Isabiau, and Ysabiau.

4. Identified simply as "Mahaut fileresse de soie" in 1300.

5. Identified as "ouvrière de soie" in 1300.

6. Probably related to Guillaume and Robert du Vergier, who made cloth of gold; and possibly identical with Thomasse du Jardin, ouvrière de soie: Appendix 3, part A, nos. 8, 16; Appendix 5, no. 114 (Vergier could mean "orchard").

Appendix 5. *Ouvriers/Ouvrières de Soie* in the Parisian Tax Assessments

	Forename	Surname	Profession	Tax (in deniers)	Average Tax 1297–1300 (in deniers)	Street	Year/Folio[1]	Parish/Quête[2]	Location on Fig. 19 (S1/S2)	Location on Fig. 26 (SJ/SL)
1	Guillaume	le Breton[3]	ouvrier de soie	24	24	rue du Roi-de-Cézile (Sicile)	1300 f. 275v	Par. S. Gervais, 4		SJ
2	Guillaume[4]	Viel	ouvrier de soie; purse maker	24	24	rue de Bière	1297 f. 81 1298 f. 135	Par. S. Merri, 4	S1	
3	Jehan	de Crosettes	ouvrier de soie; maker (i.e., weaver) of "draps de soie"	30 24	27	rue du Fossez S. Germain	1298 f. 124v 1299 f. 154	Par. S.-Germain-l'Auxerrois, 2		SL
4	Vincent	de Gonnesse	ouvrier de soie	72	72	rue Viez du Temple, outside the walls	1300 f. 275v	Par. S. Gervais, 4		
5	Yvonnet	le Breton	ouvrier de soie	24	24	rue et ruelle S. Bon	1300 f. 261	Par. S. Merri, 1	S1	
6	Aalis	de Chanevieres	ouvrière de soie	72	72	rue du Temple, outside the walls	1298 f. 111v	Par. S. Merri, 3		SL
7	Aalis	de Monz	ouvrière de soie; mercer	96 120	108	rue des Marmousez	1297 f. 61v 1298 f. 122	Par. S.-Pierre-aux-Boeufs	S2	

8	**Aalis**	**de Saint Joce**	**ouvrière de soie; purse maker**	288 / 288	288	rue Guillaume Bourdon	1298 f. 99 / 1299 f. 156v	Par. S.-Germain-l'Auxerrois, 3		SL
9	Aalis	de Vile-le-Roy	ouvrière de soie	24	24	rue Trousse-Nonnains, near rue Frépillon	1299 f. 180	Par. S.-Nicolas-des-Champs, 1		
10	Aalis	la Maçonne	ouvrière de soie	24 / 72 / 72	56	rue S. Martin	1297 f. 80v / 1299 f. 175v / 1300 f. 253	Par. S. Laurent	S1	SJ
11	Aalis	l'Englaiche	ouvrière de soie	24	24	rue Quincampoix	1300 f. 259	Par. S.-Nicolas-des-Champs, 2	S1	
12	Dame Ade		ouvrière de soie	24	24	rue de l'Hirondelle	1300 f. 292v	Par. S.-André-des-Arts	S2	
13	Adeline		ouvrière de soie	720	NA	?	1296 f. 28	Par. S.-Geneviève-des-Ardents	S2	
14	Adeline	de Mauregart	ouvrière de soie	36	36	rue des Cordeliers	1300 f. 292v	Par. S. Cosme		
15	Adeline	d'Orliens	ouvrière de soie	24	24	rue du Grenier S. Lazare (or Guernier de S. Ladre)	1300 f. 255v	Par. S.-Nicolas-des-Champs, 1		SL
16	**Agnes**	**de Biauvez**	**ouvrière de soie; maker of tissu de soie**	24 / 36	30	rue des Escoufles	1299 f. 200 / 1300 f. 276v	Par. S. Gervais, 4		SJ

Appendix 5 (continued)

	Forename	Surname	Profession	Tax (in deniers)	Average Tax 1297–1300 (in deniers)	Street	Year/Folio[1]	Parish/Quête[2]	Location on Fig. 19 (S1/S2)	Location on Fig. 26 (SJ/SL)
17	Agnes	de la Cele	ouvrière de soie	96	96	rue Guillaume Joce	1298 f. 114; 1299 f. 191v	Par. S.-Jacques-de-la-Boucherie, 1	S1	
18	**Agnes**	**de Pertes**	**ouvrière de soie; fileresse de soie**	96 72 96 96	90	rue des Petits Champs	1297 f. 51; 1298 f. 112; 1299 f. 189; 1300 f. 265v	Par. S. Merri, 4	S1	
19	Agnes	de Venyse	ouvrière de soie	96 24	60	rue Mau-conseil	1299 f. 167; 1300 f. 245v	Par. S. Eustache (or Huitace), 3	S1	SL
20	Agnes	la Charpentiere	ouvrière de soie	24	24	rue Espaulart	1298 f. 134v	Par. S. Merri, 3	S1	SJ
21	Agnes	le Moi	ouvrière de soie	84	84	rue des Poulies	1299 f. 154v	Par. S.-Germain-l'Auxerrois, 2		SL
22	Agnesot		ouvrière de soie	24	NA	Grant or Petit Marivas	1292 f. 41v	Par. S.-Jacques-de-la-Boucherie, 2	S1	
23	Alison		ouvrière de soie	12	NA	rue Mau-Conseil	1292 f. 3v	Par. S. Eustache (or Huitace)	S1	SL

24	Ameline	de la Porte	ouvrière de soie	96	96	rue Pierre-au-Lart	1300 f. 264v	Par. S. Merri, 3	SI	SJ
25	**Ameline**	**de Macy**	**ouvrière de soie; fileresse de soie**	36 72 60	56	rue d'Averon	1299 f. 154v 1298 f. 98 1300 f. 233v	Par. S.-Germain-l'Auxerrois, 2		SL
26	Ameline	de Plailli	ouvrière de soie	24	24	rue Viez du Temple	1299 f. 206	Par. S. Paul (or S. Pôl), 2		SJ
27	Ameline	de Rueul	ouvrière de soie	24	24	rue de la Petite Bouclerie	1298 f. 133v	Par. S. Merri, 3	SI	SJ
28	Amice		ouvrière de soie	24	24	rue du Roi-de-Cézile (Sicile)	1299 f. 199	Par. S. Gervais, 4		SJ
29	anonymous		ouvrière de soie	24	24	rue Frogier l'Asnier	1299 f. 198v	Par. S. Gervais, 2		
30	anonymous		ouvrière de soie	24	24	rue Alexandre l'Anglais	1298 f. 147	Par. S.-Geneviève-du-mont, 1		
31	anonymous		ouvrière de soie	108	108	rue du Temple, outside the walls	1300 f. 260	Par. S.-Nicolas-des-Champs, 3		SL
32	Auberée	la Cristaliere	ouvrière de soie	24	24	rue Pierre-au-Lart	1300 f. 264v	Par. S. Merri, 3	SI	SJ
33	Aveline	de Brie	ouvrière de soie	24	24	rue de Frépillon	1299 f. 178v	Par. S.-Nicolas-des-Champs, 1		SJ

Appendix 5 (continued)

	Forename	Surname	Profession	Tax (in deniers)	Average Tax 1297–1300 (in deniers)	Street	Year/Folio[1]	Parish/Quête[2]	Location on Fig. 19 (S1/S2)	Location on Fig. 26 (SJ/SL)
34	Avice		ouvrière de soie	72	72	rue de la Porte Baudéer	1298 f. 120	Par. S. Paul (or S. Pôl), 2		SJ
35	Basile		ouvrière de soie	120	120	rue des Gravilliers	1299 f. 179	Par. S.-Nicolas-des-Champs, 1		SL
36	Bietriz		ouvrière de soie	24	24	rue Frogier l'Asnier	1299 f. 198v	Par. S. Gervais, 2		
37	Bietriz	la Champenaise	ouvrière de soie	24	24	rue du Fauconnier	1300 f. 280v	Par. S. Paul (or S. Pôl), 1		
38	Benoite	la Beguine	ouvrière de soie	108 72 72	72	rue des Gravilliers	1296 f. 9 1298 f. 179 1300 f. 256v	Par. S.-Nicolas-des-Champs, 1		SL
39	Cateline		ouvrière de soie	60	NA	rue S. Martin	1292 f. 23v	Par. S.-Leu-S.-Gilles	S1	SJ
40	Catherine		ouvrière de soie	24	24	rue de la Petite Bouclerie	1300 f. 262v	Par. S. Merri, 3	S1	SJ
41	Chrétienne		ouvrière de soie	24	24	Grant or Petit Marivas	1298 f. 136	Par. S.-Jacques-de-la-Boucherie, 3	S1	

42	Climence	de Gornai	**ouvrière de soie; maker of tissu de soie**	36 72 48	52	rue des Petits Champs	1297 f. 80v 1299 f. 188v 1300 f. 265v	Par. S. Merri, 4	S1	
43	Climence	de Plailli	**ouvrière de soie; fileresse de soie**	24 60	42	rue des Petits Champs	1299 f. 188v 1300 f. 265v	Par. S. Merri, 4	S1	
44	Coleite		ouvrière de soie	24	24	rue de Gloriette	1297 f. 69v	Par. S.-Germain-l'Auxerrois, 3		SL
45	Denise	Cotele	ouvrière de soie	60	60	rue Chapon	1299 f. 179v 1300 f. 257	Par. S.-Nicolas-des-Champs, 1		SL
46	Erembourc	de Senliz	ouvrière de soie	60	60	rue du Viez Cimetière S. Jehan	1298 f. 139	Par. S.-Jehan-en-Grève, 2		
47	Erembourc	la Riaude	ouvrière de soie	96	96	rue de la Harpe	1299 f. 218	Par. S. Severin, 3	S2	
48	Ermanjart	Lanurée	ouvrière de soie	120	120	rue du Figuier	1300 f. 280v	Par. S. Paul (or S. Pôl), 1		
49	Eustache (or Huitace)	de Caan	**ouvrière de soie; fileresse de soie**	36	36	rue des Petits Champs	1297 f. 80v 1298 f. 135	Par. S. Merri, 4	S1	

Appendix 5 (continued)

	Forename	Surname	Profession	Tax (in deniers)	Average Tax 1297–1300 (in deniers)	Street	Year/ Folio[1]	Parish/Quête[2]	Location on Fig. 19 (S1/S2)	Location on Fig. 26 (SJ/SL)
50	**Flandrine**	**d'Amiens**[5]	**ouvrière de soie; mercer**	144	144	rue de la Calandre	1298 f. 122 1300 f. 285v	Par. S.-Germain-le-Vieux	S2	
51	Florence		ouvrière de soie	24	NA	rue de la Savonnerie	1292 f. 43	Par. S.-Jacques-de-la-Boucherie, 3		
52	**Genevieve**	**de Meudon**	**ouvrière de soie; fileresse de soie**	36 24 24	28	rue de la Petite Bouclerie	1297 f. 79v 1298 f. 133v 1300 f. 262v	Par. S. Merri, 3	S1	SJ
53	Genevieve	de Vanves	ouvrière de soie	72	72	rue du Paon	1299 f. 220v	Par. S. Cosme		
54	Dame Gile		ouvrière de soie	24	24	rue au Cerf	1297 f. 69v	Par. S.-Germain-l'Auxerrois, 3		SL
55	Gile		ouvrière de soie	48	48	rue de la Hyaumerie	1300 f. 269v	Par. S.-Jacques-de-la-Boucherie, 2	S1	
56	**Gile**	**de Bondies**	**ouvrière de soie; weaver**	288 24	156	rue de la Hyaumerie	1298 f. 118 1299 f. 193v	Par. S.-Jacques-de-la-Boucherie, 2	S1	

57	Goncelyne	la Poucarde	ouvrière de soie	120	120	rue du Temple	1298 f. IIIv	Par. S. Merri, 3		
58	Hellote	l'Englaiche	ouvrière de soie	36	36	rue S. Geneviève	1298 f. 147	Par. S.-Geneviève-du-Mont, 1		
59	Helloÿs	de Betisi	ouvrière de soie	60	60	rue du Temple hors les murs	1300 f. 259v	Par. S.-Nicolas-des-Champs, 3		SL
60	Helloÿs	d'Escan	ouvrière de soie	24	24	rue du Grenier S. Lazare (or Guernier de S. Ladre)	1299 f. 178	Par. S.-Nicolas-des-Champs, 1		SL
61	Helloÿs	la Normande	ouvrière de soie	24	24	rue Porte Foin	1300 d. 260	Par. S.-Nicolas-des-Champs, 3		
62	Isabel[6]	Alixandre	ouvrière de soie	24	24	rue Frépillon	1300 f. 256	Par. S.-Nicolas-des-Champs, 1		
63	**Isabel**	**de Glatigni**	**ouvrière de soie; fileresse de soie; silk dyer**	92 24 36	30	rue Geoffroi l'Angevin	1296 f. 15 1299 f. 186v 1300 f. 263	Par. S. Merri, 3		SJ
64	Jacqueline		ouvrière de soie	24	24	rue Jehan Palée	1298 f. 129v	Par. S.-Leu-S.-Gilles	Si	
65	Jacqueline		ouvrière de soie	0	NA	rue Hue-Leu (list of the dead)	1300 f. 303v	Par. S.-Leu-S.-Gilles		SL
66	Jacqueline		ouvrière de soie	24	NA	rue de la Croix du Tiroir	1292 f. 9	Par. S.-Germain-l'Auxerrois, 3		SL

Appendix 5 (continued)

	Forename	Surname	Profession	Tax (in deniers)	Average Tax 1297–1300 (in deniers)	Street	Year/ Folio[1]	Parish/Quête[2]	Location on Fig. 19 (S1/S2)	Location on Fig. 26 (SJ/SL)
67	Jacqueline	la Mau Petite	ouvrière de soie	120 96	108	rue du Grenier S. Lazare (or Guernier de S. Ladre)	1298 f. 178 1300 f. 255v	Par. S.-Nicolas-des-Champs, 1		SL
68	Jacquelot[7]		ouvrière de soie	36	36	rue des Escoufles	1300 f. 276v	Par. S. Gervais, 4		SJ
69	Jehanne		ouvrière de soie	24	24	rue Guillaume Bourdon	1298 f. 125	Par. S.-Germain-l'Auxerrois, 3		SL
70	Jehanne		ouvrière de soie	24	24	rue Jehan Pain-Mollet	1299 f. 183v	Par. S. Merri, 1	S1	
71	Jehanne		ouvrière de soie	96	96	rue du Temple, outside the walls	1299 f. 186v	Par. S. Merri, 3		SL
72	Jehanne	d'Arraz	ouvrière de soie	60	60	rue Tirechape	1297 f. 69v	Par. S.-Germain-l'Auxerrois, 3		SL
73	Jehanne	de Dangu	ouvrière de soie	24	24	rue Geoffroi l'Angevin	1298 f. 133v	Par. S. Merri, 3		SJ
74	Jehanne	de Galardon	ouvrière de soie	36	36	rue Pierre-au-Lart	1299 f. 187v	Par. S. Merri, 3	S1	SJ

#										
75	Jehanne	de Rueil	ouvrière de soie	24	24	rue d'Averon	1299 f. 154v	Par. S.-Germain-l'Auxerrois, 2		SL
76	Jehanne	la Beguine	ouvrière de soie	72	72	rue du Four?	1300 f. 243	Par. S. Eustache (or Huitace), 1		SL
77	Jehanne	la Beguine	ouvrière de soie	24	24	rue S. Estienne-des-Grés	1299 f. 222	Par. S. Benoît. 2		
78	Jehanne	la Cloatiere	ouvrière de soie	24	24	rue de la Barre-du-Bec	1298 f. 132v	Par. S. Merri, 2		SJ
79	Jehanne	la Fort	ouvrière de soie	24	24	rue Perronele de S.Pol	1299 f. 203v	Par. S.-Jehan-en-Grève, 3		SJ
80	Jehanne	la Fourniere	ouvrière de soie	24	24	Cour Pierre-la-Pie	1299 f. 193	Par. S.-Jacques-de-la-Boucherie, 2		
81	Jehanne	la Petite	ouvrière de soie	60	60	Porte du Temple	1300 f. 258	Par. S.-Nicolas-des-Champs, 2		SL
82	Jehanne/Jehannette	la Borgoigne	ouvrière de soie	84	NA	rue Neuve S. Merri	1292 f. 37 1296 f. 16	Par. S. Merri, 4	S1	SJ
83	Jehannete		ouvrière de soie	36	NA	rue Guillaume Bourdon	1292 f. 8	Par. S.-Germain-l'Auxerrois, 3		SL
84	Jehannette		ouvrière de soie	24	24	rue aux Fèves	1299 f. 211	Par. S.-Germain-le-Vieux	S2	
85	Jehannette		ouvrière de soie	24	24	rue Pierre-au-Lart?	1297 f. 82	Par. S.-Jacques-de-la-Boucherie, 3	S1	SJ

Appendix 5 (continued)

	Forename	Surname	Profession	Tax (in deniers)	Average Tax 1297–1300 (in deniers)	Street	Year/Folio[1]	Parish/Quête[2]	Location on Fig. 19 (S1/S2)	Location on Fig. 26 (SJ/SL)
86	Jehanne		ouvrière de soie	24	NA	rue de la Barillerie	1292 f. 60	Par. S. Barthelémy	S2	
87	Julienne	de Marli	ouvrière de soie	24	24	rue de Froit Mantel	1298 f. 124	Par. S.-Germain-l'Auxerrois, 1		SL
88	Mabile		ouvrière de soie	36	NA	rue S.-Germain-l'Auxerrois	1292 f. 12	Par. S.-Germain-l'Auxerrois, 4		SL
89	Mabile	de Monci	ouvrière de soie	24	24	rue de Gloriette	1298 f. 125	Par. S.-Germain-l'Auxerrois, 3		SL
90	Mabile	l'Escuiere	ouvrière de soie	84	84	rue des Gravilliers	1296 f. 9v	Par. S.-Nicolas-des-Champs, 1		SL
91	**Mahaut**	**aus Cholez**	**ouvrière de soie; fileresse de soie**	192	192	rue des Cordeliers	1299 f. 220v 1300 f. 292v	Par. S. Cosme		
92	Marguerite	de Gonsain vile	ouvrière de soie	36 48	48	rue de la Petite Bouclerie /Rosiers	1292 f. 37 1299 f. 199v	Par. S. Merri, 4; Par. S. Gervais, 4	S1 in 1292	SJ

93	Marguerite	de la Cele	ouvrière de soie	24	24	rue du Grenier S. Lazare (or Guernier de S. Ladre)	1300 f. 255v	Par. S.-Nicolas-des-Champs, 1		SL
94	Marguerite	de Limesus	ouvrière de soie	36	NA	rue Tirechape	1313 f. 3v	Par. S.-Germain-l'Auxerrois, 3		SL
95	Marguerite	la Paridane	ouvrière de soie	24	24	rue S. Geneviève	1298 f. 147	Par. S.-Geneviève-du-Mont, 1		
96	Marie		ouvrière de soie	24	24	Truanderie	1300 f. 246v	Par. S. Eustache (or Huitace), 4	S1	SL
97	Marie	de Laingni	ouvrière de soie	240	240	rue de la Bretonnerie	1299 f. 203	Par. S. Jehan-en-Grève		
98	Marie	des Cordeles	ouvrière de soie	72	72	rue Frépillon	1299 f. 178v 1300 f. 256	Par. S.-Nicolas-des-Champs, 1		
99	Marie	du Val	ouvrière de soie	24	24	rue Pierre-au-Lart	1298 f. 134v	Par. S. Merri, 3	S1	SJ
100	Marie	la Champenoise	ouvrière de soie	24	24	rue du Temple	1298 f. 134	Par. S. Merri, 3		
101	Dame Marie	la Coquesse	ouvrière de soie	240	240	rue Pierre-au-Lart	1300 f. 264v	Par. S. Merri, 3	S1	SJ
102	Martine		ouvrière de soie	24	24	rue Frogier l'Asnier	1298 f. 137v	Par. S. Gervais, 2		

Appendix 5 (continued)

	Forename	Surname	Profession	Tax (in deniers)	Average Tax 1297–1300 (in deniers)	Street	Year/ Folio[1]	Parish/Quête[2]	Location on Fig. 19 (S1/S2)	Location on Fig. 26 (SJ/SL)
103	Dame Nicole		ouvrière de soie	0	NA	list of the dead	1300 f. 303v	Par. S. Opportune	S1	
104	Nicole	de Traies/de Troyes	ouvrière de soie	144	144	Near rue du Four	1299 f. 164 1300 f. 243	Par. S. Eustache (or Huitace), 1		SL
105	Dame Odierne		ouvrière de soie	36	36	rue de la Viez Monnaie	1299 f. 193	Par. S.-Jacques-de-la-Boucherie, 2	S1	
106	Dame Odierne	de Roissy	ouvrière de soie	126	NA	rue du Figuier	1313 f. 33	Par. S. Paul (or S. Pôl), 1		
107	Dame Osane		ouvrière de soie	60	60		1300 f. 244	Par. S. Eustache (or Huitace), 2		SL
108	Perrenele	de Dammartin	ouvrière de soie	36	36	rue des Gravilliers	1299 f. 179	Par. S.-Nicolas-des-Champs, 1		SL
109	Perrenele	de Moisseles	ouvrière de soie	36	36	rue du Grenier S. Lazare (or Guernier de S. Lazare)	1300 f. 255v	Par. S.-Nicolas-des-Champs, 1		SL
110	Richelot	de Fontenay	ouvrière de soie	36	36	rue S. Martin	1298 f. 135	Par. S.-Jacques-de-la-Boucherie, 1	S1	SJ

111	Sabeline		ouvrière de soie	48	48	rue Chapon	1299 f. 179v	Par. S.-Nicolas-des-Champs, 1	SL
112	Sanceline		ouvrière de soie	36	36	rue de Gloriette	1297 f. 69v	Par. S.-Germain-l'Auxerrois, 3	SL
113	Sanceline	la Cosarde[8]	ouvrière de soie	192 24	108	rue du Temple, outside the walls	1299 f. 186v; 1300 f. 263v	Par. S. Merri, 3	
114	Thomasse	du Jardin[9]	ouvrière de soie	108	108	rue Quincampoix	1299 f. 182	Par. S.-Nicolas-des-Champs, 2	Si
115	Thomasse	la Beguine	ouvrière de soie	72	72	rue de la Barre-du-Bec	1298 f. 111	Par. S. Merri, 2	SJ
116	Thomasse	la Normande	ouvrière de soie	96	96	rue des Cordeliers	1299 d. 220v	Par. S. Cosme	
117	Thomasse	la Platriere	ouvrière de soie	24	24	rue Où l'en Cuist les Oës	1299 f. 174v	Par. S.-Leu-S.-Gilles	Si
118	Tyfainne		ouvrière de soie	24	NA	rue de Hosteriche	1292 f. 5	Par. S.-Germain-l'Auxerrois, 2	SL

Names in bold = individuals identified as "ouvriers"/"ouvrières de soie" in one tax assessment but with more specific professional identification/s in one or more other tax assessments. The first 5 individuals on the list were men; the rest were women.

118 ouvriers/ouvrières de soie (5 men/113 women).

Average tax 1297–1300: 57.5 deniers = 4.8 sous.

12 ouvrières (and 2 ouvriers) identified with at least one other profession in another tax assessment. 7 of those 12 ouvrières (58.33%) = throwsters; thus an estimated 58.33% of the 113 ouvrières (66 ouvrières) were probably throwsters. 2 of the 12 (16.66%) = weavers of tissu de soie; thus an estimated 16.66% of the 113 ouvrières (19 ouvrières) were probably weavers of tissu de soie. 1 each of the 12 (8.33%) = a weaver, a mercer, and a purse maker; thus an estimated 8.33% of the 113 ouvrières (9 ouvrières) probably practiced each of those trades.

Appendix 5 (continued)

36 of the 118, or 30%, resided in zone S1.

7 of the 118, or 6%, resided in zone S2.

26 of the 118, or 22%, resided in zone SJ (22% of the 113 women *ouvrières de soie* also in that zone)

41 of the 118, or 35%, resided in zone SL (35% of the 113 women *ouvrières de soie* also in that zone).

Note: The orthography of the words "ouvrier" and "ouvrière" was not stable; I have standardized the spellings here, simply distinguishing between the masculine and feminine forms.

1. Folio number references are to folio numbers in the original manuscripts of the 7 Parisian tax assessments (1292, 1296, 1297, 1298, 1299, 1300, 1313). For the 1292 tax assessment readers can consult the 1991 revised edition of Géraud, and for the 1296, 1297, and 1313 assessments, readers can consult Michaëlsson's editions; all four of these editions provide folio numbers in the margins. The assessments of 1298–1300 remain unpublished in AN KK 283.

2. For the purposes of the tax assessments, larger parishes were divided into different "quêtes." I give the numbers of the quêtes because they are useful for narrowing down the physical location of taxpayers. For a map of the various parishes and quêtes in 1300, see Bourlet and Bethe, "Création des plans," 163. This map is also available on the Alpage website: http://alpage.huma-num.fr/documents/Illustration_colloque/BOURLET_Paroisses_1300.pdf (accessed September 9, 2015).

3. Possibly the same as the weaver Guillaume le Breton, "qui fait dras de soie," who was taxed on the rue/ruelle S. Bon, in the parish of S. Merri, in 1298: AN KK 283 f. 132v; Appendix 3, part A, no. 7.

4. Names highlighted in bold face type signal individuals who were identified as *ouvrier/ouvrière de soie* in one tax assessment, but for whom a more specific profession was indicated in another tax assessment.

5. No surname/place-name in 1300.

6. This name had a variety of spellings, including Isabiau, Ysabiau, and Yzabiau. I have standardized with a single spelling.

7. Possibly a man. This individual is described as "qui oeuvre soie" so the professional name is of no help in determining his or her gender.

8. No surname/place-name in 1300.

9. Possibly the same as the throwster Thomasse du Vergier (which could mean orchard): Appendix 4, no. 92.

Notes

INTRODUCTION

1. On the thirteenth-century industries of Lucca, Venice, Bologna, and Genoa, see Molà, *The Silk Industry*, 3. For a discussion of some of the smaller thirteenth-century industries in Italy, see ibid., 4.

2. By 1260 Cologne was producing simple, non-luxurious, non-patterned silks as well. Edler, "The Silk Trade of Lucca," 21; Howell, *Women, Production, and Patriarchy*, 131–132.

3. Molà, *The Silk Industry*, 22.

4. Tognetti, "The Development of the Florentine Silk Industry," 62; Jacoby, "Silk Economics and Cross-Cultural Artistic Interaction," 223–228; Mazzaoui, "Artisan Migration and Technology"; Molà, "L'industria della seta a Lucca."

5. Noiriel, *Le creuset français*; Noiriel, "L'histoire est un sport de combat." For a bibliography of French scholarship on immigration up to 2006, see Bibliothèque Nationale de France, direction des collections, Département philosophie, histoire, science de l'homme, "Immigration en France."

6. Sahlins, *Unnaturally French*; Dubost and Sahlins, *Et si on faisait payer les étrangers?*

7. Anderson, "Nation-States and National Identity," 8; Frémont, "La terre," 30–32.

8. "À quelques rare exceptions près, chaque famille française plonge les racines de son arbre généalogique dans la terre paysanne": Frémont, "La terre," 20.

9. Roux, *Paris in the Middle Ages*, 47. On foreigners, most especially Italians, remaining in Paris for only a "short sojourn," see ibid., 74. On Italians being "poorly integrated" into Parisian society, see Bove, *Dominer la ville*, 64.

10. Pomian, "Francs et gaulois," 80; Noiriel, "Difficulties in French Historical Research on Immigration," 30.

11. Bourlet, "Le *Livre des métiers*," 37.

12. Jordan, *Louis IX and the Challenge of the Crusade*, 173–181; Bove, *Dominer la ville*, 173–200.

13. Bove, *Dominer la ville*, 52.

14. The total amount of money collected in those eight years, 80,000 livres parisis, was equal to 100,000 livres tournois, which is what the taxpayers owed the king. Taxpayers were assessed in livres parisis; 4 livres parisis = 5 livres tournois. In both monetary systems, 12 deniers = 1 sou, and 20 sous (or 240 deniers) = 1 livre. The average tax was 1 livre parisis.

15. Bourlet and Layec, "Densités de population et socio-topographie," 224. Four of the tax assessments (1292, 1296, 1297, and 1313) have been published: Géraud, ed., *Paris sous Philippe-le-Bel*, 1–179; Michaëlsson, ed., *Livre de la taille . . . 1296*; Michaëlsson, ed., *Livre de la*

taille . . . 1297; Michaëlsson, ed., *Livre de la taille . . . 1313*. Segments of the 1296–1300 assessments concerning foreign Lombards have also been published: Piton, *Les lombards*, 124–156. The unpublished assessments of 1299 and 1300 provide the greatest amount of detail concerning the professions of individuals; they, along with the assessments of 1296–1298, are in a single manuscript: AN KK 283.

    16. Vale, *The Princely Court*, 77.

    17. Ibid., 78.

    18. Lachaud, "Les textiles dans les comptes des hôtels royaux et nobiliaires." On Sweden: *Diplomatarium norvegicum*, 3:271 (postmortem inventory of Blanche of Namur, queen of Sweden and Norway, who died in 1363 or 1364). On Savoy: ADS, 7 MI 3, roll 6, register 42 (April 28, 1396–May 16, 1398), view 164. I wish to thank Camilla Luise Dahl for the reference to Blanche of Namur, and Nadège Gauffre-Fayolle, who shared with me her transcription of parts of the accounts from the court of Savoy.

    19. "Le premier compte de Geoffroi de Fleuri, argentier du roi Philippe le Long, pour les six derniers mois de l'année 1316," in Douët-d'Arcq, ed., *Comptes de l'argenterie*, 57; London, National Archives, Public Records Office, E 361/3, rots. 2, 3v, 6v, 22v and E 361/9, rots. 3, 5, 7v, 10 (English royal wardrobe accounts from the 1330s); *Diplomatarium norvegicum*, 3:271 (postmortem inventory of Blanche of Namur, queen of Sweden and Norway, who died in 1363 or 1364; Blanche probably brought this piece of Parisian silk to Scandinavia at the time of her marriage in 1335); ADS, 7 MI 3, roll 6, register 42 (April 28, 1396–May 16, 1398), view 164.

CHAPTER I

    1. For a summary discussion of all of the scholarly attempts to estimate the population of Paris around the year 1300, see Bourlet and Layec, "Densités de population et socio-topographie," 230–233.

    2. For references to sources that referred to the lower portion of the Grand Rue (now the rue Saint Denis) as "La Sélerie," or "The Street of the Saddle Makers," see Géraud, ed., *Paris sous Philippe-le-Bel*, 258.

    3. Our evidence concerning foreign servants in the French royal household is extremely limited, but we do know that Eleanor of Castile, the daughter of King Ferdinand III of Castile who married King Edward I of England in 1254, had two Iberian gardeners at her estate at Langley and a worker at Leeds named "Ferrando of Spain." Parsons, ed., *The Court and Household of Eleanor of Castile*, 75, 104; Harvey, *Mediaeval Gardens*, 78. See also Tolley, "Eleanor of Castile and the 'Spanish Style.'"

    4. Nolan, *Queens in Stone and Silver*, 122–129.

    5. Ibid., 136–140.

    6. The textile on Jean's and Blanche's tombs very much resembles that worn by the king or prince in a manuscript executed in Castile at the time of Alfonso X (r. 1252–1284); it also resembles the textile depicted on the pillows and underlying drapery in the tomb sculpture of Eleanor of Castile, queen of England, who died in 1290. Like these textiles, the silk in which Fernand de la Cerda was buried included alternating heraldic symbols, but they were framed by shields rather than by squares or diamonds. Lachaud, "Textiles, Furs and Liveries," 37–38, 416; Carretero, *Museo de Telas Medievales*, 32–33, 39–41; *Libro de ajedrez*, fol. 148v, image reproduced in Constable, "Chess and Courtly Culture in Medieval Castile," 337.

    7. Cohen, *The Sainte-Chapelle*, 201–202.

8. Katz, "The Final Testament of Violante de Aragón," 54.

9. Ward, "Fables for the Court," 197–198; Martin, "Cinq portraits."

10. Daumet, "Louis de la Cerda." On Béthencourt and De la Sale, see Beazley, "The French Conquest of the Canaries."

11. Leroy, "Le royaume de Navarre aux XIIIe–XIVe siècles," 157–158.

12. Kinoshita, "Translatio/n, Empire, and the Worlding of Medieval Literature."

13. Lalou, ed., *Les comptes sur tablettes de cire*, 857, 863; Leroy, "Le royaume de Navarre aux XIIIe-XIVe siècles," 155, 158, 159; Langlois, *Le règne de Philippe III*, 97–107.

14. Leroy, "Les juifs de Navarre à la fin du XIVe siècle," 116.

15. Dunbabin, *The French in the Kingdom of Sicily*; Dunbabin, *Charles I of Anjou*.

16. On Charles I, see Dunbabin, *Charles I of Anjou*. On the hotel of the king of Sicily and Marguerite of Burgundy's occupancy there, see Bove, "Typologie spatiale des hôtels aristocratiques à Paris (1300, 1400)," 289. On Charles II of Anjou and Paris, see Dunbabin, *The French in the Kingdom of Sicily*, 43.

17. Dunbabin, *The French in the Kingdom of Sicily*, 210. Aquinas, of course, was also from the *regno*, but his arrival in Paris predated Charles I of Anjou's conquest of the realm.

18. Proctor-Tiffany, "Lost and Found."

19. Dunbabin, *The French in the Kingdom of Sicily*, 275–276.

20. Farmer, "Aristocratic Power and the 'Natural' Landscape," 644; Dunbabin, *The French in the Kingdom of Sicily*, 101–120.

21. Dunbabin, *The French in the Kingdom of Sicily*, 115.

22. Bove, "Typologie spatiale des hôtels aristocratiques à Paris (1300, 1400)," 280–290. Bove's map of the locations of the residences in Paris is available on the Alpage website: alpage.tge-adonis.fr/documents/illustration_colloque/BOVE_HOTEL_1300.pdf (accessed September 1, 2015).

23. In 1309, King Philip the Fair conducted an inquest into foreign Lombard business practices and patterns of settlement in France. The administrators of the inquest, who were specifically instructed to ask how long each Italian merchant or moneylender had resided in France and whether or not he was married to a Frenchwoman, found that most foreign Lombards residing in Paris had been in France between five and twenty years and that only the poorest of them married Frenchwomen: Bautier, "I lombardi," 45. Gandoufle d'Arcelles (or Gandolfo di Arcelli), who was from Piacenza, had lived in Paris for at least twelve years when he died, and as far as we can tell he never married. Similarly, the Florentine Lippo di Fede del Segna remained in France for thirty years, leaving his wife behind in Italy the entire time: Terroine, "Études sur la bourgeoisie parisienne," part 2, 53; Roncière, *Un changeur florentin*, 179–194.

24. "Carta civium astensum," 521–522. For further discussion of these pawnbrokers, see main text of Chapter 5, discussion preceding note 49.

25. Terroine, "Études sur la bourgeoisie parisienne," part 1, 60–61.

26. Géraud, ed., *Paris sous Philippe-le-Bel*, 1–4, 176; Farmer, *Surviving Poverty in Medieval Paris*, 13.

27. Sivéry, *L'économie du royaume de France*, 243.

28. Piton, *Les lombards*, 125, 128, 142, 149, 151; Michaëlsson, ed., *Livre de la taille . . . 1313*, xvi–xviii.

29. Pegolotti, "Spices." See also Heyd, *Histoire du commerce du Levant*, 2:563–711.

30. Mirot, ed., "Inventaire mobilier."

31. When they appear in the assessments, Biche and Mouche, or Mouchet, are always in the parish of Saint-Germain-l'Auxerrois, and their tax assessment is well above the average of 1 livre in 1297–1300. Géraud, ed. *Paris sous Philippe-le-Bel*, 1 ("Biche, le lombart . . . 40 livres"). Lists of foreign Lombards in the 1296–1300 Parisian tax assessments: Piton, *Les lombards*, 124 (1296: "Mouchet . . . 82.5 livres"), 135 (1298: Mouche is not taxed, but his nephew Vanne is), 140 (1299, "Messire Mouche" is identified as "gentil home" and thus not taxed).

32. Strayer, *The Reign of Philip the Fair*, 50–51, 156–157; Favier, *Philippe le Bel*, 18–19; Bigwood, "La politique de la laine" (1937), 96–98; Piton, *Les lombards*, 124 (Gui Fauconnier taxed in 1296, 2 taxpayers away from Mouchet); 129 (Gui Fauconnier and Quinquenelle le lombart taxed right next to each other); 135 (Gui Fauconnier taxed in 1298, 3 taxpayers away from Mouche's nephew Vanne); 146 (Gui le Fauconnier taxed in 1300).

33. On Betin, see Strayer, *The Reign of Philip the Fair*, 74; and Piton, *Les lombards*, 114–119; on the others, see Appendix 1, part A, nos. 9, 12, 16, 34, 44.

34. Strayer, *The Reign of Philip the Fair*, 74; Piton, *Les lombards*, 114–119.

35. Piton, *Les lombards*, 149. On the *maltôte*, see Hélary, "Revolution militaire, revolution fiscale?" 242.

36. Lambertini, "Giles of Rome," section 6, "Ethics and Political Theory"; Briggs, *Giles of Rome's "De regimine principum*," 10.

37. McVaugh, "Surgical Education," 291–293.

38. Courtenay, *Parisian Scholars in the Early Fourteenth Century*, 115–116, 118, 120; Courtenay, "Spanish and Portuguese Scholars at the University of Paris," 113.

39. Courtenay, "The Parisian Franciscan Community in 1303"; Courtenay, "Between Pope and King."

40. Accounts from the household of Artois indicate that between 1292 and 1328 Count Robert II of Artois and his daughter, Countess Mahaut, bought a large portion of their woolens in Douai, Ghent, Arras, Saint-Omer, Malines, and Ypres. Nevertheless, some of the better woolens were purchased in Paris: Richard, *Une petite-nièce*, 158–195. On the Hall of Brussels, and aristocratic households that bought their Brabantine wool in Paris, see Bautier, "La place de la draperie brabançonne," 38–39; on Countess Mahaut's purchases in Paris of wool from Brussels, see Richard, *Une petite-nièce*, 161, 195.

41. On aristocrats and kings shopping in Paris, see Vale, *The Princely Court*, 351–354; Lysons, ed., "Copy of a Roll of Purchases"; London, British Library, Add. 7966A, fol. 156; Lachaud, "Textiles, Furs and Liveries," 121–122; Piponnier, *Costume et vie sociale*, 27, 41; *De Rekeningen der Graven en Gravinnen*, 1:516; PdC A 151/91; PdC A 263, fol. 21v; PdC A 270, fol. 25v; Brussels, Archives générales du Royaume, CC 1, membrane 19; and Ghent, Rijksarchief, fonds Gaillard 33; fonds Gaillard 52, membranes 5, 7; fonds Saint-Genois, 668.

42. Dunbabin, *The French in the Kingdom of Sicily*, 42.

43. Geijer, "Broderies françaises du haut gothique," 32–35.

44. Campbell, "Paris, miroir ou lumière"; Farmer, "*Biffes, Tiretaines,* and *Aumonières*," 83–88.

45. See main text of this chapter, at notes 72–77, 80–82.

46. Farmer, "*Biffes, Tiretaines,* and *Aumonières*," 74–78; Belhoste, "Paris grand centre drapier au Moyen Âge"; Chorley, "The Cloth Exports of Flanders and Northern France."

47. Michäelsson, "Les noms d'origine dans le rôle de la taille"; Cazelles, *Nouvelle histoire de Paris*, 142–143; Lorentz, Sandron, and Lebar, *Atlas de Paris au Moyen Âge*, 69–70; Roux, *Paris in the Middle Ages*, 46–47.

48. Michäelsson, ed., *Livre de la taille . . . 1297*, 31.

49. See main text of this chapter, at note 76.

50. See introduction, note 15 for a discussion of the locations of the seven assessments and of the editions of four of the seven assessments.

51. Bove, *Dominer la ville*, 57, 59.

52. In 1297 approximately 35 percent of taxpayers overall were identified with place-name surnames, such as "Marques of Lucca" or "Guy the Burgundian": Michaëlsson, ed., *Livre de la taille . . . 1297*. I thank my research assistant, Sarah Hanson, for making these calculations. For a breakdown of surnames among male and female taxpayers, see Bourlet, "L'anthroponymie à Paris," 20, 25.

53. PdC A 361, fol. 20; PdC A 374, fols. 25, 29; PdC A 378, fol. 15v; PdC A 403, fol. 19; PdC A 444, fols. 26v, 27; PdC A 458; PdC A 474, fol. 255; *De Rekeningen der Graven en Gravinnen*, 1:259, 274, 284, 285, 304, 368; "Inventaire et vente après décès des biens de la reine Clémence de Hongrie veuve de Louis le Hutin, 1328," in Douët-d'Arcq, ed., *Nouveau recueil de comptes*, 78.

54. In the Parisian tax assessments there was an increasing tendency, between 1292 and 1300, for a surname to be inserted between the forename and the name of the individual's profession; this was especially true for men. These men, it would seem, did not inherit a surname from their progenitors: Bourlet, "L'anthroponymie à Paris," 20.

55. Kedar, "Toponymic Surnames as Evidence of Origin," 123–129.

56. Appendix 1, part A.

57. Ibid., nos. 23, 65.

58. Viard, *Documents parisiens du règne de Philippe VI*, 1:105; Géraud, ed., *Paris sous Philippe-le-bel*, 176: "Berthelemi le lombart" (Appendix 1, part A, no. 14) was assessed for the highest tax of anyone who was assessed in Saint Marcel. Given the fact that Italian names were "frenchified" in French sources, it seems possible that Berthelin and Berthelemi were two versions of the same name.

59. Farmer, "*Biffes, Tiretaines*, and *Aumonières*," 78n32; Lebailly, "Raoul, Comte d'Eu," 2:49. In 1328 Countess Mahaut of Artois bought "une thiretaine de saint marchel" from "Berthelot chastainis": PdC A 458, fol. 30v. *Tiretaine* of Saint Marcel was also specifically identified in the postmortem inventory of Queen Clémence of Hungary—four of her thirty-five garments were made with that textile: "Inventaire et vente après décès des biens de la reine Clémence de Hongrie, veuve de Louis le Hutin, 1328," in Douët-d'Arcq, ed., *Nouveau recueil de comptes*, 70–71.

60. PdC A 334, fol. 28v.

61. PdC A 374, fol. 29; Richard, *Une petite-nièce*, 7.

62. PdC A 351, ed. Richard, *Une petite-nièce*, 396–397. "Jaque Fene lombart de Saint Marcel" should read instead "Jaque Feve lombart de Saint Marcel."

63. Hoshino, *Industria tessile*, 23–24.

64. Farmer, "*Biffes, Tiretaines*, and *Aumonières*," 75–78.

65. On the use of worsted for hose and cutting on the diagonal, see Crowfoot, Pritchard, and Staniland, *Textiles and Clothing*, 39, 185. The Parisian guild statutes for the makers of hose (the "chaussiers") mentioned only silk and linen: *Livre des métiers*, ed. Lespinasse and Bonnardot, 114.

66. *Livre des métiers*, ed. Lespinasse and Bonnardot, 115–116; Appendix 1, part A, nos. 18, 20, 64, 84, 105.

67. Géraud, ed., *Paris sous Philippe-le-bel*, 3, 4: Estienne le chaucier, Pierre le chaucier.

68. Géraud, ed., *Paris sous Philippe-le-bel*, 88, 99; Michaëlsson, ed., *Livre de la taille . . . 1296*, 129, 130; Michaëlsson, ed., *Livre de la taille . . . 1297*, 115–116; AN KK 283, fols. 113, 136, 190v, 191; Michaëlsson, ed., *Livre de la taille . . . 1313*, 128, 129, 140: Anfroy le chauchier; Beneoit le chaucier; Estienne le chaucier; Gervese le chaucier; Gilebert le chaucier; Guiart le boçu, chaucier; Henri le chaucier; Hugues le chaucier; Jehan le chaucier; Jehan de Beauvez, chaucier; Jehan de Bretueil, chaucier; Jehan de la Sale, chaucier; Mahy le chaucier; Nicolas Prévost, chaucier; Nouve le chaucier; Perronnele la chauciere; Pierre de Vitry, chaucier; Remon/Remont le chaucier; Robin Naperon, chaucier; Ruffin le chaucier; Symon le chaucier, and others.

69. Appendix 1, part A, nos. 30, 31, 60, 67, 80, 112.

70. Six of the eight were taxed as "bourgeois of Paris"; the other two were taxed as foreign Lombards: Appendix 1, part A, nos. 10, 49, 73, 79, 85, 90; Piton, *Les lombards*, 137.

71. Some of the earliest known plate armor was made at the end of the thirteenth century: Pfaffenbichler, *Medieval Craftsmen*, 8–9.

72. Gauffre-Fayolle, "Broder à la cour de Savoie," 46, citing Lespinasse, ed., *Les métiers et corporations de la ville de Paris*, 2:321.

73. Loisne, "Une cour féodale," 109, 142.

74. Pfaffenbichler, *Medieval Craftsmen*, 33.

75. Appendix 1, part A, nos. 31, 80.

76. The four Iberian men living on the Street of the Saddle Makers (or the Grand Rue/ rue Saint Denis) were, on the west side of the street, Anciau of Aragon, chest maker ("bahu-tier") and Richart of Aragon, chest maker ("coffrier"/"bahutier"), who paid taxes in the fifth quête of the parish of Saint-Germain-l'Auxerrois; on the east side of the street, Phelippe of Aragon, saddle maker, and Pierre of Aragon, felt and blanket maker, paid taxes on the Grand Rue in the second quête of the parish of Saint-Jacques-de-la-Boucherie. The leather workers who did not reside on that street were Guillaume of Spain and Guillot of Spain, both cordovan leather workers, and Jehan of Aragon, chest maker: Appendix 1, part B, nos. 1, 8, 11, 12, 16, 21, 23. For a map showing that the division between the fifth quête of Saint-Germain-l'Auxerrois and the second quête of Saint-Jacques-de-la-Boucherie ran up the middle of the Grand Rue, see Bourlet and Layec, "Densités de population et socio-topographie," 238; also accessible online at http://alpage.huma-num.fr/documents/Illustration_colloque/BOURLET_Quetes_1300.pdf (accessed September 2, 2015).

77. *Livre des métiers*, ed. Lespinasse and Bonnardot, 185.

78. Ghent, Rijksarchief, fonds Gaillard 33; Richard, *Une petite-nièce*, 128, citing PdC A 199. In 1297, Gautier of Brussels paid the extremely high tax of 44 livres. It was the highest tax paid by anyone on either side of the part of the Grand Rue that was dominated by saddle makers, etc.: Michaëlsson, ed., *Livre de la taille . . . 1297*, 30–32, 122–124.

79. Payments made to Gautier of Brussels: *Het memorial*, 84; PdC A 37; PdC A 133; and possibly London, British Library, Add. 7966A, fol. 156 (saddles ordered in Paris for Queen Marguerite of England from "William" of Brussels). Payments to Pierre of Utrecht: PdC A 171, 173, 189/3, 192, 195, 218, 228. Payments made to Renier of Utrecht: PdC A 329, fol. 23; PdC A 483.

80. "Le premier compte de Geoffroi de Fleuri, argentier du roi Philippe le Long (1316)," in Douët-d'Arcq, ed., *Comptes de l'argenterie*, 44, 51, 62; PdC A 374, fol. 13 (1319); Lebailly, "Raoul, Comte d'Eu," 2:48.

81. Depping, ed., *Réglemens*, 228, footnote citing ordonnance of 1345.

82. Fagniez, *Études sur l'industrie*, 113. On the importation of goat skins from Spain, see also Crowfoot, Pritchard, and Staniland, eds., *Textiles and Clothing*, 104, 136–137; and Cherry, "Leather," 308.

83. Appendix 1, part B, nos. 5, 14.

84. Depping, ed., *Réglemens*, 367–369.

85. Cohen, *By the Sword*, 113–118. Sölingen and Toledo are still world leaders in the production of swords and knives. On Seigen, see Pounds, "Steelmaking," 11:470.

86. Schubert, *History of the British Iron and Steel Industry*, 118.

87. Appendix 1, part B, nos. 3, 7, 9.

88. Depping, ed., *Réglemens*, 357, n. 3.

89. Appendix 1, part A, nos. 33, 38; part B, no. 24.

90. Bautier and Bautier, "Contribution à l'histoire du cheval," part 3, 13, 17–23, 63–70.

91. Ibid., 68.

92. Loisne, "Une cour féodale," 136; Richard, *Une petite-nièce*, 124; PdC A 312, described in Richard, *Inventaire-sommaire*, 1:277; PdC A 284, described in Richard, *Inventaire-sommaire*, 1:261, for 1311; PdC A 374, fol. 13 for 1319; PdC A 389 for 1320; Lebailly, "Raoul, Comte d'Eu," 1:218–219.

93. Farmer, "Aristocratic Power and the 'Natural' Landscape," 644n2, 672; *Registre criminel du Châtelet de Paris*, 2:447.

94. Nine Cypriots show up in the tax assessments: Appendix 1, part C, nos. 15–23. On the tenth Cypriot, Bienvenue de Chypres, see Richard, ed., "Documents des XIIIe et XIVe siècles relatifs à l'hôtel de Bourgogne," 152–154; and PdC A 187/1. Beginning in 1302, Bienvenue was supported on a pension, and one reference to her pension identifies her as "Bienvenue de Chypre": PdC A 184 (1302); PdC A 209 (1305).

95. In his 1283 commission as concièrge for the Count of Artois, Mahy of Arras was identified as a goldsmith. In the Parisian tax assessment of 1313, he was identified as a mercer. In 1294, he supplied both gold vessels and silks to the Countess of Flanders: PdC A 28, described in Richard, *Inventaire-sommaire*, 1:44; Ghent, Rijksarchief, fonds Gaillard 52; Michaëlsson, ed., *Livre de la taille . . . 1313*, 124. For a discussion of Jehanne l'Espicière's role as concièrge of the Hôtel d'Artois in Paris, see Farmer, "Merchant Women and the Administrative Glass Ceiling," 100.

96. PdC A 224 (1307), described in Richard, *Inventaire-sommaire*, 1:223.

97. Richard, "Documents des XIIIe et XIVe siècles relatifs à l'hôtel de Bourgogne," 152–154; discussed by Farmer in "Merchant Women and the Administrative Glass Ceiling," 99. Count Robert II of Artois died in 1302, before Madame Bienvenue completed her account, in 1303; the count was succeeded by his daughter, Countess Mahaut. Madame Bienvenue indicates that the expenses were for "l'ostel mons. d'Artoys" (for the residence of Monsieur of Artois), thereby indicating that the account was for expenses predating Count Robert II's death in 1302.

98. Appendix 1, part C, nos. 42–47.

99. Ibid., no. 14. On the use of "Babylon" for Old Cairo, see Sheehan, *Babylon of Egypt*.

100. "Compte de l'hôtel du roi pour le terme de la Saint-Jean 1313," in *Comptes royaux (1285–1314)*, ed. Fawtier and Maillard, 2:777, #27722.

101. Guillaume de Saint-Pathus, *Vie de Saint Louis*, 21. A royal account from 1308 makes reference to the children of thirteen baptizati who had been brought back by Louis IX, so in this case as well we can be sure that their origins were in the Levant; they were living in Rouen: Lalou, ed., *Les comptes sur tablettes de cire*, 817, #131; 879, #139.

102. Appendix 1, part C, nos. 48–50.

103. Hersente la Mahommette: Archives des Quinze-Vingts, ms. 5878, fols. 129–131v (microfiche available at the Institut de recherche et d'histoire des textes in Paris).

104. Appendix 1, part C, nos. 48, 50. Jacques Mahommet, taxed in 1313, but with no specified profession, was included among the weavers moved by Queen Jeanne of Burgundy to Gray, in Burgundy, in 1318: Michaëlsson, ed., *Livre de la taille . . . 1313*, 164; Bautier, "Une opération de décentralisation industrielle," 661.

105. Appendix 1, part C, no. 49.

106. Ibid., nos. 1–13, 24–29.

107. Lalou, ed., *Les comptes sur tablettes de cire*, 850, #25; Perry, *John of Brienne*; Bove, "Typologie spatiale des hôtels aristocratiques à Paris (1300, 1400)," 280.

108. Appendix 1, part C, nos. 3, 9.

109. Géraud, ed., *Paris sous Philippe-le-Bel*, 178 ("Lyon, d'Acre, mire, sa fame Bien-li-Viengne, 5s; Amendant, fuils Lion d'Acre, 8 s."). On the importance of Acre and its destruction, see Graboïs, "The Idea of Political Zionism," 67.

110. For the area around the rue de la Buffeterie, I am counting the cloister of Saint Opportune, the rue Saint Opportune, the rue des Petits Soliers, the rue des Arcis, the rue Saint Merri, the cloister of Saint Merri, the rue de la Buffeterie, the Grand and Petit Marivaux, and the rue de la Viez-Monnaie. On foreign Lombards residing in these two zones, see Piton, *Les lombards*, 127–152. Italians taxed as bourgeois of Paris residing in the zone near the Buffeterie: Appendix 1, part A, nos. 19, 28, 33, 38, 45, 54, 60, 64, 81, 84, 85, 88, 89, 98, 100, 101, 106, 120, 126. Italians taxed as bourgeois of Paris residing in the zone around the Petit-Pont: Appendix 1, part A, nos. 1, 2, 10, 18, 21, 27, 32, 35, 39, 40, 47–49, 52, 53, 55–58, 77, 80, 90, 95, 102–105, 116.

111. On endogamous marriages, see discussion of Ugolino Belloni's daughter in the next paragraph.

112. Mirot, "Études lucquoises 1," 55; Maddocks, "The Rapondi"; Schmitt et al., eds., *La leyenda de la Santa Faz.*

113. Mirot, "La fondation de la chapelle du Volto Santo," 22.

114. Ibid., 13; Molinier, ed., "Inventaire du trésor de l'Église du Saint-Sepulcre de Paris," 253, notes: "Cy gist Bernard Bellenaty jadis marchand de Lucques et bourgeois de Paris, qui trespassa l'an de grace 1380 . . . Ci gist Jacqueline fille de Hugelin Blon, marchand de Lucques et bourgeois de Paris, femme dud. Bernard, laquelle trespassa l'an 1353."

115. On Caucinel, see the text of this chapter preceding note 34; on the Spifami, see Mirot, "Études lucquoises 1," 76, 82–83.

116. Mirot, "La fondation de la chapelle du Volto Santo," 14.

117. Mirot, "Études lucquoises 1," 68n3; Bove, *Dominer la ville*, 475–476; AN S 3376, documents 24, 27, 33; AN LL 782, fols. 54v–55.

118. Mirot, "La fondation de la chapelle du Volto Santo," 21; Molinier, ed., "Inventaire du trésor," 251n1, 274.

119. Mirot, "La fondation de la chapelle du Volto Santo," 21. On Guillaume Toussac's status as an *échevin*, see Bove, *Dominer la ville*, 213. For more discussion of Barthelemy and Agnes Castaing, see Chapter 5, text preceding notes 126–129.

120. Guillaume de Saint-Pathus, *Miracles de Saint Louis*, 83–85.

121. Ibid., 85–86.

122. Appendix 1, part C, nos. 16, 17, 19, 21, 23. For further discussion of this group, and of the toponymic surname "de Limesi/s," see Chapter 3, text preceding notes 91–95.

123. Depping, ed., *Réglemens*, 357, 367–369, 379–380, 383–384; *Livre des métiers*, ed. Lespinasse and Bonnardot, 115–116; Appendix 1, part A, nos. 18, 20, 30, 31, 64, 67, 84, 105, 112; part B, nos. 3, 5, 14, 26; part C, no. 16.

124. *Livre des métiers*, ed. Lespinasse and Bonnardot, 115, note e.

125. Dunbabin, *The French in the Kingdom of Sicily*, 85–86.

126. Farmer, "Aristocratic Power and the 'Natural' Landscape," 644.

127. Courtenay, "Between Pope and King," 578n5.

CHAPTER 2

1. Ghent, Rijksarchief, fonds Gaillard 52, membrane 8. See notes 23 and 25 below on the identity of the silk.

2. Ciocîltan, *The Mongols and the Black Sea Trade*, 61–140.

3. Reyerson, "Commerce and Communications," 54–55.

4. Ghent, Rijksarchief, fonds Gaillard 52, membranes 7–8. On silk tablet weaving in the households of aristocratic women, see the section of this chapter that precedes note 96. It is clear that there was tablet weaving in Isabel of Luxembourg's household; this same account includes a purchase of tablets and blades for tablet weaving ("tavieles et espees"): ibid., membrane 5.

5. Edler De Roover, "Andrea Banchi"; Jacks and Caferro, *The Spinelli of Florence*, 82–91; Molà, *The Silk Industry*; Gargiolli, ed., *L'arte della seta in Firenze*.

6. On raw silk from China, the Caspian region, and southern Italy, see note 7. On raw silk from the Levant, Byzantium, and the Greek Mediterranean, see Jacoby, "Dalla materia prima," 271; Jacoby, "Silk Production in the Frankish Peloponnese"; and Balard, *La Romanie génoise*, 2:724–725.

7. Edler De Roover, "Andrea Banchi," 237–239; Lopez, "China Silk in Europe," 73–74; Balard, *La Romanie génoise*, 2:724–730; Reyerson, "Medieval Silks in Montpellier," 128–129; Racine, "Le marché génois de la soie," 405. Scholars are not in complete agreement that the fiber referred to as "seta canjia" was from Ganja in Azerbaijan. Virgil Ciocîltan proposes, instead, that it might have been from Gangea in Caucasian Armenia: *The Mongols and the Black Sea Trade*, 102n180.

8. Edler, "The Silk Trade of Lucca," 59; Edler De Roover, *L'arte della seta*, 25. Throughout the twentieth century and into the twenty-first, the owners of silk-throwing mills in England and France continued to import skeins of previously reeled silk: Rayner, *Silk Throwing*, 12–19; visit to Moulinage de la Rive, Yssingeaux, France, April 2014. Since World War II, China and Brazil have dominated the market for reeled raw silk: Gilonne, *Soieries de Lyon*, 1:79–80; visit to Moulinage de la Rive. David Jacoby and Luca Molà found some evidence for the importation of silk cocoons to medieval and Renaissance Venice. In 1362, moreover, a Lucchese merchant in Paris had in stock both reeled raw silk and silk cocoons. Nevertheless, the importation of silk cocoons must have been the exception, since the fifteenth-century author of *L'arte della seta in firenze* included no description of reeling silk from cocoons: Jacoby, "Dalla materia prima," 247; Molà, *La comunità dei lucchesi a Venezia*, 211–214; Mirot, ed., "Inventaire mobilier," 164, 166; Gargiolli, ed., *L'arte della seta in firenze*.

9. Rayner, *Silk Throwing*, 12–13.

10. Reyerson, "Medieval Silks in Montpellier," 128n49.

11. Pegolotti, *La pratica della mercatura*, 382; cited by Lopez, "China Silk in Europe," 75.

12. Currie, "Silk," 36.

13. Rayner, *Silk Throwing*, 13; Li, *China's Silk Trade*, 77.

14. In addition to the citations in notes 2, 6, and 7, see Pegolotti, *La pratica della mercatura*, 24, 35, 59, 64, 71. On the importance of Famagusta after the fall of Acre in 1291, see Jacoby, "The Venetians in Byzantine and Lusignan Cyprus." On silk cocoons that were imported to Venice, see Jacoby, "Dalla materia prima," 274; and Molà, *La comunità dei lucchesi a Venezia*, 211–214. On the purchase of "cooked" silk in Byzantium, see Pegolotti, *La pratica della mercatura*, 36. On the purchase of dyed silk, see ibid., 59, 78 ("seta chemisi," "seta carmusi"). On the sale of previously twisted silk in France, see Ciano, ed., *La "Pratica di mercatura" datiniana*, 76.

15. Lopez, "Nouveaux documents sur les marchands italiens en Chine"; Balard, *La Romanie génoise*, 2:727–730.

16. Late fourteenth-century letters in the Datini archive indicate that silk from Granada was going to Paris, but it is not clear if that would have been the case around the year 1300. Florence Edler De Roover's studies of the Lucchese and Florentine cloth industries suggested that the output (and perhaps quality) of Iberian raw silk increased around the end of the fourteenth century. See Melis and Frangioni, *I mercanti italiani*, 155, 163; Edler De Roover, "Lucchese Silk," 2909; Edler De Roover, "Andrea Banchi," 238; Balard, *La Romanie génoise*, 2:731–732; Edler De Roover, *L'arte della seta*, 25–27; Hoshino, "La seta in Valdinievole," 171–176; and Molà, *La comunità dei lucchesi a Venezia*, 210–221, 292–293. On the high quality of fifteenth-century silk fiber from Modigliano, in Tuscany, and from Iberia, and on the continued availability of Caspian silks in the fifteenth century, see Gargiolli, ed., *L'arte della seta in firenze*, 108.

17. Balard, *La Romanie génoise*, 2:727–728; Lopez, "China Silk in Europe," 73; Jacoby, "Dalla materia prima," 271.

18. Florentines selling fiber north of the Alps: Pegolotti, *La pratica della mercatura*, 228, 243, 254, 255; Lopez, "China Silk in Europe," 74. Genoese selling silk north of the Alps: Balard, *La Romanie génoise*, 2:730. Genoese and Venetians delivering raw silk to Flanders: Ciano, ed., *La "Pratica di mercatura" datiniana*, 73: "Le ghalee portano . . . seta grossa, come ghella" (the galleys [from Genoa and Florence that go to Bruges] carry . . . raw silk, such as that of Gilan province). Venetians selling raw silk in Paris, Flanders, and London: Pegolotti, *La pratica della mercatura*, 144, 148, 151, cited by Jacoby, "Dalla materia prima," 275.

19. Guérin, *"Avorio d'ogni ragione,"* 170–171 (Guérin argues that the Genoese were sailing through the Straits of Gibraltar by the 1240s); Reyerson, "Commerce and Communications," 70 (Reyerson argues for regular voyages through the straits after 1277).

20. Lopez, "China Silk in Europe," 74.

21. Balard, *La Romanie génoise*, 2:730: in 1288 the Genoese sold 39 percent of their raw silk to merchants from Florence, Pistoia, and Piacenza. On Montpellier, see Reyerson, "Medieval Silk in Montpellier," 128.

22. See note 18 above.

23. The entire entry of the Parisian tariff list reads, "La livre de soye escreue, ligée et catonière, III d.—La livre de soie mermite de gerant et pampée": "Tarif des marchandises qui se vendaient à Paris," ed. Douët-d'Arcq, 223. See note 24 on "mermite" and "gerant." It was R.-H. Bautier who argued convincingly that this tariff list must date from the first half of the fourteenth century: "La Place de la draperie brabançonne," 36n. On "seta leggia," see Balard, *La Romanie génoise*, 2:724–725; and Edler De Roover, *L'arte della seta*, 25. On "seta catanji," see Molà, *The Silk Industry*, 56. According to a fifteenth-century Florentine treatise on silk production "seta catanji" fetched the same price as "seta leggi" and a significantly higher price than silk from Catanzaro ("seta Catanzane"): Gargiolli, ed., *L'arte della seta in firenze*, 105, 108.

24. On raw silk from Malmistra and from Georgia, for which the Italian term was "seta jurea" or "seta juree," see Racine, "Le marché génois de la soie," 406, 407, 415.

25. Ghent, Rijksarchief, fonds Gaillard 52, membrane 8: "Item . . . pour soie delivre a Paris et achetee en la foire de Lagny a Cote Salmon de Luke, 132 livres 5 onches de soie, 20 sous tornois la livre . . . et est ceste soie appielee *lissee*; item 84 livres 2 onches de soie et couste chacune livre 25 sous tournois . . . et est ceste soie appielee *Katonie*; item 56 livres 12 onches de soie et couste li livre 33 sous tornois . . . et est ceste soie appiele *nikolie*." I am assuming that the scribe of the final account misread the purchase account from the fair, and thus "lissee" should read "liggee" (silk of Lahijan). It is also possible that "Nikolie" should read "Nikosie," which would mean that the third silk came from Nicosia, Cyprus.

26. Ghent, Rijksarchief, fonds Gaillard 52, membrane 7. We know it was raw silk because Mahy of Arras paid to have it thrown.

27. Mirot, ed., "Inventaire mobilier," 164.

28. In 1275 the mercers complained to the provost of Paris that throwsters were pawning or selling off the mercers' good fiber to Lombards and Jews, replacing part of their good silk with waste silk ("quant aucuns des merciers de la ville de Paris bailloient leur soie escrue por ouvrer . . . il [les fillerresses] le engagoient ou vendoient chiez Lombars ou chiez juyfs, ou leur eschangoient la bonne soie . . . a bourre de saie"). The Lombards and Jews who purchased the fiber must have traded more broadly in raw silk fiber: Fagniez, ed., *Documents relatifs à l'histoire de l'industrie*, 1:277–278. The same issue came up again in the statutes for the weavers of silk head coverings, which were written at some point between 1280 and 1300: *Livre des métiers*, ed. Lespinasse and Bonnardot, 84, statute 8. On the date of these statutes, see Bourlet, "Le *Livre des métiers*," 37, 41.

29. Géraud, ed., *Paris sous Philippe-le-Bel*, 1–4, 176.

30. Michaëlsson, ed., *Livre de la taille . . . 1296*, 269–275.

31. Ibid., 272; Terroine, "Étude sur la bourgeoisie parisienne," part 2.

32. Géraud, ed., *Paris sous Philippe-le-Bel*, 1–3; Michaëlsson, ed., *Livre de la taille . . . 1296*, 270–272. The Lombard section of the 1296 tax assessment included a separate list of twelve Lucchese merchants and merchant companies; one other company was also identified as being from Lucca. Similarly, the 1296 tax assessment had a separate section listing five Venetians or Venetian companies, and one other Lombard taxpayer was also identified as a Venetian: Michaëlsson, ed., *Livre de la taille . . . 1296*, 271–273. See also Racine, "Paris, rue des Lombards," 95.

33. Géraud, ed., *Paris sous Philippe-le-Bel*, 3–4; Michaëlsson, ed., *Livre de la taille . . . 1296*, 273–275.

34. The tax assessments include the names of thirteen stocking/hosiery makers (*chaussiers*) who resided on the Cité, the Petit-Pont, or the Left Bank within a few blocks of the Petit-Pont. Some of them show up in more than one assessment: Géraud, ed., *Paris sous Philippe-le-Bel*, 140, 145, 148, 150, 151, 152; Michaëlsson, ed., *Livre de la taille . . . 1296*, 203, 204, 214, 216, 221, 231; Michaëlsson, ed., *Livre de la taille . . . 1297*, 202, 204, 213; AN KK 283, fols. 89v, 137, 144, 146, 216, 217, 218v, 219, 284, 292. On the use of silk in the making of hosiery, see *Livre des métiers*, ed. Lespinasse and Bonnardot, 114.

35. Ghent, Rijksarchief, fonds Gaillard 52, membrane 7. Mahy of Arras, Phelippe Anketin, and Jehan le Pellier were all identified as mercers in the Paris tax assessments: Appendix 2, part A, no. 55; part B, nos. 50, 66. On Mahy of Arras's identity as a goldsmith, see PdC A 28, PdC A 32.

36. Ghent, Rijksarchief, fonds Gaillard 52, membrane 3.

37. Currie, "Silk," 10–11; Hills, "From Cocoon to Cloth," 63–64; Rayner, *Silk Throwing*, xiii; oral communication from Sophie Desrosiers.

38. Edler De Roover, *L'arte della seta*, 43–44.

39. Ghent, Rijksarchief, fonds Gaillard 52, membrane 7.

40. For lists of throwsters and weavers, see Appendices 3 and 4. The dyers were Hervé le Breton, Isabel de Glatigni, Jehan de Roan/Roem, Jehan d'Ouville, Michiel Du Buot, and Noël de Chesnai: Michaëlsson, ed., *Livre de la taille . . . 1296*, 18, 21; Michaëlsson, ed., *Livre de la taille . . . 1313*, 142; AN KK 283, fols. 111v, 134v, 188, 189v, 263v, 264, 266. My assumption that the women who were described as "qui carie soie" were silk weavers is based, first, on similarities between the French word *carier* and the Sicilian word *careri* ("silk weaver"), which was derived from the Arabic words *harir* and *harrar*, which mean "silk" and "silk weaver," respectively: Dozy, *Supplément aux dictionnaires*, 263–264. I thank R. Steven Humphreys for this reference. A Parisian statute from 1324 supports this reading: the mercers wanted to prevent silk workers from mixing silk fiber with other fiber and from using an inferior silk fiber, known as "flourin," which came from broken cocoons. Since the primary thrust of the statute was addressed at final products—silk thread or silk textiles—the main workers who were being addressed would have been the throwsters ("filleresses") and weavers. The terms "fillerresse de soie" and "soye a filler" are used elsewhere in this set of statutes, so it appears that "de faire soye carier" meant "to arrange for silk to be woven": Fagniez, ed., *Documents relatifs à l'histoire de l'industrie*, 2:59–61. This reading is also supported by the fact that in 1299 Count Robert II of Artois bought silk cloth from Lucca called "carraires de Luque": Loisne, "Une cour féodale," 122 (transcription of PdC A 2, fol. 24).

41. Appendix 5. For further discussion of the underrepresentation of women, and of the "ouvrières de soie," see Chapter 4. On specific crafts that were practiced by *ouvriers/ouvrières de soie*, see Appendix 5.

42. See text of Chapter 4 just before table 3 for further discussion concerning numbers of women in the silk industry.

43. On the modern system of evaluating raw silk fiber, see Currie, "Silk," 25; on inspections by silk merchants in fifteenth-century Florence, see Edler De Roover, "Andrea Banchi," 241.

44. Gargiolli, ed., *L'arte della seta in firenze*, 102–108.

45. Jacks and Caferro, *The Spinelli of Florence*, 83.

46. On the weighing of silk fiber in Venice before and after it went out to the homes of winders, see Molà, "Le donne nell'industria serica veneziana," 428–429.

47. "Rosete pignerresse de soie," AN KK 283, fol. 276.

48. On the use of waste-silk yarn, see *Livre des métiers*, ed. Lespinasse and Bonnardot, 77 (statute no. 4 of the statutes for "Ouvriers de Draps de soye . . . de veluyaus et de boursserie en lice"): "Item, que nuls . . . ne pourra ne ne devra ouvrer . . . de soye canete, se ce n'est en meneure; car ourture de canete est fausse, se ce n'est en draps a deus ourtures" (Moreover, no one should work with waste-silk yarn, if this is not a minor work; because warping with waste-silk yarn is false, unless it is a cloth woven with two warp beams). On the use of waste silk as stuffing in padded clothing that went under armor, see Depping, ed., *Réglemens*, 371; and Richard, *Une petite-nièce*, 223. Desrosiers has found that waste silk was used for the weft of velvets, which were woven with two warp beams: "Sur l'origine d'un tissu qui a participé à la fortune de Venise," 39.

49. Jean de Meung recommended that women create thick tresses with "soie blonde borriaus": *Roman de la rose*, ed. Marteau, 3:234, verse 13893; cited in Richard, *Une petite-nièce*, 367.

50. Oral communication from Sophie Desrosiers.

51. John of Garland, *Dictionarius*, ed. Hunt, 201. In his description of the textiles produced by women silk weavers, Garland mentioned only narrow ware items. On Paris in the 1220s as the place and date of the *Dictionarius*, see Hunt's introduction to this text: ibid., 192. For a general introduction to Garland's work, and the emphasis, in the work, on crafts and trades in Paris, see Lachaud, "La première description des métiers de Paris."

52. *Livre des métiers*, ed. Lespinasse and Bonnardot, 68, 70. On the dating of the statutes see Bourlet, "Le *Livre des métiers*," 35–40.

53. Oral communication from Sophie Desrosiers. Flavio Crippa proposed that in Calabria silk may have been thrown through an ancient method of thigh spinning, but there is no evidence that thigh spinning was a local tradition in Paris: "Dal baco al filo," 15–16.

54. "Quiconques veut estre Fillaresse de soie a grans fuiseaus, a Paris, c'est a savoir desvudier, filer, doubler et retordre": *Livre des métiers*, ed. Lespinasse and Bonnardot, 68.

55. Ibid., 70–72.

56. "Richeut de Saint Denis, file au touret," "Jehanne qui file au touret," "Marie la ravace qui file au touret": AN KK 283, fols. 80v, 136v, 140.

57. Rayner, *Silk Throwing*, 22–24. According to the Parisian guild statutes, reeling ("desvudier") was one of the tasks of the silk throwsters working with "large spindles." It is possible, however, that the throwsters assigned the task of winding and reeling to specialized employees or apprentices: *Livre des métiers*, ed. Lespinasse and Bonnardot, 68. One silk reeler ("Haouys de chailloel desvuide soie") does show up in the tax assessments: AN KK 283, fol. 265. In Lucca silk winders, who were known as *incannaresse*, constituted a large portion of the population of silk workers: Edler, "The Silk Trade of Lucca," 59.

58. Rayner, *Silk Throwing*, 26–27; Gargiolli, ed., *L'arte della seta in firenze*, 6.

59. Hills, "From Cocoon to Cloth," 68. The statutes of the makers of silk alms purses forbade the use of untwisted silk yarn ("nulles mestresses ne ouvrières dou dit mestier ne puent ne ne doivent faire euvre de soye deffillées, dites aumosnières et boursses sarrazinoises, pour ce que la soye n'est pas filée ne retorsse" [no mistress or worker of the said craft can or should make a work with untwisted silk of the said alms purses and saracen purses, because such silk is not twisted or retwisted]). Presumably the concern was that the purses would not be strong enough. Depping, ed., *Réglemens*, 385.

60. Cardon, *La draperie au Moyen Âge*, 273, fig. 105; Desrosiers, *Soieries et autres textiles*, 485.

61. On doubled yarns in taffeta, see Gargiolli, ed., *L'arte della seta in firenze*, 75; and Savary, *Le parfait negociant*, part 1, book 2, chap. 9, p. 81. On doubled yarn in lampas weave, see Desrosiers, *Soieries et autres textiles*, cat. nos. 153, 154, pp. 284, 286. On doubled and tripled yarns in velvet pile, see Desrosiers, "Sur l'origine d'un tissu qui a participé à la fortune de Venise," 38.

62. Rayner, *Silk Throwing*, 25. For examples of nubby silk cloth woven from yarns that had been poorly thrown, see Crowfoot, Pritchard, and Staniland, *Textiles and Clothing*, 92. Jacques Savary, who wrote a French manual for entrepreneurs in the seventeenth century, was well aware that the quality of a final silk product depended on the quality of the job that was done by the throwsters—although by his time, throwing had been mechanized in France: Savary, *Le parfait negociant*, part 2, book 1, chap. 7, 92.

63. Farmer, "*Biffes, Tiretaines* and *Aumonières*," 85, 86, 88.

64. "Le premier compte de Geoffroi de Fleuri, argentier du roi Philippe le Long pour les six derniers mois de l'année 1316," in Douët-d'Arcq, ed., *Comptes de l'argenterie*, 57; London,

National Archives, Public Records Office, E 361/3, rots. 2, 3v, 6v, 22v and E 361/9, rots. 3, 5, 7v, 10; *Diplomatarium norvegicum*, 3:271; ADS, 7 MI 3, roll 6, register 42 (April 28, 1396–May 16, 1398), view 164: "item pour 6 aunes de soye roge vert et pers de Paris." I wish to thank Camilla Luise Dahl for the reference to Blanche of Namur and Nadège Gauffre-Fayolle, who shared with me her transcriptions of passages from the accounts of the court of Savoy that mentioned Parisian silk products.

65. Savoy: ADS, 1 MI 33, bobine 2 up to view 109, then bobine 3 at view 54, account number 27 (December 12, 1370–October 14, 1372), view 174; ADS 1 MI 90, roll 3, register 34 (August 8, 1377–August 8, 1382), view 145; ADS 7 MI 3, rolls 6, 7, register 43 (May 16, 1398–September 1, 1400), view 260. London: Dale, "London Silkwomen," 330, citing British Library, Ms. Cotton, Vespasian E, ix, fols. 86–110, a treatise called "The Noumbre of Weyghtes." Part of this treatise has been edited, but the section on silk yarn is not in the edition: Hall and Nicholas, eds., *Select Tracts and Table Books*, 12–20; "Wardrobe Account for Thomas of Lancaster, Duke of Clarence, c. 1418–21," in Woolgar, *Household Accounts from Medieval England*, 2:662 (reference to silk yarn from Paris).

66. Coyecque, ed., *Recueil des actes notariés*, 1:481, #2592 (1543).

67. Edler De Roover, *L'arte della seta*, 43–44.

68. PdC A 474, f. 16: "pour iiii pieces et une aune de chendal no laves des langes . . . pour iiii pieces et demy de chendal no lavez des langes" (for 4 pieces and 1 ell of unwashed cendal . . . for 4 and a half pieces of unwashed cendal); Ghent, Rijksarchief, fonds Gaillard 52, membrane 7: "une pieche de soie esorne."

69. Edler De Roover, *L'arte della seta*, 43.

70. Ghent, Rjiksarchief, fonds Gaillard 52, membrane 7.

71. Mercers' statutes of 1324, nos. 5, 6, Fagniez, ed., *Documents relatifs à l'histoire de l'industrie*, 2:59–60.

72. Fagniez, *Études sur l'industrie*, 238.

73. AN KK 283 fols. 15, 15v, 111, 134v, 188, 189v, 263v, 264, 266 (some dyers were taxed in more than one year); Michaëlsson, ed., *Livre de la taille . . . 1313*, 142.

74. The 1427 *catasto* of Florence indicated that there were 211 silk weavers, four companies of silk dyers, and three individual silk dyers: Edler De Roover, *L'arte della seta*, 32; and ibid., introduction by Bruno Dini, p. x.

75. AN KK 283 fols. 15, 15v, 111, 134v, 188, 189v, 263v, 264, 266 (some dyers were taxed in more than one year). The one dyer who shows up in the tax assessment of 1313 was located in the Lombard zone just south of the rue de la Buffeterie: Michaëlsson, ed., *Livre de la taille . . . 1313*, 142.

76. AN KK 283, fols. 111v, 134v, 188, 189v, 263v, 264, 266. In all cases, when calculating averages taxes for groups that included taxpayers who appeared in more than one tax assessment, I first averaged the individual's tax assessments and then counted that taxpayer only once.

77. Appendix 3, parts A and B.

78. Gargiolli, ed., *L'arte della seta in firenze*, 14–15; Currie, "Silk," 31; Edler De Roover, *L'arte della seta*, 43.

79. Gilonne, *Soieries de Lyon*, 1:343.

80. Beaumont-Maillet, *L'eau à Paris*, 63; Benoît, "En eaux troubles," 72–73. The wool dyers on the right bank concentrated in the zone south of the Porte-Saint-Antoine, near the convent of the Beguines: Gourmelon, "L'industrie et le commerce des draps," 24–25.

81. Cardon, *Natural Dyes*, 345–346, 615.

82. For the contrast between Florentine wool dyers, who worked with only one color, and the silk dyers, who worked with the full palette of colors, see Edler De Roover, *L'arte della seta*, 31, 43–47. On the complexities of the recipes for the various colors, see Gargiolli, ed., *L'arte della seta in firenze*, 50–63.

83. Cardon describes how some modern indigo dyers determine when a dye bath is ready for the fiber by smelling the solution: *Natural Dyes*, 348.

84. "Grano," which was made from dried insects that grew on oak trees around the Mediterranean, was the most expensive and fashionable dye of the thirteenth and early fourteenth centuries. In the late fourteenth century another expensive red dye made from another insect, which grew primarily in the Caspian Sea region and in Anatolia, became fashionable. Molà, *The Silk Industry*, 110.

85. Fagniez, ed., *Documents relatifs à l'histoire de l'industrie*, 2:64; London, National Archives, Public Records Office, E 361/3, rot. 6v ("xiiii ulñ demi in grano panni paris' in serico rad' " [4 and one half ells of striped silk cloth of Paris dyed *in grano*]).

86. Ghent, Rijksarchief, fonds Gaillard 52, membrane 7: "Item pour soie ki fu portee en Flandre et raportee a Paris pour taindre, vi s[ous]" (Again, for silk that was transported to Flanders and transported back to Paris to be dyed, 6 sous).

87. Loesch, *Die Kölner Zunfturkunden*, 1:191n1.

88. On veils woven with gold thread, see Guillaume de Nangis, "Listoire du roy Phelippe," 497; on narrow ware, see Desrosiers, *Soieries et autres textiles*, 158–159, 162 and "Le premier compte de Geoffroi de Fleury argentier du roi Philippe le Long pour les six derniers mois de l'année 1316," in Douët-d'Arcq, ed., *Comptes de l'argenterie*, 44, 66 ("Pour le petit Daufin, une aloière et 1 tissu ferré d'argent"; "pour 4 tissus d'or esmailliez, 20 s pour pièce . . . pour 3 tissus d'or esmailliez, 16 s pour pièce . . . pour 12 tissus à pelles, ferrez d'argent").

89. Thirteenth-century Venetian silk and gold cloth: Desrosiers, *Soieries et autres textiles*, 256; Costantini, "Uno sciamito del XIII secolo," 4. Silk and gold cloth of Lucca: Desrosiers, *Soieries et autres textiles*, 345, 349 (technical description of cat. nos. 187, 189); Wardwell, " '*Panni Tartarici*,' " 96. Much like Italian cloth of gold of this period, Central Asian cloth of gold was woven with gold thread spun with gilded animal substratum, which was then wrapped around a cotton core or woven directly into the fabric: Wardwell, " '*Panni Tartarici*,' " 96.

90. On the metallic thread on an embroidery that was probably made in Paris, see Geijer, *Textile Treasures of Uppsala Cathedral*, 24.

91. Jacoby, "Cypriot Gold Thread." Anna Muthesius describes the metallic thread on the central panel of the Grandson Antependium, which was probably made in Cyprus soon after the fall of Acre in 1291, as silver-gilt wire over a yellow silk core: *Studies in Silk in Byzantium*, 241.

92. "Que nulz ne nulle ne soit si hardiz de faire ne de faire faire, d'acheter ne de vendre tissuz a or, se il ne sont tissuz dedens fine soye, et que les tissuz qui d'or seront faiz soient faiz de tel or qu'il soient souffisans, c'est assavoir or que l'en appelle de Chippre et or de Paris. Et que nulz ne nulle ne soit si hardiz de mesler autre or avecques yceus ne de mettre y or de Luques": Fagniez, ed., *Documents relatifs à l'histoire de l'industrie*, 2:62.

93. Ghent, Rijksarchief, fonds Gaillard 52, membrane 3; *Livre des métiers*, ed. Lespinasse and Bonnardot, 63–66, See Bourlet, "Le *Livre des métiers*," 35–40 on the dating of the statutes.

94. Eight women, and no men, "qui file l'or" show up in the Parisian tax assessments: Géraud, ed., *Paris sous Philippe-le-Bel*, 56, 159; Michaëlsson, ed., *Livre de la taille . . . 1296*, 98; AN KK 283, fols. 132, 135, 181, 187v, 188v, 194, 258v, 265; Michaëlsson, ed., *Livre de la taille . . .*

1313, 122. On Italian women who spun gold thread, see Strocchia, *Nuns and Nunneries*, 35, 120–122; and Bonds, "Genoese Noblewomen and Gold Thread Manufacturing," 79–81.

95. Ghent, Rijksarchief, fonds Gaillard 52, membrane 3: "bastons dor," "bastons dargent," "pour un paire de forces pour taillier or et pour fusois dachier pour filer or" (for a pair of metal cutters to cut gold and for steel spindles to spin gold).

96. On aristocratic women and tablet weaving, see Crowfoot, Pritchard, and Staniland, eds., *Textiles and Clothing*, 131; Ghent, Rijksarchief, fonds Gaillard 52, membrane 5; PdC A 178, cited by Richard, *Une petite-niece*: "Le xxie jour de février [1302], paia Garsie à un mestre de Paris par le commandement maistre [Thierry] pour une espée d'ivroire pour madame la contesse et pour uns taveles d'ivoire à ouvrer de soie" (February 21 [1302], by the command of master [Thierry], Garsie paid a master in Paris for an ivory weaver's blade for madame the countess and for some ivory tablets for working with silk). This passage is very important for establishing that the term "tavele" referred to the physical item (the "tablet") that was used to make the narrow ware and not simply to the finished narrow ware product, as Godefroy assumed: Godefroy, *Dictionnaire* 7:658. By extension, the fact that "taveles" were tablets for tablet weaving indicates that narrow ware that was described as having been made "au tavel" was tablet-woven.

Other evidence concerning textile activities of French and Francophone aristocratic women includes purchases in 1294 by Isabel of Luxembourg, Countess of Flanders, of silk and gold thread and of the tools to make gold thread; the construction of what appears to have been a draw loom for Countess Mahaut of Artois in 1304; Marguerite of Sicily's testamentary gift of all of her gold thread and pearls to "Hugueite ma ouvrière de soie"; the purchase of two ivory reeling devices in 1317 and 1318 for King Philip V's household (one of the reeling devices was for Queen Jeanne of Burgundy); and the presence of a reeling device in the posthumous estate of Queen Clémence of Hungary, who died in 1328: Ghent, Rijksarchief, fonds Gaillard 52; Richard, *Une petite-nièce*, 368; Dehaisnes, *Documents*, 1:166; Douët-d'Arcq, ed., *Nouveau recueil de comptes*, 3, 7, 82.

97. Depping, ed., *Réglemens*, 370–373, 379–387; *Livre des métiers*, ed. Lespinasse and Bonnardot, 72–74, 113–116, 168–174. Stocking makers: computerized list generated from the tax assessments by Caroline Bourlet. On arms makers as embroiderers, see Gauffre-Fayolle, "Broder à la cour de Savoie," 45–47; and Chapter 1 above, main text preceding note 72. On *crépines* in the late thirteenth and fourteenth centuries, see Enlart, *Manuel d'archéologie française*, 181. On gold and silk hats, see Chapter 5, main text preceding notes 67–70.

98. "Textrices, que texunt serica texta, proi[i]ciunt fila deaurata officio cavillarum et percutiunt subtegmina cum linea spata. De textis vero fiunt cingula et crinalia divitum [Ms devitum] mulierum et stole sacerdotum": John of Garland, *Dictionarius*, ed. Hunt, 201.

99. *Livre des métiers*, ed. Lespinasse and Bonnardot, 74–75. On the dating of these statutes, see Bourlet, "Le *Livre des métiers*," 37, 41.

100. Appendix 3, part C.

101. *Livre des métiers*, ed. Lespinasse and Bonnardot, 66–68. On numbers of makers of *laz de soie* and *dorelotiers* (13 women, 41 men), see Appendix 3, part D.

102. For multiple references to silver and gold thread in *tissu/z de soie*, see Godefroy, *Dictionnaire*, 10:772. On *tissu/z de soie* as ribbon or laces, see "Pour un tissu de soie ynde, pour faire les fermillez d'icelles heures" (for a blue ribbon, to make the ties for this [book of] hours): Prost and Prost, eds., *Inventaires mobiliers*, 2:14.

103. Crowfoot, Pritchard, and Staniland, eds., *Textiles and Clothing*, 130–131.

104. Ibid., 24, 130; Collingwood, *The Techniques of Tablet Weaving*.

105. Piponnier, "Usages et diffusion de la soie," 793–794; "D'un tissut d'or avoit chain-ture," *Richard le beau,* Turin ms. f. 130v, cited by Godefroy, *Dictionnaire,* 10:772.

106. In 1294, for instance, the Countess of Flanders paid a Beguine of Douai for some orphreys destined for the Franciscans of that town: Ghent, Rijksarchief, fonds Gaillard 52, membrane 3.

107. "Un orfrois fait au tavel de l'ouvrage de Paris semé a fleur de lis aux armes de France": Molinier, ed., "Inventaire du trésor de l'Église du Saint-Sepulcre de Paris," no. 13, p. 251. See also nos. 4, 5, 6, 11–12, 14, 18, 38, 188, 233, 390, 391 on pp. 250–252, 254, 269, 273, 285. See note 96 for a discussion of why I am assuming that "fait au tavel" meant "tablet woven."

108. Ghent, Rijksarchief, fonds Gaillard 52, membrane 5: "a une femme ki ploie bourses pour iiii tissus vers, le tissus ix sous . . . montent xxxvi sous" (to a woman who weaves [?] purses, 9 sous each for 4 green "tissus" . . . for a total of 36 sous).

109. Jolivet, "Pour soi vêtir honnêtement," vol. 2, annexes, pp. 38–40. In 1425 King Henry VI of England, who held authority over Paris at the time, approved a new set of statutes for the weavers of "tissus de soye": Longnon, ed., *Paris pendant la domination anglaise,* 200–202. In the 1370s and 1380s the court of Savoy also purchased narrow ware (called "bisette") from Paris: ADS, 1 MI 33, bobine 2 up to view 109 then bobine 3 starting at view 54, account number 27 (December 12, 1370–October 14, 1372), view 258; 7 MI 3, rolls 2, 3, register number 37.1 (February 23, 1386–March 25, 1389), view 13. I thank Nadège Gauffre-Fayolle for these references.

110. For a list of the women who wove silk head coverings and who were described as "qui carie soie," see Appendix 3, part B. See above, note 40, for my translation of "qui carie soie" as "silk cloth weaver." On the fourteenth-century Beguine who wove *cendal,* see "Jehanne des Granches beguine, pour la soye facon de deux brayes de cendal, lun pour le comte d'anjou, lautre pour le comte d'Estampes": "Compte de M. Estienne Lafontaine," ed. Leber, 94.

111. Becker and Wagner, *Pattern and Loom,* 1.

112. *Livre des métiers,* ed. Lespinasse and Bonnardot, 83–84.

113. Bourlet, "Le *Livre des métiers.*"

114. Heckett, "Some Hiberno-Norse Headcoverings."

115. Guillaume de Nangis, "Listoire du roy Phelippe," 497; "Dit du mercier," ed. Ménard, 798.

116. Molà, "Le donne nell'industria serica veneziana," 439.

117. Appendix 3, part B. On "qui carie soie," see above, note 40.

118. See Chapter 4, note 4.

119. *Livre des métiers,* ed. Lespinasse and Bonnardot, 76–78.

120. Ibid., 77.

121. On separate warpers in Florence, see Edler De Roover, *L'arte della seta,* 49–52. On weavers sometimes doing the warping, see Cardon, *La draperie au Moyen Âge,* 318; and Massa, *La "fabbrica" dei velluti genovesi,* 51. On the predominance of men rather than women in this guild of silk weavers, see main text of this chapter, just before note 131, and Appendix 3, part A.

122. On rewinding onto bobbins and placing the bobbins onto a frame with upright or horizontal pegs to hold them in place, see Cardon, *La draperie au Moyen Âge,* 322–325; and Edler De Roover, *L'arte della seta,* 49.

123. Cardon, *La draperie au Moyen Âge,* 325.

124. Ibid., 332–333. Most warping frames were actually rectangular, with two pegs on the bottom horizontal bar, which created a second "cross" to prevent the warp yarns from crossing

each other. In such cases, the end point of the length of the warp was at the second of those two bottom pegs. The illustration from fifteenth-century Florence does not show those two bottom pegs.

125. Cardon, *La draperie au Moyen Âge*, 361, 392, fig. 137.

126. Ibid., 345–352, 365.

127. One silk dalmatic in the Cluny museum in Paris, which may have been woven in Paris in the first third of the fourteenth century, had a warp thread count of 32–36 threads per centimeter; at that thread count, a warp with 1,900 single threads would have been 53–59 centimeters in width: Desrosiers, *Soieries et autres textiles*, 165. In the mid-fourteenth century Lucca had a minimum width requirement of 44.287 centimeters for narrow *cendal* and 59.05 centimeters for narrow baldachins, heavy and light satins, and a number of other cloths: Monnas, "Loom Widths and Selvedges," 36–37. In fifteenth-century Florence, brocades had a thread count of 1,800 warp ends (45 turns of 20 bobbins): Gargiolli, ed., *L'arte della seta in firenze*, 71.

128. Cardon, *La draperie au Moyen Âge*, 317, 373.

129. Edler De Roover, *L'arte della seta*, 52; Cardon, *La draperie au Moyen Âge*, 368.

130. *Livre des métiers*, ed. Lespinasse and Bonnardot, 76–78.

131. Appendix 3, part A.

132. Molà, *The Silk Industry*, 8.

133. On the entry exam for this guild, see *Livre des métiers*, ed. Lespinasse and Bonnardot, 76; on other guilds requiring an exam, see Fagniez, *Études sur l'industrie*, 93–94.

134. Desrosiers, "Sur l'origine d'un tissu qui a participé à la fortune de Venise," 40–41. The statutes for the Parisian guild of makers of "draps de soye" and velvet mentioned looms with two warp beams: weavers were not allowed to mix "soie canete" (presumably yarn formed from silk waste) with good silk, unless the loom had two warp beams: *Livre des métiers*, ed. Lespinasse and Bonnardot, 77.

In her article on the origins of European velvet weaving, Desrosiers expressed a small doubt as to whether Parisian velvet was made of silk. Count Robert II of Artois's commission in 1292 of twenty-seven saddles that were decorated with "veluau de soie" (silk velvet) puts that doubt to rest. For other responses to Desrosiers's doubts, see Farmer, "*Biffes, Tiretaines,* and *Aumonières,*" 83–84. Since publishing that article I have reinterpreted the activities of makers of "tissuz de soie" (they made narrow ware, not silk cloth) and of *ouvriers/ouvrières de soie* (most were not weavers), and I have added makers of *drap d'or* to my list of weavers, thus the statistics on silk weavers on p. 83 of that article are not accurate.

135. The statutes mentioned looms with two warp beams in the context of whether or not it was ever permitted to weave with waste silk: "Item, que nuls . . . ne pourra ne ne devra ouvrer ou dit mestier, de quel euvre que ce soit, de soye canete . . . car ourture de canete est fausse, se *ce n'est en draps a deus ourtures* [italics added]" (see note 48 for translation); *Livre des métiers*, ed. Lespinasse and Bonnardot, 77, statute 4. On the use of two warp beams in the weaving of velvets, see Desrosiers, "Sur l'origine d'un tissu qui a participé à la fortune de Venise," 41.

136. Desrosiers, "Sur l'origine d'un tissu qui a participé à la fortune de Venise," 35; Monnas, "Developments in Figured Velvet Weaving," 64.

137. Lysons, ed., "Copy of a Roll of Purchases," 301, 308.

138. Richard, *Une petite-nièce*, 126–127, citing PdC A, 132; Ghent, Rijksarchief, fonds St.-Genois, 668 (quittance from Count Guy of Flanders). On Amauri of Amiens, see Appendix 2, part A, no. 7.

139. Ghent, Rijksarchief, fonds Gaillard 52, membrane 10. On Ymbert (or Imbert) of Lyon's identity as a mercer, see Appendix 2, part A, no. 25. In 1313 both Ymbert of Lyon and "les fames aus II Jehans de Lyons" (the widows, most likely, "of the two Jehans of Lyon") were taxed on the rue Troussevache. Ymbert (whose profession was not identified) paid the extremely high tax of 90 livres and the two widows paid another high tax, of 60 livres. The probable familial relationship among the men named Jehan of Lyon and Ymbert of Lyon emerges in a discussion of their apparent descendants—two Ymberts and a Jehan—in a fragmentary Parisian tax assessment of 1355. At the beginning of a list naming the eight prominent merchants who were to take responsibility for handing over the taxes that were collected in the parish of Saint-Pierre-des-Arcis, on the Île-de-la-Cité, the assessment included the names of "sire Ymbert de Lions . . . Ymbert de Lions, son fils . . . Jehan de Lions, son filz." The fact that the three Lyon men were now taxed in the parish of Saint-Pierre-des-Arcis rather than on the rue Troussevache is indicative of the emerging importance of the mercery in the gallery of the Palais Royale: Michaëlsson, ed., *Livre de la taille . . . 1313*, 132; Moranvillé, "Un rôle d'impôt à Paris," 9.

140. Dehaisnes, *Documents*, 1:133, cited by Monnas, "Developments in Figured Velvet Weaving," 64. Monnas points out that in the 1317 royal account, striped velvet was so common that the record keeper mentioned when pieces of velvet were *not* striped: Monnas, "Developments in Figured Velvet Weaving," 64; Douët-d'Arcq, ed., *Nouveau recueil de comptes*, 1, 2, 7.

141. Géraud, ed., *Paris sous Philippe-le-Bel*, 29; AN KK 283, fol. 192.

142. Géraud, ed., *Paris sous Philippe-le-Bel*, 29; Richard, *Une petite-nièce*, 127–128.

143. Munro, "Medieval Woollens," 194.

144. Becker and Wagner, *Pattern and Loom*, 314–319, 334–335.

145. Desrosiers, "Trois representations d'un métier à la tire."

146. Becker and Wagner, *Pattern and Loom*, 334. A text from 1335 describing a draw loom in Lucca indicates that it had pulleys and a pulley box: Monnas, "Developments in Figured Velvet Weaving," 76n11: "cum pectine, cassio et subiis et una licciatura, cum ramis et plumbis et tabulis, cum girellis, stanghis, et cum toto fornimento" (tentative translation by Monnas: "with a reed, pulley box and beams, and a harness, with pulley and tail cords and lingoes and a comber board, with pulleys, shafts, and all the (necessary) equipment").

147. Richard, *Une petite-nièce*, 368, citing PdC A 201: "Pour fair 1 mestier avoekes madame, pour faire viii/xx vergiaus et II/c poulietes, xxvii jumeles, et le havestre de bos lau eles sont fremees, xxii s. vii d." (To make a loom with madame: to make 160 rods and 200 pulleys, 27 pairs, and the wooden hook where they are attached—22 sous, 7 deniers). I have not worked out all of the mechanical details of this text. The text seems to imply that the countess herself participated in the construction of the loom.

148. On the consumption of luxury silk from Paris, see references above in note 64. The best evidence for the production of cloth of gold and velvet in Paris is that concerning taxpayers who were identified as makers of those textiles: Appendix 3, part A, nos. 3, 4, 8, 12, 13, 15, 16.

CHAPTER 3

1. AN KK 283, fols. 110v, 184v; Appendix 1, part A, no. 126; Appendix 3, part A, no. 3. Another Rolant of Venice paid taxes in 1299, on the rue Jehan le Comte, but his tax of only 2 sous indicates that he cannot have been the same as the Rolant of Venice who had resided on the rue Saint Merri and the rue de la Buffeterie between 1292 and 1298: Appendix 1, part A,

no. 127. In the years 1297–1300 several weavers of silk narrow ware paid taxes that were equal to or higher than the tax paid by Gautier the Burgundian: Appendix 3, part C, no. 17; part D, nos. 30, 34, 53.

2. Tognetti, "Development of the Florentine Silk Industry," 62; Mazzaoui, "Artisan Migration"; Jacoby, "Silk Economics," 223–228; Molà, "Industria della seta"; Molà, *The Silk Industry*, 3–29.

3. *Livre des métiers*, ed. Lespinasse and Bonnardot. On the dating of the statutes, see Bourlet, "Le *Livre des métiers*."

4. On Lucca, see Dini, "L'industria serica in Italia," 94; and Edler De Roover, "Lucchese Silks," 2920. On Venice, see Dini, "L'industria serica in Italia," 102. On Florence, see Edler De Roover, "Andrea Banchi," 236.

5. "Nus ne nule de leur mestier ne puet ourdir en ourture de tissus . . . ne en autre euvre quelle que elle soit, fil ne flourin aveques cuer de soie": *Livre des métiers*, ed. Lespinasse and Bonnardot, 158, statute 3. On the dating of the mercers' statutes, see Bourlet, "Le *Livre des métiers*," 37, 41.

6. "Nus ne nulle ne puet faire faire ne acheter aumosnieres sarrasinoises ou il ait mellé fil ne coton aveques soie": *Livre des métiers*, ed. Lespinasse and Bonnardot, 158, statute 10.

7. "Pour 8 onces de fuille dor et dargent achater par Est. Chevalier que furent baillies a Belun pour ouvrer": PdC A, 448, fol. 26v.

8. "A Estienne Chevalier pour taveles et espees a ouvrer pour ladite [*sic*] Belun": ibid. Jules-Marie Richard mistakenly assumed that the "Belun" in this passage was an embroiderer, but it is clear from the context that the reference is to Lando Belloni: Richard, *Une petite-nièce*, 205. For a discussion of tablet weaving, see main text of Chapter 2, discussion preceding notes 104–107. On the meaning of "tavele," see Chapter 2, note 96.

9. PdC A 474, fol. 25: "A dit Etene [le furbisseur/orfevre] pour ferrer 1 tissus de soie que Belon fit ou il mist dargent une once . . . xi s" ([Paid] 11 sous . . . to the said Etienne [the sword polisher/goldsmith] to garnish with one ounce of silver a piece of silk narrow ware that Belloni made); PdC A 403, fol. 19: "A Laude belun pour 3 samiz pour le cier du char et pour la tinture: 16 lb 10 s" (Paid 16 livres, 10 sous to Lando Belloni for 3 samites for the seat of the cart, and for the dyeing).

10. Fagniez, *Études sur l'industrie*, 74n1, citing AN 5223, fol. 13v.

11. *Livre des métiers*, ed. Lespinasse and Bonnardot, 67 (statute 10), 159 (statute 14). For further discussion, see Farmer, "Les privilèges des métiers."

12. On the history and importance of the provost of the merchants and the *échevins*, see main text of introduction, discussion preceding note 12.

13. "Quant aucuns des merciers de la ville de Paris baillioent leur soie escrue por ouvrer, pour labourer ou pou filler . . . il le engagoient ou vendoient chiez Lombars ou chiez juyfs, ou leur eschangoient la bonne soie que il leur bailloient . . . a bourre de saie, et l'atornoient et apportoient en lieu de la bonne soie a celui qui la leur avoit baillée. . . . Item, quant il avoient vendue ou engagié ycelle soie que l'en leur avoit ballié pour labourer et pour filer, et cil qui la leur avoit baillée venoit a eus, et leur demandoit sa soie, il disoient qu'il l'avoient perdue et adirée, et que volontiers leur rendroient et paieroient l'argent que elle valoit apres leurs vies, et que il n'avoient de quoi paier; pour laquele [chose] cilz qui li avoit baillié la soie pour labourer et pour filer les traioient en cause pardevant nous, et estoient plaintis d'eles, et leur demandoient icele soie, et eles respondoient que eles l'avoient adirée, et que il n'avoient de coi paier la valeur": Fagniez, ed., *Documents relatifs à l'histoire de l'industrie*, 1:277–278.

Statute 9 of the original statutes for the guild of "Fillerresses de soye a grans fuiseaus," written between 1266 and 1275, had already prohibited throwsters from using silk that had been put out to them as a pledge for money loans, but the statute did not name the mercers as the silk owners to whom the damage was done, nor did it single out Jews and Lombards as the moneylenders. *Livre des métiers*, ed. Lespinasse and Bonnardot, 69, statute 9. On the dating of the statutes for the throwsters, see Bourlet "Le *Livre des métiers*," 35–41.

14. Fagniez, ed., *Documents relatifs à l'histoire de l'industrie*, 1:278.

15. On banishment as a sanction for debt, see Claustre, *Dans les geôles*, 44–47. Claustre claims that Paris, which had no commune, never practiced banishment for debt, but this text indicates that the picture is more complicated than she suggests.

16. Fagniez, ed., *Documents relatifs à l'histoire de l'industrie*, 2:59–60 (statutes 1, 9, 10). By this time debtors' law also involved the possible seizure of body and possessions, but such seizure was contingent upon the nonpayment of the debt. In these statutes, by contrast, the bodies and possessions of the guilty parties are placed under the "the mercy" or the "will" of the king regardless of any conditions. Claustre, *Dans les geôles*, 243–246.

17. Mayade-Claustre, "Le corps lié de l'ouvrier," 387.

18. December 4, 1340: "Fu amenée en notre prison [that of the abbey of Saint-Martin-des-Champs] Denise, fame Nicolas Lelegat, notre sergent, pour cause de ce que Phelipote la monine [who had been accused of working with stolen silk] l'avoit accusée, disant que elle lui avoit vendu la soie que emblée avoit, et que ladite Denise estoit commune recelaresse de apprentisses et autres fames ouvrieres de soie, qui lui portent soie que emblée ont à leurs mestres et mestresses, et que ladicte Denise lui avoit dit que elle lui portast hardiement de la soie, et que elle lui baudroit l'argent": Tanon, ed., *Histoire des justices des anciennes églises*, 533. The possibility that servants were stealing silk fiber had been raised in a statute from 1324, which prohibited moneylenders from accepting silk fiber from servants and underaged individuals: Fagniez, *Documents relatifs à l'histoire de l'industrie*, 2:60 (statute 10). For an example of a servant who stole some silk narrow ware from her employer, see *Régistre criminel du Châtelet de Paris*, 1:198.

19. Rayner, *Silk Throwing*, 19, 25, 34–35; Savary, *Le parfait negociant*, part 2, book 1, chap. 7, 93–94.

20. Serjeant, *Islamic Textiles*, 199; Molà, "Le donne nell'industria serica veneziana," 429–430; Savary, *Le parfait negociant*, part 2, book 1, chap. 7, 94.

21. *Livre des métiers*, ed. Lespinasse and Bonnardot, 83, statute 5: "Item, il est ordené que nule mestresse ne ouvriere du mestier ne pevent acheter soie de Juys, de filerresses ne de nul autre, fors de marcheanz tant seulement." Ibid., 83–84, statute 8: "Item, il est ordené que nule mestresse ne alouée du mestier desus dit ne peut ne ne doit metre euvre que ele face, soit ourdie ou sanz ourdir, ou faite ou a fere, en gages a juif, a lombart, ne a nul autre maniere de gent. Et se ele le faisoit, toutes les foiz que ele le feroit et ele en seroit reprise, ele paieroit dis solz d'amende: des quiex li Rois auroit sis solz, et les mestresses qui garderoient le mesiter IIII s."

22. On poor people and debt in medieval France, see Claustre, *Dans les geôles*. See also Chapter 5.

23. One Beguine who was identified in 1298 as a throwster was identified in 1299 as a "seller" of silk, so it seems that a few throwsters were able to move out of the position of economic dependency vis-à-vis the mercers. Miller, *The Beguines of Medieval Paris*, 65.

24. It is possible that some of the purse weavers in the guild of "Ouvriers de draps de soye, et de veluyaus et de boursserie en lice" were women. However, since another guild of makers of silk alms purses ("Faiseuses d'aumônières sarrazinoises") was formed around the year 1300, it is impossible to tell which of the silk purse makers and retailers who show up in the

tax assessments were members of the guild of makers of "draps de soye" and velvet. I have, for that reason, left the purse weavers out of my analysis. For the statutes of the other guild of purse makers, see Depping, ed., *Réglemens*, 382–386.

25. *Livre des métiers*, ed. Lespinasse and Bonnardot, 76–78.

26. "A tous ceus qui ces lettres verront Jehan Loncle, garde de la prevosté de Paris salut. Comme les bonnes gens merciers de la ville de Paris se feussent traiz pardevers nous et nous eussent signifié et donné a entendre que en la marchandise et ou mestier de ladicte mercerie plusieurs malefaçons dommageuses a tout le commun peuple estoient faites de jour en jour par deffaut de gardes convenables qui n'estoient paz oudit mestier et si grandement que, se remede n'y estoit miz, grief et dommage en pourroit venir . . . et pour ce nous eussent requis et supplié que nous . . . voussissiens sur ce prouveoir de remede convenable": Fagniez, ed., *Documents relatifs à l'histoire de l'industrie*, 2:58.

27. Fagniez, ed., *Documents relatifs à l'histoire de l'industrie*, 2:59–60, statutes 1, 9, 10.

28. Ibid., 2:59–61, statutes 2, 5, 6, 17, 19.

29. For complaints about similar deceptions, see Savary, *Le parfait negociant*, part 2, book 1, chap. 7, 95. On the deceptions that were especially possible when silk was dyed black, see Fagniez, ed., *Documents relatifs à l'histoire de l'industrie*, 2:60, statute 6; Savary, *Le parfait negociant*, part 2, book 1, chap. 7, 95; and Massa, *La "fabbrica" dei velluti genovesi*, 50.

30. Fagniez, ed., *Documents relatifs à l'histoire de l'industrie*, 2:58–65 (statutes 2 and 3 concern weaving; 4, 5, and 6 concern dyeing, as does statute 31, which places the bodies and possessions of offenders at the mercy of the king); Lespinasse, ed., *Les métiers et corporations de la ville de Paris*, 242–248. Placing bodies and possessions at the mercy of the king is also mentioned in four statutes (1, 9, 10, 12) that focus on the sale, theft, subcontracting, or corruption of raw silk: 1—unauthorized use of silk fiber as a form of payment; 9—taking silk from someone who is not the merchant of the silk in order to throw it; 10—buying silk from an underaged seller or from a servant; 12—selling various kinds of waste silk. Statutes 30 and 32, which also imposed the harshest punishment, attempted to prevent Parisian mercers from sharing business assets or business interests with Lombard merchants, presumably because this enabled the foreign Lombards to evade forms of taxation that applied only to them. On the red dye known as "grainne" "grano," "grana," or "kermes," see Cardon, *Natural Dyes*, 609–619.

31. *Livre des métiers*, ed. Lespinasse and Bonnardot, 158; see also main text of this chapter, discussion preceding notes 8 and 9.

32. Ibid., 158–159.

33. "Tous les lieux de la Ville de Paris où l'en fait et exerce ledit mestier et marchandise": Lespinasse, ed., *Les métiers et corporations de la ville de Paris*, 248. I cite Lespinasse's edition here because Fagniez did not print statutes 37 and 38 of the 1324 statutes.

34. "[Pourront aller visiter par tous les lieux de la Ville de Paris] . . . et aient avecq eulx un sergent de Chastellet ou plusieurs . . . pour eulz garder de force et de violence": Lespinasse, ed., *Les métiers et corporations de la ville de Paris*, 248, statute 37.

35. Fagniez, *Études sur l'industrie*, 305–306: two employees in a goldsmith's workshop refused to open a door for the jurors of their guild, who then sought assistance from the Châtelet in order to complete their statutory visitation.

36. Recent historians have made a similar argument concerning Jehan Boinbroke, the famous merchant and wool entrepreneur of Douai, who was once portrayed as an entrepreneur who controlled wool workers through a putting-out system but is now seen as both a merchant and an artisan. Derville, "Les draperies flamandes"; Roch, *Un autre monde du travail*, 101–103.

37. On the risks involved in dyeing silk, see Muthesius, "Silk in the Medieval World," 349.

38. In fifteenth-century Florence a piece of taffeta took four or five weeks to weave; more complex brocades could take up to six months: Goodman, "Cloth, Gender and Industrial Organization," 240. Parisian silks would not have been as intricate as the complex brocades or figured velvets of fifteenth-century Florence, but the velvet and cloth of gold would have taken more time than was necessary for weaving a monochrome piece of taffeta.

39. Appendix 2.

40. The thirteenth-century "Dit des marcheans" by Phelippot highlighted the rues Troussevache and Quincampoix "por la mercerie achater": Poëte, *Vie d'une cité*, 1:219. Many wealthy bourgeois citizens of thirteenth-century Paris owned more than one property, so it is impossible to know if a tax address was both a shop/workshop and a residence. However, since tax assessors would have come around during normal working hours, we can assume that in most cases a tax address was also a working address.

41. Appendix 2, part A. I thank my research assistant, Sarah Hanson, for assisting me in creating separate lists of mercers in various neighborhoods and in ensuring that those lists included only one entry for each individual mercer. Before calculating the average tax assessment for any one group, I first calculated the average annual assessment for each individual who paid taxes more than once between 1297 and 1300.

42. In 1292 members of the Dammartin family resided in two separate households on the rue de la Courroierie in the Troussevache mercery, as did the widow of a member of the Toussac family; the rue Troussevache included three households of the Toussac family. In that year, none of the professions of these individuals was mentioned, but four were later identified as mercers, as was one additional member of the Toussac family living in the Troussevache mercery: Géraud, ed., *Paris sous Philippe-le-Bel*, 90–91; Appendix 2, part A, nos. 13, 15, 42, 48, 53. On Parisian families, including those mentioned here, whose members held positions as *échevins* or as provosts of the merchants, see Bove, *Dominer la ville*, esp. 643–646.

43. Appendix 2, part A, nos. 4, 7, 13, 22, 41, 44, 47, 55; Ghent, Rijksarchief, fonds Gaillard 52, membranes 3, 5, 7; Ghent, Rijksarchief, fonds St.-Genois, no. 668; PdC A 2, fol. 28v, described by Richard, *Inventaire-sommaire*, 1:8; PdC A 242, described by Richard, *Inventaire-sommaire*, 1:233; PdC A 151/19; Parsons, *The Court and Household of Eleanor of Castile*, 84, 102. Jehan of Lyon was never identified in the tax assessments as a mercer, but we know he sold velvet to the Countess of Flanders and that he lived on the rue Troussevache: Ghent, Rijksarchief, fonds Gaillard 52, membrane 10; Michaëlsson, ed., *Livre de la taille . . . 1313*, 132. In 1313 both Ymbert of Lyon and "les fames aus II Jehans de Lyons" (the widows, most likely, "of the two Jehans of Lyon") were taxed on the rue Troussevache. Like Jehan of Lyon, Jehan le Roumain was never identified in the tax assessments as a mercer, but his widow Eustache (or Huitace) was (Appendix 2, part A, no. 9). Moreover, we know that Jehan le Roumain was himself a mercer because he sold mercery goods to the English queen, Eleanor of Castile: Parsons, *The Court and Household of Eleanor of Castile*, 84, 102.

44. In May 1303, the mercer Ymbert (or Imbert) of Lyon, who resided on the rue Troussevache, joined a group of approximately twenty Parisian elites who, in the presence of King Philip the Fair, borrowed 2,500 livres tournois from an Italian banking company, probably to help finance the military attack against Pope Boniface VIII that King Philip was planning for later that year: Lalou, Bautier, and Maillard, *Itinéraire de Philippe IV*, 2:216–217. On Ymbert's address, see Appendix 2, part A, no. 25. On Jacquet Tabarie's location on the rue Troussevache, see Appendix 1, part C, no. 38; on his identity as a mercer: British Library, Add. 7966A, fol.

156 and Mons, Archives de l'État, chartier 485, membrane 5; on his privileges at the French royal court: Paris, Bibliothèque Nationale de France, Ms. Clairambault, 832, p. 643.

45. Appendix 2, part B.

46. *Échevin* elites in the Quincampoix mercery included several members of the Dammartin family and several members of the Espernon family; Quincampoix mercers who did business with aristocratic courts included Mahy of Arras, Jehan le Pellier, and Nicolas of Amiens: Appendix 2, part B, nos. 6, 7, 25, 38, 45, 50, 66, 69, 75, 93, 96; Ghent, Rijksarchief, fonds Gaillard 52, membrane 7.

47. Appendix 2, part C.

48. Male weavers residing in the Lombard zone: Appendix 3, part A, nos. 3, 4, 7. Other male silk workers residing in the Lombard zone: Appendix 3, part D, nos. 21, 42, and possibly 7 (whose sex cannot be determined); Appendix 5, no. 5.

49. Jehan Vanne (Appendix 2, part A, no. 43), who moved to the Lombard mercery after residing in the Troussevache mercery, was an officer of the court of King Edward I of England: see main text of this chapter, discussion preceding notes 69–70. Jehan Marcel, who resided near the church of Saint-Merri, in the Lombard mercery, sold a number of mercery goods to King Edward I in 1278: Lysons, "Copy of a Role of Purchases," 308; Appendix 2, part C, no. 16.

50. On Jehan of Rueil, see Bove, *Dominer la ville*, 646; and Appendix 2, part C, no. 9. On Jehan Marcel, see the previous note. While there were a number of *échevins* from a family surnamed Marcel, and a number of the men in that family were named Jehan, I have found no other references indicating that any of the men in that family were mercers: Frémaux, "La famille d'Étienne Marcel."

51. Appendices 4 and 5.

52. Appendix 3, parts A and B. On dyers, see Chapter 2, note 40.

53. Appendix 2, part D; Appendix 3, parts A and B; Appendices 4 and 5; Chapter 2, note 40. Mercers who did not reside in the Troussevache, Quincampoix, Lombard, or Petit-Pont mercery constituted just under 20 percent of the mercers; their average tax of 14 sous, or .7 livre, was slightly below average: Appendix 2, part E.

54. "Drap tartaire" and "nach": Jacoby, "Oriental Silks," 71–73; Desrosiers, *Soieries et autres textiles*, 312–313, #166 (burial garment of Pierre de Courpalay, abbot of Saint-Germain-des-Prés, 1334). In her path-breaking article on *panni tartarici*, Anne Wardwell assumed that all references to *panni tartarici* or *drap tartaire* referred to Central Asian silks. Account book evidence suggests, however, that the term became descriptive of a certain type of silk, which could be made in other locations as well. Thus French royal and aristocratic accounts from the early fourteenth century refer not only to "drap tartaire" and "tartaire d'outremer" but also to "drap tartaire de Lucques" or "tartaire de Lucques": Wardwell, "'*Panni Tartarici*,'" 134–144; "Compte de draps d'or et de soie rendu par Geoffroi de Fleuri argentier du Roi Philippe le Long en 1317," in Douët-d'Arcq, ed., *Nouveau recueil de comptes*, 2, 6, 15, 19 (for "tartaire de Lucques"); 2, 4, 6, 8, 9, 10, 11, 13, 14, 15, 16, 17 (for "tartaire"); PdC A 2, fol. 24, described by Richard, *Inventaire-sommaire*, 1:8 ("tartaires de Luque"); PdC A 179, no. 2, described by Richard, *Inventaire-sommaire*, 1:191 ("tartare d'outremer"); "Compte des recettes et depenses faites pour le comte de Flandre," in Dehaisnes, *Documents*, 1:71 ("un tartaire"); "Inventaire de joyaux de la contesse d'Artois (1301)," in Dehaisnes, *Documents*, 1:120 ("tartaires"); "Inventaire des biens de feu Raoul de Nesle, Connètable de France" (1302), in Dehaisnes, *Documents*, 1:133 ("1 drap tartaire oisele d'or"); Inventory of the abbey of Longchamps (1305) (AN K 37, no. 2), ed. Hippolyte Cocheris, *Histoire de la ville, et de tout le diocèse de Paris*, 4:263 ("noir tartaire");

Testament of Marie, widow of Robert Evrout (1316) (AN L 840 #100), ed. Terroine, in "Recherches sur la bourgeoisie," 4:133.

55. On the meaning of "Turkey," see Jacoby, "Oriental Silks," 75. See notes 66, 79, and 83 below for evidence of the presence in northern France of silk textiles from Lucca, the Levant, and Venice. French references to textiles from "Turkey" include: "Compte de draps d'or . . . par Geoffroi de Fleuri" (1317), in Douët-d'Arcq, ed., *Nouveau recueil de comptes*, 5, 7, 9, 12, 13; "Inventaire de feu Raoul de Nesle," ed. Dehaisnes, *Documents*, 1:136; and "Tarif des marchandises qui se vendaient à Paris," ed. Douët-d'Arcq, 224. On silks from Montpellier, see "Tarif des marchandises qui se vendaient à Paris," ed. Douët-d'Arcq, 221. On the weaving of silk in Montpellier, see Reyerson, "Medieval Silks in Montpellier," 123, 132, 133. Reyerson notes (p. 126) and the account book evidence seems to confirm that silk merchants of Montpellier did not have many trade contacts with Paris. R.-H. Bautier established that the Parisian tariff list that mentions Montpellier silk dates from the first half of the fourteenth century rather than the end of the thirteenth: "La place de la draperie brabançonne," 36.

56. Desrosiers, "Draps d'Areste (II)"; Reyerson, "Medieval Silks in Montpellier," 124. See note 87 below for evidence of late thirteenth- and early fourteenth-century cloth of Aresta in northern France.

57. On twelfth-century French references to these silks, see Burns, *Sea of Silk*, 28–29, 34–35, 44–45.

58. Desrosiers, "Draps d'Areste (II)," 111, 113; Desrosiers, "Draps d'Areste (III)." In the twelfth century, the famous Cistercian abbot, Bernard of Clairaux, was buried with two different pieces of *drap d'Areste* from Iberia: Desrosiers, "Draps d'Areste (II)," 111.

59. Lachaud, "Textiles, Furs and Liveries," 37–38, 416. See also Chapter 1, note 6 and fig. 3.

60. Muthesius, *Studies in Silk in Byzantium*, 192; Molinier, ed., *Inventaire du trésor du Saint Siège*, 110, #1193–1195; "Inventaire et vente après décès des biens de la reine Clémence de Hongrie veuve de Louis le Hutin 1328," in Douët-d'Arcq, ed., *Nouveau recueil de comptes*, 87: "tapis velu de Roumenie" (it is not clear if this last textile was made of silk).

61. On the cultivation of silkworms in southern Italy, see Sakellariou, *Southern Italy in the Late Middle Ages*, 379. On silk textile production in southern Italy after the conquest by Charles of Anjou, see Yver, *Le commerce et les marchands dans l'Italie méridionale*, 92–93; and *I registri della Cancelleria Angioina*, ed. Filangieri et al., 26.

62. On *cendals* from Cologne, see Edler, "The Silk Trade of Lucca," 21; and Howell, *Women, Production, and Patriarchy*, 131–132. References in Pope Boniface VIII's papal inventory to "frixium de alamania" ("border trim from Germany") are probably to half-silk narrow ware from Cologne: Molinier, *Inventaire du trésor du Saint-Siège*, 117, #1319, 1321. For material evidence, see Desrosiers, *Soieries et autres textiles*, 258–262, #137–141.

63. Molinier, *Inventaire du trésor du Saint-Siège*, 84, 85, 90, 91, 99 (#829, 832, 892, 908, 910, 1009, 1010); "Compte de l'argenterie d'Étienne de la Fontaine (1352)," in Douët-d'Arcq, ed., *Comptes de l'argenterie*, 158; Grandson Antependium (fig. 20).

64. Jacoby, "Cypriot Gold Thread." I thank David Jacoby for sharing the manuscript version of this article with me.

65. See main text of Chapter 1, discussion preceding notes 54–56.

66. Lucchese silks show up in the following: Loisne, "Une cour féodale," 122 (transcription of PdC A 2 fol. 24—"carraires de Luque," purchased in 1299); Fawtier and Maillard, eds., *Comptes royaux (1285–1314)*, 2:544, #24033; 2:546, #24069, 24071, 24072; "Tarif des marchandises qui se vendaient à Paris," ed. Douët-d'Arcq, 224 ("quartelle de Lucque"); and "Inventaire

de feu Raoul de Nesles," (1302), ed. Dehaisnes, *Documents*, 1:133. See also references to "tartaires de Luque" in note 54.

67. In 1284 the Parisian Parlement ruled that ultramontane merchants who resided in Paris with their wives and children could be taxed among the bourgeois of Paris rather than as foreign merchants: Fagniez, ed., *Documents relatifs à l'histoire de l'industrie*, 1:298. Additionally, the king sometimes extended privileges of citizenship to Italian entrepreneurs in Paris: Viard, ed., *Documents parisiens du règne de Philippe VI*, 1:104–105.

The Lombard section of the 1296 tax assessment included a separate list of twelve Lucchese merchants and merchant companies; one other company was also identified as being from Lucca: Michaëlsson, ed., *Livre de la taille . . . 1296*, 271–272 (reedited in Piton, *Les Lombards*, 125–127).

68. Marques de Luques, rue Troussevache, 1292, 1296–1299 (identified as mercer in 1299); Mahaut, widow of Marques de Luques, 1300: Appendix 1, part A, nos. 109, 110; Appendix 2, part A, no. 49 (Appendix 2 gives only the 1299 tax reference for Marques because he was identified as a mercer in that year only).

69. Appendix 1, part A, no. 64; Appendix 2, part A, no. 43.

70. On Vanne's membership in the Bellardi Company, see Lachaud, "Textiles, Furs and Liveries," 74; Sutton, *The Mercery of London*, 41, citing London, National Archives, Public Records Office, E 101/126/6 (an inquest of 1294 involving payments by London mercers to Jehan Vanne); and Lloyd, *Alien Merchants*, 184, 202. The tax assessments also made reference to Vanne's connection with the Bellardi Company: AN KK 283, fol. 267v ("Jacques bon dos . . . Jehan Vane, balart, son gendre") and Michaëlsson, ed., *Livre de la taille . . . 1313*, 140 ("Vanne, belart"). On Vanne's status as "valet" of King Edward I of England, see Lachaud, "Textiles, Furs and Liveries," 74, citing London, National Archives, Public Records Office, E 101 363/24/78. Vanne shows up in the English royal wardrobe account of 1303–1304 as a supplier of textiles, spices, and furs: London, National Archives, Public Records Office, E 101/366/4. On his role as guardian of the king's exchange, see Piton, *Les lombards*, 35.

71. Mirot, "Études lucquoises I," 56, 68n3; AN S 3380, liasse 5, doc. 6: vidimus of Bonvis Bondos's testament of 1306; the document affirms that Bonvis Bondos was from Lucca and that he owned a property adjacent to one that was owned by Jacques Bondos. The proximity of the two properties suggests that the two men were probably related to each other. Further evidence that Jacques was also probably from Lucca is suggested by the fact that he had three Lombard sons-in-law, one of whom—Jehan Vanne—was clearly from Lucca. Also, at one point Phelippe of the company of l'Espine, who was from Lucca, resided in Jacques's house: Michaëlsson, ed., *Livre de la taille . . . 1296*, 271 (also printed in Piton, *Les lombards*, 125, 126); AN KK 283, fol. 267v. For further discussion of Bonvis Bondos, see main text of this chapter, discussion preceding notes 115–125.

72. AN KK 283, fol. 194 (Appendix 2, part C, no. 5).

73. PdC A 361, fol. 20; PdC A 374, fols. 25, 29; PdC A 378, fol. 15v; PdC A 403, fol. 19; PdC A 444, fols. 26v, 27; PdC A 458, fol. 24; PdC A 474, fol. 25; *De Rekeningen der Graven en Gravinnen*, 1:516; Dehaisnes, *Documents*, 1:259, 274, 284, 285, 304, 368; "Inventaire et vente après décès des biens de la reine Clémence de Hongrie veuve de Louis le Hutin, 1328," in Douët-d'Arcq, ed., *Nouveau recueil de comptes*, 78; Lebailly, "Raoul, Comte d'Eu," 2:94 (edition of AN JJ 269, at fol. 47); account of the confraternity of Saint-Jacques-aux-Pelerins (1318–1324), partial edition in Bordier and Brièle, eds., *Les archives hospitalières de Paris*, 2:17.

74. AN S 3380, liasse 6, doc. 5: a property located on the Petit or the Grant Marivas that was sold in 1328 was described as being adjacent to that of Lande Belon.

75. Ugolino's son-in-law owned properties on the Petit or the Grant Marivas and the rue Pierre-au-Let; both were in the Lombard mercery. Mirot, "La fondation de la chapelle du Volto Santo," 9, 13.

76. Mirot, "La fondation de la chapelle du Volto Santo," 5–6, 21–28. On Lando's status as "bourgeois of Paris," see PdC A 483 (1328).

77. Mirot, "Études lucquoises I," 74n5.

78. Appendix 2, part B, no. 5.

79. For written evidence concerning Mongol cloth of gold, see above, note 54. For physical evidence for both Mongol cloth of gold and silk from the Levant, see Desrosiers, *Soieries et autres textiles*, 284–285, 287–291. Account book evidence for silk from the Levant: Fawtier and Maillard, eds., *Comptes royaux (1285–1314)*, 2:544, #24034; 2:546, #24067; "Tarif des marchandises qui se vendaient à Paris," ed. Douët-d'Arcq, 224 ("quartel d'outremer"); Dehaisnes, *Documents*, 1:133 ("quarriaus d'uevre sarrazinoise").

80. Appendix 1, part C, nos. 38–41; Appendix 2, part A, no. 4, 41. Phelippe does not show up in Appendix 2 because the tax assessments identified him as a merchant of wimples rather than as a mercer. Jehan Tabarie the younger does not show up in Appendix 2 because he was not identified as a mercer in the tax assessments, but his widow was, and he apparently shows up as a mercer in the 1294 account of the Countess of Flanders (see note 81). We can assume that Jehan Tabarie the elder was the father of Jehan Tabarie the younger because the elder moved to the residence of the younger after the younger and his wife died. I am assuming that Phelippe, who resided in the Quincampoix mercery, was related to the others because, like Jehan Tabarie the elder, he specialized in women's head coverings. The 1313 tax assessment included a Jacquet Tabarie, who may have been identical with Jehan Tabarie the elder, but he may have been a grandson as well: Michaëlsson, ed., *Livre de la taille* . . . 1313, 133 (Appendix 1, part C, no. 38). Jacquet is not identified in the 1313 tax assessment as a mercer, but we find a Jacquet Tabarie in an account of Queen Margaret of England, from 1300–1301: British Library Ad. 7966A, fol. 156.

81. Ghent, Rijksarchief, fonds Gaillard 52, membranes 3, 5, 10 (in 1294 the Countess of Flanders purchased head coverings, barbettes, and *cendal* from Jehan Tabarie and crêpe from "fil tabarie"—presumably Jehan Tabarie the younger); PdC A 2, fol. 24v (in 1298 the Countess of Artois purchased head coverings from Jacques Tabarie); London, British Library, Add. 7966A, fol. 156 (in 1300–1301 Queen Margaret of England purchased jewels and textiles from "Jaketum de Tabarie"); Mons, Archives de l'État, chartrier 485, membrane 5 (in 1313 executors for the Countess of Hainaut paid Jehan Tabarie for various head coverings).

82. The list, which dates from the second decade of the fourteenth century, mentions Jacquet Tabarie: Paris, Bibliothèque Nationale de France, MS. Clairambault, 832, p. 643.

83. "Tarif des marchandises qui se vendaient à Paris," ed. Douët-d'Arcq, 224; "Compte de l'exécution du testament de Mathilde de Béthune épouse de Gui, comte de Flandre" (1264), in Dehaisnes, *Documents*, 1:61; "Inventaire des biens de feu Raoul de Nesle, connétable de France" (1302), in Dehaisnes, *Documents*, 1:134; "Compte de draps d'or . . . par Geoffroi de Fleuri" (1317), in Douët-d'Arcq, ed., *Nouveau recueil de comptes*, 8, 13.

84. The Lombard section of the Parisian tax assessment of 1296 had a separate section listing five Venetians or Venetian companies; one other Lombard taxpayer was also identified as a Venetian: Michaëlsson, ed., *Livre de la taille* . . . 1296, 271, 273 (also edited in Piton, *Les lombards*, 125, 127).

85. Jacques/Jacquet de Venyse: Appendix 1, part A, no. 121 (and possibly no. 122 as well); Appendix 2, part B, no. 35.

86. See main text of this chapter, discussion preceding notes 110–113.

87. "Tarif des marchandises qui se vendaient à Paris," ed. Douët-d'Arcq, 224; "Inventaire des biens de feu Raoul de Nesle, connétable de France" (1302), in Dehaisnes, *Documents*, 1:134; AN L 870, no. 59, fol. 9 (1342 inventory of liturgical objects at the abbey of Saint-Martin-des-Champs in Paris).

88. Michaëlsson, ed., *Livre de la taille . . . 1297*, 119. On the goldsmiths' fourteenth-century claim to the right to engage in mercery work while paying the tax for goldsmiths' work, see Fagniez, *Études sur l'industrie*, 382–383.

89. Appendix 1, part C, no. 16.

90. Jehan's name appears on a list of members of the embroiderers' guild that was compiled around 1300: Depping, ed., *Réglemens*, 380.

91. Appendix 1, part C, nos. 17, 19, 21, 23.

92. See main text of this chapter, discussion preceding notes 113–115.

93. In 1282 the Count and Countess of Artois assigned rights over the castellany of Moulins, in the Auvergne, to Jehan of Cyprus, Geoffrey of Cyprus, Bertaut of Lymesi, and nine other individuals, who, like Jehan, Geoffrey, and Bertaut, were probably furnishers of luxury goods to the comital household: PdC A 1; summarized by Richard, *Inventaire-sommaire*, 1:3.

94. After they settled in Cyprus in 1191, the English and French colonizers renamed the Greek town of Nemesos "Limezun" or "Limasson." According to George Hill, after that renaming, Greek authors (and presumably Greek speakers as well) accepted the change of the initial letter from N to L, but they retained the Greek ending of "os." Thus for Greek speakers, Nemesos became "Lemesos" or, on occasion, "Lemeso": Hill, *A History of Cyprus*, 2:15; Hill, "Two Toponymic Puzzles."

95. Mahy of Lymesis was identified as a goldsmith one year and as a mercer the next: AN KK 283, fols. 113v, 191v. Thomas of Lymesis was identified as a goldsmith: ibid., fol. 191v.

96. "Veluyau des armes du roy, les fleurs de lys d'or de Chypre broudées de pelles": "Inventaire des armeures de Louis X," in Gay and Stein, *Glossaire archéologique du Moyen Âge*, 1:61; "un nassis d'or de Cipre": "Inventaire . . . de la reine Clémence de Hongrie," in Douët-d'Arcq, ed., *Nouveau recueil de comptes*, 78 ("Veluyau" was velvet; "Nassis" was a type of cloth of gold).

97. "Que nulz ne nulle ne soit si hardiz de faire ne de faire faire, d'acheter ne de vendre tissuz a or, se il ne sont tissuz dedens fine soye, et que les tissuz qui d'or seront faiz soient faiz de tel or qu'il soient souffisans, c'est assavoir or que l'en appelle de Chippre et or de Paris. Et que nulz ne nulle ne soit si hardiz de mesler autre or avecques yceus ne de mettre y or de Luques": Fagniez, ed., *Documents relatifs à l'histoire de l'industrie*, 2:62 (statute 20).

98. According to Anna Muthesius, the metallic thread in the embroidery in the central panel of the Grandson Antependium (fig. 20), for which there are strong indications that it was made in Cyprus in the 1290s, consists of silver-gilt wire over a yellow silk core. According to Agnes Geijer, the cope of Bishop Fulk of Uppsala, embroidered in France in the third quarter of the thirteenth century, was made with "lamina cut from sheets of pure gold" that was wrapped around a silk core. The metallic thread of both embroideries was attached by underside couching: Muthesius, *Studies in Silk in Byzantium*, 241; Geijer, *Textile Treasures of Uppsala Cathedral*, 24. These descriptions do not seem to have drawn on the latest scientific analysis of medieval gold and gilded threads. There is, of course, no way to definitively conclude that the threads employed in Parisian and Cypriot embroideries were considered to be "or de Chypre" or "or de Paris," but David Jacoby has found conclusive evidence that "or de Chypre" was of high value and thus was probably not the cheaper gilded animal membrane, as earlier

historians often maintained: Jacoby, "Cypriot Gold Thread." For a description of scientific techniques for analyzing gold thread, see Jaro, "Gold Embroidery and Fabrics in Europe." Jaro's assumption that threads made of gilded animal membrane were known as "or de chypre" should be ignored.

99. Desrosiers, *Soieries et autres textiles*, 345, 349 (technical description of cat. nos. 187, 189); Wardwell, "'*Panni Tartarici*,'" 96. Much like Italian cloth of gold of this period, Central Asian cloth of gold was made with a gilded animal substratum, which was then wrapped around a cotton core or woven directly into the fabric: Wardwell, "'*Panni Tartarici*,'" 96.

100. Appendix 1, part C, no. 35; Parsons, ed., *The Court and Household of Eleanor of Castile*, 84, 102 ("Johanne le Romeyn mercatore Paris"). Jehan was not identified in the Paris tax assessments as a mercer, but his widow, Eustache (or Huitace), was: Appendix 1, part C, no. 32; Appendix 2, part A, no. 9.

101. For a discussion of the Toucy family, which left Byzantium after 1261, migrating first to the kingdom of southern Italy and then, in the case of two family members, on to France, see Dunbabin, *The French in the Kingdom of Sicily*, 150–151, 266–267.

102. Appendix 1, part C, no. 32; Appendix 2, part A, no. 9.

103. Appendix 2, part A, no. 54 (identified as a mercer in 1300). We know Nicole was a widow because Aalis Gros-Parmi was identified as her daughter in 1296 and 1299: Michaëlsson, ed., *Livre de la taille . . . 1296*, 22; AN KK 283, fol. 191v. On narrow ware from Cologne, see note 62.

104. Appendix 2, part B, no. 88.

105. Appendix 1, part B, no. 20; Appendix 2, part E, no. 19. In 1296 the combined tax of Gracien and his son-in-law was more than twice the average.

106. Michiel d'Espaigne corroyer, residing on the rue du Grenier-Saint-Lazare: Appendix 1, part B, no. 27.

107. That makes a total of 19. Of the 23 individuals in table 2, I have not included Eustache (or Huitace) la Roumainne, because she took her place-name from her husband so she may not have been from the Byzantine empire; Jacquet of Tabarie, because he may be identical with Jehan of Tabarie; Rogier of Germany, because we do not know if he was from Cologne; and Jehan of Apulia, because he resided outside of the three prestigious merceries.

108. Appendix 2, part D, no. 32.

109. Jehan Tabarie the older, Jehan Tabarie the younger, Jehan Vanne, Lando Belloni, Jehan le Roumain, Jehan of Cyprus, and Bertaut of Lymesi. Three of the men (Jehan Vanne, Jehan Tabarie, and Jehan le Roumain) conducted business with the English royal court, and two (Lando Belloni and Jehan/Jacquet Tabarie) conducted business with the French royal court.

110. Appendix 1, part A, nos. 115, 117 (as well as Appendix 3, part A, no. 1; Appendix 5, no. 19).

111. On the various meanings of *ouvrière de soie*, see the entries in bold letters in Appendix 5.

112. Géraud, ed., *Paris sous Philippe-le-Bel*, 70; AN KK 283, fols. 181v, 259; Appendix 3, part A, nos. 8, 16.

113. Appendix 1, part C, nos. 20, 22 (and Appendix 3, part C, no. 21; Appendix 5, no. 94).

114. Jehan de Lymesis: Appendix 1, part C, no. 18.

115. On Jehan Vanne's relation to Jacques Bondos, see AN KK 283, 267v: "Jacques Bondos, 21 L [his tax is 21 livres]; Jehan Vanne balart son gendre 7 L 10 s [his tax is 7 livre, 10 s.]."

116. In his testament Bonvis gave to the church of Saint-Jacques-de-la-Boucherie a house that was adjacent to one belonging to Jacques Bondos. Since Bonvis had always paid taxes on the south side of the street, where the tax assessors usually referred to a property belonging to Jacques Bondos as the terminal point of a unit of the tax assessment, we can assume that these two houses were on the south side: AN S 3380, liasse 5, no. 6, dossier on the Maison de la Nef Argent on the rue des Lombards (this is a vidimus of Bonvis Bondos's testament, dated 1306); AN KK 283, fol. 18v.

117. Bonvis Bondos on the south side of the street (living in a property adjacent to one belonging to Jacques Bondos but not usually occupied by Jacques): Michaëlsson, ed., *Livre de la taille . . . 1296*, 142; AN KK 283, fols. 115, 194, 270. In 1296 Bonvis's segment of the street was defined as stretching from the house of Geoffroi Dammartin to that of Jacques Bondos; in 1298 (fol. 115) that same segment was defined as stretching along the Buffeterie from Geoffroi Dammartin's house to the rue de la Viez Monnaie, which intersected with the rue de la Buffeterie on the south side. Jacques Bondos residing on the north side of the street: Michaëlsson, ed., *Livre de la taille . . . 1296*, 130; AN KK 283 fols. 113v, 267v. In 1296 and 1298 (fol. 113v) this side of the Buffeterie was referred to as "devers Troussevache"—the side closest to the rue Troussevache, which was to the north of the Buffeterie. Jehan Vanne on the rue de la Buffeterie: AN KK 283, fol. 267r; Michaëlsson, ed., *Livre de la taille . . . 1313*, 140. By 1313, Jehan Vanne had apparently relocated to the south side of the rue de la Buffeterie.

118. *Livre des métiers*, ed. Lespinasse and Bonnardot, 115.

119. The statutes for the hosiers' guild mentioned hosiery made of silk and linen: *Livre des métiers*, ed. Lespinasse and Bonnardot, 114, statute 4. Account book evidence suggests that quite a lot of hosiery was made with wool: PdC A 316, fol. 17v; PdC A 329, fol. 17; PdC A 334, fol. 28.

120. Géraud, ed., *Paris sous Philippe-le-Bel*, 88, 99; Michaëlsson, ed., *Livre de la taille . . . 1296*, 129, 130; AN KK 283, fols. 113, 136, 190v, 191, 267v; Michaëlsson, ed., *Livre de la taille . . . 1313*, 128, 129, 137, 140. Pasquier le Chaucier (AN KK 283, fols. 191, 267v) was identified in the statutes for the hosiers' guild as a Lombard: *Livre des métiers*, ed. Lespinasse and Bonnardot, 115.

121. Appendix 1, part A, nos. 18, 105.

122. The relationship between the two properties was described when Bonvis donated his property to the church of Saint-Jacques-de-la-Boucherie: Mirot, "Études lucquoises 1," 68n3; AN S 3380, liasse 5, no. 6.

123. In 1296, Richard, the son of Jehan des Lesches, was listed just after Bonvis Bondos, at the end of the block that ended at the property of Jacques Bondos; in 1300 the son of Jehan des Lesches was again listed right next to Bonvis Bondos, at the very end of the block, and he was identified as a gold beater: Michaëlsson, ed., *Livre de la taille . . . 1296*, 142; AN KK 283, fol. 270. In 1299 Bonvis Bondos and "Coluche le lombart kalendreeur" appeared together at the end of that block: AN KK 283, fol. 194.

124. On mangles and silk production, see Mainoni, "La seta in Italia," 381–382.

125. Jacoby, "Silk in Western Byzantium."

126. Molà, *La comunità dei lucchesi a Venezia*, 27.

127. Molà, *The Silk Industry*, 4, 12.

128. Ibid., 4–8, 12, 23; Chevalier, *Tours: Ville Royale*, 267–269.

129. *Ordonnances des rois de France*, 20:592.

130. Desrosiers and Eichler, "Luxurious Merovingian Textiles," 2.

131. In 1430 the guild of silk entrepreneurs of Florence requested that three of its members seek out some gold beaters and bring them back to Florence; in the sixteenth century, moreover, the city of Mantua issued a number of different relocation charters to several different

groups of gold beaters from Milan and Venice, but the craft never took off: Edler De Roover, *L'arte della seta*, 87; Molà, *The Silk Industry*, 27.

132. Bautier, "Une opération de décentralisation industrielle"; Molà, *The Silk Industry*, 29–32.

133. *Livre des métiers*, ed. Lespinasse and Bonnardot, 33, 78.

134. "Le premier compte de Geoffroi de Fleuri, argentier du roi Philippe le Long pour les six derniers mois de l'année 1316," in Douët-d'Arcq, ed., *Comptes de l'argenterie*, 57.

135. The Parisian silk that originally belonged to Edward II passed into the inventory of possessions of Edward III as well: London, National Archives, Public Records Office, E 361/3, rots. 2, 3v, 6v, 22v; E 361/9, rots. 3, 5, 7v, 10. On Blanche of Namur's postmortem inventory, see *Diplomatarium norvegicum*, 271. I thank Camilla Luise Dahl for the reference to Blanche of Namur.

136. ADS, 7 MI 3, roll 6, register number 42 (April 28, 1396–May 16, 1398), view 164: "item pour 6 aunes de soye roge vert et pers de Paris." I thank Nadège Gauffre-Fayolle, who shared with me her transcription of this part of the accounts from the court of Savoy.

137. *Livre des métiers*, ed. Lespinasse and Bonnardot, 66, 68, 70, 74, 78, 83, 158.

138. Ibid., 66–72, 74–78, 83–84, 157–159.

139. Ibid., 68, 70, 78, 158.

140. See, on this point, Stella, "Travail, famille et maison," 43; and Reyerson, "Adolescent Apprentice/Worker," 356.

141. Stella, "Travail, famille et maison," 37; Reyerson, "Adolescent Apprentice/Worker," 355; Fagniez, *Études sur l'industrie*, 61, 62, 70, 73 (citing AN Y 5221, fol. 122; 5222, fol. 83; 5224, fol. 75v, 5226); Mayade-Claustre, "Le corps lié de l'ouvrier," 394 (citing AN Y 5220, fol. 213v).

142. Stella, "Travail, famille et maison," 43; Geremek, *Le salariat dans l'artisanat parisien*, chap. 3.

143. Fagniez, *Études sur l'industrie*, 74 (citing AN Y 5223, fol. 13v).

144. Appendix 2, part A, nos. 4, 9.

145. See above notes 80 and 81.

146. See main text of this chapter, discussion preceding note 117.

147. AN KK, fols. 181v, 259; Appendix 3, part A, nos. 8, 16.

CHAPTER 4

1. Ghent, Rijksarchief, fonds Gaillard 52, membranes 3, 5.

2. On the predominance of women in the silk industry of early modern Lyon, see Hafter, *Women at Work*, 13. On Florence, see main text of this chapter, discussion preceding notes 8 and 9.

3. Appendices 3, 4, 5. These numbers include an estimated 66 *ouvrières de soie* who probably worked as throwsters and 9 who probably worked as weavers of silk cloth. See the text at the end of Appendix 5 for a discussion of how I arrived at these estimates. There are no appendices for the gold beaters and gold spinners. I have derived their numbers (23 male/1 female gold beaters; 8 female gold spinners) from computer databases that were created for me by Caroline Bourlet of the Institut de recherche et d'histoire des textes. For gold beaters (some of whom show up in more than one tax assessment), see Michaëlsson, ed., *Livre de la taille . . . 1296*, 118; Michaëlsson, ed., *Livre de la taille . . . 1297*, 290, 291, 302, 336; AN KK 283, fols. 108,

109, 112v, 132, 173v, 174, 177v, 181v, 189, 192v, 245, 246, 255, 258v, 259, 262v, 264v, 266v, 269v; and Michaëlsson, ed., *Livre de la taille . . . 1313*, 78, 99, 139. For the gold spinners (some of whom show up in the assessments more than once), see Géraud, ed., *Paris sous Philippe-le-Bel*, 56; Michaëlsson, ed., *Livre de la taille . . . 1296*, 98; AN KK 283, fols. 132, 135, 181, 187v, 194; and Michaëlsson, ed., *Livre de la taille . . . 1313*, 122.

4. Based on what we know about how many women were in the embroiderers' guild (79) versus how many showed up in the tax assessments (13), we can assume that women artisans in the silk crafts who showed up in the tax assessments constituted only 16–17 percent of the total number of silk women. For the list of women and men who were in the embroiderers' guild around 1300, see Depping, ed., *Réglemens*, 379–380. For a list of women embroiderers who showed up in the tax assessments, see Farmer, "Medieval Paris and the Mediterranean," 395n39. For men who worked in the silk industry, I am estimating that those who showed up in the tax assessments constituted at least 25 percent of the men who worked in silk, but those who showed up in the assessments may have constituted a much larger proportion than this.

5. I have calculated these numbers from the computer-generated alphabetized list of women who showed up in the tax assessment of 1300, which was originally produced by Caroline Bourlet for Janice Archer, who supplied me with a copy. The 1300 tax assessment included 1,554 women, of whom 387 were identified unambiguously with a profession and 378 were given surnames that might have been descriptions of their professions. My numbers for women in the silk professions include 15 unambiguous mercers plus 9 ambiguous mercers, 37 throwsters, 38 *ouvrières de soie*, 6 makers of *tissu/z de soie*, 4 makers of silk ribbons and laces (2 unambiguous, 2 ambiguous), 2 women who "carie soie," and 2 gold thread spinners. So counting artisans alone, there were 87 women whose professions were identified unambiguously as silk professions, plus another 2 whose profession was identified ambiguously; and when we add in the mercers, there were 102 silk women whose professional identity was listed unambiguously and another 11 who were identified ambiguously with silk professions. There were 49 unambiguous *regratières* and another 26 women for whom the term *regratière* occurred as a surname. With the exception of mercers, nearly all of the women in the silk-making professions were described with an unambiguous phrase ("qui carie soie," "qui file soie"), thus the silk artisans tend to be overrepresented in the unambiguous group, since a phrase cannot be mistaken for a mere surname.

6. In her study of women's work in the Parisian tax assessments, Janice Archer also found a predominance of silk workers, followed by *regratières*. In several earlier articles, I drew on her statistics, but my calculations have now changed in several significant ways from those of Archer. First, rather than counting the total number of listings of women in a given profession over the four-year period from 1297 to 1300 and then coming up with an average number for each year, I have counted each individual taxpayer in each of the seven tax assessments, taking care to count each individual only once; for those individual taxpayers who were listed in more than one assessment, I have first calculated each person's average tax assessment for the 1297–1300 period before attempting to calculate the average tax assessment for any group as a whole. Second, I have come up with a much smaller number of women who were silk weavers than Archer suggested, and than I originally thought, because I am now convinced that weavers of *tissu/z de soie* wove narrow ware rather than cloth and because I have found that only a small proportion of the *ouvrières de soie* may have been weavers (see note 3 and the text at the end of Appendix 5): Archer, "Working Women," 111–117, 179, 315, 316; Farmer, "*Biffes, Tiretaines*, and *Aumonières*," 82–83; Farmer, "Merchant Women and the Administrative Glass Ceiling," 101, 108n80.

7. Goodman, "Cloth, Gender and Industrial Organization." Women silk workers in early modern Lyon also lacked labor status, largely entering the trade through their husbands or fathers but never attaining positions as guild masters themselves: Hafter, *Women at Work*, 131.

8. Goodman does not actually discuss the gendered constitution of the *setaioli*, but in his work as well as the work of Florence Edler De Roover and Philip Joshua Jacks and William Caferro, the assumption seems to be that all of the *setaioli* were male. Edler De Roover, *L'arte della seta*, 13–23; Jacks and Caferro, *The Spinelli of Florence*, 78–93.

9. Goodman, "Cloth, Gender and Industrial Organization," 231–234. Goodman expressed some surprise concerning the predominance of male throwsters in the fifteenth century. I think it is pretty clear that the expense and complexity of the throwing machines explain that predominance.

10. Goodman, "Cloth, Gender and Industrial Organization," 241–244.

11. In her seminal study of women and labor status in medieval Leiden and Cologne, Martha Howell emphasized independent ownership of raw materials and control of the final product that went to market as the key elements in labor status. *Women, Production, and Patriarchy*, 24.

12. There was a similar gendered division of labor between gold beaters and gold thread spinners in Florence and Venice. Edler De Roover, *L'arte della seta*, 87–98; Molà, "Le donne nell'industria serica veneziana," 423.

13. *Livre des métiers*, ed. Lespinasse and Bonnardot, 74–75.

14. Ibid., 66–68. Four of the jurors of this guild, whose names were inscribed in the margins of the original manuscript, were identified as "dorelotier": ibid., 68n.

15. Ibid., 76–78.

16. Ibid., 83–84. Women also did most of the veil weaving in early modern Venice. Molà, "Le donne nell'industria serica veneziana," 435–437.

17. For my argument that "qui carie soie" refers to weavers of silk cloth, see Chapter 2, note 40.

18. The surviving tax assessments of 1296–1300 represent five out of eight years in which taxes were collected. The total amount collected was 100,000 livres tournois, or 80,000 livres parisis, and c. 10,000 individuals were taxed in each of the 8 years. Thus the average tax paid per person per year was 1 livre parisis. Archer, *Working Women*, 154.

19. Gourmelon, "L'industrie et le commerce des draps," 10.

20. "A une pauve fame ki file soie, xvi s.": Ghent, Rijksarchief, fonds Gaillard 52, membrane 3.

21. Fagniez, ed., *Documents relatifs à l'histoire de l'industrie*, 1:277–278; *Livre des métiers*, ed. Lespinasse and Bonnardot, 69 (statute 9), 83–84 (statute 8).

22. The twelfth-century French romance author Chrétien de Troyes also associated women silk workers with poverty, but this was before a silk industry emerged in Paris: Burns, *Sea of Silk*, 65–66. On consumer debt among artisans, see Mayade-Claustre, "Le corps lié de l'ouvrier"; and Chapter 5.

23. *Livre des métiers*, ed. Lespinasse and Bonnardot, 68 (statute 1), 70 (statute 1), 83 (statute 1).

24. "Pour qu'ele sache fere le mestier bien et loialment": *Livre des métiers*, ed. Lespinasse and Bonnardot, 83 (statute 1); for the makers of "tissuz de soie": ibid., 74 (statute 1).

25. "Quiconques voudra tenir ledit mestier comme mestre, il convendra que il le sache faire de touz poinz, de soy, sanz conseil ou ayde d'autruy, et que il soit a ce examinez par les gardes du mestier. Et se il est trouvé souffisant, si comme dessus est dit, il convendra que il

achate le dit mestier du Roy ou de son lieutenant, souz quele juridicion que il soit en la Chastelerie de Paris; et en paiera a nostre seigneur le Roy, pour l'achat dudit mestier, xx s., et aus dites gardes x s. pour leur paine": *Livre des métiers,* ed. Lespinasse and Bonnardot, 76 (statute 1).

26. Fagniez, *Études sur l'industrie,* 93.

27. The statutes for the guild of makers of "draps de soye," velvet and woven purses mentioned looms with two warp beams in the context of whether or not it was ever permitted to weave with waste silk: "Item, que nuls . . . ne pourra ne ne devra ouvrer ou dit mestier, de quele euvre que ce soit, de soye canete . . . . car ourture de canete est fausse, se *ce n'est en draps a deus ourtures*" (italics added): *Livre des métiers,* ed. Lespinasse and Bonnardot, 77 (statute 4). On the use of two warp beams in the weaving of velvets, see Desrosiers, "Sur l'origine d'un tissu qui a participé à la fortune de Venise," 41.

28. Richard, *Une petite-nièce,* 368, citing PdC A 201: "Pour fair 1 mestier avoekes madame, pour faire viii/xx vergiaus et II/c poulietes, xxvii jumeles, et le havestre de bos lau eles sont fremees, xxii s. vii d." (To make a loom with madame: to make 160 rods and 200 pulleys, 27 pairs, and the wooden hook where they are attached—22 sous, 7 deniers). The text seems to imply that the countess herself participated in the construction of the loom.

29. The need for a furnace is implied in discussions of boiling while dyeing and cooking: Gargiolli, ed., *L'arte della seta in firenze,* 12–16, 30–40, 48–49, 51–52.

30. See main text of Chapter 3, discussion preceding notes 134–136.

31. *Livre des métiers,* ed. Lespinasse and Bonnardot, 77 (statutes 5, 6).

32. Ibid., 33 (statute 6).

33. Ibid., 7 (statute 21).

34. On mercers who served as *échevins* or who were related to *échevins,* see main text of Chapter 3, discussion preceding notes 42, 46, 50.

35. "Li quel IIII proud'omme seront esleu du commun du mestier et amené devant vous pour jurer sur Sains que il bien et loiaument garderont ledit mestier, et raporteront au prevost ou a son commandement toutes les forfaitures et mesprentures qu'i trouveront faites ou mestier desus dit": *Livre des métiers,* ed. Lespinasse and Bonnardot, 159 (statute 14).

36. "les quex [preud'home] li prevoz de Paris met et oste a son plesir": *Livre des métiers,* ed. Lespinasse and Bonnardot, 67 (statute 10).

37. Hosted by the provost: *Livre des métiers,* ed. Lespinasse and Bonnardot, 69 (statute 11), 71 (statute 10). No mention of election: ibid., 75 (statute 9), 84 (statute 10).

38. Ibid., 69–72.

39. Ibid., 84 (statute 10), and marginal note, printed just below statute 10, naming four women who "sont jurées de cest mestier" in 1296.

40. See note 5 of this chapter.

41. Bove, *Dominer la ville.*

42. Endrei, "Manufacturing a Piece of Woolen Cloth," 21. The count of wool spinners is based on a search for "fileresse," "fileresse a la quenouille," "fileresse a la touret," and "fileresse de laine" in the computer-generated lists of women in the Paris tax assessments of 1292–1313.

43. Gourmelon, "L'industrie et le commerce de draps," 56.

44. Guillaume de Saint-Pathus, *Les miracles de Saint Louis,* 128, 132, 135, 177: two of the Parisian women in these stories spun wool and two of them combed it; one of the combers lived for thirty years with the weaver for whom she worked. Fagniez, *Études sur l'industrie,* 70 (citing and partially transcribing AN Y 5226, April 23, 1407): an eight-year-old girl was apprenticed to a draper in order to learn how to card and spin.

45. See the preceding note, as well as Boutaric, *Actes du Parlement de Paris*, 1:400, no. 575. In 1285 Parlement decided that wool dyers were allowed to have in their workshops tools for preparing wool, such as spinning wheels. This suggests that some wool spinners worked for dyers.

46. It was also the case in Rouen that carders and spinners were often trained and employed in the workshops of drapers, with the wives of the drapers overseeing the training: Roch, "Femmes et métiers en Normandie." I thank Professor Roch for sending me this paper.

47. On limits on numbers of apprentices, see *Livre des métiers*, ed. Lespinasse and Bonnardot, 68 (statute 2), 70 (statute 3), 74 (statute 2), 83 (statute 4).

48. Fagniez, *Études sur l'industrie*, 58 (citing and partially transcribing AN Y 5227). On the guild regulation regarding numbers of apprentices, see *Livre des métiers*, ed. Lespinasse and Bonnardot, 74 (statute 2). At least four other women who made silk narrow ware appeared before the civil court of the Parisian Châtelet in the late fourteenth and early fifteenth centuries in order to deal with issues regarding their apprentices: Fagniez, *Études sur l'industrie*, notes on pages 58, 59, 62, 73 (citing AN Y 5221, fols. 98, 122; Y 5224, fol. 75v; Y 5227).

49. Appendix 5, nos. 8, 97, 101; Appendix 4, no. 49.

50. Appendix 5, no. 63. For a good discussion of the advantages of putting others to work, see Hutton, *Women and Economic Activities*, 105.

51. ADS, 1 MI 33, bobine 2 up to view 109; continuation at bobine 3, from view 54, account number 27 (December 12, 1370–October 14, 1372), views 174, 175; ADS, 1 MI 90, roll 3, register 34 (August 8, 1377–August 8, 1382), views 145, 185; ADS, 7 MI 3, rolls 6, 7, register number 43 (May 16, 1398–September 1, 1400), view 260; Dale, "London Silkwomen," 330, citing British Library, Ms. Cotton, Vespasian E, ix, fols. 86–110, a treatise called "The Noumbre of Weyghtes." Part of this treatise was edited by Hall and Nicholas in *Select Tracts and Table Books*, 12–20, but the edition does not include the section that mentions silk yarn from Paris. I thank Nadège Gauffre-Fayolle for providing me with transcriptions of the Savoy accounts.

52. Farmer, "*Biffes, Tiretaines*, and *Aumonières*," 88.

53. Ibid., 88; Parsons, ed., *The Court and Household of Eleanor of Castile*, 130; Molinier, "Inventaire du trésor de l'église du Saint-Sepulcre de Paris," nos. 4, 5, 6, 11–14, 18, 38, 188, 233, 390, 391, pp. 250–252, 254, 269, 273, 285; ADS, 1 MI 33, bobine 2 up to view 109; bobine 3, from view 54, account 27 (December 12, 1370–October 14, 1372), view 258; ADS, 7 MI 3, rolls 2, 3, register 37.1 (February 23, 1386–March 25, 1389), view 132. Both of the Savoy passages refer to "bisete" of Paris; in the second case, it was "bisete d'or." Bisete was apparently narrow ware: Gay and Stein, *Glossaire archéologique du Moyen Âge*, 1:159. On the accounts of Burgundy, see Prost and Prost, *Inventaires mobiliers*, 1:434, no. 2307.

54. PdC A 189/3 (identifying Aliz of Basoches as "ouvrière de soie"); PdC A 286, described by Richard, *Inventaire-sommaire*, 1:198, 262; PdC A 329, fol. 22.

55. Ghent, Rijksarchief, fonds Gaillard 52, membrane 3; Prost and Prost, eds., *Inventaires mobiliers*, 1:434, no. 2307.

56. Kowaleski and Bennett, "Crafts, Guilds, and Women."

57. *Livre des métiers*, ed. Lespinasse and Bonnardot, 68, 70, 74, 83, 207; Depping, ed., *Réglemens*, 382–386.

58. They were the "crespiniers"—makers of women's silk hairnets—and the embroiderers: *Livre des métiers*, ed. Lespinasse and Bonnardot, 72–73; Depping, ed., *Réglemens*, 380–382. On the evidence that the "crespiniers" were women, see Archer, "Working Women," 192.

59. Miller, *The Beguines of Medieval Paris*, 70.

60. Symon Male-Vie had been identified as a mercer in 1292; in 1297, 1299, and 1300, Gile paid above-average taxes of 40–84 sous, but her profession was not identified. Her tax in 1298, when she was identified as a gold beater, was 75 sous (or 3.75 livres), and in 1313, when she was identified as a mercer, it was 300 sous, or 15 livres: Géraud, ed., *Paris sous Philippe-le-Bel*, 86; *Livre de la taille . . . 1297*, 110; AN KK 283, fols. 112v, 190, 266v; Michaëlsson, ed., *Livre de la taille . . . 1313*, 125; Appendix 2, part B, nos. 17, 94.

61. Appendix 2; Archer, "Working Women," 138.

62. Archer, "Working Women," 158, 315.

63. See Appendix 2 for the raw data from which these statistics have been calculated.

64. Appendix 2, part A, nos. 47, 54. The other ten mercers who paid more than 11 livres in at least one of the tax assessments of 1297–1300 were Geoffroi of Dammartin, Guarnot of Lyon, Imbert of Lyon, Jehan Vanne, Phelippe Anquetin, Richard des Polies, Jehan of Esparnon, Jehan le Pellier, Olivier Chief-de-fer, and Thibaut of Flori: Appendix 2, part A, nos. 13, 16, 25, 43, 55, 66; part B, nos. 45, 50, 73, 95. We know that Marie Osane never married because when she first appeared in the tax assessments, in 1292, she was identified as "Marie, fille Osane": Géraud, ed., *Paris sous Philippe-le-Bel*, 91.

65. Paris, Archives de l'Assistance Publique, Fonds St.-Jacques, no. 14, discussed by Miller, *The Beguines of Medieval Paris*, 77.

66. PdC A, 151/19.

67. Prost and Prost, eds., *Inventaires mobiliers*, 2:22, no. 134.

68. Delisle, *Mandements*, 361, 541, 646, 702, 730, 731, 757, 758, 772, 795 (nos. 715, 1039, 1361, 1242, 1439, 1440, 1507, 1508, 1545, 1603); Prou, *Étude sur les relations politiques*, 170 (no. 84); Prost and Prost, eds., *Inventaires mobiliers*, 1:158, 166, 495 (nos. 911, 943, 2630); AN KK 242, fols. 17v, 48, 66, 68; ADS, 1 MI 28, bobine 1, account 20.b (January 24, 1380–March 28, 1380), view 10.

69. AN KK 242, fols. 17v, 48, 66, 68. On Dino Rapondi's career, see Lambert, *The City, the Duke, and Their Banker*.

70. Prou, *Étude sur les relations politiques*, 170 (no. 84).

71. Delisle, *Mandements*, 772 (no. 1545).

72. Farmer, "Merchant Women and the Administrative Glass Ceiling."

73. Shennan Hutton has argued that although there were a few prominent women merchants in medieval Ghent, women cloth sellers had a structural disadvantage because they were relegated to less prestigious market space than were cloth merchants who were men: "Men, Women, and Markets." On women mercers in London, see Sutton, "Two Dozen and More Silkwomen." On women selling silk in Montpellier, see Reyerson, *Business, Banking, and Finance*, 44.

74. See main text of this chapter, discussion preceding notes 8–10.

75. A number of recent studies have shown that Florentines sometimes softened the effects of this law through their own testamentary choices, but the law of succession nevertheless had a profound effect in marginalizing daughters and widows vis-à-vis the men in their families. Chabot, "La loi du lignage."

76. Olivier-Martin, *Histoire de la coutume*, 2:219–220 (2:239–240 in the reprint edition).

77. Ibid., 2:266, 271–272 (2:290, 295–296 in the reprint edition).

78. Le Roux de Lincy, *Histoire de l'Hôtel de Ville de Paris*, part 2, 120.

79. Archer, "Working Women," 142.

80. Ibid., 142–146.

81. Olivier-Martin, *Histoire de la coutume*, 2:368–369 (2:396–397 in the reprint edition). At the end of the thirteenth century and in the early decades of the fourteenth the aldermen in the Parloir aux Bourgeois overrode testaments in order to enforce the principle of equal inheritance among heirs of the same degree of kinship: Olivier-Martin, *Histoire de la coutume*, 2:377–378 (2:405–406 in the reprint edition); Le Roux de Lincy, *Histoire de l'Hôtel de Ville de Paris*, part 2, p. 121.

82. Archer, "Working Women," 141.

83. Olivier-Martin, *Histoire de la coutume*, 2:468 (2:496 in the reprint edition). See also Caroline Jeanne, who claims, on the basis of an examination of late fourteenth- and fifteenth-century documents of practice, that "dans les affaires concernant leur famille d'origine, succession des parents ou d'un membre de la fratrie par example, les veuves semblent tenir leur place au même titre que leurs frères et soeurs." She also claims that widows had more freedom of independent action than did their married sisters, who were always accompanied by their husbands: "Seules ou accompagnées?" paragraph 11.

84. Archer, "Working Women," 141.

85. On Marie Osane, see main text of this chapter, discussion preceding note 64.

86. On Mahy of Arras and his wife, see main text of Chapter 2, discussion preceding note 35. On the spice dealers Pierre Vaillant and his wife, Jeanne l'Espicière, both of whom were major suppliers for the Countess of Artois, see Farmer, "Merchant Women and the Administrative Glass Ceiling," 100; on Geneviève la Fouacière, see ibid., 95; on wives of prominent merchants who were moneylenders or money changers (it is unclear which), see ibid., 102n6. On Jehan le Houssereau, a linen weaver whose wife sold used clothing, see Fagniez, *Études sur l'industrie*, 74 (citing AN Y 5223, fol. 13v).

87. *Livre des métiers*, ed. Lespinasse and Bonnardot, 62 (statute 8), 102 (statute 7), 189 (statute 9), 190 (statute 16). See also Roux, "Les femmes dans les métiers."

88. Prost and Prost, eds., *Inventaires mobiliers*, 1:364, #1972.

89. Olivier-Martin, *Histoire de la coutume*, 2:200–201 (2:220–222 in the reprint edition). The fragmentary documents of practice show that married women did indeed usually appear in court with their husbands: Fagniez, *Études sur l'industrie*, 61, 75, 59 (citing AN Y 5222, fol. 83; Y 5223, fol. 13v; Y 5227).

90. Olivier-Martin, *Histoire de la coutume*, 2:204 (2:224 in reprint edition); Fagniez, ed., *Fragment d'un répertoire*, 2–3.

91. Olivier-Martin, *Histoire de la coutume*, 2:205 (2:225 in reprint edition).

92. On Douai, see Kittell, "The Construction of Women's Social Identity"; and Kittell, "Guardianship over Women." On Ghent, see Hutton, *Women and Economic Activities*, 35–36. On France in the sixteenth century, see Hafter, *Women at Work*, 41–42. On the ribbon makers' guild in 1600, see Fagniez and Funck-Brentano, *La femme et la société française*, 111; and *Livre des métiers*, ed. Lespinasse and Bonnardot, 66–68, 74–75.

93. Fagniez, *Études sur l'industrie*, 73 (partial transcription of AN Y 5221, fol. 122).

94. Ibid., 62 (partial transcription of AN Y 5221, fol. 90).

95. Ibid., 58 (partial transcription of AN Y 5227). On the guild regulation for numbers of apprentices, see *Livre des métiers*, ed. Lespinasse and Bonnardot, 74 (statute 2). On London widows who had apprentices, see McIntosh, *Working Women*, 138; and Sutton, "Two Dozen and More Silkwomen."

96. Coyecque, *Recueil des actes notariés*, 1:251, 330, 595, 648 (nos. 1279, 1739, 3250, 3554); vol. 2, #4680, 5601. All of the "tissutiers de soie" in these examples are male. No. 1739 (1:330)

involves a widow, but the masculine of "tissutier" makes it clear that the deceased husband was the ribbon maker.

97. Miller, *The Beguines of Medieval Paris*.

98. Paris, Archives de l'Assistance Publique, Fonds St.-Jacques, no. 14, discussed by Miller, *The Beguines of Medieval Paris*, 77, 214n123.

99. Pegolotti, *La pratica della mercatura*. On Pegolotti's career as a factor for the Bardi Company, see p. xvii.

100. De Roover, *Money, Banking and Credit*, 44n20.

101. Mirot, ed., "Inventaire mobilier," 163.

102. See main text of this chapter, discussion preceding notes 57–58.

103. On Cologne and Rouen as the only other towns with female guilds, see Kowaleski and Bennett, "Crafts, Guilds and Women." On all of the women's guilds in Cologne involving silk making, linen yarn production, or the spinning of gold thread, see Howell, *Women, Production, and Patriarchy*, 124; and Loesch, *Die Kölner Zunfturkunden*, 2:154, no. 378 (the source clarifies that the yarn makers' guild was involved in the making of linen yarn). On the women's guilds of Rouen, see Roch, "Femmes et métiers en Normandie."

104. My graduate student Sarah Hanson is writing a dissertation on prominent women wool merchants in Douai: "Gender, Work, and Economic Power: Elite Women in Late Medieval Douai" (in progress). See also Dhérent, "L'assise sur le commerce des draps à Douai." On Rouen, see Roch, "Femmes et métiers en Normandie." On early modern Paris and Amsterdam, see Sargentson, *Merchants and Luxury Markets*, 18–23, 136; Jones, *Sexing la Mode*, 96–98; and Van den Heuvel, *Women and Entrepreneurship*, 203, 263–264.

105. Hafter, *Women at Work*, 42.

106. On Ghent, see above, note 73.

107. On the lucrative nature of these positions, see Bove, *Dominer la ville*, 69–105, 269–291.

108. Farmer, "Merchant Women and the Administrative Glass Ceiling," 89–90; Bove, *Dominer la ville*, 69–114, 269–291.

109. *Registre criminel du Châtelet*, 1:195–201; "Registre criminel de Saint-Martin-des-Champs," ed. Tanon, *Histoire des justices*, 533.

CHAPTER 5

1. *Livre des métiers*, ed. Lespinasse and Bonnardot, 208. For further discussion, see main text of this chapter, discussion preceding notes 67–74.

2. Fagniez, *Documents relatifs à l'histoire de l'industrie*, 1:277–278; *Livre des métiers*, ed. Lespinasse and Bonnardot, 83–84 (statutes 5, 8). See also main text of Chapter 3, discussion preceding notes 13–14 and 21.

3. Some documents also refer to "Cahorsins" as specialized moneylenders. The term may have originally referred to people from Cahors, in southern France, but it seems to have become a more generic term that applied to moneylenders from the Piedmont as well: Grunwald, "Lombards, Cahorsins and Jews," 393.

4. Shatzmiller, *Shylock Reconsidered*; Nahon, "Le crédit et les juifs"; Jordan, "An Aspect of Credit."

5. Claustre, *Dans les geôles*, 47–50; Jordan, *Women and Credit*, 19–20.

6. Bove, *Dominer la ville*, 97, 101–106. On the market in rents as a form of credit in late medieval Paris, see Roux, "Le côut du logement," 247.

7. In early fourteenth-century Manosque, the average value of Lombard loans was twice that of Jewish loans, and while humble people constituted the majority of those who borrowed from Jews, they constituted only 40 percent of those who borrowed from Lombards. Shatzmiller, *Shylock Reconsidered*, 90–91.

8. Toch, *The Economic History of European Jews*, 87–89. On Jewish moneylending in late tenth-century France and Germany, see ibid., 97–98. On the initial arrival of Lombard moneylenders north of the Alps, see main text of this chapter, discussion preceding note 49.

9. Chazan, *Medieval Jewry*, 17.

10. Ibid., 34–35; Graboïs, "L'abbaye de Saint-Denis et les juifs." On Jewish loans to the Count of Champagne, see Taitz, *The Jews of Medieval France*, 114. Champagne, at that time, was not part of the French kingdom.

11. Jordan, *French Monarchy*, 30–33.

12. Ibid., 39–40.

13. Not all of the attrition of the Jewish community in Paris should be attributed to the 1182–1198 expulsion and return; nor was the attrition constant or unidirectional in the thirteenth century. In 1211 and again in 1258 the community probably shrank again when some Parisian religious leaders (and their families) migrated to Palestine; and the royal policies discussed in the main text of this chapter, in the section preceding notes 16–19, probably created attrition. By contrast, in the 1220s and 1230s, under the intellectual leadership of r. Yehiel of Paris, the Parisian Jewish community must have seen some growth, since we are told that he had 300 followers. For differing reasons the community probably grew after 1290, when some of the Jews who were expelled from England came to Paris, showing up in the tax assessments of 1292, 1296, and 1297. See Krauss, "L'émigration de 300 rabbins en Palestine"; Nahon, "La communauté juive de Paris," 155; and Prawer, *History of the Jews in the Latin Kingdom*, 274. The tax assessments of 1292 and 1296 included at least 9 Jews who were identified as "l'Anglais/e" (the English man/woman): Loeb, "Le role des juifs de Paris," 66–70.

14. Jordan, *French Monarchy*, 21; Loeb, "Le role des juifs de Paris." For the figure of 300–330 Jews in 1296, I am rounding off from an estimate of 3.7 to 4 people per household. Both Roblin and Nahon interpreted the difference between the 125 named individuals in the 1292 tax assessment to 86 named individuals in 1296 as evidence of a significant decline in the size of the Parisian Jewish community, but it is more likely that the tax assessors of 1296 (and 1297) were simply more inclined to name only one person per household than they had been in 1292, when there were 86 Jewish households: Loeb, "Le role des juifs de Paris," 70–71; Nahon, "La communauté juive de Paris"; Roblin, *Les juifs de Paris*, 18; Géraud, ed., *Paris sous Philippe-le-Bel*, 178–179.

15. Roblin, *Les juifs de Paris*, 12–18.

16. Jordan, *French Monarchy*, 95.

17. On the invitation of 1225, see "Carta civium astensum"; and Bordone, "Introduzione," 9. Petit-Dutaillis also linked the invitation of the Lombards to the 1223 seizure of Jewish assets: *Étude sur la vie*, 417–418.

18. Jordan, *French Monarchy*, 129–130.

19. Ibid., 129–132, 144–145; Jordan, "An Aspect of Credit," 141.

20. Graboïs, "Du crédit juif à Paris."

21. Jordan, "An Aspect of Credit," 143–146, 151.

22. See main text of this chapter, discussion preceding note 34.

23. Nahon, "Le crédit et les juifs," 1126–1127.

24. Jordan, "An Aspect of Credit," 142.

25. On widows, see Jordan, "Jews on Top," 52, 55.

26. Reyerson, *Business, Banking, and Finance*, 68. While Jews extended 33 percent of the total number of recorded loans in Montpellier in 1293–1294 and 1301–1302, those loans constituted only 20 percent of the total value of recorded loans in those years.

27. Jordan, "An Aspect of Credit," 146; Jordan, "Jews on Top," 48; Shatzmiller, *Shylock Reconsidered*, 97–99; Abulafia, *Christian-Jewish Relations*, 79–80.

28. Nahon, "Le crédit et les juifs," 1124; Jordan, "Jews on Top," 53; Jordan, "An Aspect of Credit," 149.

29. Luce, "Catalogue des documents du Trésor des Chartes," 28–29.

30. Jordan, "Jews on Top," 53–55.

31. Loeb, "Le role des juifs de Paris," 64–65. One mother-son unit paid a tax of 24.5 pounds in 1292: ibid., 70. On the average taxes of foreign Lombards from Piacenza, see note 53.

32. Rigord, "Philippidos," 25; Claustre, *Dans les geôles*, 32, 322.

33. Versions of the story that identified the Jewish culprit as a moneylender and the Christian enabler as a woman who had pawned her clothing included: "Extraits d'un chronique anonyme française," 132–133; "De miraculo hostiae," 32; and the liturgical office of the convent of the Billettes: Dehullu, "L'affaire des Billettes," 134. In the late fourteenth century, Jewish moneylenders in Paris were still accepting used clothing as pledges on loans: see main text of this chapter, discussion preceding notes 109 and 111.

34. "Chronique rimée attribuée à Geoffroi de Paris," 119, lines 3121–3127, 3762–3765. English translation by Richard Howard, quoted by Shatzmiller, *Shylock Reconsidered*, 98.

35. Appendix 3, parts B and C; Appendices 4 and 5. Three of the eight women who spun gold thread (Aveline, Marguerite/Marguerite de Moncy, and Jehanne) resided in that section of Paris: AN KK 283, fols. 135, 187v, 188v, 265; Michaëlsson, ed., *Livre de la taille . . . 1313*, 122. The other two areas of Paris with Jewish residents were the rue de l'Atacherie, which was just south of the main Lombard area of town, and the Petit-Pont, which was also a Lombard area of town.

36. There were clusters of 4–6 Lombards on the rue Neuve Saint Merri, the rue de la Voirrerie, the rue Viez du Temple, and the rue de la Brétonnerie, and 1 or 2 Lombards on the rue aux Jongleurs, the rue Saint Martin, the rue du Temple, and at the rue de la Porte-Baudéer. Piton, *Les lombards*, 126–127, 129, 132, 135–136, 138, 142–144, 149–151.

37. Piton, *Les lombards*, 129–134; Loeb, "Le role des juifs de Paris," 63–65.

38. For examples of foreign Lombard brothers in the tax assessments of 1296–1300, see Piton, *Les lombards*, 124, 125, 130, 131, 135, 140, 141, 150. For nephews, see ibid., 132, 135, 138. In 1309, King Philip the Fair conducted an inquest into foreign Lombard business practices and patterns of settlement in France. The administrators of the inquest, who were specifically instructed to ask how long each Italian merchant or moneylender had resided in France and whether or not he was married to a Frenchwoman, found that most foreign Lombards residing in Paris had been in France between five and twenty years, and that only the poorest of them married Frenchwomen: Bautier, "I lombardi," 45. Gandolfo di Arcelli had lived in Paris for at least twelve years when he died, and as far as we can tell he never married. Similarly, the Florentine Lippo di Fede del Segna remained in France for thirty years, leaving his wife behind in Italy the entire time: Terroine, "Études sur la bourgeoisie parisienne," part 2, 53; Roncière, *Un changeur florentin*, 179–194.

39. See main text of Chapter 1, discussion preceding note 116.

40. For Jordan's argument about anomie and Jewish credit, see his "Jews on Top," 50.

41. Géraud, ed., *Paris sous Philippe-le-Bel*, 3.

42. *Registre criminel du Châtelet*, 2:525–533. On the fifteenth-century case, see Fagniez, ed., *Documents relatifs à l'histoire de l'industrie*, 2:204–205. Further evidence for liaisons between Italian men and Parisian maidservants emerges from a property dispute between two men from Lucca who resided in Paris in the 1360s. In an effort to discredit his adversary in court, one of the disputants claimed that the other had been sleeping with a female servant who worked for his landlord: Mirot, ed., "Inventaire mobilier," 163. For a broader perspective on the illegitimate children of Florentine merchants (with some discussion of those who were conceived when merchants were away from home on business), see Kuehn, *Illegitimacy in Renaissance Florence*, 117, 137.

43. Tanon, *Histoire des justices des anciennes églises*, 471–473, 492–493, 508–509, 524. In one other case, a Lombard was accused of severely beating a woman and cutting her hair; apparently they were not related to each other: ibid., 504.

44. De Roover, *Money, Banking and Credit*, 99–112; Bigwood, *Régime juridique*. On the Bellardi and their presence in Paris, see main text of Chapter 3, discussion preceding note 70. On the Anguissola and Scotti, see Bautier, "Les marchands et banquiers de Plaisance." On the Tolomei and Gran Tavola of Siena (also known as the Bonsignori), see Bautier, "Les Tolomei de Sienne aux foires de Champagne"; and English, *Enterprise and Liability*. On the presence of these companies in late thirteenth-century Paris, see Géraud, ed., *Paris sous Philippe-le-Bel*, 2, 3 ("Escoz" [Scotti], "Anguisseus"); Piton, *Les lombards*, 125, 127, 131, 133, 137, 142, 143, 147, 148, 149 ("Escoz," "Anguissoles," "Grant Table"; "Binde" [who was a member of the Gran Tavola]; Berthelemi de Senne [Tolomei of Siena]); and Michaëlsson, ed., *Livre de la taille . . . 1313*, 140 ("Vanne, Belart" [Jehan Vanne, of the Bellardi Company]).

45. Bordone, "Introduzione," 9–10; Bordone, "I lombardi in Europa," 10–12.

46. De Roover, *Money, Banking and Credit*, 100–101, 113–114.

47. On the late fourteenth century, see Kohn, "Le statut forain," 12.

48. In 1308 Countess Mahaut of Artois borrowed 1,000 livres tournois from three men from Asti, Asignel and his nephews Alexander and Boniface: PdC A 242; described by Richard, *Inventaire-sommaire*, 1:233.

49. "Carta civium astensum."

50. Bautier, "Le marchand lombard."

51. Bigwood and Grunzweig, eds., *Les livres*, 1:139, 189, 203 (nos. 477, 614, 658); 2:261.

52. There were eight major companies from Piacenza: the Gaignebiens, Scotti, Anguissola, Cavassole, Chapon, Borins, Rustigaz, and that of Gandolfo di Arcelli: Terroine, "Études sur la bourgeoisie parisienne," part 1, 67. Additionally, there were two other foreign Lombards from Piacenza: Aubertin Plesantin and Oudart le Lombart, Plesantin. On the Paris locations and tax payments of these ten taxpayers/companies, see Piton, *Les lombards*, 124–126, 130–132, 135–137, 141–143, 148–150.

53. Terroine, "Études sur la bourgeoisie parisienne," part 1, 65; Géraud, ed., *Paris sous Philippe-le-Bel*, 2; Piton, *Les lombards*, 126, 130, 136, 142, 148.

54. Testament of Gandolfo di Arcelli, in Piton, *Les lombards*, 161–165. I have calculated the averages from the tax payments indicated in Piton's edition of the tax lists of foreign Lombards (see the preceding note).

55. Ibid.

56. Bigwood and Grunzweig, eds., *Les livres*, vol. 1, nos. 477, 614, 658. The descriptions of the pledged items mention silk, silver, and pearls.

57. On co-borrowers, see Claustre, "Vivre à crédit dans une ville sans banque," 589.

58. Bigwood and Grunzweig, eds., *Les livres*, vol. 1, nos. 431, 435, 443, 449, 459, 461, 500, 521, 554, 555, 609, 654, 659, 665.

59. Bigwood and Grunzweig, eds., *Les livres*, vol. 1, no. 480. Another debt that was in arrears involved only a woman, but it was for her rent rather than for a loan: ibid., no. 621.

60. Bigwood and Grunzweig, eds., *Les livres*, vol. 1, no. 584.

61. There may have been some Italian moneylenders active in Paris, even in years when no royal contracts were in effect, but none of the sources concerning them, or the royal contracts themselves, tells us anything about the actual clients. In the 1340s and 1350s a number of Lombard usurers who were active in France paid fines or had their goods confiscated for exercising their trade, but I have found no evidence linking those particular lenders to Paris. Moranvillé, ed., "Extraits des journaux du trésor," 156, 159, 192, 199, 201 (nos. 12, 13, 24, 172, 191, 198).

62. Appendices 4 and 5. Two of the eight gold spinners (Clarice and Maheut) resided in this relatively large part of Paris, as did 33 percent of the weavers of silk head coverings and 17 percent of the weavers of *tissu de soie*: Géraud, ed., *Paris sous Philippe-le-Bel*, 56; Michaëlsson, ed., *Livre de la taille . . . 1296*, 98; Appendix 3, parts B and C.

63. These included Biche, Mouche, Vanne their nephew, Gui Fauconnier, and Quinquenelle. See Chapter 1, notes 31 and 32.

64. Géraud, ed., *Paris sous Philippe-le-Bel*, 1 (I am not counting, in the parish of Saint Eustach —[or "Saint Huitace"] the female employee of Raimbaud or the man who had already fled town); Piton, *Les lombards*, 124, 127, 129, 130.

65. Piton, *Les lombards*, 129–130.

66. Bigwood and Grunzweig, eds., *Les livres*, 1:123–209.

67. "Item, que nus ne nules n'envoient leur aprantices ne leur ouvrieres chés juies ne chiés orieres ne chiés mercier, por aprendre ledit mestier, se leur fames ne sevent du mestier": *Livre des métiers*, ed. Lespinasse and Bonnardot, 208 (statute 8).

68. *Livre des métiers*, ed. Lespinasse and Bonnardot, 207 (statute 1).

69. A statute for the mercers' guild, written before 1275, indicates that items with pearls were to be made with silk or waste silk; and another statute for the mercers' guild, from 1324, specified that narrow ware made with gold was to be woven only with fine silk: *Livre des métiers*, ed. Lespinasse and Bonnardot, 158 (statute 5); Fagniez, ed., *Documents relatifs à l'histoire de l'industrie*, 2:62.

70. "[Paid to Jehan Viel of Troussevache, bourgeois of Paris, 10 livres for] 2 hats of goldwork with pearls and pearlwork" (deux chapiaus d'orfaverie a peles et a perlerie): PdC A 242, described by Richard, *Inventaire-sommaire*, 1:233.

71. Baumgarten, *Mothers and Children*, chap. 4.

72. Géraud, ed., *Paris sous Philippe-le-Bel*, 179; Loeb, "Le role des juifs de Paris," 64 (tax assessments of 1292, 1296).

73. For three beautiful examples of medieval Jewish engagement rings from 1300 to 1348, see Descatoire, *Trésors de la Peste Noire*, 22–23. All three rings are inscribed with Hebrew letters spelling out "Mazel tov." According to the Fourth Lateran Council, Jews were required to wear special hats, but illustrated Jewish manuscripts, which depict Jews wearing pointed hats, indicate that this was not simply an idea that was imposed from the outside: Strauss, "The 'Jewish Hat.'" For good examples of representations of Jewish hats in Jewish art, see the fourteenth-century Bird's Head Haggadah and the Leipzig Mahzor: Shatzmiller, *Cultural Exchange*, figs. 17, 18, pp. 94, 95.

74. Leroy, "Quelques pièces de vêtement à la cour de Navarre," 395n10.

75. Géraud, ed., *Paris sous Philippe-le-Bel*, 178.

76. See Appendix 4.

77. AN KK 283, fols. 50v, 111v.

78. "Belon, fille Michiel le Convert": Depping, ed., *Réglemens*, 379. Silk and gold thread were the only materials that were mentioned in the statutes for the embroiderers' guild: ibid., 381.

79. Michaëlsson, ed., *Livre de la taille . . . 1297*, 110; AN KK 283, fols. 112v, 190, 230, 266.

80. "Jehanne la Converte et Jehan Hardi son mari": Michaëlsson, ed., *Livre de la taille . . . 1313*, 133.

81. The 42 sous is the combination of the tax that the deceased Estienne paid as a "mort" (20 sous: fol. 230) and that which his widow, Mahaut, paid (22 sous: fol. 190).

82. There were 5,979 taxpayers in 1313, who generated a total of 10,000 livres parisis, so the average household tax payment was 1.67 l. p. However, taxpayers were assessed in livres tournois. One livre parisis was worth 1.25 livres tournois, so the average tax in livres tournois was 2.09 l. t.: Michaëlsson, ed., *Livre de la taille . . . 1313*, xiii, xiv. There is no sense in trying to directly compare Jehanne and Jehan's tax assessment to that of Estienne and Mahaut, since the currency had been debased in the intervening years between 1300 and 1313.

83. Boutaric, *Actes du Parlement de Paris*, 2:94 (no. 3982 [1312]). On the new "Halle" of Paris, built by King Louis IX, see Martineau, *Les Halles de Paris*, 25–27.

84. Golb, *Jews in Medieval Normandy*, 262.

85. Gutmann, *The Jewish Sanctuary*, plates 33, 48.

86. Goitein, *Mediterranean Society*, 1:430nn9, 13.

87. Munro, "Medieval Woollens," 193.

88. Toch, *The Economic History of European Jews*, 21–23.

89. Jacoby, "Silk in Western Byzantium"; Toch, *The Economic History of European Jews*, 30–32; Goitein, *Mediterranean Society*, 1:84, 87, 88, 90, 104, 116, 128.

90. Toch, *The Economic History of European Jews*, 31; Adler, *Itinerary of Benjamin of Tudela*, 35, 40, 43.

91. Toch, *The Economic History of European Jews*, 50–51, 148; Reyerson, "Medieval Silks in Montpellier," 122–123.

92. Leroy, "Quelques pièces de vêtement à la cour de Navarre," 394; Leroy, "Recherches sur les juifs de Navarre" (includes an edition of an inventory of Dueña Encave's shop).

93. On the two immigrations, see above, note 13. On continued contacts, see Prawer, *History of the Jews in the Latin Kingdom*, 286–289.

94. Géraud, ed., *Paris sous Philippe-le-Bel*, 178 ("Lyon, d'Acre, mire, sa fame Bien-li-Viengne, 5s; Amendant, fuils Lion d'Acre, 8 s.") On the importance of Acre and its destruction, see Graboïs, "The Idea of Political Zionism," 67.

95. Golb, *Jews in Medieval Normandy*, 253–296.

96. Zimmels, *Ashkenazim and Sephardim*, 16–17.

97. Luce, "Catalogue des documents du Trésor des Chartes," 28.

98. Jordan, *French Monarchy*, 202–213, 215, 223–224, 230–237.

99. There is scholarly disagreement concerning the nature and extent of the exodus of 1322: Brown, "Philip V, Charles IV, and the Jews of France"; Jordan, "Home Again."

100. Kohn, *Juifs de la France du Nord*, 171; Kohn, "Les juifs de Paris."

101. Chazan, *Medieval Jewry*, 203; Kohn, *Juifs de la France du Nord*, 23.

102. Chazan, *Medieval Jewry*, 202; Kohn, "Les juifs de la France du Nord à travers les archives du Parlement," 37.

103. In 1311, Philip the Fair declared that Italian moneylenders could charge annual interest rates of 15 percent at the Champagne Fairs and 20 percent elsewhere in France: Henneman, "Taxation of Italians by the French Crown," 26. On the Jewish lender who charged one penny per pound, see Kohn, "Les juifs de la France du Nord à travers les archives du Parlement," 37.

104. Kohn, *Juifs de la France du Nord*, 101–102, 118–119.

105. Ibid., 96, 134–139.

106. Ibid., 102.

107. Teilhard de Chardin, ed., "Registre de Barthélemi de Noces," part 2, 569–571. On Precieuse's status as a widow, see Moranvillé, ed., "Extraits de Journaux du Trésor," 375 (no. 278): "De Preciosa, uxore quondam Abrahe de Pont à Morson, Judea, pro exemptione sua ab aliis Judeis" (1378).

108. *Registre criminel du Châtelet*, 2:47, 156, 212.

109. Fagniez, *Études sur l'industrie*, 317–318.

110. For another study of positive relations that arose between Jewish lenders and Christian borrowers, see Shatzmiller, *Shylock Reconsidered*.

111. Kohn, "Les juifs de la France du Nord à travers les archives du Parlement," 133 (cat. no. 462).

112. Douët-d'Arcq, ed., *Choix de pièces inédites*, 2:225–227.

113. During his twenty-eight-year sojourn in France, most of which was spent in and around Paris, the Florentine money changer and moneylender Lippo di Fede del Sega had to rely, on several occasions, on money that was sent to him from home: Roncière, *Un changeur florentin*, 188.

114. Henneman, "Taxation of Italians," 26; *Ordonnances des rois de France*, 1:96, 298–300.

115. Henneman, "Taxation of Italians," 21, 26–28; Strayer, "Italian Bankers and Philip the Fair," 115–116; Bautier, "Le marchand lombard," 77. On diminishing resources among foreign Lombards in France, see the main text of this chapter, discussion preceding note 120.

116. Henneman, "Taxation of Italians," 29.

117. Ibid., 30.

118. Ibid., 31, 34.

119. Ibid., 33.

120. Bautier, "Le marchand lombard," 76–77.

121. English, *Enterprise and Liability*, 113–114.

122. Members of the Spifami, Forteguerra, Cenami, and Rapondi families—all of them from Lucca—served as furnishers and creditors to royal and aristocratic courts in the late fourteenth century; and Florentine furnishers who provided credit for the Duke of Berry included at least three members of the di Cino family and one member of the Pazzi family. By the late fourteenth century, members of the Belloni, Spifami, and Cenami families of Lucca had married Frenchwomen and settled permanently in Paris. Mirot, "Études lucquoises 1," 74, 76, 79, 82–83; Lehoux, "Le Duc de Berri," 41–42.

123. Kohn, "Le statut forain," 12. For general background on the Garetti family, see Bordone and Spinelli, *Lombardi in Europa nel Medioevo*, 180–183.

124. *Registre criminel du Châtelet*, 1:254–268 (in 1389 Marguerite of Bruges, the wife of a Parisian horse merchant, was imprisoned and hanged for instigating a deadly assault on her neighbor, Colin le Rotisseur, who, along with his wife, had once shared meals and relationships of god-parenting with Marguerite and her husband; the relationship between the two couples

had gone sour after Marguerite and her husband borrowed some money from the other couple); 1:197 (in 1390 Marion du Val, a servant and petty thief, pawned to a woman who made purses a golden rod that she stole from her employer); Terroine and Fossier, eds., *Chartes et documents de l'abbaye de Saint-Magloire*, 88 (discussion of the postmortem inventory of Gérard of Montaigu, a lawyer in Parlement who also engaged in pawnbroking); Moranvillé, ed., "Extraits de Journaux du Trésor," 388, no. 358 (a priest is identified as a usurer in 1392). For more examples, see the discussions of the Duke of Berry and Barthelemy Castaing in the next two paragraphs of this chapter, and Claustre, "Vivre à crédit dans une ville sans banque."

125. Lehoux, "Le Duc de Berri."

126. Lehoux, "À Paris sous Philippe VI."

127. Barthelemy's executors included three Italians, one of whom appears to have been from Florence, and he had conducted business with Florentines before his death. Lehoux posits that he may have been Genoese, but the social connections point in the direction of Florence. It is clear that the identification of Barthelemy as a spice dealer was more than just window dressing; the inventory of his goods begins with an assessment of his spices. Lehoux, "À Paris sous Philippe VI," 56–57.

128. "Tapiz sarrazinois des trois Roys de Coulongne"; "un petit viel corsset à fille"; "la moitié d'une veille cote rouge à fame": Lehoux, "À Paris sous Philippe VI," 62.

129. Lehoux, "À Paris sous Philippe VI," 61–62.

130. The court confirmed a sentence by the provost of Paris, who had ruled in favor of Furquin and his wife, Jehanne, because Denise the Moneychanger, who had received a deposit of 200 florins from Jehanne, would not return the money to Furquin and Jehanne. Boutaric, *Actes du Parlement de Paris*, 2:271 (no. 5694 [1319]).

CONCLUSION

1. ADS, 7 MI 3, roll 6, register number 42 (April 28, 1396–May 16, 1398), view 164. I wish to thank Nadège Gauffre-Fayolle for sharing with me her transcription of this document.

2. For a survey of the crises that afflicted Paris in the fourteenth and fifteenth centuries, along with relevant bibliography, see Jones, *Paris: Biography of a City*, 62–95. For a list of aristocratic residences and a chart showing the increase in the number of elite residences between 1300 and 1400, see Bove, "Typologie spatiale des hôtels aristocratiques à Paris (1300, 1400)," 263, 280–290. For a richly illustrated guide to the artistic accomplishments of the years 1380 to c. 1407, see Taburet-Delahaye, dir., *Paris-1400*.

3. Taburet-Delahaye, dir., *Paris-1400*, 98–111.

4. Ibid., 87–90, 100–101, 126.

5. Beaune, "Paris au temps de Charles VI," 23.

6. Delisle, *Mandements*, 772 (no. 1545).

7. Gibbons, "The Queen as 'Social Mannequin,'" 376, 391–392.

8. Taburet-Delahaye, dir., *Paris-1400*, 262–263, 280–281, 292–293.

9. Paris, Bibliothèque Nationale de France, MS. fr. 23279, fol. 19, color reproduction in Crane, *The Performance of Self*, plate 1. For the argument that the embroidered animal is indeed a tiger, see Famiglietti, *Royal Intrigue*, xv.

10. Taburet-Delahaye, dir., *Paris-1400*, 119. The velvet is part of the permanent collection of the Musée des Tissus in Lyon (Inv. 25688). For a detailed discussion of the uncertainty concerning the patron for whom the silk was woven, and the time when it was probably

produced, see Monnas, "Developments in Figured Velvet Weaving," 72–73. For a chronological list of Charles VI's favorite emblems, mottoes, and colors, see Taburet-Delahaye, dir., *Paris-1400*, 376–379.

11. Crane, *The Performance of Self*, 15–20; Taburet-Delahaye, dir., *Paris-1400*, 119, 376–379. For references to embroiderers, see "Le XVIIe compte de Guillaume Brunel, argentier du roi Charles VI, pour le terme de la Saint-Jean 1387," in Douët d'Arcq, ed., *Nouveau recueil de comptes*, 192–201; Gibbons, "The Queen as 'Social Mannequin,'" 385; and Dehaisnes, *Documents*, 2:710, 736.

12. Gibbons, "The Queen as 'Social Mannequin,'" 385.

13. Taburet-Delahaye, dir., *Paris-1400*, 124 (color reproduction of London, British Library, Harley 4431, t. 1, fol. 3).

14. Dehaisnes, *Documents*, 2:710, 736; Paris, Bibliothèque Nationale de France, MS. fr. 23279, fol. 19, reproduced in Crane, *The Performance of Self*, plate 1.

15. Favier, *Paris au XVe siècle*, 147–171; Jones, *Paris: Biography of a City*, 77–83; Schnerb, *Les Armagnacs et les Bourguignons*; Schnerb, "Les insurrections à Paris," 260.

16. Reynolds, "'Les Angloys'"; Thompson, *Paris and Its People Under English Rule*, 13–14, 218–220; Favier, *Paris au XVe siècle*, 177–191; Jones, *Paris: Biography of a City*, 83–84.

17. Favier, *Paris au XVe siècle*, 241; Jones, *Paris: Biography of a City*, 85.

18. *Journal d'un bourgeois de Paris*, ed. Beaune, 415. See also 381, 426. On the identity of the author, see 11–13.

19. Jones, *Paris: Biography of a City*, 86–87.

20. Chevalier, *Tours, ville royale*, 241, 259.

21. *Ordonnances des rois de France*, 20:592; and see main text of Chapter 3, discussion preceding notes 128 and 129.

22. Document edited in Franklin, *Dictionnaire historique des arts*, 63–65. The *ordonnance* makes no reference to silk cloth weavers, silk throwsters, or weavers of silk narrow ware. However, the silence concerning throwsters and weavers of narrow ware is probably due to the fact that most of the workers in those two industries were women, and thus they were exempt from military obligations. We do know that in 1425 King Henry VI of England had approved statutes for makers of silk narrow ware ("tissu de soie"): Longnon, ed., *Paris pendant la domination anglaise*, 200–201.

23. Eheberg, *Verfassungs-, Verwaltungs-, und Wirtschaftsgeschichte*, 267. "Parissyde" (Paris silk) is grouped with "Bastside," which is a reference to raw silk (that is to say, silk that has been reeled into skeins but not yet degummed), so the Paris silk is probably silk yarn. In his discussion of this reference Rolf Sprandel did not distinguish between yarn and cloth: "Die wirtschaftlichen Beziehungen zwischen Paris und dem deutschen Sprachraum," 307.

24. Favier, ed., *Les contribuables parisiens*. The assessment of 1421 included 1,332 names, those of 1423 and 1438, 502 and 579 names.

25. Sargentson, *Merchants and Luxury Markets*, 18–23, 136. On the presence of prominent women entrepreneurs in the seventeenth century, see the engraving by Abraham Bosse of the Gallery of the Palais de Justice (c. 1638), Metropolitan Museum of Art, accession number 22.67.16. The engraving depicts several merchants in the gallery, including a "lingère" selling fine linens and laces.

26. Jones, *Sexing la Mode*, 96–98; Truant, "La maîtrise d'une identité?"; Farmer, "Merchant Women and the Administrative Glass Ceiling," 100–101.

27. Drouault, "Le travail de la soie."

Bibliography

ARCHIVAL SOURCES

Arras, Archives du Pas-de-Calais, Centre Mahaut d'Artois
    Série A—Household accounts and financial documents of the lords of Artois (PdC A)
Brussels, Archives générales du Royaume
    CC 1
Chambéry, Archives départementale de Savoie (ADS)
    Microfilm series 1 MI 28—extraordinary accounts of the Count of Savoy
    Microfilm series 1 MI 33—accounts of the household of the Countess of Savoy
    Microfilm series 1 MI 90—accounts of the treasury of the County of Savoy
    Microfilm series 7 MI 3—accounts of the treasury of the County of Savoy
Ghent, Rijksarchief
    Fonds Gaillard 33, 52
    Fonds St.-Genois 668
London, British Library
    Add. 7966A
London, National Archives, Public Records Office
    E 361/3
    E 361/9
    E 101/366/4
Mons, Archives de l'État
    Chartrier 485
Paris, Archives de l'Assistance Publique
    Fonds St.-Jacques, no. 14
Paris, Archives Nationales de France (AN)
    KK 242
    KK 283, Role de la taille de Paris (1296–1300)
    L 870
    LL 782
    S 3376
    S 3380
Paris, Archives des Quinze-Vingts
    MS. 5878 (microfiche available at the Institut de recherche et d'histoire des textes, Paris)
Paris, Bibliothèque Nationale de France
    MS. Clairambault, 832
    MS. fr. 23279

PRINTED PRIMARY SOURCES

Adler, Marcus N. *The Itinerary of Benjamin of Tudela: Critical Text, Translation and Commentary.* New York: P. Feldheim, 1965.

Bigwood, Georges, and Armand Grunzweig, eds. *Les Livres des comptes des Gallerani.* 2 vols. Brussels: Palais des académies, 1961.

Boutaric, M. E. *Actes du Parlement de Paris.* 2 vols. Paris: Henri Plon, 1863.

"Carta civium astensum." In Charles Petit-Dutaillis, *Étude sur la vie et le règne de Louis VIII (1187–1226),* 521–522. Paris: Emile Bouillon Editeur, 1894.

"Chronique rimée attribuée à Geoffroi de Paris." In *Recueil des historiens des Gaules et de la France,* 22:87–166.

Ciano, Cesare, ed. *La "Pratica di mercatura" datiniana (secolo XIV).* Biblioteca della rivista Economia e storia, 9. Milan: Giuffrè, 1964.

"Le compte Lucas Borgne tailleur nostre sire le roy [1335–42]." Ed. Constant Leber. In *Collection des meilleurs dissertations, notices et traités particulier,* 19:79–89. Paris: G.-A. Dentu, 1838.

"Compte de M. Estienne Lafontaine argentier du roi pour l'an MCCCL (1350–51)." Ed. Constant Leber. In *Collection des meilleurs dissertations, notices et traités particulier,* 19:89–110. Paris: G.-A. Dentu, 1838.

Coyecque, Ernest, ed. *Recueil des actes notariés relatifs à l'histoire de Paris et de ses environs au 16e siècle.* 2 vols. Paris: Imprimerie Nationale, 1905, 1923.

"De miraculo hostiae." In *Recueil des historiens des Gaules et de la France,* 22:32–33.

De Rekeningen der Graven en Gravinnen uit het Henegouwsche Huis. Ed. J. Smit. 3 vols. Werken van het Historisch Genootschap, gevestigd te Utrecht, 3rd ser. xlvi, liv, lxix. Amsterdam and Utrecht, 1924–1939.

Dehaisnes, M. le Chanoine. *Documents et extraits divers concernant l'histoire de l'art dans la Flandre, l'Artois et le Hainaut.* 2 vols. Lille: Impr. L. Danel, 1886.

Delisle, Léopold. *Mandements et actes divers de Charles V. (1364–1380): Recueillis dans les collections de la Bibliothèque Nationale.* Paris: Imprimerie nationale, 1874.

Depping, Georges Bernard, ed. *Réglemens sur les arts et métiers de Paris, rédigés au 13 siècle, et connus sous le nom du* Livre des métiers *d'Étienne Boileau: Publiés, pour la première fois en entier, d'après les manuscrits de la Bibliothèque du roi et des Archives du royaume, avec des notes et une introduction.* Paris: Impr. de Crapelet, 1837.

Diplomatarium norvegicum: Oldbreve til kundskab om Norges indre og ydre forhold, sprog, slægter, sæder, lovgivning og rettergang i middelalderen. Vol. 3. Ed. Christian Christoph Andreas Lange, Carl Richard Unger, and Norsk Historisk Kjeldeskrift-Institutt. Christiania: Malling, 1855.

"Dit du mercier." Ed. Philippe Ménard. In *Mélanges de langue et de littérature du Moyen Âge et de la Renaissance offerts à Jean Frappier,* 2:797–818. Geneva: Droz, 1970.

Douët-d'Arcq, L., ed. *Choix de pièces inédites relatives au règne de Charles VI.* Paris: Jules Renouard, 1863–1864.

———. *Comptes de l'argenterie des rois de France.* Paris: Jules Renouard, 1851.

———. *Nouveau recueil de comptes de l'argenterie des rois de France.* Paris: Librairie Renouard, H. Loones, successeur, 1874.

Eheberg, K. Th. *Verfassungs-, Verwaltungs-, und Wirtschaftsgeschichte der Stadt Strassburg bis 1681.* Strasbourg, 1899.

"Extraits d'un chronique anonyme française finissant en M.CCC.VII." In *Recueil des historiens des Gaules et de la France*, 21:130–137.

Fagniez, Gustave, ed. *Documents relatifs à l'histoire de l'industrie et du commerce en France*. 2 vols. Paris: Alphonse Picard et Fils, Editeurs, 1898.

———. *Fragment d'un répertoire de jurisprudence parisienne au XVe siècle*. Paris: Daupeley-Gouverneur, 1891.

Favier, Jean, ed. *Les contribuables parisiens à la fin de la Guerre de Cent Ans, les rôles d'impôt de 1421, 1423 et 1438*. Paris: Droz, 1970.

Fawtier, Robert, and François Maillard, eds. *Comptes royaux (1285–1314)*. 3 vols. Paris: Imprimerie Nationale, 1953–1956.

Gargiolli, Girolamo, ed. *L'arte della seta in firenze: Trattato del secolo xv*. Florence: G. Barbèra, 1868.

Géraud, Hercule, ed. *Paris sous Philippe-le-Bel: D'après des documents originaux et notamment d'après un manuscript contenant le rôle de la taille imposée sur les habitants de Paris en 1292*. Paris: Crapelet, 1837. Reprint ed. with introduction and index by Caroline Bourlet and Lucie Fossier. Tübingen: Max Niemeyer Verlag, 1991.

Guillaume de Nangis. "Listoire du roy Phelippe filz de Monseigneur Saint Loys." In *Recueil des historiens des Gaules et de la France*, 20:467–539.

Guillaume de Saint-Pathus. *Les miracles de Saint Louis*. Ed. Percival B. Fay. Paris: H. Champion, 1931.

———. *Vie de Saint Louis*. Ed. H.-François Delaborde. Paris: Alphonse Picard et fils, 1899.

Hall, Hubert, and Frieda J. Nicholas, eds. *Select Tracts and Table Books Relating to English Weights and Measures (1100–1742)*. Camden: Miscellany, 1929.

Het memorial van Jehan Makiel, klerk en ontvanger van Gwijde van Dampierre (1270–1275). Ed. J. Buntinx. Brussels: Commission Royale d'Histoire, 1944.

John of Garland. *Dictionarius*. Ed. Tony Hunt. In *Teaching and Learning Latin in Thirteenth-Century England*, 1:191–203. Rochester, NY: D. S. Brewer, 1991.

Journal d'un bourgeois de Paris: De 1405 à 1449. Ed. Colette Beaune. Paris: Librairie générale française, 1990.

Lalou, Elisabeth, ed. *Les comptes sur tablettes de cire de la chambre aux deniers: De Philippe III le Hardi et de Philippe IV le Bel (1282–1309)*. Paris: Diffusion de Boccard, 1994.

Lespinasse, René de, ed. *Les métiers et corporations de la ville de Paris, tome II, Orfèvrerie, sculpture, mercerie, ouvriers en métaux, bâtiment et ameublement*. Paris: Imprimerie Nationale, 1892.

Le livre des métiers d'Étienne Boileau. Ed. René de Lespinasse and François Bonnardot. Paris: Imprimerie Nationale, 1879.

Loesch, Heinrich von, ed. *Die Kölner Zunfturkunden nebst anderen Kölner Gewerbeurkunden bis zum Jahre 1500*. 2 vols. Bonn: Harsteins Verlag, 1907.

Longnon, Auguste, ed. *Paris pendant la domination anglaise (1420–1436): Documents extraits des registres de la Chancellerie de France*. Paris: C. H. Champion, 1878.

Lysons, Samuel, ed. "Copy of a Roll of Purchases Made for the Tournament in Windsor Park in the Sixth Year of King Edward I, Preserved in the Record Office at the Tower." *Archaeologia* 17 (1814): 297–310.

Michaëlsson, Karl, ed. *Le livre de la taille de Paris l'an 1296*. Göteborg: Almqvist & Wiksell, 1958.

———. *Le livre de la taille de Paris l'an 1297*. Göteborg: Elanders Boktryckeri Aktiebolag, 1962.

————. *Le livre de la taille de Paris: L'an de grâce 1313.* Göteborg: Wettergren & Kerbers Förlag, 1951.

Mirot, Léon, ed. "Inventaire mobilier chez un marchand lucquois à Paris en 1362." In "Études lucquoises 4: Les Cename, Appendix III." *Bibliothèque de l'École des chartes* 91 (1930): 160–168.

Molinier, Emile, ed. "Inventaire du trésor de l'Église du Saint-Sepulcre de Paris, 1379." *Mémoires de la Société de l'histoire de Paris et de l'Île-de-France* 9 (1882): 239–286.

————. *Inventaire du trésor du Saint Siège sous Boniface VIII (1295).* Paris: Daupeley-Gouverneur, 1888.

Moranvillé, H., ed. "Extraits des journaux du trésor (1345–1419)." *Bibliothèque de l'École des chartes* 49 (1888): 149–214, 368–437.

————. "Un rôle d'impôt à Paris au XIVe siècle." *Bulletin de la Société de l'histoire de Paris et de l'Île-de-France* 15 (1888): 3–9.

Ordonnances des rois de France de la troisième race, recueillies par ordre chronologique. Ed. Eusèbe-Jacob de Laurière et al. 22 vols. Paris, 1723–1849.

Parsons, John Carmi, ed. *The Court and Household of Eleanor of Castile in 1290: An Edition of British Library, Additional Manuscript 35294 with Introduction and Notes.* Toronto: Pontifical Institute of Mediaeval Studies, 1977.

Pegolotti, Francesco Balducci. *La pratica della mercatura.* Ed. Allan Evans. Cambridge, MA: Mediaeval Academy of America, 1936.

————. "Spices." Translated from *La pratica della mercatura* by Robert S. Lopez and Irving W. Raymond. In *Medieval Trade in the Mediterranean World,* 109–114. New York: Columbia University Press, 1955.

Prost, Bernard, and Henri Prost, eds. *Inventaires mobiliers et extraits des comptes des ducs de Bourgogne de la maison de Valois (1363–1477).* 2 vols. Paris: E. Leroux, 1902, 1913.

Recueil des historiens des Gaules et de la France. 24 vols. Ed. Martin Bouquet et al. Paris, 1738–1904.

Registre criminel du Châtelet de Paris: Du 6 septembre 1389 au 18 mai 1392. 2 vols. Ed. Société des bibliophiles françois. Paris: C. Lahure, 1861, 1864.

I registri della Cancelleria Angioina. Vol. 9. Ed. Riccardo Filangieri. Naples: L'Accademia Pontaniana, 1957.

Richard, Jules-Marie, ed. "Documents des XIIIe et XIVe siècles relatifs à l'hôtel de Bourgogne (ancien hôtel d'Artois) tirés du Trésor des chartes d'Artois." *Bulletin de la Société de l'histoire de Paris et de l'Île-de-France* 17 (1890): 137–158.

Rigord, Guillaume. "Philippidos, libri xii." In *Oeuvres de Rigord et de Guillaume le Breton,* vol. 1, ed. H. François Delaborde, 1–167. Paris: Librairie Renouard, 1882.

Le Roman de la Rose: Par Guillaume de Lorris et Jean de Meung. 5 vols. Ed. and trans. Pierre Manteau. Paris: P. Daffis (vols. 2–5). Orleans: H. Herluison, 1878. Reprint, Nendeln: Kraus Reprint, 1970.

Savary, Jacques. *Le parfait negociant, ou instruction generale pour ce qui regarde le commerce.* 2nd ed. Paris: Louis Billaine, 1679.

Schmitt, Jean-Claude, Maria Gabriella Critelli, Marie-Thérèse Gousset, and Marie-Hélène Tesnière, eds. *La Leyenda de la Santa Faz.* Salamanca: Biblioteca Apostolica Vaticana & Ediciones de Arte y Bibliofilia S.A., 2010.

Tanon, Louis. *Histoire des justices des anciennes églises et communautés monastiques de Paris, suivie des registres inédits de Saint-Maur-des-Fossés, Sainte-Geneviève, Saint-Germain-des-Prés et du registre de Saint-Martin-des-Champs.* Paris: L. Larose et Forcel, 1883.

"Tarif des marchandises qui se vendaient à Paris à la fin du XIIIe siècle." Ed. L. Douët-d'Arcq. *Revue archéologique*, IXe année (1852): 213–228.

Teilhard de Chardin, Emmanuel, ed. "Registre de Barthélemi de Noces, officier du duc de Berri, (1374–1377)." *Bibliothèque de l'École des chartes* 52 (1891): 220–258, 517–572.

Terroine, Anne, and Lucie Fossier, eds. *Chartes et documents de l'abbaye de Saint-Magloire*. Vol. 3. Paris: CNRS, 1976.

Viard, Jules Marie Édouard, ed. *Documents parisiens du règne de Philippe VI de Valois (1328–1350): Extraits des registres de la chancellerie de France*. 2 vols. Paris: Honoré Champion, 1899, 1900.

Woolgar, C. M., ed. *Household Accounts from Medieval England*. 2 vols. Oxford: Oxford University Press, 1992.

SECONDARY SOURCES

Abulafia, Anna Sapir. *Christian-Jewish Relations, 1000–1300: Jews in the Service of Medieval Christendom*. New York: Pearson Education, 2011.

Anderson, Perry. "Nation-States and National Identity." Review of *The Identity of France*, vol. 2, *People and Production*, by Fernand Braudel, trans. Sian Reynolds, *London Review of Books* 13/9 (1991): 3–8.

Archer, Janice Marie. "Working Women in Thirteenth-Century Paris." PhD diss., University of Arizona, 1995.

Balard, Michel. *La Romanie génoise: (XIIe–début du XVe siècle)*. 2 vols. Rome: École française de Rome, 1978.

Bartlett, Robert. *The Making of Europe: Conquest, Colonization and Cultural Change, 950–1350*. Princeton: Princeton University Press, 1993.

Baumgarten, Elisheva. *Mothers and Children: Jewish Family Life in Medieval Europe*. Princeton, NJ: Princeton University Press, 2004.

Bautier, Anne-Marie. "Contribution à l'histoire du cheval au Moyen Âge." Parts 1 and 2. *Bulletin philologique et historique (jusqu'à 1610) du comité des travaux historiques et scientifiques* (1978): 209–249.

Bautier, Anne-Marie, and Robert-Henri Bautier. "Contribution à l'histoire du cheval au Moyen Âge." Part 3. *Bulletin philologique et historique (jusqu'à 1610) du comité des travaux historiques et scientifiques* (1980): 7–72.

Bautier, Robert-Henri. "I lombardi e i problemi del credito nel regno di Francia nei secoli XIII e XIV." In *L'uomo del banco dei pegni: "Lombardi" e mercato del denaro nell' Europa medievale: Antologia di storia medievale*, ed. Renato Bordone, 23–57. Turin: Scriptorium, 1994.

———. "Le marchand lombard en France aux XIIIe et XIVe siècles." *Actes des congrès de la Société des historiens médiévistes de l'enseignement supérieur public* 19 (1988): 63–80.

———. "Les marchands et banquiers de Plaisance." In *Il "Registrum Magnum" del commune di Piacenza: Atti del covegno internazionale di studio (Piacenza, 1985)*, 182–215. Piacenza: Cassa di Risparmio di Piacenza, 1985. Reprinted in Bautier, *Commerce méditerranéen et banquiers italiens au Moyen Âge*. Chap. 1. Aldershot: Variorum, 1992.

———. "Une opération de décentralisation industrielle sous Philippe V: L'installation de drapiers parisiens à Gray (1318)." *Bulletin philologique et historique (jusqu'à 1610) du Comité des travaux historiques et scientifiques* 2 (1971): 645–664.

———. "La place de la draperie brabançonne et plus particulierement bruxelloise dans l'industrie textile du Moyen Âge." *Annales de la Société royale d'archéologie de Bruxelles, volume jubilaire* 51 (1962–1966): 31–63. Reprinted in Bautier, *Sur l'histoire économique de la France médiévale: La route, la fleuve, la foire.* Chap. 10. Aldershot: Variorum, 1991.

———. *Sur l'histoire économique de la France médiévale: La route, le fleuve, la foire.* Aldershot: Variorum, 1991.

———. "Les Tolomei de Sienne aux foires de Champagne." In Bautier, *Commerce méditerranéen et banquiers italiens au Moyen Age.* Chap. 8. Aldershot: Variorum, 1992.

Beaumont-Maillet, Laure. *L'Eau à Paris.* Paris: Hazan, 1991.

Beaune, Colette. "Paris au temps de Charles VI." In Élisabeth Taburet-Delahaye, dir., *Paris-1400: Les arts sous Charles VI*, 21–25. Éditions de la Réunion des musées nationaux. Paris: Fayard, 2004.

Beazley, C. Raymond. "The French Conquest of the Canaries in 1402–6, and the Authority for the Same." *Geographical Journal* 25/1 (1905): 77–81.

Becker, John, with the collaboration of Donald B. Wagner. *Pattern and Loom: A Practical Study of the Development of Weaving Techniques in China, Western Asia and Europe.* 2nd ed. Copenhagen: Rhodos, 2009.

Belhoste, Jean-François. "Paris grand centre drapier au Moyen Âge." *Fédération des Sociétés historiques et archéologiques de Paris et de l'Île-de-France: Mémoires* 51 (2000): 31–48.

Benoît, Paul. "En eaux troubles . . ." In *Paris au Moyen Âge: Recherches recentes.* Special issue of *Histoire et images médiévales* 9 (2007): 68–75.

Bibliothèque Nationale de France, direction des collections, Département philosophie, histoire, science de l'homme. "Immigration en France: Histoire, société, communautés: Bibliographie selective." November 2006. www.bnf.fr/documents/biblio_immigration_2.rtf. Accessed February 18, 2016.

Bigwood, Georges. "La politique de la laine en France sous les règnes de Philippe le Bel et de ses fils." *Revue belge de philologie et d'histoire* 15 (1936): 79–102, 429–457; 16 (1937): 95–118.

———. *Le régime juridique et économique du commerce de l'argent dans la Belgique du Moyen Âge.* Brussels: Hayez, 1920.

Bonds, William M. "Genoese Noblewomen and Gold Thread Manufacturing." *Medievalia et humanistica* 17 (1966): 79–81.

Bordier, Henri, and Léon Brièle, eds. *Les archives hospitalières de Paris.* 2 vols. Paris: H. Champion, 1877.

Bordone, Renato. "Introduzione." In *L'uomo del banco dei pegni: "Lombardi" e mercato del denaro nell' Europa medievale: Antologia di storia medievale*, ed. Renato Bordone, 5–21. Turin: Scriptorium, 1994.

———. "I lombardi in Europa: Uno sguardo d'insieme." In *Lombardi in Europa nel Medioevo*, ed. Renato Bordone and Franco Spinelli, 9–39. Milan: Franco Angeli, 2005.

Bordone, Renato, and Franco Spinelli. *Lombardi in Europa nel Medioevo.* Milan: Franco Angeli, 2005.

Bourlet, Caroline. "L'anthroponymie à Paris à la fin du XIIIe siècle d'après les rôles de la taille du règne de Philippe le Bel." In *Genèse médiévale de l'anthroponymie modern*, ed. Monique Bourin and Pascale Chareille, vol. 2, part 2, 9–44. Tours: Université François Rabelais, 1992.

———. "Le *Livre des métiers*, dit d'Étienne Boileau, et la lente mise en place d'une législation écrite du travail à Paris (fin XIIIe–début XIVe siècle)." *Médiévales* 69 (2016): 19–48.

Bourlet, Caroline, and Anne-Laure Bethe. "Création des plans de référence pour la fin du Moyen Âge: Îlots, voirie, paroisses et quêtes." In *Paris de parcelles en pixels: Analyse géomatique de l'espace parisien médiévale et moderne*, ed. Hélène Noizet, Boris Bove, and Laurent Costa, 155–165. Paris: Presses Universitaires de Vincennes, 2013.

Bourlet, Caroline, and Alain Layec. "Densités de population et socio-topographie: La géolocalisation du rôle de taille de 1300." In *Paris de parcelles en pixels: Analyse géomatique de l'espace parisien médiévale et moderne*, ed. Helene Noizet, Boris Bove, and Laurent Costa, 215–237. Paris: Presses Universaires de Vincennes, 2013.

Bove, Boris. *Dominer la ville: Prévôts des marchands et échevins parisiens de 1260 à 1350*. Paris: Editions du CTHS, 2004.

———. "Les hôtels de Paris vers 1300." http://alpage.huma-num.fr/documents/Illustration _colloque/BOVE_Hotels1300_p264.pdf. Accessed February 18, 2016.

———. "Les hôtels de Paris vers 1400." http://alpage.huma-num.fr/documents/Illustration _colloque/BOVE_Hotels1400_p264.pdf. Accessed February 18, 2016.

———. "Typologie spatiale des hôtels aristocratiques à Paris (1300, 1400)." In *Paris de parcelles en pixels: Analyse géomatique de l'espace parisien médiévale et moderne*, ed. Hélène Noizet, Boris Bove, and Laurent Costa, 257–292. Paris: Presses Universitaires de Vincennes, 2013.

Briggs, Charles F. *Giles of Rome's "De regimine principum": Reading and Writing Politics at Court and University, c. 1275–c. 1525*. Cambridge: Cambridge University Press, 1999.

Brown, Elizabeth A. R. "Philip V, Charles IV, and the Jews of France: The Alleged Expulsion of 1322." *Speculum* 66/2 (1991): 294–329.

Burns, E. Jane. *Sea of Silk: A Textile Geography of Women's Work in Medieval French Literature*. Philadelphia: University of Pennsylvania Press, 2009.

Campbell, Marian. "Paris, miroir ou lumière pour l'orfèvrerie anglaise vers 1300?" In *1300: L'art au temps de Philippe le Bel, actes du colloque international, Grand Palais, 1998*, ed. Danielle Gaborit-Chopin and François Avril, 203–218. Paris: École du Louvre, 2001.

Cardon, Dominique. *La draperie au Moyen Âge: Essor d'une grande industrie européenne*. Paris: CNRS Ed., 1999.

———. *Natural Dyes: Sources, Tradition, Technology, and Science*. London: Archetype, 2007.

Carretero, Concha Herrero. *Museo de Telas Medievales, Monasterio de Santa María la Real de Huelgas*. Madrid: Patrimonio Nacional, 1988.

Cazelles, Raymond. *Nouvelle histoire de Paris, de la fin du règne de Philippe Auguste à la mort de Charles V, 1223–1380*. Paris: Hachette, 1972.

Chabot, Isabelle. "La loi du lignage: Notes sur le système successoral florentin (XIVe/XVe–XVIIe siècle)." *Clio: Femmes, genre, histoire* 7 (1998): 2–13.

Chazan, Robert. *Medieval Jewry in Northern France: A Political and Social History*. Baltimore: Johns Hopkins University Press, 1973.

Cherry, John. "Leather." In *English Medieval Industries*, ed. John Blair and Nigel Ramsay, 295–318. London: Hambledon Press, 1991.

Chevalier, Bernard. *Tours, ville royale (1356–1520)*. Paris: Vander/Nauwelaerts, 1975.

Chorley, Patrick. "The Cloth Exports of Flanders and Northern France During the Thirteenth Century: A Luxury Trade?" *Economic History Review*, n.s. 40/3 (1987): 349–379.

Ciocîltan, Virgil. *The Mongols and the Black Sea Trade in the Thirteenth and Fourteenth Centuries*. Trans. Samuel Willcocks. Leiden: Brill, 2012.

Claustre, Julie. *Dans les geôles du roi: L'emprisonnement pour dette à Paris à la fin du Moyen-Âge*. Paris: Publications de la Sorbonne, 2007.

———. "Vivre à crédit dans une ville sans banque." *Le Moyen Âge* 119/3–4 (2013): 567–596.

Cocheris, Hippolyte, ed. *Histoire de la ville, et de tout le diocèse de Paris par l'Abbé Lebeuf, Nouvelle édition annotée et contiuée jusqu'à nos jours par Hippolyte Cocheris.* 7 vols. Paris, 1863–1891.

Cohen, Meredith. *The Sainte-Chapelle and the Construction of Sacral Monarchy.* Cambridge: Cambridge University Press, 2015.

Cohen, Richard. *By the Sword: A History of Gladiators, Musketeers, Samurai, Swashbucklers, and Olympic Champions.* New York: Random House, 2002.

Collingwood, Peter. *The Techniques of Tablet Weaving.* London: Faber and Faber, 1982.

Constable, Olivia Remie. "Chess and Courtly Culture in Medieval Castile: The 'Libro de ajedrez' of Alfonso X, el sabio." *Speculum* 82/2 (April 2007): 301–347.

Costantini, Marta Cuoghi. "Uno sciamito del XIII secolo." *Arte tessile rivista-annuario del Centro italiano per lo studio della storia del tessuto* 1 (1990): 4–8.

Courtenay, William J. "Between Pope and King: The Parisian Letters of Adhesion of 1303." *Speculum* 71/3 (1996): 577–605.

———. "The Parisian Franciscan Community in 1303." *Franciscan Studies* 53/1 (1993): 155–173.

———. *Parisian Scholars in the Early Fourteenth Century: A Social Portrait.* Cambridge: Cambridge University Press, 1999.

———. "Spanish and Portuguese Scholars at the University of Paris in the Fourteenth and Fifteenth Centuries: The Exchange of Ideas and Texts." In *Medieval Iberia: Changing Societies and Cultures in Contact and Transition*, ed. Ivy A. Corfis and Ray Harris-Northall, 110–119. Woodbridge, UK: Tamesis, 2007.

Crane, Susan. *The Performance of Self: Ritual, Clothing, and Identity During the Hundred Years War.* Philadelphia: University of Pennsylvania Press, 2002.

Crippa, Flavio. "Dal baco al filo." In *La seta in Italia dal medioevo al seicento: Dal baco al drappo*, ed. Luca Molà, Reinhold C. Mueller, and Claudio Zanier, 3–33. Venice: Fondazione Cini, 2000.

Crowfoot, Elisabeth, Frances Pritchard, and Kay Staniland, eds. *Textiles and Clothing: c. 1150–c. 1450.* London: Museum of London, 1992. Reprint, Woodbridge, Suffolk: Boydell Press, 2002, 2004.

Currie, Ronald. "Silk." In *Silk, Mohair, Cashmere and Other Luxury Fibers*, ed. Robert Franck, 1–67. Cambridge: Woodhead Publishing, 2000.

Dale, Marian K. "The London Silkwomen of the Fifteenth Century." *Economic History Review* 4 (1932–1934): 324–335.

Daumet, Georges. "Louis de la Cerda ou d'Espagne." *Bulletin hispanique* 15/1 (1913): 38–67.

De Roover, Raymond. *Money, Banking and Credit in Mediaeval Bruges: Italian Merchant Bankers, Lombards and Money-Changers.* Cambridge, MA: Mediaeval Academy of America, 1948.

Derville, Alain. "Les draperies flamandes et artésiennes vers 1250–1350: Quelques considérations critiques et problématiques." *Revue du Nord* 54/215 (1972): 353–370.

Descatoire, Christine. *Trésors de la peste noire: Erfurt et Colmar: Exposition présentée du 25 avril au 3 septembre 2007 au Musée national du Moyen-Âge-Thermes et Hôtel de Cluny.* Paris: Réunion des musées nationaux, 2007.

Desrosiers, Sophie. "Les draps d'Areste: De nouvelles soieries à la mode en Occident aux XIIe–XIIIe siècles." In *L'innovation technique au Moyen Âge: Actes du VIe Congrès international d'Archéologie Médiévale (1–5 Octobre 1996, Dijon-Mont Beuvray-Chenôve-Le Creusot-Montbard)*, 43–44. Caen: Société d'archéologie médiévale, 1998.

———. "Draps d'Areste (II): Extension de la classification, comparaisons et lieux de fabrication." *Techniques & culture* 34 (2005): 89–119.

———. "Draps d'Areste (III): Singularité et origine des tisserands." In *Islamische Textilkunst des Mittelalters: Aktuelle Probleme*, 181–192. Riggisberger Berichte 5. Riggisberg: Abegg-Stiftung, 1997.

———. *Soieries et autres textiles de l'Antiquité au XVIe siècle, catalogue [du] Musée national du Moyen Âge—Thermes de Cluny*. Paris: Réunion des musées nationaux, 2004.

———. "Sur l'origine d'un tissu qui a participé à la fortune de Venise: Le velours de soie." In *La seta in Italia dal medioevo al seicento: Dal baco al drappo*, ed. Luca Molà, Reinhold C. Mueller, and Claudio Zanier, 35–61. Venice: Marsilio, 2000.

———. "Trois representations d'un métier à la tire florentin du XVe siècle." *Bulletin de liaison du Centre international d'étude des textiles anciens* 71 (1993): 36–47.

Desrosiers, Sophie, and Antoinette Rast Eichler. "Luxurious Merovingian Textiles Excavated from Burials in the Saint Denis Basilica, France in the 6th–7th Century." Paper presented at the Textile Society of America Symposium Proceedings on September 1, 2012. digital-commons.unl.edu/tsaconf/675. Accessed February 27, 2016.

Dehullu, Joanie. "L'affaire des Billettes: Une accusation de profanation d'hosties portées contre les juifs à Paris, 1290." *Bijdragen* 56/2 (1995): 133–155.

Dhérent, Catherine. "L'assise sur le commerce des draps à Douai en 1304." *Revue du Nord* 65/257 (1983): 369–397.

Dini, Bruno. "L'industria serica in Italia, secc. XIII–XV." In *La seta in Europa, sec. XIII–XX: Atti della Ventiquattresima settimana di studi, 4–9 maggio 1992*, ed. Simonetta Cavaciocchi, 91–123. Florence: Le Monnier, 1993.

Dozy, Reinhart Pieter Anne. *Supplément aux dictionnaires arabes*. Vol. 1. Leiden: Brill, 1887.

Drouault, Célia. "Le travail de la soie, une voie pour l'exercice de la liberté individuelle des femmes à Tours au XVIIIe siècle." *Annales de Bretagne et des pays de l'ouest* 114 (2007): 159–168.

Dubost, Jean-François, and Peter Sahlins. *Et si on faisait payer les étrangers?: Louis XIV, les immigrés et quelques autres*. Paris: Flammarion, 1999.

Dunbabin, Jean. *Charles I of Anjou: Power, Kingship and State-Making in Thirteenth-Century Europe*. New York: Longman, 1998.

———. *The French in the Kingdom of Sicily, 1266–1305*. Cambridge: Cambridge University Press, 2011.

Edler, Florence Marguerite. "The Silk Trade of Lucca During the Thirteenth and Fourteenth Centuries." PhD diss., University of Chicago, 1930.

Edler De Roover, Florence. "Andrea Banchi, Florentine Silk Manufacturer and Merchant in the Fifteenth Century." *Studies in Medieval and Renaissance History* 3 (1966): 223–285.

———. *L'arte della seta a Firenze nei secoli XIV e XV*. Ed. Sergio Tognetti. Florence: Leo S. Olschki Editore, 1999.

———. "Lucchese Silk." *Ciba Review* 80 (1950): 2902–2936.

Endrei, Walter. "Manufacturing a Piece of Woolen Cloth in Medieval Flanders: How Many Work Hours?" In *Textiles of the Low Countries in European Economic History: Proceedings of the Tenth International Economic History Congress Session B-15*, ed. Erik Aerts and John Munro, 14–23. Leuven: Leuven History Press, 1990.

English, Edward D. *Enterprise and Liability in Sienese Banking, 1230–1350*. Cambridge, MA: Medieval Academy of America, 1988.

Enlart, Camille. *Manuel d'archéologie française depuis les temps mérovingiens jusqu'à la Renaissance, tome 3—le costume.* Paris: A. Picard, 1916.

Fagniez, Gustave. *Études sur l'industrie et la classe industrielle à Paris au XIIIe et au XIVe siècle.* Paris: F. Vieweg, 1877. Reprint, New York: Burt Franklin, 1970.

Fagniez, Gustave, and Frantz Funck-Brentano. *La femme et la société française dans la première moitié du XVIIe siècle.* Paris: Librairie Universitaire J. Gamber, 1929.

Famiglietti, R. C. *Royal Intrigue: Crisis at the Court of Charles VI, 1392–1420.* New York: AMS Press, 1986.

Farmer, Sharon. "Aristocratic Power and the 'Natural' Landscape: The Garden Park at Hesdin, ca. 1291–1302." *Speculum* 88/3 (2013): 644–680.

———. "*Biffes, Tiretaines,* and *Aumonières*: The Role of Paris in the International Textile Markets of the Thirteenth and Fourteenth Centuries." In *Medieval Clothing and Textiles,* ed. Robin Netherton and Gale R. Owen-Crocker, 2:73–89. Woodbridge: Boydell and Brewer, 2006.

———. "Medieval Paris and the Mediterranean: The Evidence from the Silk Industry." *French Historical Studies* 37/3 (2014): 383–419.

———. "Merchant Women and the Administrative Glass Ceiling in Thirteenth-Century Paris." In *Women and Wealth in Late Medieval Europe,* ed. Theresa Earenfight, 89–108. New York: Palgrave Macmillan, 2010.

———. "Les privilèges des métiers, l'integration verticale, et l'organisation de la production des textiles de soie à Paris au XIIIe et XIVe siècles." *Médiévales* 69 (2016): 71–86.

———. *Surviving Poverty in Medieval Paris: Gender, Ideology, and the Daily Lives of the Poor.* Ithaca, NY: Cornell University Press, 2002.

Favier, Jean. *Paris au XVe siècle, 1380–1500.* Paris: Hachette, 1974.

———. *Philippe le Bel.* Paris: Fayard, 1978.

Franck, R. R., ed. *Silk, Mohair, Cashmere and Other Luxury Fibres.* Cambridge: Woodhead Publishing, 2001.

Franklin, Alfred. *Dictionnaire historique des arts, métiers, et professions exercés dans Paris depuis le treizième siècle.* Paris: H. Welter, 1906.

Frémaux, Henri. "La famille d'Étienne Marcel, 1250–1397." *Mémoires de la Société de l'histoire de Paris et de l'Île-de-France* 30 (1903): 175–242.

Frémont, Armand. "La terre." In *Les lieux de mémoire,* vol. 3, part 2, *Les France: Traditions,* ed. Pierre Nora, 18–55. Paris: Gallimard, 1992.

Gauffre-Fayolle, Nadège. "Broder à la cour de Savoie entre 1300 et 1430: De l'armurier au brodeur ou de la difficulté à recruter des artisans." In *Les acteurs de la broderie: Qui brode quoi et pour qui?,* ed. Danièle Véron-Denise and Françoise Cousin, 45–54. Saint-Maur-des-Fossés: Éditions SÉPIA, 2012.

Gay, Victor, and Henri Stein. *Glossaire archéologique du Moyen Âge et de la Renaissance.* 2 vols. Paris: Librairie de la Société Bibliographique, 1887, 1928.

Geijer, Agnes. "Broderies françaises du haut gothique conservées en Suède." In *Festschrift Ulrich Middeldorf,* ed. Antje Kosegarten and Peter Tigler, 32–38. Berlin: Walter de Gruyter, 1968.

———. *Textile Treasures of Uppsala Cathedral from Eight Centuries.* Stockholm: Almqvist & Wiksell, 1964.

Geremek, Bronislaw. *Le salariat dans l'artisanat parisien au XIIIe–XVe siècles.* Trans. Anna Posner and Christiane Klapisch-Zuber. Paris: Mouton, 1982.

Gibbons, Rachel C. "The Queen as 'Social Mannequin': Consumerism and Expenditure at the Court of Isabeau of Bavaria, 1393–1422." *Journal of Medieval History* 26/4 (2000): 371–395.

Gilonne, Georges. *Soieries de Lyon: Documents techniques et pratiques sur l'art et la fabrication des soieries, tissus à mailles, tulles, dentelles, et leur utilisation dans la nouveauté.* 2 vols. Lyon: Éditions du Fleuve, 1948.

———, ed. *Dictionnaire pratique des tissus.* Lyon: Éditions Bosc frères et Riou, 1930.

Godefroy, Frédéric. *Dictionnaire de l'ancienne langue française et de tous ses dialectes du IXe au XVe siècle.* 11 vols. Paris: F. Vieweg, 1881–1902. http://www.lexilogos.com/francais_diction naire_ancien.htm. Accessed February 27, 2016.

Goitein, Shelomo Dov. *A Mediterranean Society: The Jewish Communities of the Arab World as Portrayed in the Documents of the Cairo Geniza,* vol. 1, *Economic Foundations.* Berkeley: University of California Press, 1999.

Golb, Norman. *The Jews in Medieval Normandy: A Social and Intellectual History.* New York: Cambridge University Press, 1998.

Goodman, Jordan. "Cloth, Gender and Industrial Organization: Towards an Anthropology of Silk Workers in Early Modern Europe." In *La seta in Europa, sec. XIII–XX: Atti della Ventiquattresima settimana di studi, 4–9 maggio 1992,* ed. Simonetta Cavaciocchi, 229–245. Florence: Le Monnier, 1993.

Gourmelon, Roger. "L'industrie et le commerce des draps à Paris du XIIIe au XVIe siècle." PhD diss., École des chartes, 1950. Microfilm, Bibliothèque Nationale de France, 76 mi 10.

Graboïs, Aryeh. "L'abbaye de Saint-Denis et les juifs sous l'abbatiat de Suger." *Annales: Histoire, Sciences Sociales* 24/5 (1969): 1187–1195.

———. "Du crédit juif à Paris au temps de Saint Louis." *Revue des études juives* 129 (1970): 5–22.

———. "The Idea of Political Zionism in the Thirteenth and Early Fourteenth Centuries." In *Festschrift Rëuben R. Hecht,* 67–79. Jerusalem: Korén Publishers, 1979.

Grunwald, Kurt. "Lombards, Cahorsins and Jews." *Journal of European Economic History* 4/2 (1975): 393–398.

Guérin, Sarah M. *"Avorio d'ogni ragione*: The Supply of Elephant Ivory to Northern Europe in the Gothic Era." *Journal of Medieval History* 36/2 (2010): 156–174.

Gutmann, Joseph. *The Jewish Sanctuary.* Iconography of Religions 23/1. Leiden: Brill, 1983.

Hafter, Daryl M. "Artisans, Drudges, and the Problem of Gender in Pre-Industrial France." *Annals of the New York Academy of Sciences* 441/1 (1985): 71–88.

———. *Women at Work in Preindustrial France.* University Park: Penn State University Press, 2007.

Harvey, John. *Mediaeval Gardens.* Beaverton, OR: Timber Press, 1981.

Heckett, Elizabeth. "Some Hiberno-Norse Headcoverings from Fishamble Street and St. John's Lane, Dublin." *Textile History* 18 (1987): 159–174.

Hélary, Xavier. "Revolution militaire, revolution fiscale?" In *Monnaie, fiscalité et finances au temps de Philippe le Bel: Journée d'études du 14 mai 2004,* ed. Philippe Contamine, Jean Kerhervé, and Albert Rigaudière, 229–254. Paris: Comité pour l'histoire économique et financière de la France, 2007.

Henneman, John B., Jr. "Taxation of Italians by the French Crown (1311–1363)." *Mediaeval Studies* 31 (1969): 15–43.

Heyd, Willhelm. *Histoire du commerce du Levant au Moyen-Âge.* 2 vols. Trans. Furcy Raynaud. Leipzig: Otto Harrassowitz, 1923, 1936.

Hill, George Francis. *A History of Cyprus: 1192–1432,* vol. 2, *The Frankish Period.* 1948. Cambridge: Cambridge University Press, 2010.

———. "Two Toponymic Puzzles: 1. Nemesos-Limassol. 2. Leukosia-Nicosia." *Journal of the Warbourg Institute* 2 (1939): 375–379.

Hills, Richard Leslie. "From Cocoon to Cloth: The Technology of Silk Production." In *La seta in Europa, sec. XIII–XX: Atti della Ventiquattresima settimana di studi, 4–9 maggio 1992*, ed. Simonetta Cavaciocchi, 59–90. Florence: Le Monnier, 1993.

Hoshino, Hidetoshi. *Industria tessile e commercio internazionale nella Firenze del tardo medioevo.* Ed. Franco Franceschi and Sergio Tognetti. Biblioteca Storica Toscana, Serie I, vol. 39. Florence: Leo S. Olschki, 2001.

———. "La seta in Valdinievole nel basso Medioevo." In Hoshino, *Industria tessile e commercio internazionale.*

Howell, Martha C. *Women, Production, and Patriarchy in Late Medieval Cities.* Chicago: University of Chicago Press, 1986.

Hutton, Shennan. "Men, Women, and Markets: The Gendering of Market Space in Late Medieval Ghent." In *Urban Space in the Middle Ages and the Early Modern Age*, ed. Albrecht Classen, 409–432. New York: Walter de Gruyter, 2009.

———. *Women and Economic Activities in Late Medieval Ghent.* New York: Palgrave Macmillan, 2011.

Jacks, Philip Joshua, and William Caferro. *The Spinelli of Florence: Fortunes of a Renaissance Merchant Family.* University Park: Penn State University Press, 2001.

Jacoby, David. "Cypriot Gold Thread in Late Medieval Silk Weaving and Embroidery." In *Deeds Done Beyond the Sea: Essays on William of Tyre, Cyprus and the Military Orders Presented to Peter Edbury*, ed. Susan B. Edgington and Helen J. Nicholson, 101–114. Burlington, VT: Ashgate, 2014.

———. "Dalla materia prima ai drappi tra bisanzio, il levante e Venezia: La prima fase dell'industria serica veneziana." In *La seta in Italia dal medioevo al seicento: Dal baco al drappo*, ed. Luca Molà, Reinhold C. Mueller, and Claudio Zanier, 265–304. Venice: Marsilio, 2000.

———. "Oriental Silks Go West: A Declining Trade in the Later Middle Ages." In *Islamic Artefacts in the Mediterranean World*, ed. Catarina Schmidt and Gerhard Wolf, 71–88. Venice: Marsilio, 2010.

———. "Silk Economics and Cross-Cultural Artistic Interaction: Byzantium, the Muslim World, and the Christian West." *Dumbarton Oaks Papers* 58 (2004): 197–240.

———. "Silk in Western Byzantium Before the Fourth Crusade." *Byzantinische Zeitschrift* 84–85 (1991–1992): 462–463.

———. "Silk Production in the Frankish Peloponnese: The Evidence of Fourteenth-Century Surveys and Reports." In *Travellers and Officials in the Peloponnese: Descriptions-Reports-Statistics*, ed. H. A. Kalligas, 41–61. Monembasia: Monembasia Omilos, 1994.

———. "The Venetians in Byzantine and Lusignan Cyprus: Trade, Settlements, and Politics." In *La Serenissima and la Nobilissima: Venice in Cyprus and Cyprus in Venice*, ed. Angel Nicolauou Konnari, 59–100. Nicosia: Bank of Cyprus Cultural Foundation, 2009.

Jaro, Marta. "Gold Embroidery and Fabrics in Europe: XI–XV Centuries." *Gold Bulletin* 23 (1990): 40–57.

Jeanne, Caroline. "Seules ou accompagnées? Les veuves parisiennes et leurs fratries à la fin du Moyen Âge." *Médiévales* 54 (2008): 69–82.

Jolivet, Sophie. "Pour soi vêtir honnêtement à la cour de monseigneur le duc de Bourgogne: Costume et dispositif vestimentaire à la cour de Philippe le Bon de 1430 à 1455." 2 vols. PhD diss., Université de Bourgogne, 2003.

Jones, Colin. *Paris: Biography of a City*. New York: Penguin, 2004.

Jones, Jennifer Michelle. *Sexing La Mode: Gender, Fashion and Commercial Culture in Old Regime France*. New York: Berg, 2004.

Jordan, William Chester. "An Aspect of Credit in Picardy in the 1240s: The Deterioration of Jewish-Christian Credit Relations." *Revue des études juives* 142 (1983): 141–152.

———. *The French Monarchy and the Jews: From Philip Augustus to the Last Capetians*. Philadelphia: University of Pennsylvania Press, 1989.

———. "Home Again: The Jews in the Kingdom of France, 1315–1322." In *The Stranger in Medieval Society*, ed. F. R. P. Akehurst and S. C. Van d'Elder, 27–45. Minneapolis: University of Minnesota Press, 1997.

———. "Jews on Top: Women and the Availability of Consumption Loans in Northern France in the Mid-Thirteenth Century." *Journal of Jewish Studies* 29 (1978): 39–56.

———. *Louis IX and the Challenge of the Crusade*. Princeton, NJ: Princeton University Press, 1981.

———. *Women and Credit in Pre-Industrial and Developing Societies*. Philadelphia: University of Pennsylvania Press, 1993.

Katz, Melissa R. "The Final Testament of Violante de Aragón (c. 1236–1300/01): Agency and (dis)Empowerment of a Dowager Queen." In *Queenship in the Mediterranean: Negotiating the Role of the Queen in the Medieval and Early Modern Eras*, ed. Elena Woodacre, 51–71. New York: Palgrave Macmillan, 2013.

Kedar, Benjamin Z. "Toponymic Surnames as Evidence of Origin: Some Medieval Views." *Viator* 4 (1973): 123–130.

Kinoshita, Sharon. "Translatio/n, Empire, and the Worlding of Medieval Literature: The Travels of Kalila Wa Dimna." *Postcolonial Studies* 11/4 (2008): 371–385.

Kittell, Ellen E. "The Construction of Women's Social Identity in Medieval Douai: Evidence from Identifying Epithets." *Journal of Medieval History* 25/3 (1999): 215–227.

———. "Guardianship over Women in Medieval Flanders: A Reappraisal." *Journal of Social History* 31/4 (1998): 897–930.

Kohn, Roger S. "Les juifs de la France du Nord à travers les archives du Parlement de Paris (1359?–1394)." *Revue des études juives* 141 (1985): 5–138.

———. *Les juifs de la France du Nord dans la seconde moitié du XIVe siècle*. Louvain: E. Peeters, 1988.

———. "Les juifs de Paris (1359?–1394): Problèmes de topographie urbaine." *Proceedings of the Seventh World Congress of Jewish Studies* (1981): 1–8.

———. "Le statut forain: Marchands étrangers, lombards et juifs en France royale et en Bourgogne (seconde moitié du XIVe siècle)." *Revue historique de droit français et étranger* 61/1 (1983): 7–24.

Kowaleski, Maryanne, and Judith M Bennett. "Crafts, Gilds, and Women in the Middle Ages: Fifty Years After Marian K. Dale." *Signs* 14/2 (1989): 474–501.

Krauss, Samuel. "L'émigration de 300 rabbins en Palestine en l'an 1211." *Revue des études juives* 82 (1926): 333–352.

Kuehn, Thomas. *Illegitimacy in Renaissance Florence*. Ann Arbor: University of Michigan Press, 2002.

Lachaud, Frédérique. "La première description des métiers de Paris: Le *Dictionarius* de Jean de Garlande (vers 1220–1230)." *Consommer en ville au Moyen Âge*, special issue of *Histoire urbaine* 16/2 (2006): 91–114.

———. "Les textiles dans les comptes des hôtels royaux et nobiliaires (France et Angleterre, XIIe au XIVe siècle)." *Bibliothèque de l'École des chartes* 161 (2006): 71–96.

———. "Textiles, Furs and Liveries: A Study of the Material Culture of the Court of Edward I (1272–1307)." PhD diss., St. John's College, Oxford University, 1992.

Lalou, Elisabeth, Robert-Henri Bautier, and François Maillard, eds. *Itinéraire de Philippe IV le Bel (1285–1314)*. 2 vols. Mémoires de l'Académie des inscriptions et belles-lettres, t. 37. Paris, 2007.

Lambert, Bart. *The City, the Duke, and Their Banker: The Rapondi Family and the Formation of the Burgundian State (1384–1430)*. Turnhout, Belgium: Brepols, 2006.

Lambertini, Roberto. "Giles of Rome." In *The Stanford Encyclopedia of Philosophy*, ed. Edward N. Zalta. Last modified Winter 2014. http://plato.stanford.edu/archives/win2014/entries/giles/. Accessed February 27, 2016.

Langlois, Ch.-V. *Le règne de Philippe III le Hardi*. Paris: Hachette et cie, 1887. Reprint, Geneva: Mégariotis Reprints, 1979.

Lebailly, Emilie. "Raoul, Comte d'Eu et de Guines, Connetable de France (1290–1345): Une vie, un office, un milieu." 2 vols. PhD diss., Université de Paris IV, 2004. Dissertation available for consultation at the Institut de recherche et d'histoire des textes, Paris.

Lehoux, Françoise. "Le duc de Berri, les juifs et les lombards." *Revue historique* 215/1 (1956): 38–57.

———. "À Paris sous Philippe VI: Les opérations d'un lombard." *Annales: Économies, Sociétés, Civilisations* 9/1 (1954): 55–62.

Le Roux de Lincy, Antoine. *Histoire de l'Hôtel de Ville de Paris: Suivi d'un essai sur l'ancien gouvernement municipal de cette ville*. Paris: J. B. Dumoulin, 1846.

Leroy, Béatrice. "Les juifs de Navarre à la fin du XIVe siècle: À propos d'une adjudication à Estella en 1383." *Revue du monde Musulman et de la Méditerranée* 63/1 (1992): 115–121.

———. "Quelques pièces de vêtement à la cour de Navarre à la fin du XIVe siècle." In *Milieux naturels, espaces sociaux: Études offertes à Robert Delort*, ed. Élizabeth Mornet and Franco Morenzoni, 393–400. Paris: Publications de la Sorbonne, 1997.

———. "Recherches sur les juifs de Navarre à la fin du Moyen Âge." *Revue des études juives* 140 (1981): 319–432.

———. "Le royaume de Navarre aux XIIIe–XIVe siècles: Un exemple d'état gouverné par des étrangers." In *Actes des congrès de la Société des historiens médiévistes de l'enseignement supérieur public: 30e congrès, Göttingen, 1999*, 155–164. Paris: Publications de la Sorbonne, 2000.

Li, Lillian M. *China's Silk Trade: Traditional Industry in the Modern World, 1842–1937*. Cambridge, MA: Harvard University Press, 1981.

Lloyd, T. H. *Alien Merchants in England in the High Middle Ages*. New York: St. Martin's Press, 1982.

Loeb, Isidore. "Le rôle des juifs de Paris en 1296 et 1297." *Revue des études juives* 1 (1880): 61–71.

Loisne, M. Le Comte de. "Une cour féodale vers la fin du XIIIe siècle: L'hôtel de Robert II, Comte d'Artois." *Bulletin philologique et historique du Comité des travaux historiques et scientifiques* (1918): 84–143.

Lopez, Robert Sabatino. "China Silk in Europe in the Yuan Period." *Journal of the American Oriental Society* 72/2 (1952): 72–76.

———. "Nouveaux documents sur les marchands italiens en Chine à l'époque mongole, communication du 11 février 1977." *Comptes rendus des séances de l'Académie des Inscriptions et Belles-Lettres* 2 (1977): 445–458.

Lorentz, Philippe, Dany Sandron, and Jacques Lebar, eds. *Atlas de Paris au Moyen Âge: Espace urbain, habitat, société, religion, lieux de pouvoir.* Paris: Parigramme, 2006.

Luce, Simeon. "Catalogue des documents du Trésor des chartes relatifs aux juifs sous le règne de Philippe le Bel." *Revue des études juives* 2 (1881): 15–72.

Maddocks, Hilary. "The Rapondi, the Volto Santo di Lucca, and Manuscript Illumination in Paris ca. 1400." In *Patrons, Authors and Workshops: Books and Book Production in Paris Around 1400*, ed. Godfried Croenen and Peter Ainsworth, 91–122. Leuven, Belgium: Peeters, 2006.

Mainoni, Patrizia. "La seta in Italia fra XII e XIII secolo: Migrazioni artigiane e tipologie seriche." In *La seta in Italia dal medioevo al seicento: Dal baco al drappo*, ed. Luca Molà, Reinhold C. Mueller, and Claudio Zanier, 365–399. Venice: Marsilio, 2000.

Martin, Henry. "Cinq portraits du XIIIe siècle: Marie de Brabant; Blanche de France; Jean II de Brabant; Robert II d'Artois; Adenet Le Roi, ménestrel." *Société Nationale des Antiquaires de France, Centenaire: Recueil de mémoires* (1904): 269–279.

Martineau, Jean. *Les Halles de Paris, des origines à 1789: Evolution matérielle, juridique et économique.* Paris: Éditions Montchrestien, 1960.

Massa, Paola. *La "fabbrica" dei velluti genovesi: Da Genova a Zoagli.* Zoagli: Libri Scheiwiller, 1981.

Mayade-Claustre, Julie. "Le corps lié de l'ouvrier: Le travail et la dette à Paris au XVe siècle." *Annales: Histoire, Sciences Sociales* 60/2 (2005): 383–408.

Mazzaoui, Maureen Fennell. "Artisan Migration and Technology in the Italian Textile Industry in the Later Middle Ages (1100–1500)." In *Strutture familiari, epidemie, migrazioni nell'Italia medievale*, ed. Rinaldo Comba, Gabriella Piccinni, and Giuliano Pinto, 519–534. Naples: Edizioni scientifiche italiane, 1984.

McIntosh, Marjorie Keniston. *Working Women in English Society, 1300–1620.* New York: Cambridge University Press, 2005.

McVaugh, Michael. "Surgical Education in the Middle Ages." *Dynamis. Acta Hispanica ad Medicinae Scientiarumque Historiam Illustrandam* 20 (2000): 283–304.

Melis, Federigo, and Luciana Frangioni. *I mercanti italiani dell'Europa medievale e rinascimentale.* Florence: Le Monnier, 1990.

Michaëlsson, Karl. "Les noms d'origine dans le rôle de la taille parisien de 1313." *Symbolae philologicae Gotoburgenses*, Acta universitatis Gotoburgensis 56/3 (1950): 357–400.

Miller, Tanya Stabler. *The Beguines of Medieval Paris: Gender, Patronage, and Spiritual Authority.* Philadelphia: University of Pennsylvania Press, 2014.

Mirot, Léon. "Études lucquoises 1: La colonie lucquoise à Paris du XIIIe au XVe siècle." *Bibliothèque de l'École des chartes* 88 (1927): 50–86.

———. "Études lucquoises 2: Les Isbarre, monnayeurs royaux." *Bibliothèque de l'École des chartes* 88 (1927): 275–314.

———. "Études lucquoises 3: La société des Raponde-Dine Raponde." *Bibliothèque de l'École des chartes* 89 (1928): 299–389.

———. "Études lucquoises 4: Les Cename." *Bibliothèque de l'École des chartes* 91 (1930): 100–168.

———. "La fondation de la chapelle du Volto Santo en l'Église du Saint Sepulcre à Paris." *Bollettino storico Lucchese* 6/1 (1934): 1–28.

Molà, Luca. *La comunità dei lucchesi a Venezia: Immigrazione e industria della seta nel tardo medioevo.* Venice: Istituto veneto di scienze, lettere ed arti, 1994.

————. "Le donne nell'industria serica veneziana del Rinascimento." In *La seta in Italia dal Medioevo al Seicento. Dal baco al drappo*, ed. Luca Molà, Reinhold C. Mueller, and Claudio Zanier, 423–459. Venice: Marsilio, 2000.

————. "L'industria della seta a Lucca nel tardo Medioevo: Emigrazione della manodopera e creazione di una rete produttiva a Bologna e Venezia." In *La seta in Europa sec. XIII–XX: Atti della Ventiquattresima settimana di studi, 4–9 maggio 1992*, ed. Simonetta Cavaciocchi, 435–444. Florence: Le Monnier, 1993.

————. *The Silk Industry of Renaissance Venice*. Baltimore: Johns Hopkins University Press, 2000.

Molà, Luca, Reinhold C. Mueller, and Claudio Zanier, eds. *La seta in Italia dal Medioevo al Seicento: Dal baco al drappo*. Venezia: Marsilio, 2000.

Monnas, Lisa. "Developments in Figured Velvet Weaving in Italy During the 14th Century." *Bulletin de liaison du Centre international d'étude des textiles anciens* 63–64 (1986): 63–100.

————. "Loom Widths and Selvedges Prescribed by Italian Silk Weaving Statutes, 1265–1512: A Preliminary Investigation." *Bulletin de liaison du Centre international d'étude des textiles anciens* 66 (1988): 35–44.

————. "Textiles for the Coronation of Edward III." *Textile History* 32/1 (2001): 2–35.

Munro, John. "Medieval Woollens: Textiles, Technology and Organisation." In *Cambridge History of Western Textiles*, vol. 1, ed. D. T. Jenkins, 181–227. Cambridge: Cambridge University Press, 2003.

Muthesius, Anna. "Silk in the Medieval World." In *Cambridge History of Western Textiles*, vol. 1, ed. D. T. Jenkins, 325–354. Cambridge: Cambridge University Press, 2003.

————. *Studies in Silk in Byzantium*. London: Pindar Press, 2004.

Nahon, Gérard. "La communauté juive de Paris au XIIIe siècle: Problèmes topographiques, démographiques et institutionnels." *Actes du 100e congrès national des sociétés savantes, Paris, 1975, 2, Études sur l'histoire de Paris et de l'Île-de-France*. Paris, 1978.

————. "Le crédit et les juifs dans la France du XIIIe siècle." *Annales: Histoire, Sciences Sociales* 24/5 (1969): 1121–1148.

Noiriel, Gérard. *Le creuset français: Histoire de l'immigration, XIXe–XXe siècle*. Paris: Seuil, 1988.

————. "Difficulties in French Historical Research on Immigration." *Bulletin of the American Academy of Arts and Sciences* 46/1 (1992): 21–35.

————. "L'histoire est un sport de combat." *Vacarme* 32/3 (2005): 6–14.

Nolan, Kathleen. *Queens in Stone and Silver: The Creation of a Visual Imagery of Queenship in Capetian France*. New York: Palgrave Macmillan, 2009.

Olivier-Martin, François. *Histoire de la coutume de la prévôté et vicomté de Paris*. 2 vols. Paris: Editions Cujas, 1972. First printed by E. Leroux in 1922.

Perry, Guy J. M. *John of Brienne: King of Jerusalem, Emperor of Constantinople, c. 1175–1237*. Cambridge: Cambridge University Press, 2013.

Petit-Dutaillis, Charles. *Étude sur la vie et le régne de Louis VIII (1187–1226)*. Geneva: Slatkine, 1975. First published by Bouillon in 1894.

Pfaffenbichler, Matthias. *Medieval Craftsmen: Armourers*. London: British Museum Press, 1992. First published by University of Toronto Press, 1992.

Piponnier, Françoise. *Costume et vie sociale: La cour d'Anjou XIVe–XVe siècle*. Paris: Mouton, 1970.

————. "Usages et diffusion de la soie en France à la fin du Moyen Age." *La seta in Europa sec. XIII–XX: Atti della Ventiquattresima settimana di studi, 4–9 maggio 1992*, ed. Simonetta Cavaciocchi, 785–800. Florence: Le Monnier, 1993.

Piton, Camille. *Les lombards en France et à Paris*. Paris: Honoré Champion, 1892.

Poëte, Marcel. *Une vie d'une cité: Paris de sa naissance à nos jours*. 2 vols. Paris: Auguste Picard, 1924.

Pomian, Krzysztof. "Francs et gaulois." In *Les lieux de mémoire* III, 1: *Les France: Conflits et pariages*, ed. Pierre Nora, 41–105. Paris: Gallimard, 1992.

Pounds, Norman J. G. "Steelmaking." In *Dictionary of the Middle Ages*, vol. 11, ed. Joseph Strayer, 469–472. New York: Scribner, 1988.

Prawer, Joshua. *The History of the Jews in the Latin Kingdom of Jerusalem*. Oxford: Clarendon Press, 1988.

Proctor-Tiffany, Mariah. "Lost and Found: Visualizing a Medieval Queen's Destroyed Objects." In *Queenship in the Mediterranean: Negotiating the Role of the Queen in the Medieval and Early Modern Eras*, ed. Elena Woodacre, 73–96. New York: Palgrave Macmillan, 2013.

Prou, Maurice. *Étude sur les relations politiques du pape Urbain V avec les rois de France Jean II et Charles V (1362–1370)*. Paris: F. Vieweg, 1887.

Racine, Pierre. "Le marché génois de la soie en 1288." *Revue des études sud-est-européennes* 8 (1970): 403–417.

———. "Paris, rue des Lombards (1280–1340)." In *Comunita forestiere e "nations" nell'Europe dei secoli XIII–XVI*, ed. Giovanni Petti Balbi, 95–111. Naples: Liguori Editore, 2001.

Rayner, Hollins. *Silk Throwing and Waste Silk Spinning*. London: Scott, Greenwood, 1903.

Reyerson, Kathryn. "The Adolescent Apprentice/Worker in Medieval Montpellier." *Journal of Family History* 17/4 (1992): 353–370.

———. *Business, Banking, and Finance in Medieval Montpellier*. Toronto: Pontifical Institute of Mediaeval Studies, 1985.

———. "Commerce and Communications." In *The New Cambridge Medieval History*, vol. 5, ed. David Abulafia, 50–70. Cambridge: Cambridge University Press, 1999.

———. "Medieval Silks in Montpellier: The Silk Market ca. 1250–ca. 1350." *Journal of European Economic History* 11 (1982): 117–140.

Reynolds, Catherine. " 'Les Angloys, de leur droicte nature, veullent toujours guerreer': Evidence for Painting in Paris and Normandy c. 1420–1450." In *Power, Culture and Religion in France, c. 1350–1550*, ed. Christopher Allmand, 37–55. Woodbridge: Boydell Press, 1989.

Richard, Jules-Marie. *Inventaire-sommaire des archives départementales antérieurs à 1799: Pas-de-Calais-Archives Civiles, Série A*. 2 vols. Arras: Imprimerie de la Société du Pas-de-Calais, 1878.

———. *Une petite-nièce de Saint Louis: Mahaut, comtesse d'Artois et de Bourgogne (1302–1329). Étude sur la vie privée, les arts et l'industrie, en Artois et à Paris au commencement du XIVe siècle*. Paris: H. Champion, 1887.

Roblin, Michel. *Les juifs de Paris: Démographie, économie, culture*. Paris: A. et J. Picard, 1952.

Roch, Jean-Louis. *Un autre monde du travail: La draperie en Normandie au Moyen Âge*. Mont-Saint-Aignan: Presses universitaires de Rouen et du Havre, 2013.

———. "Femmes et métiers en Normandie au Moyen Âge." Paper delivered at the 48th Congrès des sociétés historiques et archéologiques de Normandie, Bellême, September 2013.

Roncière, Charles de la. *Un changeur florentin du Trecento: Lippo di Fede del Sega (1285 env.–1363 env.)*. Paris: SEVPEN, 1973.

Roux, Simone. "Le côut du logement ordinaire à Paris au XVe siècle." *D'une ville à l'autre: Structures matérielles et organisation de l'espace dans les villes européennes (XIIIe–XVIe siècle)*. Actes du colloque de Rome 122 (1984–1989): 243–263.

———. "Les femmes dans les métiers parisiens: XIIIe-XVe siècles." *Clio: Femmes, genre, histoire* 3 (1996): 2–12.

———. *Paris in the Middle Ages*. Trans. Jo Ann McNamara. Philadelphia: University of Pennsylvania Press, 2009.

Sahlins, Peter. *Unnaturally French: Foreign Citizens in the Old Regime and After*. Ithaca, NY: Cornell University Press, 2004.

Sakellariou, Eleni. *Southern Italy in the Late Middle Ages: Demographic, Institutional and Economic Change in the Kingdom of Naples, c. 1440–c. 1530*. Leiden: Brill, 2012.

Sargentson, Carolyn. *Merchants and Luxury Markets: The Marchands Merciers of Eighteenth-Century Paris*. Malibu, CA: J. Paul Getty Museum, 1996.

Schnerb, Bertrand. *Les Armagnacs et les Bourguignons: La maudite guerre*. Paris: Librairie académique Perrin, 1988.

———. "Les insurrections à Paris au temps de la guerre civile entre Armagnacs et Bourguignons." In *Le Paris du Moyen Âge*, ed. Boris Bove and Claude Gauvard, 237–262. Paris: Belin, 2014.

Schubert, John Rudolph Theodore. *History of the British Iron and Steel Industry from c. 450 B.C. to A.D. 1775*. London: Routledge and Kegan Paul, 1957.

Serjeant, Robert Bertram. *Islamic Textiles: Material for a History up to the Mongol Conquest*. Beirut: Librairie du Liban, 1972.

Shatzmiller, Joseph. *Cultural Exchange: Jews, Christians, and Art in the Medieval Marketplace*. Princeton, NJ: Princeton University Press, 2013.

———. *Shylock Reconsidered: Jews, Moneylending, and Medieval Society*. Berkeley: University of California Press, 1990.

Sheehan, Peter. *Babylon of Egypt: The Archaeology of Old Cairo and the Origins of the City*. New York: American University in Cairo Press, 2010.

Sivéry, Gérard. *L'économie du royaume de France au siècle de Saint Louis (vers 1180–vers 1315)*. Lille: Presses Universitaires de Lille, 1984.

Sprandel, Rolf. "Die wirtschaftlichen Beziehungen zwischen Paris und dem deutschen Sprachraum im Mittelalter." *Vierteljahrschrift für Sozial- und Wirtschaftsgeschichte* 49 (1962): 289–319.

Stella, Alessandro. "Travail, famille et maison: Formes et raisons du placement dans les sociétés traditionnelles." *Médiévales* 15/30 (1996): 35–44.

Strauss, Raphael. "The 'Jewish Hat' as an Aspect of Social History." *Jewish Social Studies* 2/1 (January 1942): 59–72.

Strayer, Joseph. "Italian Bankers and Philip the Fair." *Explorations in Economic History* 7 (1969): 113–121.

———. *The Reign of Philip the Fair*. Princeton, NJ: Princeton University Press, 1980.

Strocchia, Sharon T. *Nuns and Nunneries in Renaissance Florence*. Baltimore: Johns Hopkins University Press, 2009.

Sutton, Anne F. *The Mercery of London: Trade, Goods and People, 1130–1578*. Burlington, VT: Ashgate, 2005.

———. "Two Dozen and More Silkwomen in Fifteenth-Century London." *Ricardian* 16 (2006): 1–8.

Taburet-Delahaye, Élisabeth, dir. *Paris-1400: Les arts sous Charles VI. Catalogue de l'exposition du Musée du Louvre, 26 mars-12 juillet 2004*. Paris: Fayard, Réunion des musées nationaux, 2004.

Taitz, Emily. *The Jews of Medieval France: The Community of Champagne*. Westport, CT: Greenwood Press, 1994.

Terroine, Anne. "Études sur la bourgeoisie parisienne: Gandoufle d'Arcelles et les compagnies placentines à Paris (fin du XIIIe siècle)." *Annales d'histoire sociale* 8/1 (1945): 54–71; 8/2 (1945): 53–74.

———. "Recherches sur la bourgeoisie parisienne au XIIIe siècle." 4 vols. PhD diss., École des chartes, 1940. Copy available at the Institut de recherche et d'histoire des textes, Paris.

Thompson, Guy Llewelyn. *Paris and Its People Under English Rule: The Anglo-Burgundian Regime, 1420–1436*. Oxford: Clarendon Press, 1991.

Toch, Michael. *The Economic History of European Jews: Late Antiquity and Early Middle Ages*. Leiden: Brill, 2013.

Tognetti, Sergio. "The Development of the Florentine Silk Industry: A Positive Response to the Crisis of the Fourteenth Century." *Journal of Medieval History* 31/1 (2005): 55–69.

Tolley, T. "Eleanor of Castile and the 'Spanish Style.'" In *England in the Thirteenth Century: Proceedings of the 1989 Harlaxton Symposium*, ed. W. M. Ormrod, 167–192. Stamford, CT: Boydell & Brewer, 1991.

Truant, Cynthia. "La maîtrise d'une identité? Corporations féminines à Paris aux XVIIe et XVIIIe siècles." *Clio: Femmes, genre, histoire* 3 (1996): 55–70.

Vale, Malcolm G. A. *The Princely Court: Medieval Courts and Culture in North-West Europe, 1270–1380*. New York: Oxford University Press, 2001.

Van den Heuvel, Danielle. *Women and Entrepreneurship: Female Traders in the Northern Netherlands, c. 1580–1815*. Amsterdam: Aksant, 2007.

Ward, Susan Leibacher. "Fables for the Court: Illustrations of Marie de France's *Fables* in Paris, BN, ms. Arsenal 3142." In *Women and the Book: Assessing the Visual Evidence*, ed. Lesley Janette Smith and Jane Taylor, 190–203. London: British Library, 1997.

Wardwell, Anne E. "'*Panni Tartarici*': Eastern Islamic Silks Woven with Gold and Silver (13th and 14th Centuries)." *Islamic Art* 3 (1988–1989): 95–173.

Woodacre, Elena. *Queenship in the Mediterranean: Negotiating the Role of the Queen in the Medieval and Early Modern Eras*. New York: Palgrave Macmillan, 2013.

Yver, Georges. *Le commerce et les marchands dans l'Italie méridionale au XIIIe et au XIVe siècle*. New York: Fontemoing, 1903.

Zimmels, Hirsch Jakob. *Ashkenazim and Sephardim: Their Relations, Differences, and Problems as Reflected in the Rabbinical Responsa*. Hoboken: KTAV Press, 1996.

Index

Acre, 31, 40, 45, 89, 94, 157; immigrants from, 32, 191–93; Lyon of, Jewish physician, 32, 157, 192, 199 n.13

Alès, town in southern France, 39, 88, 94

Alfonso of Spain, 14, 16

Amauri of Amiens, mercer, 70, 84, 128, 200

apprenticeship, 103–4, 132–33, 152–53. *See also* guilds

Apulia, Jehan of, mercer, 92, 97, 227

Aragon, 12, 29–30, 36; immigrants from, 28, 35, 186–88; Richart of, chest maker, 12, 23, 28, 31, 188

Armenia, 87. *See also* Ayas; Cilician Armenia

armorers, 27–28, 59, 174, 177, 180–82

Artois: Countess Mahaut of, 26, 28, 30, 54, 72, 77, 93, 116, 126, 129, 152; Count Robert II of, 18, 27, 30, 70–71, 128

Asia Minor, silk textiles from, 87

Asti, moneylenders and pawnbrokers of, 148, 162

Ayas, in Cilician Armenia, 38, 40, 45

Babylon (old Cairo), immigrant from, 31, 193

Barthelemy Castaing, Italian spice dealer and moneylender, 34, 163

Bartlett, Robert, 36

Bautier, Robert-Henri, 148

Beguine/s, 61–62, 133, 246, 256–58, 261, 263, 265, 270, 275, 279. *See also* Jehanne du Faut; Marie Osane

Belloni: Lando, mercer from Lucca, 24, 33, 77, 83, 92, 100, 102; Ugolino, Lando's brother, 33, 92

Berry, Jean, Duke of, 159, 163, 165–66

Betin Caucinel of Lucca, mint master, 20, 33

Bigwood, Georges, 147

Bologna, silk industry of, 101

Bonaventure, Franciscan theologian, 20

Bondos: Bonvis, mercer from Lucca, 91–93, 99–100, 221; Jacques, 33, 91, 93, 99–100

Bourbon, Louis II, Duke of, 30, 166

Bourlet, Caroline, 8, 64

Bove, Boris, 19

Bruges, 40, 46–48

Burgundy, duke of, 126, 128–29; John the Fearless, 165–67; Philip the Good, 62

Byzantine empire (former), 36

Byzantium, 45, 156

Cairo. *See* Babylon

Caspian Sea region, silk from, 38–39, 41–42, 45–46. *See also* Central Asia, silk from; Ganja; Georgia; Gilan province; Lahijan; Malmistra

Castile, 12–13, 29–30, 36. *See also* Cerda, Fernand de la

Central Asia, silk from, 47. *See also* Caspian Sea region; Ganja; Georgia; Gilan province; Lahijan; Malmistra; silk cloth, *nach*; silk cloth, *panni tartarici*

Cerda: Alfonso de la, 14, 16; Fernand de la, crown prince of Castile, 13–14, 16, 282 n.6; Louis de la, 14, 16

Champagne, Fairs, 46–47. *See also* Lagny-sur-Marne

Châtelet of Paris, 79–80, 83, 115, 121, 136

chest maker/s, 12, 23, 28, 35

China: silk fiber from, 39, 41–42, 45–47; silk textiles from (*see* silk cloth, *nach*; silk cloth, *panni tartarici*); Tsatlee reel from, 45

Christine de Pisan, 166–67

Cilician Armenia, 38, 45

Acknowledgments

It is a pleasure to thank the many individuals, groups, and institutions that have helped bring this book to fruition. First and foremost, I thank two wonderfully generous French scholars: Caroline Bourlet and Sophie Desrosiers. Caroline was one of the original creators of a computerized database of the Parisian tax assessments of 1292–1313, without which this project would have been impossible. Over the past decade she has generously responded to my numerous requests for newly generated lists of Parisians with particular surnames indicating place of origin, or with surnames and professional names indicating craft and professional activities. I have also benefited from her deeply researched scholarship on the crafts and trades of medieval Paris, as well as from her seminar "Paris au Moyen Âge." Sophie Desrosiers's scholarship on the archaeology and technology of medieval textiles has been essential to this project from the beginning. Since we first met in October 2013 moreover, she has been exceedingly generous in commenting on my work and arranging opportunities for me to learn more about the physical processes of silk production; it has been a great pleasure sharing her friendship, camping out on her cousin's floor in the Massif Central, and introducing her to the beaches of Santa Barbara.

I am indebted to the Guggenheim Foundation and the National Endowment for the Humanities, which supported the early research for this project. During the final year of writing, the project benefited as well from a 2013–2014 EURIAS fellowship at the Institut d'Études Avancées de Paris (France), with the support of the European Union's 7th Framework Programme for research, and from funding from the French state managed by the Agence Nationale de la Recherche, programme "Investissements d'avenir" (ANR-11-LABX-0027–01 Labex RFIEA+). I thank all of my colleagues at the IEA-Paris, most especially the director, Gretty Mirdal, whose own work with Turkish immigrants in Denmark led to some insightful questions and a total revamping of the final section of Chapter 1 of this book. Six research grants from the Academic Senate at the University of California, Santa Barbara provided funds for multiple research trips to the UK, France, and Belgium, for the maps and images in the book, and for the work of my research assistant, Sarah Hanson, whom I also thank. Sarah pored over several printed resources relating to the Parisian tax records in order to arrive at some of the statistics in the book; she also helped transform my somewhat messy endnotes into a presentable bibliography and provided early assistance in creating some of the appendices.

For sharing their unpublished or very recently published scholarship, I thank Nadège Gauffre-Fayolle, David Jacoby, Tanya Stabler Miller, Jean-Louis Roch, and Joseph Shatzmiller. For sharing her database on women in the Parisian tax assessments, I thank Janice Archer. For advice on scholarship on Jewish-Christian relations, I thank Elisheva Baumgarten. For valuable references to archival and primary sources, I thank Nadège Gauffre-Fayolle and Camilla Luise Dahl. For fruitful comments on earlier drafts of chapters, I thank Sophie Desrosiers, Ed English, Shennan Hutton, David Jacoby, Maureen Miller, Ann Plane, Jean-Claude Schmitt, participants in the California Medieval Seminar, participants in Didier Lett's seminar "Famille, parenté et genre au Moyen Âge," and participants in the seminar "Paris au Moyen Âge." For help with Arabic terminology, I thank R. Stephen Humphreys. For insightful comments on the manuscript as a whole, I thank the anonymous reader at the University of Pennsylvania Press and Nicole Archambeau. In addition to catching a number of errors, they prodded me to weave the individual chapters into a much more coherent whole. Finally, I thank my daughter, Roxana, whose first trip to Europe coincided with the beginning of this project. Her companionship then, and on subsequent trips, transformed travel for work into hilarious adventures. She contributed to this book, moreover, by patiently assisting with archival photography.

9 780812 248487